VICTORY THROUGH HARMONY

Victory through Harmony

THE BBC AND POPULAR MUSIC IN WORLD WAR II

Christina L. Baade

OXFORD
UNIVERSITY PRESS

OXFORD
UNIVERSITY PRESS

Oxford University Press, Inc., publishes works that further
Oxford University's objective of excellence
in research, scholarship, and education.

Oxford   New York
Auckland   Cape Town   Dar es Salaam   Hong Kong   Karachi
Kuala Lumpur   Madrid   Melbourne   Mexico City   Nairobi
New Delhi   Shanghai   Taipei   Toronto

With offices in
Argentina   Austria   Brazil   Chile   Czech Republic   France   Greece
Guatemala   Hungary   Italy   Japan   Poland   Portugal   Singapore
South Korea   Switzerland   Thailand   Turkey   Ukraine   Vietnam

Published by Oxford University Press, Inc.
198 Madison Avenue, New York, New York 10016

www.oup.com

Library of Congress Cataloging-in-Publication Data
Baade, Christina L.
Victory through harmony : the BBC and popular music in World War II / Christina L. Baade.
   p.   cm.
Includes bibliographical references and index.
ISBN 978-0-19-537201-4 (alk. paper)
1. Radio and music—Great Britain.   2. British Broadcasting Corporation—History.
3. World War, 1939–1945—Music and the war.   4. Popular music—Great Britain—1941–1950—History and
criticism.   I. Title.
ML68.B33 2012
791.440941'09044—dc22   2011009138

Publication of this book was supported by the AMS 75 PAYS Endowment of
the American Musicological Society, funded in part by the National
Endowment for the Humanities and the Andrew Mellon Foundation.

1 3 5 7 9 8 6 4 2

Printed in the United States of America

For Alana

Acknowledgments

HAVING LIVED WITH the material in this book for more than a decade, I have many individuals and institutions to thank. First, I thank the head archivist, Jacqueline Kavanagh, and staff of the BBC Written Archives Centre in Caversham for their knowledgeable, efficient, and resourceful assistance. Their support, particularly that of Mike Websell and Louise North, was invaluable. I would also like to thank the staff of the National Sound Archive in London, whose resources I turned to repeatedly over the years, as well as the staff of the British Library Newspaper Library. My thanks to Robert Tame of IPC Media, Inc., who granted permission for me to obtain microfilms of crucial years of the *Melody Maker* from the British Library Newspaper Library, easing the task of transatlantic research. Finally, a special word of thanks to several hardworking librarians for their kind and expert assistance: Geri Laudati and Steve Sundquist of Mills Music Library at the University of Wisconsin–Madison, and Laurie Crompton and Kim Pickett of Mills Library at McMaster University.

This book is built upon the scaffolding of my doctoral dissertation at the University of Wisconsin–Madison. My heartfelt thanks go to my adviser, Susan Cook, for all her support, mentoring, and challenging questions. I also thank the distinguished members of my dissertation committee, Michele Hilmes, Pamela Potter, Charles Dill, and David Crook, in whose seminar I first explored this topic. I am grateful for funding I received from the Wisconsin Alumni Research Foundation and Vilas Graduate Fellowships, as well as a travel grant from the University of Wisconsin–Madison Graduate School. At Madison, I was surrounded by an amazing community, both within the university and without. I thank my fellow graduate students Jess Courtier, Maya Gibson, Shersten Johnson, Eden Kainer, Anna Nekola, Rebecca Oettinger, and Liz Paley for many thoughtful conversations and Andrea Broaddus, Tim Dean, Laura Dresser, Sandy Thistle, Sara van Cleef, and the members of my band Yid Vicious, especially Daithi Wolfe, Mike Pollay, and Jon Pollack, for all their moral support. I also remember my bandmate Dave Austin, whose 2009 passing is mourned by all who knew him.

This project transformed into the present book during my time at McMaster University, supported by friends, colleagues, and funding from the McMaster Arts Research

Board and the Canadian Social Sciences and Humanities Research Council. I am grateful to the students who have worked, with grace, patience, and initiative, as my research assistants during this process: Paul Aitken, Carolyn Kotva, and especially Mary Clements. I owe a special word of thanks to Claudia Manley for her marvelous help in editing the final manuscript; to Robert Greenway, who waded through the BBC Programmes as Broadcast logs at the Written Archives Centre; to Jeannette Jackson and Helena Collins for their always kindly and efficient administrative support; and to Tracy Reynolds, who took wonderful care of my son during the sabbatical when I completed the manuscript. I am grateful to many colleagues from McMaster for their mentoring, sharp insights, and friendship, including Jim Deaville, Susan Fast, Catherine Graham, Janice Hladki, Graham Knight, Liss Platt, Christine Quail, and Sandy Thorburn. My thanks to many friends in Hamilton and beyond for their moral support: Scott Annandale, Nadine Attewell, Norma Coates, Lane Dunlop, Judy Eaton, Tina Fetner, Melinda Gough, Katie Keenleyside, Claudia Manley, Jenny Martin, Richard Nagel, Jeff Pollock, and Renee Sgroi. Farther afield, I am deeply grateful to Jenny Doctor for her inspiring support throughout this project; to Annie Randall for her encouragement and feedback at several critical moments; to Louis Niebur for sharing enthusiasms for British music, film, and the BBC; to Matt Baumer and Jane Potter-Baumer for friendship during our sojourn in Tennessee; and to Anne van Allen-Russell and John Russell for hosting me so graciously in London. At Oxford University Press, I thank the anonymous reviewers for their feedback, and I am indebted to Norm Hirschy for his enthusiastic support, wise guidance, and patience throughout the process.

I thank the BBC Written Archives Centre for permission to quote BBC copyright material and Mrs. Mardie Gorman for permission to quote from Cecil Madden's Wartime Radio Diary, housed at BBC Written Archives Centre. Extracts from Mass-Observation Archive materials are reproduced with permission of Curtis Brown Group Limited, London on behalf of the Trustees of the Mass Observation Archive (copyright © The Trustees of the Mass Observation Archive). I thank the following for permission to reproduce photographs: Getty Images (figures 2.1, 4.1, 6.3, and 8.2), the BBC Photo Library (figures 4.4, 5.2, 6.2, and 8.1), and Mr. Charles and Mrs. Penny Chilton (figure 5.1). I am especially grateful to Mr. and Mrs. Chilton for sharing a photograph from their family collection.

At last, my deep appreciation goes to my family for their love and support throughout the process. I thank my sister, Angela, for her friendship and many insights into singing voices and my parents for their unflagging encouragement and a generous gift of travel funds during my graduate years. I also thank my son, Ernst, for being such a delight over the three years since his birth and for helping me to keep life and work in their proper perspective. At last, I thank my wife, Alana, who read many chapters of this book, for being the best partner imaginable across borders, career changes, and the new territories of parenthood: this book is for you.

Contents

About the Companion Website

www.oup.com/us/victorythroughharmony
Oxford University Press has created a password-protected website to accompany *Victory through Harmony*, which features sound examples of songs and instrumental numbers discussed throughout this book. Given the unfamiliarity to contemporary readers of many of the wartime BBC's most popular performers and musical genres, the companion website is an invaluable tool in conveying an aural snapshot of the period. It is hoped that readers will listen as they read and then be inspired to explore the music further, aided in part by this book's selected discography.

Sound examples available online are signaled in the text with Oxford's symbol ●. Access with **username Music3** and **password Book3234.**

Abbreviations

AEFP	Allied Expeditionary Forces Programme
AFN	[United States] Army Forces Network
AFRS	[United States] Armed Forces Radio Service
ARC	American Red Cross
BBC	British Broadcasting Corporation
BBC WAC	British Broadcasting Corporation Written Archives Centre
BEF	British Expeditionary Forces
CBC	Canadian Broadcasting Corporation
DMPC	Dance Music Policy Committee
EEU	Empire Entertainments Unit
ENSA	Entertainments National Service Association
GFP	General Forces Programme
GOS	General Overseas Service
MOI	Ministry of Information
MP	Member of Parliament
MPA	Music Publishers' Association
MWYW	*Music While You Work*
NSA	National Sound Archive
OB	Outside Broadcast
ODJB	Original Dixieland Jazz Band
RAF	Royal Air Force
RRC	*Radio Rhythm Club*
SHAEF	Supreme Headquarters Allied Expeditionary Force
USO	United Service Organizations

VICTORY THROUGH HARMONY

INTRODUCTION: "VICTORY THROUGH HARMONY"

IN JUNE 1941, the producer Wynford Reynolds invoked the slogan "Victory through Harmony" to describe the ultimate goal of "one of the most popular wartime features" aired by the British Broadcasting Corporation, *Music While You Work (MWYW)*.[1] The phrase was an apt description of the radio series, which deployed live popular music in the service "of increasing war production," but it also resonated with the populist regard for the Second World War as a "People's War," in which ordinary British people united in the common cause of victory against the Axis and of building a better post-war society at home.

As demonstrated by the symbolic importance of *MWYW*, and its ubiquity in factories and homes, popular music broadcasting by the BBC played a crucial role in promoting national unity and morale during the war. With its monopoly on broadcasting in the United Kingdom and tradition of public service, the BBC was a central institution in British life. By the beginning of the war, it reached the homes of 34 to 40 million listeners (i.e., 70–80 percent of Britain's total population), it was the largest employer of musicians in the nation, and its fees for compositions and popular songs represented 54 percent of the Performing Rights Society's income.[2] Through the mass, boundary-crossing medium of radio and an intimate domestic address, the BBC connected listeners to the imagined community of the nation, an entity whose culture it actively helped to define.[3] Unsurprisingly for a sound-based medium, music constituted a significant component of the BBC's cultural offerings.

The onset of war significantly altered the BBC's approach to popular music broadcasting. Before the war, the BBC aired theater organs and sophisticated dance bands as respectable middlebrow entertainment, but it regarded popular music as ancillary to classical music, the promotion of which was central to its mission of cultural uplift. During the war, however, it recognized the morale-building value of popular music. Popular music could draw listeners together in shared affinities while its broadcast helped the BBC demonstrate its regard for special groups involved in the war effort, such as factory workers and members of the forces, as well as the public as a whole. The BBC accomplished these aims not only by airing professional musicians but also by featuring a range of amateur singers and bands in outside broadcasts, transmitted on the spot from factories and military camps "somewhere in England." With titles like *Works Wonders* and *Private Smith Entertains*, such programming enacted the sense of egalitarianism, community, and participation so important to the People's War. Indeed, whether it was amateurs or stars performing, the audience often joined in; the sing-along became a regular trope in wartime film and in broadcasts before live audiences.[4]

The sound of a multitude of voices joined together in singing popular songs like "Roll Out the Barrel" and "We'll Meet Again" offered participants and listeners a living enactment of the sentiments conveyed in Reynolds's slogan, "Victory through Harmony." Indeed, harmony offers a useful metaphor for the interrelation of individuals in a civilized nation. Nonmusical uses of the term invoke notions of agreement, accord, and congruity, but in music theory, harmony "denote[s] a system of structural rules" that prescribe how notes are combined, based upon hierarchies of voices, chords, and musical events.[5] The harmonic system requires not uniform consonance but rather the resolution of dissonance, which by its very difference reinforces the tonal center.[6]

Although the slogan "Victory through Harmony" emphasized unity based upon shared values and aims, it also operated in more prescriptive terms: good wartime British citizens were expected to look past their self-interest and contribute cheerfully to the war effort.[7] Nonetheless, the push toward national unity, coupled with wartime movements of troops and civilians, also revealed differences and discord, not all of which were easily contained by traditional social hierarchies or resolved into political consensus. War service and evacuations brought different classes into unprecedented contact; the presence within the United Kingdom of Commonwealth troops revealed the true diversity of British subjects; and a variety of political perspectives, including an admiring fascination for the Soviet Union, vied for attention. The contributions of men in reserve occupations and women doing traditionally male work existed uneasily with idealized wartime traits—virility, temperance, cheer, and bravery—that were gendered masculine and drew upon the figure of the soldier-hero.[8] Finally, many British observers regarded conscientious objectors, "loose" women, and what eventually became more than 1 million American GIs stationed in the country (nearly 10 percent of whom were African American) to be in such dissonance with British wartime norms as to be utterly alien.

Thus, while the BBC's broadcast of popular music could be understood as furthering the unifying, populist aims conveyed in the slogan "Victory through Harmony," it also revealed the dissonances and discords of the nation. For example, Vera Lynn, with her working-class roots, heartfelt voice, and sentimental repertory, is remembered now as one of the most iconic singers of the war, but she was also one of its most controversial. In 1942, her popular radio show, *Sincerely Yours—Vera Lynn*, became the focal point for a broad debate about appropriate entertainment for the forces, which led to a BBC ban on "demoralizing" music: male crooners, overly sentimental female singers, and "slushy" songs. Later in the war, to the delight of youths, swing enthusiasts, and working-class listeners, the BBC aired visiting Americans like Bing Crosby and Glenn Miller's Army Air Force Band with the aim of fostering Anglo-American cooperation; however, recognizing Americanization as a threat to a distinct British common culture, it also promoted British-style popular music. Detractors, both within and without the BBC, faulted crooners as the effeminate other to the soldier-hero; swing and jazz as the African American other to straightforward British dance music; and theater organs as the lowbrow other to uplifting classical music. For some, the BBC's embrace of morale-building popular music during "a war in defense of civilization" represented not a turn to democratic populism but the tyranny of mindless mass culture.[9]

The BBC's wartime approach to popular music did not merely cater to the majority, nor did it represent top-down propaganda; rather, it operated in dialogue with a diversity of voices, including listeners, the press, governmental authorities, and the music industry, which included the Musicians' Union, music publishers, and gramophone companies. Moreover, while listeners and critics tended to regard the BBC as a cohesive entity (and, indeed, it presented itself as such), it was a complex organization, with numerous divisions, departments, and a staff that grew to more than 11,000 during the war.[10] They, too, offered competing—and cooperative—visions of how best popular music could serve the nation in wartime. Finally, especially because the BBC emphasized live over recorded musical performance, the personae, repertories, and stylistic choices of dance bandleaders, jazz musicians, vocalists, and theater organists, as well as the input of producers and gramophone records recitalists, all played critical roles in meaning-making during the war. Although established systems and hierarchies rendered this multitude of voices into overall harmony, popular music broadcasting at the BBC was no stable category but rather, to paraphrase Stuart Hall, a site to contest what values, identities, and tastes were most essential to a nation bent on victory.[11]

"The Kaleidoscopic Panorama"

"A kind of idle, restless attentiveness is bred towards the kaleidoscopic panorama that jigs behind that bland clock-face," wrote Rose Macaulay in "The BBC and War Moods."[12] The wireless offered a portal into a sonically variegated world that ranged, depending upon the listener's tastes, between pleasant, familiar patterns and cacophony. Although the BBC throughout the war increased the representation of recordings broadcast, whether in gramophone programs or in prerecorded broadcasts, live performance was the standard for music broadcasting: thus, Macaulay's restlessly attentive listener was almost certain to hear a broadcast performance unfolding in real time.

Popular music at the BBC was administered by the Variety Department and divided into two main categories: dance bands and theater organs, both of which played repertory that ranged from arrangements of light classical works to straightforward

renditions of popular songs. Many famous "name" bands further extended their repertory to include a few commercial swing numbers and possibly even one or two "hot"
numbers played in a style that might earn praise from jazz enthusiasts. They also featured a battery of vocalists: "straight" singers, crooners, and close-harmony ensembles.
Bands remained the chief employers for popular singers during the war, but a few
broke away to pursue solo careers. Several singers, most notably Vera Lynn and Anne
Shelton, starred in their own BBC series, which were directed to the forces overseas
and at home.

In addition to the large, mainstream dance orchestras, the BBC broadcast a range of
smaller, more specialized bands. These included Edmundo Ros's influential rumba
band, which helped feed a wartime vogue for Latin music; Victor Silvester's popular
strict-tempo Ballroom Orchestra; and Harry Parry's Radio Rhythm Club Sextet, which
brought small-group swing to the mainstream audience. The relative popularity of the
last two bands demonstrated the conservative tastes of most BBC listeners: on *Radio
Rhythm Club (RRC)*, Parry's band attracted audiences that hovered around 8 percent
while the audience for *BBC Dancing Club*, which featured Silvester and his band, regularly exceeded 20 percent. Here follows a tour of the BBC's popular music panorama by
way of six representative recordings made between October 1939 and September 1942
by five leading soloists and bands: Sandy Macpherson at the theater organ, Geraldo
and His Orchestra, Lynn, Silvester, and Parry.

Theater Organ: Sandy Macpherson, "I'll Play to You" (sound example 0.1)◐

Sandy Macpherson, who became the BBC's resident theater organist in 1938, was one
of the most recognizable and beloved broadcasters during the Second World War. In
the first month of the war, he made more than fifty broadcasts; from 1940, he broadcast several overseas and domestic "messages programs," which relayed dedications
along with song requests; and his weekly postbag numbered in the thousands.[13]
Macpherson was by no means the only broadcasting organist: the BBC featured
dozens, often in "outside broadcasts" from the cinemas where they were resident, and
they were well liked throughout the war by a majority of listeners.[14] In a September
1942 novelty release, "Sandy Forges Signatures," Macpherson registered the organ's
ubiquity on the radio by playing and announcing the signature tunes of five other
famous theater organists, including "Keep Smiling," the signature of his predecessor,
Reginald Foort. "The 'forgeries' are so good as to almost defy detection," observed
Gramophone.[15]

Macpherson concluded the disc by announcing in his warm, clear voice, "And now
I'll play to you, 'I'll Play to You,' my own signature tune, which some of you may have
heard before." The tune, a waltz of Macpherson's own composition, would indeed have
been familiar, since it opened and closed nearly every broadcast that he made. Only
twenty-four bars long, the F-major waltz offered reassuring symmetry in its ABA
structure and paired four-bar phrases. Its repetitions reinforced by generous doses of
tremulant and rubato, "I'll Play to You" established familiarity for listeners and created
the sense of brief, nearly instantaneous, return.[16]

Dance Band: Geraldo and His Orchestra, "We Must All Stick Together"
(sound example 0.2)◐ and "Russian Lullaby" (sound example 0.3)◐

Dance bands defined popular music at the BBC from the 1920s until well after the war. Their studio performances and outside broadcasts from exclusive venues like the Savoy Hotel brought the glamour of the metropolis to listeners at home. Geraldo entered the pantheon of broadcasting "name" leaders during the 1930s, but it was during the war, when he gained a long-term BBC contract (lasting from 1941 until 1944), that his band came to the fore. His performing forces ranged from a small swing-oriented band-within-a-band to a "concert orchestra," which included a full complement of strings. At the beginning of the war, the instrumentation for Geraldo's dance band featured four brass, four reeds with the occasional addition of a flute, and a rhythm section with piano, guitar, drums, and string bass. By the end of the war, he had adopted a six-brass, five-reed instrumentation, which more closely resembled large American swing bands, like Glenn Miller's. Two recordings demonstrate Geraldo's stylistic range, along with his growing internalization of the big-band swing idiom: "We Must All Stick Together," recorded in October 1939, and "Russian Lullaby," from April 1942.

The quickstep "We Must All Stick Together" by Ralph Butler and Raymond Wallace, which exhorted listeners to unite, "never mind the old school tie," was one of many peppy, patriotic numbers churned out by songwriters in the initial months of the war. Geraldo and his band offered a crisp, animated rendition at tempo fast enough to permit four full statements of the chorus and one of the verse in the space of a three-minute side of a 78-rpm disc. In a manner typical of dance-band recordings since the 1920s, instrumental statements of the chorus framed the vocal section, which featured Cyril Grantham's rousing, clearly enunciated declamation of the verse (a brief cloud of minor in an otherwise major key song) and chorus in his manly baritone, repeated by a male ensemble with a clipped delivery. The first chorus featured a signature device for Geraldo: the trumpets, mutes in, playing a staccato, virtuosically triple-tongued version of the melody. The recording's overall mood was jaunty, yet resolved—a perfect realization of the cheerful, temperate heroism that the lyrics urged listeners to embrace.[17]

Geraldo's adventurous arrangement of Irving Berlin's "Russian Lullaby" contrasted strikingly with "We Must All Stick Together," both for its treatment of the singer and for its deployment of swing arranging techniques. Berlin's song, which portrayed a "Russian rose" with her infant near the "dreamy Volga" in the verse and her lullaby in the chorus, promising "soon we'll see a land that's free," resonated with the British fascination for their Soviet allies. After a lushly scored introduction, which with its high woodwinds and pedal tones in the now-three-man trombone section trendily evoked a Rachmaninovian mood, Geraldo's highly regarded vocalist Dorothy Carless launched into the verse, an undulating waltz. At the end of her performance, a screaming trumpet, jungle toms, and trombone chorus executed a dramatic transition to a common-time, swung version of the tune. In contrast to Grantham's clipped accents, Carless crooned; where the sectional playing had been crisp and straight, now it had a driving, assured swing.[18] Geraldo continued to switch between these and other styles, but he (and other mainstream band-leaders) embraced swing with increased enthusiasm from 1942.

Vocal Soloist: Vera Lynn, "We'll Meet Again" (sound example 0.4)◗

For many in Britain, "We'll Meet Again" was the song of the war, and the singer they associated most closely with it was Vera Lynn. Lynn closed every program of her famous wartime series, *Sincerely Yours*, with the song, and she performed it frequently, accompanied only by a pianist, in the intimate vocal feature, *Starlight*, which was broadcast to the troops overseas. Accompanied on the novachord, a type of electric organ, by the keyboardist Arthur Young, Lynn's recording of the song in November 1939, early in her solo career, anticipated the intimate style of her *Starlight* performances. Penned by the ace British songwriting team of Ross Parker and Hugh Charles, the song tapped into a wartime mood that would become far more prevalent than jingoism: the longing of loved ones separated by war. The song, which incorporated the slogan "keep smiling" into its text, remained steadfastly in D major throughout, but the frequent chromatic notes in the melody and the affecting catches in Lynn's sweet, slightly nasal delivery transformed it from patriotic exhortation to a brave, human declaration of hope. (The lower keys she favored also made it easy for amateurs to sing along.) Lynn's diction was clear, her expression heartfelt, and her relation to the text utterly sincere.[19] No wonder wartime audiences embraced her.

Strict-Tempo Dance Music: Victor Silvester and His Ballroom Orchestra, "Yours"

While a wide audience loved Lynn and other crooners, there was another sizable public that appreciated Silvester's strict-tempo dance music precisely because it excluded vocalists. Silvester was a leading ballroom dance instructor, and he had been making recordings that suited his exacting standards for correct tempos and steady, clear rhythm since 1936. His November 1941 recording of "Yours," a song closely associated with Lynn, exemplified his methods. Originally composed in 1930 by Gonzalo Roig, the song had been recently revived with new English lyrics by Jack Sherr. For his version, Silvester stripped away the rhythmically confusing habanera rhythm, substituting a steady foxtrot accompaniment (he did record a small selection of tangos and rumbas as well). He also removed the verse, permitting four straightforward statements of the chorus, with the most utilitarian of intros and codas. Following Silvester's established formula, the violinist Oscar Grasso and the saxophonist E. O. Pogson traded the melody in each chorus, playing with the "schmaltzy" vibratos that Silvester regarded as critical to his sound, while Eddie Macaulay, the first pianist, provided the "lemonade," an obbligato above the melody (sound example 0.5).[20] ◗ While swing enthusiasts regarded strict-tempo dance music as "unbelievably dull," "Yours" and other Silvester numbers were well played and highly favored by the mainstream.[21]

Swing: Harry Parry and His Radio Rhythm Club Sextet, "I've Found a New Baby" (sound example 0.6)◗

With swing a minority taste in Britain at the beginning of the war, the bandleader who did the most to bring it to widespread popularity was Harry Parry, a Welsh clarinetist who came to lead *RRC*'s house band in 1940. The iteration of the RRC Sextet that played its first recording session in January 1941 included Parry, the outstanding pianist George Shearing, vibraphonist Roy Marsh, guitarist Joe Deniz, bassist Tom Bromley, and drummer Ben Edwards, who also played recording dates for Silvester. Parry's instrumentation owed a great deal to Benny Goodman's Sextet, which included the vibraphonist Lionel Hampton and Charlie Christian on guitar. For critics like Edgar Jackson, the group's first recording "prove[d]...that British boys *can* hold their own with the Americans when it comes to getting the real thing in improvised jazz on to the wax."[22]

Certainly, the recording of Spencer Williams's jam-session staple, "I've Found a New Baby," was exciting. The band took a breakneck tempo, which, though it limited nuance for some players, did not hinder the group's cohesion. Following choruses by Parry and Shearing, the sextet engaged in increasingly riff-oriented collective improvisation, and the rhythm players each took brief, understated solos.[23] The band's accessible exhilaration and spontaneity, which contrasted strikingly with so much music of the period, helped build a vibrant youth audience for swing during the war.

Sources

In order to understand why Lynn's singing could have inspired such ambivalence for wartime audiences or why Parry's band so thrilled young listeners, it is critical to attend to the context in which they performed, broadcast, and recorded. The work of several social historians of the period, including Asa Briggs, Angus Calder, Siân Nicholas, and Sonya Rose, as well as others working on the BBC in earlier periods, including Paddy Scannell and David Cardiff, Jenny Doctor, and D. L. LeMahieu have strongly influenced this book, but it is also deeply rooted in primary sources from the period.[24] Official voices survive in relatively complete form while others, which have been silenced or lost, have been reconstructed from ancillary material.

Documents preserved at the BBC Written Archives Centre in Caversham (BBC WAC) serve as the bass line for this work. Thanks to the BBC's formal, bureaucratic culture and its reflexive awareness of its importance in British society, it is possible to trace policy and programming decisions through meeting minutes, detailed memoranda, and artist contracts. Gaps remain, of course: several relevant artist files, for example, were "destroyed," either in collection reorganizations of the late 1940s or in the 1940 bombing of Broadcasting House in London. The archive's Special Collections also include the Wartime Radio Diary of Cecil Madden, the innovative producer who directed overseas entertainment broadcasting for the forces, giving crucial insight into his perspectives and preserving a range of important documents.

Demographic surveys by BBC Listener Research and the independent social research organization Mass-Observation comprise the next major category of material; they convey both listeners' opinions and the ways in which the BBC and other organizations regarded the public. BBC Listener Research tracked public opinion quantitatively throughout the war; more important, it also completed studies of musical genres, audience tastes, listening habits, and individual programs, which drew upon qualitative material provided by voluntary listener panels and local correspondents. These findings are supplemented by the work of Mass-Observation, which was founded in 1936 during the abdication crisis by the anthropologist Tom Harrisson and the "leftist poet and… frustrated journalist" Charles Madge, who were fascinated with "myth and superstition in national life."[25] During the war, Mass-Observation produced ambitious surveys of morale as well as detailed accounts of daily life and popular tastes in dancing and music.

The contemporary press reported upon "newsworthy" BBC music policies and programming and printed reader letters, opinion columns, and reviews. The most important press sources for this book were the BBC's weekly program guide, *Radio Times*, and the dance music weekly, *Melody Maker*. The *Radio Times* boasted the largest circulation of the periodicals examined; by 1939, it numbered 3 million copies, one-third the number of radio licenses issued in the United Kingdom.[26] It provided not only program listings and advertisements but also feature articles, an outlet for BBC publicity, and letters columns where readers aired their opinions on BBC programming. *Melody Maker* commenced publication in 1926 and continued to adapt to changing popular musical tastes until it was discontinued in 1999.[27] Under Ray Sonin's editorship during the war, *Melody Maker* provided detailed accounts of the dance band world and BBC jazz and popular music programs; passionate advocacy for American music and for the importance of musicians to the war effort; and vigorous critiques of the BBC's approach to popular music.[28]

A further eight sources were surveyed for this book: the BBC's uplift-oriented monthly, the *Listener*; the *Musical Times*, which voiced the interests of classical musicians, music scholars, and advocates for music appreciation and education; *Gramophone*, which offered comprehensive reviews of all recordings released in the United Kingdom; two trade journals, *Electrical Trading and Radio Marketing* and *Pianomaker and Music Seller*; the short-lived, but vivid, entertainment weekly *Band Wagon*; the *Dancing Times*, a journal for dance instructors, which registered trends in social dance; and *Parade*, a military weekly published in Cairo for British troops stationed in the Middle East, which included several articles on BBC overseas broadcasting along with program listings. In addition, this book draws upon the indexed paper of record, the *Times* of London, and the invaluable clippings files in the BBC WAC, which bring together articles on broadcasting from a wide range of daily and weekly publications.

Recorded performances constitute another important set of sources for this study. Some recordings of broadcasts are available in the BBC Sound Archives housed at the National Sound Archive (NSA), but the availability of popular music in this collection is limited. During the war, the BBC made increasing use of prerecorded (and rebroadcast) programming, but it rarely preserved such material—motivated, in part, by its own and the Musicians' Union's interests in maintaining the priority of live performance. The BBC did use its limited resources to preserve what it regarded as historically important broadcasts; however, few popular music programs fell into this category (e.g., there is no recording of a wartime *MWYW* program). The most effective method for remedying this gap is the use of commercial recordings from the period, which are available both through the growing number of compact disc reissues and in the original 78-rpm format, many of which are housed at the NSA.

Finally, drawing upon all these materials, this study represents a vigorous effort to locate and reconstruct the perspectives of actual listeners. Listeners sent thousands of fan and request letters directly to wartime performers, as well as more general letters of complaint and suggestion to the BBC; unfortunately, only a small number have been preserved in the BBC WAC. This gap has been supplemented partially by the NSA's invaluable Oral History of Jazz in Britain collection, which preserves the recollections of several important wartime performers, broadcasters, and fans. The most valuable and reliable sources for contemporary listener opinions are letters published in the press (culled from an array of periodicals) and BBC and Mass-Observation surveys.

While cultural memory of the Second World War in Britain has often cast popular music as a compliant soundtrack underscoring People's War themes of unity and shared sacrifice, this study aims to reveal the struggles that defined popular music at the BBC and the transformations it helped bring about. To an unprecedented degree, the wartime BBC programmed popular music and studied its audiences in order to build national unity and morale, promoting new roles for women, virile representations of masculinity, Anglo-American friendship, and pride in a common British culture. In the process, the BBC came into uneasy contact with threats of Americanization, sentimentality, and the creativity of nonwhite, racialized "Others." It responded by regulating and even censoring popular music repertories and performers while listeners, the press, and Parliament energetically debated its decisions. Organized by chronology and theme, with the central chapters invoking five important wartime music programs, this book examines popular music and jazz broadcasting at the wartime BBC as a locus where musical practice and discourse modulated the harmonies of the nation.

Chapter 1 offers a contextual account of BBC broadcasting between the wars; discusses the infusion of jazz and dance music from America into British musical life; and situates the book in relation to discourses of mass culture, modernity, and the popular. Its examination of the BBC is concerned particularly with its ideologies of cultural uplift, promotion of active listening, advocacy for (classical) music appreciation, and conceptualization of the audience. The more comprehensive discussion of dance bands and jazz in interwar British culture (necessary because of their unfamiliarity to most North American readers) is focused through the lens of broadcasting. It gives particular attention to the problem of song plugging and the BBC's turn to lighter programming during the late 1930s: these cases distilled the BBC's ambivalence about popular music, with its ties to the commercial and the American, even as it prepared for war.

Focusing on the state of popular music broadcasting during the first nine months of the war (September 1939 to May 1940), chapter 2 explores the wartime discourses that credited both music and radio with special roles in maintaining national unity and morale. This chapter first describes the BBC's uninspired initial reactions to war and the ways in which it increased dance music programming. Second, it explores the innovative Forces Programme, begun in January 1940 to serve British troops and to provide a light alternative for home listeners. The Forces Programme was significant because it represented how the BBC conceptualized a special audience (male soldiers), acknowledged background listening, and used music to serve these new priorities.

Finally, this chapter considers the 1940 song-plugging scandal, during which the BBC reaffirmed its conviction that dance music required careful control.

Chapter 3 examines *MWYW*, created by the BBC in response to the production drives spurred by the retreat at Dunkirk in June 1940. The half-hour program united ideologies of music as a force for cultural uplift with research in industrial efficiency in service of the war effort. As the program developed, it reflected societal concerns with the new female workforce, for the apathetic and unruly bodies of conscripted women threatened to slow production, detract from the nation's war effort, and even, according to Mass-Observation, undermine "the health of all democracy."[29] Prized for its tonic qualities, *MWYW* was a powerful tool for disciplining workers' bodies. Producers harnessed popular and light repertories not according to entertainment or artistic values but for their effect on production, audibility, and impact on worker morale. Nevertheless, the program also offered an escape from total control through its invocation of collective, democratic participation in the war effort and its evocation of dancing and background listening, which had become mass leisure activities during the preceding decades. This chapter argues that *MWYW* gained its symbolic significance not only because of the millions of lives it affected every day but also because of the powerful ways in which it invoked the utopian and dystopian concerns of mass modernity, including Taylorism, demography, and background listening.

Chapter 4 focuses on how wartime notions of masculinity, escapism, and morale affected the BBC's efforts to provide high-quality dance music. As Britain faced the Blitzkrieg and military defeats throughout 1940 and 1941, broadcast dance music and dancing were popular as mental, emotional, and physical escapes. Despite the recognition that dance music was an important morale booster, the government resisted classifying dance musicians as belonging to an "essential" occupation while critics held them to be unmanly shirkers. The call-up decimated the ranks of dance instrumentalists and contributed to a decline in dance band quality. To supply its needs, the BBC developed the Dance Band Scheme, which involved indefinite contracts for two bandleaders, Jack Payne and Geraldo. The two men embodied the poles of wartime dance music at the BBC: Payne espoused the unadventurous, middlebrow aesthetic favored by the Corporation while Geraldo (née Gerald Bright), who despite his exotic name spoke with a Cockney accent that marked his working-class London roots, favored a more up-to-date approach. It was Silvester who best reconciled wartime manliness with dance music, however. In *BBC Dancing Club*, a program that featured dance instruction and strict-tempo dance music that was "easy on the ears," he positioned dancing as an activity that supported wartime goals of fitness and social harmony. Whether broadcasting entertaining music for listeners or dancers, however, dance musicians had to position themselves carefully as fully masculine, British, and patriotic.

Chapter 5 focuses on the program *RRC* and its participation in discourses surrounding race and authenticity in jazz, as well as its role in popularizing swing in Britain. First broadcast in June 1940 (like *MWYW*), the program signaled the BBC's recognition of jazz as a distinct musical genre, its developing sense that jazz enthusiasts were connoisseurs, and its interest in serving young men, a crucial wartime audience. The series featured an array of informative gramophone records recitals and live performances, providing a legitimizing, mainstream site for British "rhythm club" discourse and improvised performance. Its house bandleader, Parry, played a key role in popularizing swing in Britain, a vogue that crested in 1942—several years after the "swing craze," as it has been defined traditionally, peaked in the United States. *RRC* also represented an important site where the creativity of African American and black British musicians was taken seriously, and it offered regular representations of interracial music making. This chapter situates the role of *RRC* among young enthusiasts and addresses how its participants negotiated the performance of racial and stylistic authenticity in British jazz.

Chapter 6 examines the BBC's 1942 "ban on crooners," an act of reform by highbrow idealists within the Corporation, which distilled wartime concerns with popular music, mass culture, and masculinity. With the military setbacks of 1942, vocal members of the press, government, and public argued that sentimental songs and singers demoralized the forces, frequently citing the program *Sincerely Yours*, which featured heartfelt sentiment. In July, the BBC banned "sloppy" lyrics, male crooners, and overly sentimental female singers from broadcast. Until the end of the war, the Dance Music Policy Committee vetted hundreds of songs and vocalists. While the BBC's effectiveness in ending sentimentality and crooning was questionable, the energetic public debate about sentimental music's impact on the morale and virility of fighting men demonstrated the wide range of opinions of what constituted good wartime masculinity and how best to sustain the nation's morale.

Chapter 7 focuses on women singers and the ways in which the BBC deployed their femininity in its broadcasts to forces and civilian audiences. Radio's ability to traverse great distance while maintaining an intimate address made it an ideal medium to support the morale of British troops stationed in North Africa and the Middle East. One of the most influential figures in this task was Cecil Madden, the director of the Empire Entertainments Unit (established in 1940), who made unprecedented use of women producers, announcers, and singers. While their work could be described using the "Rosie the Riveter" trope of women replacing men on the home front, their contemporaries praised their unique abilities to represent the values of home to men stationed abroad. Their songs and personalities rendered "croonettes" like Lynn and Shelton into what Madden called "radio pin-ups." Popular with troops, they attracted a very different response from civilians when in February 1944 the BBC instituted the General Forces Programme to replace the popular domestic Forces Programme in a change the BBC promised would build a sense of unity between the two fronts. Outspoken members of the public greeted women announcers and singers with outrage, as inappropriate to virile fighting men. The ambivalent response to women performers revealed the ways in which authority on the airwaves was gendered masculine, the difficulties of performing both femininity and good wartime citizenship, and the rift in taste between younger and older listeners.

Focusing on 1944, "Invasion Year," chapter 8 explores how the BBC, British musicians, and fans negotiated the "special relationship" with their American allies and the potential threat that Americanization posed to a distinctly British culture. In the months surrounding D-Day, when American soldiers, Armed Forces Radio, and bands entered Great Britain in force, British dance musicians and jazz enthusiasts welcomed the opportunity to observe American musicians in person and to meet similar-minded GIs. Meanwhile, the BBC became concerned with promoting British-style dance music, which it defined in opposition to American swing, discouraging "pseudo-American" bands, like Geraldo's. Nationalism aside, dance music's value as a morale booster existed only so long as it remained popular. In 1944, Listener Research determined that dance music had declined significantly in popularity, and programmers reduced its presence in the schedule—a decision that critics and performers, especially those who had contact with soldiers, contested strenuously.

The book concludes with a consideration of VE-Day and the initial shape of the better postwar future promised by the People's War. Near the end of the war, Listener Research began to recognize that the omnibus category of dance music was really composed of several different genres with their own distinct audiences. The BBC concluded that the youthful minority audience of swing fans, which had coalesced through *RRC* and wartime service, deserved special programming, laying the groundwork for the broadcasting of traditional jazz, skiffle, and eventually rock 'n' roll. Meanwhile, the BBC renewed its commitment to big bands and dance music, which dominated the postwar Light Programme and served as a bulwark against Americanization well into the rock era.

I think it's going to come (i.e. war). I often listen
on the wireless to crooners and I think that an
age which can not only tolerate such degenerate
artists but can actually make them rich must
inevitably be heading for Armageddon.
—an informant to Mass-Observation[1]

1

UPLIFT, DANCE MUSIC, AND THE BBC IN INTERWAR BRITAIN

IN 1939, AMID the illustrated profiles of radio stars, program schedules, and advertisements for cosmetics and soap, *Radio Pictorial*, "the Magazine for Every Listener," published a series of articles that presented a more serious role for radio. While the Right Reverend Bishop of Chelmsford, the president of the National Peace Council, insisted that "radio remains potentially an incalculable force for good," others described radio as "one of Hitler's greatest allies" and as a military tool for "the next war."[2] Garry Allighan described how radio had become a means for fascist powers to "precipitate international conflict," citing the Nazi Anschluss of Austria and the Italian invasion of Abyssinia. Radio had "become the fifth arm of defense—and the first arm of offense."[3] The focus shifted from the international to the personal in the article "Dial 999 for BBC," which explained what listeners could expect in wartime: the BBC would be reduced to a single signal, transmitted from multiple stations around the country to survive air raids; if the signal was jammed, it could be heard over the telephone.[4]

Within the BBC, preparations for war such as these had been under way since 1934, when Hitler had begun to rearm openly.[5] The planning followed two key strands. First, planners attended to the physical protection of BBC studios and transmitters from sabotage and air raids.[6] Second, they engaged in complex discussions with government and military representatives regarding the wartime role of the Corporation, for which, according to Briggs, the September 1938 Munich crisis "provided a useful dress rehearsal." The BBC initiated foreign-language news bulletins, which spread "reliable news and views" abroad, while at home it dispensed information, announcements, and orders. It also helped maintain morale, a role regarded by both government and BBC planners as crucial.[7]

The Munich crisis was only one of a series of international events that caused anxiety for the British during the late 1930s. Indeed, Tom Jeffrey has argued that the years 1936 to 1939 can be understood as a "crisis of the approach of war."[8] During the Munich crisis, Mass-Observation described the public mood:

> First...a resistance to the idea that war is coming....Secondly, that although most people are anxious and would like to know more...they are discouraged and bewildered by the official secrecy and newspaper contradictions. Thence, thirdly, comes the sense of helplessness which makes it seem to one in every two that there is nothing we can do about it.[9]

In many ways, the crisis was not simply that of imminent war but of modern life itself: its complexity, the impossibility of any individual mastering the multitude of "expert systems" that constituted it, the "extraordinary interpolation of the local and the global," and individuals' lack of control over much that influenced their lives.[10] Small wonder, then, that so many prewar planners emphasized the need for the BBC not only to provide information in times of crisis but also to offer morale-building programming. Music, with its ability to calm nerves, revitalize minds, and evoke happier times, was regarded as an especially powerful tool in supporting morale, although which music best fulfilled this purpose was subject to debate.

The reassuring qualities of entertainment existed not only for a potential war but also in dance music and variety programming during the late 1930s. While the news grew grimmer, Briggs asserted, "the ordinary daily programmes were continuing."[11] The sense of continuity involved both ongoing innovations by the Corporation and the constancy of its programming values. From its founding as a company in 1922, the BBC had developed a sense of tradition, which one critic called the "Reith Policy" after the influential Sir John Reith, who served until 1938 as the BBC's director-general.[12] For Reith, the new medium of radio offered untold possibilities that needed careful stewardship if they were not to be wasted in frivolous pursuits; the wireless enabled the best in culture to be made available to all. With its monopoly on broadcasting in Britain and goals of educating and uplifting the public, the BBC became a central institution and influential force in British national life. By the 1930s, the BBC's yearly cycles of sport and ceremony, offerings of educational talks and light entertainment, and promotion of serious music along with middlebrow dance music, helped create what D. L. LeMahieu called a "common culture," which "could exist within the context of great diversity...yet retain its value as a mutually acknowledged frame of reference."[13] This frame of reference was understood as distinctly British in character, a character set against not European fascism but standardized American mass culture, which appealed to the lowest common denominator. It was within the tradition of uplift and a specifically British common culture that the Mass-Observation informant quoted at the beginning of this chapter reacted so strongly to hearing radio crooners, referring to *them*, with their American and mass cultural connotations, as harbingers of "Armageddon," rather than news bulletins describing Hitler's growing power.

While imbued by now-traditional values, BBC programming in the late 1930s was also characterized by change. Spurred by competition from commercial stations on the Continent that targeted disaffected British listeners, the BBC formed its Listener Research Department in 1936. Under the leadership of Robert Silvey, the BBC employed demographic research, which had developed in the United States as a tool of mass-market persuasion, in order to understand its audience for the purposes of public service broadcasting. Not every department within the BBC was receptive to using listener research, however. While the Variety Department, which oversaw light entertainment, dance music, and theater organs, was notable for its early receptivity, the Music Department, which produced serious and light music, resisted subjecting its programming to analysis that emphasized audience size over content. It was not until war, with its overriding demands for programming that would demonstrably boost morale for various audiences, that Listener Research came fully into its own.

The new information that flooded into the BBC prompted constant self-assessment, which included an awareness of developments in American broadcasting. As both Michele Hilmes and Valeria Camporesi have demonstrated, American commercial broadcasters and the BBC were highly conscious of each other throughout their development, defining themselves oppositionally, with each side representing itself as the solution to the other's faults. The BBC saw American radio as chaotic, commercial, and vulgar whereas the Corporation's critics dismissed British radio as paternalistic and dull. American radio and cultural exports forced the BBC to define its mission more clearly than parliamentary review alone would have done and concomitantly to assert a British national identity.[14] Nevertheless, both critics and BBC producers admired the slick, efficiently produced American variety shows.[15] In the late 1930s, BBC staff began to draw on many of the techniques, if not content, of American radio, such as regularly scheduled series and programs built around a personality. Scholars including Scannell and Cardiff have cited *Band Waggon*, which starred the comedian Arthur Askey and featured the bandleader Phil Cardew, as a key example of the distinctly British manner (e.g., teasing the sedate announcer) in which BBC Variety adopted American techniques to reach a broad, even mass, audience.[16]

Arguably, the most significant area of American influence was popular music. Although transatlantic musical exchange dated back to colonial times, the decades after World War I signaled the growing influence of the United States, whose powerful film, recording, and song publishing industries spread its commercial, mechanized culture worldwide. As Catherine Parsonage has argued, American styles of dance music reached the British public through West End revues and touring musicians, who tended to play in exclusive venues. The BBC brought this fashionable entertainment to a broader audience until, by the early 1930s, dance music had become part of the national culture, with a BBC Dance Orchestra and an "outside broadcast" from a different West End hotel each night.

In the late 1930s, the BBC made three key changes in its approach to popular music and jazz that, in conjunction with audience research, would mature with wartime demands for morale-building entertainment. First, through the initiative of Leslie Perowne in the Gramophone Department, "the BBC became jazz-conscious in about

1937" and tempered its hostility to jazz.[17] It began to treat American swing as a specialized genre that appealed to a minority audience of connoisseurs, an approach well within its mandate of serving diverse tastes.[18] As will be discussed in chapter 5, swing programming continued to flourish during the war in the interest of serving the forces, but increasingly featuring British, not American, players. Second, the BBC in 1937 introduced a distinction in dance music between music for dancing, which included hotel relays, and music for entertainment.[19] "Music for entertainment" shows, like Geraldo's *Romance in Rhythm*, were organized into short series and featured leading bandleaders, along with several singers and even comedians.[20] Musically, they presented outstanding arrangements played by full ensembles, which usually included strings sections. "Detector," *Melody Maker*'s radio reviewer, opined that these programs "provided us not only with a good deal of music which, if at times it is rather synthetically frothy, is usually entertaining, but with moments which have been the nearest approach to real jazz I have been able to find on the air, outside of one or two weekly gramophone broadcasts."[21] Entertainment dance music programs continued during the war, with a shift to featuring women singers in addition to and even in place of bandleaders; they were especially favored in the Empire Entertainments Unit, which directed its broadcasts to troops stationed abroad. Finally, during the late 1930s, the BBC gave dance music greater prominence in its schedule. Dance music entertainment shows enjoyed prime weeknight evening slots, and the BBC even tried to relax the ban on Sunday dance music. Listeners and critics were acutely aware that the BBC had begun to make significant changes in its programming. Whatever their opinions, the listeners who wrote to the BBC and the press displayed their investment in the BBC as a national institution, a reflexive sense that they spoke for a wider audience, and a desire to influence policy. While some applauded the changes or called for more, others perceived the shift to "lighter and brighter" programming as a betrayal of BBC tradition.

The broadcasting of popular music and jazz in the late 1930s registered the degree to which BBC broadcasting—and British society—had changed since the 1920s, and it laid the groundwork for further changes during the war. When popular music acquired its wartime justification as a morale builder, listeners, BBC programmers, and performers debated which music best served the needs of the forces, war workers, and civilians. In the interwar years, popular music as broadcast by the BBC could not be classified as essential to morale (other than indirectly in planning documents), and yet, it marked the tensions between the traditions of the Reith Policy and the rapid changes of mass modernity, characterized by commoditization and Americanization. Popular music occupied an ambivalent place within the BBC, which as a central musical institution shaped the discourse on popular music in the United Kingdom—even for those who challenged the Corporation's policies. In order to provide popular music, the BBC had to negotiate with the complex and profit-driven industry of publishers, song pluggers, agents, and bandleaders, who treated popular songs as products targeted to a mass audience. For the BBC, popular music was low in the musical hierarchy and bore the taint of commercialism while serious music existed for its own sake. Institutionally, popular music was entertainment, not music, for it was programmed by the Variety Department, rather than Music Department. Public service and commercial aspects of popular music broadcasting at the BBC existed in uneasy ideological company. While the Corporation's priorities did not lie in drawing a mass audience, it became during the 1930s the central player in the British popular music industry.

The BBC and Its Audience before World War II

The BBC was founded in a tide of postwar optimism. Radio would serve to unite the people of a nation that was new to universal suffrage and help to fulfill the postwar hopes for both individual education and societal unity. First, the BBC sought to create a sense of national unity in a modern society of increasingly separate publics.[22] The technology of radio offered the unprecedented possibility of reaching the full spectrum of British society (at least all those with access to a wireless set) in a single moment. To borrow from Benedict Anderson, broadcasting with its undifferentiated address made possible an awareness that other members of the nation moved in "steady, anonymous, simultaneous activity" and an acute sense of "deep, horizontal comradeship."[23] Furthermore, the BBC organized its early schedule on a yearly basis, rather than a daily or weekly cycle, returning annually to the nation's important events, which the listening public could experience as a single entity.[24] It invented new traditions in the Hobsbawmian sense, such as when it took over the sponsorship of Henry Wood's Promenade Concerts in 1927, transforming them from a localized, London tradition into a yearly national event, which through broadcasting and the live concert offered an expression of shared British identity.[25] Through such traditions and its broad address, BBC helped develop a common culture for the nation by the 1930s.[26]

Second, the BBC engaged in a program of "uplift"; it wanted to raise the "level of taste, information and understanding" and to provide universal access to the nation's politics and culture.[27] As Reith wrote in his memoir, *Broadcast over Britain* (1925), "To have exploited so great a scientific invention for the purpose and pursuit of entertainment alone would have been a prostitution of its powers and an insult to the character and intelligence of the people."[28] The gendered nature of Reith's pronouncement was no coincidence when women (those over age thirty who held property) and working-class men had been so recently enfranchised and in a culture where the popular press was described in feminized terms.[29] A monopoly could preserve radio from the commercialism infecting the popular press and cinema and help promote higher values.[30] Like other middle-class reformers, Reith embraced "the practical utility of culture and stressed the personal and social impact of aesthetic appreciation," particularly for "the lower classes."[31]

Though paternalistic, Scannell and Cardiff have argued that the Corporation's goals were based on liberal foundations: "Its major contradiction lay in the fact that it separated culture, knowledge and political attitudes from their basis in the differing economic and social circumstances of the population."[32] In other words, the BBC did not extend its aims to righting inequalities of class, and its critics frequently accused it of elitism. Part of this charge was rooted in how the monopoly was funded. Since the BBC was not a commercial entity, it was entitled to a license fee, paid by anyone who owned a radio. Hilmes has pointed out that this was a regressive "tax" structure, since all listeners paid the same fee, no matter their income.[33] The other side of the system was that all listeners (especially, it may be argued, the less wealthy) felt a sense of ownership in the BBC, and many voiced their opinions accordingly.

Music played an important role at the BBC, which gained its corporate charter in 1927, from its earliest inception. Reith contended that part of the BBC's mission was "music for all" because music was "the common property and common enjoyment of mankind [sic]."[34] This aim was complicated by the difficulty of employing sufficient performers to fill the hours devoted to music during an era when gramophone programs were more novelty than practical alternative. Many performers avoided radio appearances, deterred by low compensation as well as the disapproval of music hall impresarios and symphonic organizations, which feared that radio would steal their audiences. In response, the BBC courted the impresarios and formed its own performing groups. Ensembles like the BBC Symphony Orchestra not only allowed the BBC to command the services of fine musicians but also provided better-rehearsed, better-quality performances than were available from London's other professional orchestras.[35]

Good performance was only one aspect of the BBC's aims for musical uplift. The other goal was to expand listeners' horizons, as Doctor has shown. The BBC presented an array of new music to British listeners thanks to the efforts of Music Department staff, most notably Edward Clark, who was well connected to those involved with it on the Continent. While some works, such as Alban Berg's Violin Concerto and *Wozzeck*, were broadcast to critical acclaim, many other broadcasts alienated listeners. In the late 1920s, the BBC kept the debate over new music visible in the letters columns of the *Radio Times*, interpreting hostile letters as a positive sign: at least people were listening and cared enough to respond.[36] In further attempts to engage listeners, the Corporation relabeled contemporary music broadcasts as "chamber music concerts" (managing, in the process, to turn chamber music into a category of strictly minority appeal), printed letters of new music enthusiasts in the *Radio Times*, and promoted the concerts in broadcast talks.[37]

Talks by the music educators Sir Walford Davies and Percy Scholes played an important role in the BBC's policy of musical uplift, and they tied the BBC to Britain's youthful music appreciation movement. They identified the selection of worthy, canonical classical music and the appropriate performance medium as critical concerns: upholding the composer's intended orchestration and shunning amateur piano arrangements, the teacher and autodidact were to turn to the gramophone and radio for their listening needs.[38] The BBC's efforts to obtain the best possible performers facilitated these aims. Its concern with promoting correct versions was displayed most strikingly when it banned "swung classics" (the adaptation of classical melodies in popular songs) during the Second World War.

Music appreciation educators democratically thought good taste to be inherent in the general population. With repeated exposure to good music, the taste for bad (i.e., popular) music would wither. For Scholes, the most important technique for becoming a good listener was the "habit of Attention"; Davies, meanwhile, called for repeated and concentrated hearings.[39] The project of attentive listening was central not only to music broadcasts but also to the BBC's broader agenda of education. Its efforts to teach proper listening techniques reflected the challenges of conceptualizing the reception of a mass mode of address within private domestic spaces. The *BBC Yearbook* of 1930, for example, instructed listeners to

> listen as carefully at home as you do in a theatre or concert hall. You can't get the best out of a programme if your mind is wandering, or if you are playing bridge or reading. Give it your full attention. Try turning out the lights so that your eye is not caught by familiar objects in the room. Your imagination will be twice as vivid.[40]

The instructions both assumed a reverential mode of concert etiquette (in contrast to the participatory atmosphere of the working-class music hall or the emotional, visual focus of the cinema) and a quiet, probably middle-class, room in which to listen (where dimmed lighting would not constrain other household activities). Moreover, the BBC expected listeners to adopt the traditions of live concerts rather than altering the concert for the home—or inventing an entirely new format. As Doctor has observed, the BBC programmed a series of concerts throughout each day, which culminated in a concert by the BBC Symphony Orchestra during the prime evening hours.[41] Despite this pattern, the BBC worked against habitual listening: few programs were aired at fixed times, and announcers did not promote upcoming programs, making it necessary for the public to plan their listening in advance. Even when the BBC sought to "lighten and brighten" its programming in the late 1930s with more regular slots and variety programs, it still frowned on background, or "tap," listening.

The fact that the BBC offered such prescriptions suggested, of course, that many listeners did not observe proper listening etiquette. Indeed, the BBC promoted attentive listening at a time when an increasing number of establishments provided background music to their patrons: whereas in 1919 the Performing Rights Society issued licenses for public performance at 4,000 establishments, by 1938 it granted more than 41,000 licenses.[42] Cinemas and music halls accounted for some of these numbers, but the figures represented even greater numbers of hotels, restaurants, and cafés. Live ensembles, ranging from quartets to large orchestras, performed much of this music, which was drawn from popular and light classical repertories. The wireless extended the ubiquity of music into the home. As Scannell and Cardiff asserted, "Most people of the time, irrespective of class, gender or education, treated the wireless as no more than a domestic utility for relaxation and entertainment—a convenience, a commodity, a cheerful noise in the background."[43] The BBC's eventual acknowledgment of background listening in its wartime programming—in the Forces Programme and with *Music While You Work*—represented a distinct policy shift from the 1930s.

While the radio served to educate the individual and address the nation at large, it also created a more orderly society by gathering listeners around what Simon Frith has called a "radio hearth."[44] Families came together to enjoy respectable entertainment at home, rather than seeking working-class diversions in the music hall and street. The wireless set moved gradually from the terrain of the middle-class, suburban, male hobbyist of the 1920s, who was more interested in the mechanics of finding a signal than in listening to programs, to become a symbol of economic attainment and an important drawing room furnishing by the late 1930s, with the Ecko set, the first truly reliable and relatively affordable radio, appearing in 1934.[45] Although a radio equaled a month's earnings for the average worker, three out of four families owned a wireless set by 1939.[46] The spread of radio and the good habits and education it provided offered hope for the nation. On the eve of the Second World War, an article in the *Times* articulated the democratizing and nation-building effects of radio:

> The ordinary working man and woman is becoming, it is said, a conscious citizen of the nation and of the world. The prevalent habit of daily listening to the news, the opportunities for cultural enjoyments, such as music and drama...tend to overcome parochialism of outlook and to do away with those class barriers which are the result of paucity of common interests. Broadcasting is thus the equalizing and unifying factor in national life.[47]

A criticism leveled frequently at the BBC, however, was that it had no regard for what its listeners, who paid a licensing fee of ten shillings a year in addition to the cost of their radio sets, wanted to hear. From the late 1920s, the BBC worked to rationalize the administration of its regional stations, which resulted by the mid-1930s in a network of six Regional Programmes, the National Programme, and the London Regional Programme (which functioned as an alternative national programme). The new system allowed listeners in most areas of Britain a choice between national and regional wavelengths, on which programmers tried to allocate contrasting offerings of serious and more popular fare.[48] Nevertheless, many listeners, especially women and the working and lower-middle classes, began turning to the entertainment offered by commercial radio, which was broadcast from Ireland and the Continent.[49]

Hilmes has pointed to "the almost total lack of consideration of women as a separately identifiable and desirable audience" in the BBC's prewar programming. While the BBC occasionally treated housewives to talks on topics such as "cooking and child-rearing," the notion of women as a special audience for entertainment remained underdeveloped—even in daytime programming, for which women constituted the largest audience.[50] The novelist Ursula Bloom explained in *Radio Pictorial*:

> I have no fault to find with the general programmes, which consist very fairly of something for everybody. But I do object to the fact that there is no common sense employed in the choosing of programmes especially for women....Women listeners have a right to expect something which will interest them and I do not think that they are being fairly treated.[51]

Nicholas has argued convincingly that, in talks and feature programs like *Women at War*, the BBC began to recognize women "as citizens in their own right, with particular, but by no means marginalised interests."[52] Later chapters will demonstrate that the wartime BBC also began to recognize women as a distinct audience in popular music programming, particularly in the program *Music While You Work*. During the 1930s, however, commercial radio broadcast in the United States and from the Continent provided a striking contrast to the BBC: as the primary household consumers, women were courted as an important audience for radio in evening as well as daytime periods. Commercial radio, the popular press with its women's pages, and advertising agencies all catered to women, even as they dismissed their audience as "an emotional, feminized mass."[53]

It was precisely the mass, commercial, even "feminized" appeal that the BBC found so problematic about American radio. By casting American radio as the dangerous and chaotic Other, Hilmes has argued that the BBC eluded scrutiny of the implications of its monopoly status and maintained its narrow policy of uplift.[54] Indeed, the arrival of commercial broadcasting, directed to British listeners from abroad, was the main catalyst for the BBC's greater responsiveness to listener tastes during the 1930s, according to Camporesi.[55] Before exploring how BBC policy changed to compete with commercial radio, this chapter will consider the place of dance music and jazz in British culture, with particular attention to broadcasting.

Dance Music and Jazz in Britain between the Wars

In the wake of the First World War, popular music in Britain was characterized by its associations with modern mass culture, American jazz, and the growing popularity of social dance. James Nott has argued that the interwar period in Britain was "crucial in the development of popular music and the popular music industry" because of the unprecedented growth of its audience, commercialization of its provision, and "use of technologies" to enable its rapid national and even global diffusion. Popular dance music took on the dual connotations of mass culture: on one hand, it appealed democratically across classes, as workers enjoyed a shorter workweek, higher average wages, and a growing leisure industry; on the other, it embodied industrial standardization, in which songs and fad dances operated as interchangeable commodities.[56]

Popular music was understood not as intrinsically British but rather as an American import. Throughout the period, American songs dominated live performance, music publishing, and gramophone recordings. Many music publishers and gramophone companies had ties with American companies; according to Nott, they imported not only American repertory and musical styles but also "aggressive 'American' marketing techniques."[57] The new imports highlighted the ways in which the United States had moved to the forefront economically and politically while Britain struggled to recover from its wartime losses. The offerings of "movies and stars, music, and all sorts of mass products" were as enticing to younger generation and working-class British citizens as they were threatening to arbiters of tastes at the BBC.[58] According to LeMahieu, "Two recurring themes within the critique of America and Americanization dovetailed into the attack on commercial culture and the mass media": the fear of "rampant materialism" and the fear that "American egalitarianism" would "undermine traditional social and cultural hierarchies."[59]

At first glance, the BBC's broadcasting of dance music may seem surprising in light of its concerns with uplifting public taste and promoting British national culture. Frith has argued, however, that from the mid-1920s, the BBC offered dance music to its largely middle-class listeners as respectable, solidly British entertainment.[60] It achieved this end through a number of strategies. First, it relayed live "outside broadcasts" not from the affordable and popular dance palais, which had spread rapidly throughout the country, but from the exclusive West End nightclubs, restaurants, and hotels that catered to the wealthy elite. Its sponsorship helped encourage polished, well-played dance music, which could attract listeners who might then turn to serious music. Second, the BBC emphasized the utility of dance music for relaxation and dancing at home, at a time when the ballroom dance profession had succeeded in promoting social dance as healthful, as "a normal part of middle class and respectable working class leisure," and as "entirely suited to the British temperament."[61] Finally, the BBC promoted dance music as distinct from "jazz," which carried associations with African American primitivism and with the illegal clubs of underground New York and London.[62] Thus, the BBC's dance music programming fell well within its public service mandate to provide the best in culture for all.

The genteel style of the dance bands broadcast by the BBC, with their lush "symphonic" arrangements, helped define a style that was understood as distinctly British. Indeed, by the 1930s, British dance bands, like those led by Bert Ambrose and Jack Hylton, were generally regarded to be superior to their American counterparts, especially in their versatility.[63] However, the BBC's broadcasting of the elite London bands also contributed to what Marcelle Nicol, "the popular Mayfair night-club hostess," called "the great industries and huge fortunes behind 'Tin Pan Alley.' "[64] Not everyone celebrated this tendency. As the *Daily Dispatch* radio critic complained in 1933, the BBC promoted songs that were "alien to the national character" and allowed the music of London night spots to dominate the nation.[65] The BBC welcomed its role in promoting good taste, but it recoiled from—and tried to limit—the ways in which it was implicated in the commercialization and Americanization of popular music in Britain.

The concerns about American influence in dance music were related not only to questions of national culture but also to issues of employment for native-born British citizens. During the 1920s, hotels recruited American bandleaders like Carroll Gibbons, and individual American players infused welcome doses of authenticity into British bands. However, critics also accused touring American bands and revues, particularly if they were African American, of taking jobs from unemployed British actors and musicians. The problems increased during the 1930s, when the advent of sound film and economic depression threatened employment for all but the elite bands and players. Semiprofessional musicians, who vastly outnumbered professional musicians, guaranteed a ready supply of cheap labor, but the blame soon centered on Americans, particularly after the American Federation of Musicians refused a performance permit to Jack Hylton and his band when they visited the United States in 1929. Although some visits, such as the 1933 tours by Louis Armstrong and Duke Ellington, were justified as bringing "new ideas" to British musicians, there was a "virtual ban on American musicians entering the country" from December 1930.[66] In 1935, with a continued lack of reciprocity for American and British touring bands, the Ministry of Labour heeded the Musicians' Union and made the ban on American bands visiting the United Kingdom comprehensive.[67] It was not until the Second World War, with the arrival of Glenn Miller's and other service bands, that major American bands would visit Britain; the ban itself was not lifted until 1954.

Before the Ministry of Labour ban, touring American bands, most notably the Original Dixieland Jazz Band (ODJB) and Paul Whiteman's orchestra, strongly influenced British popular music. In 1919, the ODJB thrilled British audiences at the London Hippodrome and the Hammersmith Palais de Danse, introducing the word "jazz" into everyday British vocabulary, cementing its connection to dancing, and spotlighting the potential for wind instruments in dance bands.[68] British dance bands drew less on the improvisational approach of the ODJB than on other, more accessible developments in America, however. Whiteman, a classically trained violist and the leading exemplar of the new formula, pioneered written arrangements of popular songs with clear rhythms, which appealed to dancers, and lush instrumentation, enabled by his large dance orchestra of strings, winds, and brass.[69] In 1920, his band gained contracts at exclusive hotels in Atlantic City and New York while their recording of "Whispering" became an unprecedented hit. His band toured Britain in 1923, playing in the *Brighter London* revue at the Hippodrome and for society's elite at the Grafton Galleries; they visited again in 1926.[70] British bands like the Savoy Orpheans and the perennially popular Hylton (the "English Paul Whiteman") patterned their instrumentation, arrangements, and classy presentations upon Whiteman's model. Whiteman influenced not only working dance bands but also serious British musicians' perspectives on jazz. The 1924 *Black's Dictionary of Music and Musicians* drew heavily upon his perspectives in its entry on jazz, one of the first definitions to appear in Britain.[71]

Jazz connoisseurs during the Second World War celebrated the socially marginal position of early jazz performers, but dance band musicians in the 1920s and 1930s provided the musical soundtrack for public and private gatherings of the elite on both sides of the Atlantic. In addition to standard dance bands, exclusive venues also provided their clientele with up-to-the-minute bands that specialized in tangos and even hot jazz. Although this was appreciated by enthusiasts for the music, the clientele of establishments like the Savoy Hotel tended to be conservative in their tastes, a tendency best demonstrated by instances when their preferences were challenged.[72] In 1928, the Savoy hired Fred Elizalde opposite a more conservative dance band. Elizalde was Spanish American and had made a name for himself as the leader of the Quinquaginta Ramblers, an amateur group composed of Cambridge University students.[73] Like many British bands in the 1920s, Elizalde's band included a contingent of Americans, who provided a modish and "authentic" presence. Before moving to the Savoy, Elizalde recorded frequently, and his band enjoyed critical acclaim as an adventurous and skilled ensemble—if for no other reason than the novelty of their being a college group. At the Savoy, Elizalde famously ignored the needs of dancers in his adventurous arrangements: "I remember the Elizalde Band...playing one [introduction] of 24 bars in 7–4 time while the dancers stood on the floor in bewilderment waiting for the comforting four in the bar!" one writer recalled in 1941.[74] Parsonage has suggested that the opposition to Elizalde was overstated to increase his "countercultural" capital, since he must have made sufficient concessions to dancers to avoid dismissal; however, the Savoy did not renew his contract in 1929, possibly because his hot tendencies led the management to treat him as "a passing novelty."[75] In contrast to Elizalde, Bert Ambrose at the Mayfair Hotel treated "hot music" as only one component of his repertory. A high-society favorite, Ambrose never forgot the needs of his audience. He described his approach to playing for King George VI: "Of course, he wasn't a very good dancer. I used to start off very slowly—all wrong of course—and then I would watch him like a hawk until he got into the swing of things and then I would increase the tempo until he went whirling away."[76]

During the interwar period, members of the working and middle classes also danced, but their experience differed significantly from that of the upper classes. Dinner and dancing at the Savoy was expensive while a nightclub like Murray's charged three guineas to join and required a five-guinea yearly membership fee, with additional charges for guests, food, and drink.[77] In contrast, public dance halls charged only six pence to two shillings for entry; their low fees were enabled by their large size (accommodating 500–2,000 people) and in the late 1920s by the emergence of chains, the largest of which was Mecca under the leadership of Carl L. Heimann.[78] From the opening of the Hammersmith Palais de Danse in 1919 to the mid-1930s, dancing became a mass leisure pursuit, with 750,000 people visiting dance halls each week. The palais de danse offered glamorous surroundings, uniformed attendants, at least two bands playing in alternation, refreshments, and theatrical lighting; it echoed the plush, exotic atmosphere of the cinema.[79] Its main attraction, however, was the enormous, sprung dance floor, where patrons pursued the demanding English style of ballroom dance; the role of music was strictly utilitarian.[80]

While palais dancers enjoyed what became known as strict-tempo dance music, the BBC brought the more complex music of exclusive nightspots to a broader public. As early as 1923, the Savoy Havana Band broadcast from the BBC studios, and the (still) British Broadcasting Company relayed performances from the Carlton Hotel. In 1924, the Savoy Orpheans aired weekly.[81] With the opening of its powerful Daventry transmitter and the opportunity to offer a choice in programs, the BBC increased its hours of dance music, and the Outside Broadcasting Unit wired a number of West End hotels and nightclubs for radio relay.[82] From the late 1920s until well into the 1930s, a different "name" band broadcast each night (except Sunday) between 10:30 p.m. and midnight.[83] Following the circular logic of consumer culture in which demand is created and then fulfilled, the system featured the most well-favored dance bands, reinforcing their popularity and increasing their audience.

In addition to regular Outside Broadcasts of dance music, the BBC contracted Jack Payne to serve as the director of the BBC Dance Orchestra in February 1928. At a point when many hotels were still advertising their American members, the BBC promoted Payne and his band as all-British and celebrated their commitment to giving "British dance tunes a good showing."[84] The characterization returned when the BBC awarded him an extended contract during the Second World War. Payne began bandleading in 1925, and he was a regular broadcaster from London's Hotel Cecil. Under his 1928 contract, the BBC asked him to provide dance music from 5:15 to 6:00 p.m. daily with a band of ten players (in the style Whiteman) as well as "a light orchestra for revues and vaudeville programmes and incidental music for radio plays, if necessary with augmented numbers."[85] Payne stayed with the BBC for four years before leaving—with a well-established reputation—to pursue his career leading a touring band. He was replaced by Henry Hall, a well-known bandleader in the Midlands, who debuted on March 15, 1932, and continued at the BBC until 1937.[86] Hall's appointment signaled the growing power of the regions and registered the active dance music culture in the north. Predictably, Hall gained wide favor over the radio, although dance music fans considered his style too conservative and preferred the BBC Dance Orchestra when it had been under Payne's control.

British enthusiasts for jazz got some exposure to the music through BBC broadcasts of innovative bandleaders like Elizalde and those, like Ambrose, who included hot music as part of their varied programs. However, the BBC generally eschewed hot jazz, and much of the British public tended to use the term "jazz" interchangeably with "dance music." Roger Pryor Dodge criticized the equation of popular music with "true jazz," arguing, "There is no important similarity between the orchestras of Paul Whiteman, Jack Hylton, etc. and such organizations as . . . *King Oliver's Jazz Band . . . Red Nichols and his Five Pennies, Duke Ellington and his Orchestra, Louis Armstrong and his Hot Five*." Like many others, Dodge's definition of true jazz was tied to notions of primitivism: it was created instinctively by "the negro and . . . lower members of the white race who have not yet lost their feeling for the primitive."[87] Although some British enthusiasts were able to hear jazz in London's underground nightclubs, amateur groups formed in the university towns, and bandleaders like Elizalde, Bert Firman, and Nat Gonella recorded American-style hot jazz, many regarded real jazz as located across the Atlantic in exotic American bodies and in glamorous locations like Harlem's nightclubs.

Dodge and others recognized that the most efficient way to access real jazz was through imported American gramophone recordings. Though difficult to obtain in Britain, a core repertory emerged, which during the war became known as "Golden Age" jazz. It was dominated by small, white, New York–based ensembles, like Red Nichols's, which played a polished version of New Orleans–style jazz. More gradually, British fans became aware of African American musicians like Fletcher Henderson, Armstrong, and Ellington.[88] From 1933, rhythm clubs, not live performance venues, provided the meeting ground for jazz-minded Britons, especially record collectors. Echoing the music appreciation movement's tactics, rhythm club meetings were organized around the ritual of the gramophone records recital, accompanied by the commentary of a knowledgeable critic, perhaps followed by a jam session.

The year 1933 was also a thrilling one for jazz enthusiasts because both Armstrong and Ellington and His Orchestra visited Britain to perform in variety theaters. Not only could fans attend the live shows, but the BBC also aired performances by both Armstrong and Ellington.[89] Nevertheless, key members of the BBC remained hostile to jazz. R. H. Eckersley, the director of entertainments, was "entirely against" hot jazz, "by which is implied definitely 'negroid' music of the Ellington-Armstrong type." He approved, however, of Hall's occasional inclusion of "clever orchestration[s] of quick music," which provided relief from repetitive popular songs and "[met] the need of a very large body of enthusiasts who are interested in the development of the so-called jazz songs."[90] It is doubtful that Hall's broadcasts did much to satisfy jazz enthusiasts, for whom the BBC's disapproval of jazz was legendary.

By the mid-1930s, the BBC was the largest employer of musicians in Britain and was at the center of the popular music industry, which included recording companies, the music hall circuit (where stage bands like Hylton's and Billy Cotton's toured), exclusive night spots, palais de danse, music publishers, the Musicians' Union, and others.[91] The BBC's investment in offering dance music from the finest establishments as a form of respectable leisure was extraordinarily successful. It created a strong national demand for the music and cemented a "national style" in dance music, which ironically was modeled on the symphonic syncopation pioneered by the American Whiteman. With its emphasis on live, as opposed to recorded, music and its resistance to "uncivilized" hot jazz, the BBC also contributed to the growth of the popular music industry, building an audience for a standardized product and serving as a conduit for music publishers to promote songs and bandleaders to gain fame, which they could then exploit in the variety circuit. Through radio, dance music for the elite transformed into a common cultural entertainment.

Broadcasting Dance Music during the Crisis of the Approach of War, 1936–39

The BBC had succeeded in its mission of providing high-quality British dance music, but its broadcasts also helped support a profitable industry. Although its staff could not banish all commercial influences from the schedule, they worked throughout the latter half of the 1930s to limit the most egregious business practices, especially song plugging. Meanwhile, Continental stations began to compete with the BBC for English-speaking listeners. Without abandoning its mandate, the Corporation had to demonstrate that it served a wider public in order to maintain its monopoly in Britain: it established the Listener Research Department and engaged in significant efforts to "lighten and brighten" its offerings, which involved innovations in dance music and jazz programming and attempts to relax its strict, Puritan Sundays. The changes were greeted with dismay by listeners who preferred the BBC's traditional offerings, while those who advocated lighter programming complained of the limited nature of the changes—often returning to the Continental stations.

In 1938, "Detector" reported that the BBC spent nearly £30,000 on its 700 yearly dance music broadcasts, reflecting a growing investment in popular music.[92] He described the average £43 per broadcast as "terrific pay," but the money had to pay administrative costs, technicians, and Performing Rights Society fees, as well as performers. For bands, the BBC fees were at best nominal. The BBC justified its low rates by pointing to the publicity that broadcasting provided, but bandleaders, who otherwise lost money when they aired, supplemented their income through song plugging.

Song plugging, of course, depended upon publishers, who paid bandleaders—or, increasingly throughout the 1930s, provided free arrangements—to ensure that songs and instrumental numbers in their catalogs would gain sufficient radio exposure to make them hits with the public.[93] A dance band used approximately eighteen arrangements in each hour-long program—and they were expensive, ranging between six and ten guineas for standard dance band instrumentations and between fifteen and twenty guineas for "feature orchestras" of thirty players.[94] Top bandleaders, especially the premier Ambrose, preferred to use arrangements made specifically for their bands; dance music fans looked approvingly upon their use as "a stylish effort."[95]

The BBC was troubled not simply by the intrusion of commercialism but also by song plugging's potential for bribery and manipulation. More important, it feared that plugging harmed the quality of dance music programs. In late 1935, Eric Maschwitz, the director of the recently formed Variety Department, asserted that it could be "largely stamped out by energetic action and reform on the part of the BBC."[96] The records of the BBC efforts over the next four years survive in several thick files at the BBC Written Archives Centre and, happily, are summarized by Scannell and Cardiff.[97] In brief, by August 1936, the BBC began to insert a clause forbidding song plugging and the acceptance of free orchestrations into bandleader contracts.[98] While established music publishers approved of requiring bandleaders to pay for arrangements, they recognized the difficulties of enforcement and the unfair advantage that noncompliant publishers might gain. Meanwhile, bandleaders asserted that the BBC should pay for the arrangements.[99] Ultimately, the BBC recognized the futility of enforcing the ban and determined that it had "no obligation...to do anything further to assist the publishers from cutting each other's throats."[100] At the end of 1938, it simply required that bandleaders submit their playlists to be vetted for a balanced representation of publishers. Song plugging had not ceased, but John Watt, the new director of Variety, asserted that vetting and the bandleaders' desires to play good material were sufficient to ensure good programs—the BBC's primary objective.[101]

Vocal choruses, and the singers who performed them, played an important role in the problems of song plugging. Singing a song's chorus impressed the title upon listeners, who might then purchase the sheet music. For a brief period in 1937, the BBC limited vocal numbers in dance music programs to one-third.[102] When quotas proved untenable, Maschwitz urged a focus upon good-quality performances, asserting, "The original prejudice against vocal refrains was...based upon bad vocalising by the second-rate bands."[103] "Bad vocalizing" was nearly synonymous with crooning, which Reith had classed dismissively with hot jazz in 1933.[104] Detractors regarded it as a dubious American import, although, as Vera Lynn pointed out, "anyone who sang with a danceband in the thirties was a crooner," since the style involved adapting one's voice to sing into a microphone.[105] BBC policy makers had attempted to ban crooning in 1935, but it proved nearly impossible to police.[106] As will be discussed in chapter 6, the problem recurred frequently during the war, coupled with anxieties about morale in the forces.

Dance bands encountered less regulation—and greater remuneration—when they broadcast over commercial stations on the Continent, including Radio Luxembourg,

Normandy, Toulouse, and Lyons. British firms sponsored the programs, which London advertising agencies produced on the model of commercial radio in the United States. From 1935, radio agents recorded the programs in London studios and sent them across the Channel on disc or sound film. They paid well because of efficient production methods, the organization of commercial programs into series, and the practice of recording for several different sponsors each week under different aliases.[107] Unsurprisingly, by the late 1930s, most popular bands aired on the Continental stations, as well as on the BBC.[108]

Listeners who tuned into Continental radio heard their favorite bands on a weekly basis and enjoyed polished, American-style presentation. Radio Luxembourg's appeal was especially strong on Sundays, when it sent out light English-language entertainment and dance music all day, in contrast to the staid BBC Sabbath. According to a 1938 survey by British advertising groups, the four major commercial stations had peak audiences of more than 6 million listeners on Sundays, with Luxembourg alone drawing 4 million listeners and outpacing the BBC. Continental stations, with their offerings of popular and light music, appealed most to the working and lower-middle classes, women, and the young.[109]

The BBC could not block the commercial broadcasts, but it could change its own programming. In 1934, the Programme Revision Committee met to evaluate the effectiveness and appeal of BBC presentations, beginning a trend toward lighter programming. Spurred, no doubt, by the Radio Manufacturers' Association 1935 critique that BBC programs were too dull (60 percent of programming time went to "cultivated entertainment," which 80 percent of listeners did not want), as well as the Ullswater Committee's inquiries into the renewal of the BBC charter (its monopoly on broadcasting in the United Kingdom), the BBC redoubled its efforts in 1936.[110] The Programme Revision Committee asserted the importance of appealing presentation, given the futility of simply "exhort[ing] listeners to listen." More important, the committee expressed the need to base its recommendations upon a clearer understanding of the composition, habits, and tastes of the audience.[111]

The BBC established its Listener Research Department in 1936, when the field of audience research was still relatively new in Britain and the work of its director, Robert Silvey, was considered pioneering—even in the United States (figure 1.1). Before Silvey's introduction of surveys, the Corporation had tracked public opinion by following the tone of the press and the content of listener letters.[112] The BBC soon recognized the publicity value of surveys. In 1939, for example, *Radio Pictorial* reported "actual figures on which the BBC are now basing programme construction" (e.g., 24 million listeners liked variety while only 2 million liked chamber music).[113] The BBC's new responsiveness was no mere propaganda, however. As the decade ended, the BBC increased the amount of variety and continuity programming that it broadcast, although it devoted somewhat less time to dance music, which had been better represented. More tellingly, it devoted greater financial resources to light entertainment, including variety, dance music, light music, and light drama, while it cut the budget for serious music.[114] Nevertheless, the BBC maintained its commitment to serving several publics—including those holding minority tastes. Simply catering to the masses, in

FIGURE 1.1 "R. J. E. Silvey (standing) has his weekly conference with Godfrey Adams, director of Programme Planning, to discuss listeners' likes and dislikes as the figures show them." (R. J. E. Silvey, "Finding Out What You Listen To," *Radio Times* [12 April 1940]: 9)

the fashion of commercial broadcasting on the American and Continental model, would have been a travesty of its mission.

Jazz fans were one group that benefited from the BBC's commitment to serving minority tastes. When the BBC began to broadcast swing in 1937, it classified the music as appealing to connoisseurs, rather than the broader public—a prudent judgment at the time in Britain.[115] The impetus came not from the top but from the advocacy of young members of the Gramophone Department: Perowne, Harman Grisewood, and later Charles Chilton.[116] Their gramophone series adopted the rhythm club style of presentation, in which the compère gave an informational talk to supplement the recordings. Perowne's *Kings of Jazz* and *Jazz Celebrities* provided "sundry biographical details of the artists," while in *Swing Time*, the critic Leonard Feather offered well-researched accounts, which he integrated "neatly and entertainingly" with the recordings.[117] Such presentations were particularly important in Britain from 1937, when gramophone companies increased their prices, putting records beyond the range of many fans.[118]

Perowne also worked with Felix Greene, the BBC's first North American representative, to bring a series of live swing relays from the United States. In cooperation with the Columbia Broadcasting System, the series *America Dances* ran from 1937 into the first year of the war. Perowne instructed that it should feature bands "giving us something we cannot get in England, i.e. Swing Music," and Greene successfully enlisted top

American swing bands, including those of Artie Shaw, Teddy Wilson, Duke Ellington, and Harry James, for the series.[119] *Melody Maker* credited the relays with bringing bands like Count Basie's and Bob Crosby's to the attention of British fans.[120] In addition to the regular presentation of established swing bands, Greene produced two live jam session relays in collaboration the clarinetist Joe Marsala, who hosted a Sunday jam session at New York's Hickory House. The BBC promoted the November 1938 and January 1939 sessions, which featured an interracial array of top American musicians with Alistair Cooke as compère, as historic events, although "Detector" reminded readers that the BBC had already broadcast jam sessions with British performers on its experimental television service.[121]

The relays received far more coverage in *Melody Maker* than in *Radio Times* or *Radio Pictorial*, for swing remained a minority taste in Britain. Feather estimated in 1939 that the average swing record sold only 500 copies in Britain while it sold 5,000 to 10,000 in the United States.[122] It often took dedication and prior knowledge to appreciate the *America Dances* relays because of both their irregular scheduling and poor sound quality.[123] The audibility of domestic broadcasts was far more reliable, but *Melody Maker* dismissed most British bands as lacking "the essential guts."[124] By late 1938, however, swing had emerged to the degree that *Radio Pictorial* initiated a short-lived column, "Swing Time Topics," while a growing number of British musicians embraced American-style swing, including Ken Johnson and His West Indian Dance Orchestra and the cooperatively run Heralds of Swing, which formed in early 1939.[125] As will be discussed in chapter 5, it was not until well into the war and the influence of *Radio Rhythm Club* and its house bandleader Harry Parry that swing in Britain finally attained something like the mass audience it enjoyed in the United States.

Most British listeners favored more conservative dance music: the sweet dance music played by the capital's "name" bands and the strict-tempo music that they heard at the palais. Victor Silvester explained:

> If you're a typical radio fan, then you consider first and foremost the entertainment value of a combination. If you're primarily a keen dancer, then you judge a band purely according to...its "danceability." And if you're not exactly a keen fan...you probably ask no more than pleasing melody plus a nice rhythmic sort of "pom, pom, pom."[126]

Silvester, whom *Radio Pictorial* described as the BBC's "right hand man" on strict-tempo dance music, broadcast several ballroom series in the late 1930s, including *For You, Madam*, a fortnightly series of lessons that "brought him—and the BBC—one of the largest individual fan-mails ever received."[127] Strict-tempo ballroom continued to be one of the most popular forms of dance music broadcast during the war, offering reassuring, familiar music to listeners.

The BBC's offerings of "dance music for entertainment" appealed to a wide spectrum of listeners. Leaders like Geraldo gained warm reviews from "Detector," who appreciated their arrangements and playing, which he compared favorably with sweet

American bands like André Kostelanetz.[128] A December 1938 broadcast of Geraldo's *Romance in Rhythm* exemplified the genre, its thirty-piece concert orchestra, mixed chorus of ten, female chorus of six, and vocal soloists demonstrating the BBC's willingness to devote greater resources to dance band broadcasting. Following the pattern established by Hylton and Payne, Geraldo's varied program included the hot classic "Tiger Rag"; recent American hits like "Music, Maestro, Please," Cole Porter's "It's D'lovely," and George Gershwin's "Summertime"; and light classical selections, like Rimsky-Korsakov's "Flight of the Bumblebee" and "Song of India" (which Whiteman had popularized in the 1920s). The program also featured a "galaxy of star vocalists," including Eve Becke and Frances Day from musical theater, the rousing dance-band vocalist Monte Ray, and the famous crooner Al Bowlly.[129] According to a wartime profile, Geraldo succeeded in achieving "universal appeal" with *Romance in Rhythm*, and he went on to become an important force in BBC dance music programming.[130]

Despite a growth in programming that spanned the spectrum of tastes and appealed to a broad audience, the BBC's changes, especially in dance band presentation and scheduling, remained controversial. For some, the changes were insufficient: *Melody Maker* and *Radio Pictorial* continued to compare the BBC unfavorably with commercial radio. "Detector" asserted, "The BBC puts on three out of four dance bands cold, or so amateurishly compèred that the listener value is half of what it might and should be."[131] Not everyone craved slick presentation, however: one listener complained to *Radio Times* about excessive announcements by dance band compères, concluding, "We can well do without our broadcasts being Americanised!"[132]

In a January 1939 issue of *Radio Pictorial*, Garry Allighan wrote a scathing "letter" to Frederick Ogilvie, who had succeeded Reith as director-general in 1938, accusing him of doing little to change his predecessor's policies. He criticized the BBC's "uplift policy," which "foisted" improvement upon listeners, and sarcastically attacked the BBC's "Sabbatarian Prejudices": "it is sinful for dance bands to broadcast dance music on Sundays, but not sinful for the BBC theatre orchestra to broadcast dance music on that day—providing it is at a tempo to which no one can dance and no satanic instruments like saxophones are used."[133] *Melody Maker* had reported hopefully in October 1938 that the BBC was relaxing its Sunday policy to include actual dance bands, but the Corporation quickly reversed its position, following protests by the Lord's Day Observance Society. Even light music troubled advocates for an observant Sunday: "We try to resign ourselves regretfully to the obvious lack of oratorios and good choral music on a Sunday...but when you start to brag about the number of your wretched 'popular light-music combinations'...we feel we must protest."[134] Despite charges of cowardice from *Melody Maker* and Allighan's well-supported claim that British listeners abandoned the Sunday BBC in droves, the restrictions on Sunday dance music did not loosen until the war.[135]

On the eve of the Second World War, the BBC sought to maintain a balance of popular and uplifting programs to meet the needs of its diverse audiences, which it had begun to understand better than ever before. It could not, of course, please everyone, and the letters columns of the *Radio Times* were filled with popular and classical music enthusiasts who articulated the need for more of their music and less of the other.

After years of effort, the BBC had given up its attempt to eradicate song plugging, choosing instead to focus on the more ambiguous goal of "program quality." Despite competition from commercial radio, it still excluded dance bands and variety from Sabbath broadcasting. As the organization at the center of the British popular music industry and the institution that had helped bring dance music into British common culture, the BBC held fast in its commitment to broadcast dance music according to the highest standards possible. Nevertheless, popular music remained a contested field at the BBC.

Conclusion

On September 1, 1939, the BBC released the new *Radio Times* issue for the forthcoming week of September 3–9. Along with the program information appeared the usual contradictory listener opinions. In the series "Adventures with a Portable," a hairdresser declared, "The only use for wireless...is to hear important news and dance music," while "Points from the Post" included one listener's statement, "For my part, I cut out Variety, dance music, cinema organs, and the news, for I hate to be reminded that civilisation has failed."[136] The declaration of war on September 3 rendered useless the programming information, but it seemed to affirm the letter writer's convictions. For many, the arrival of war represented a realization of the dread that underlay so many of the disturbing changes of modernity. However, the regular offerings of dance music and light entertainment gained new purpose with the demands on the BBC to support morale for civilians and forces. In war, after all, radio was the "fifth arm of defense."

The BBC had succeeded during its early decades in establishing traditions in uplift, listening, and music appreciation. Its promotion of dance music as a respectable and distinctly British form of entertainment belonged to these aims, which also required that the BBC resist the commercialism and Americanization of the popular music industry that grew alongside its broadcasts. With growing competition from the Continental stations during the late 1930s, the Corporation became increasingly reflexive, especially with the establishment of the Listener Research Department. The department's findings contributed to the BBC's efforts (particularly in the Variety Department) to offer dance music that would appeal to a national, even mass, audience; meanwhile, it responded in a more traditional manner to the tastes of the newly recognized minority audience of swing and jazz enthusiasts. The groundwork was laid, both for the Corporation's wartime innovations in popular music to serve new audiences, including women factory workers and men in the forces, and for the resistance to that change, rooted in the BBC traditions of public service and uplift.

"IN TEMPORE BELLI": POPULAR MUSIC FOR MORALE

IN THE PHONY WAR

IN THE DAYS leading up to the government's declaration of war on September 3, 1939, and in the weeks that followed, Britain's music press reassured readers of the value of music for a nation at war. "Music, indeed, comes right into its own in times of national menace . . . because it is the main prop of any country's morale," asserted *Melody Maker*.[1] It described the patriotic applications of music in an article entitled "Your Job Now: Musicians in Civilian Defense Worth Their Weight in Gold," which argued that "music has been used as an incentive to fighting men from time immemorial."[2] For a nation facing total war, which encompassed civilians as well as the forces, the home front was also critical. In Parliament, Lord Macmillan declared, "The maintenance of the spirit and the morale of our people on the Home Front is almost of as much consequence in the contribution to victory as the morale of our fighting services."[3]

Two days before the declaration of war, in response to Germany's invasion of Poland, Britain introduced air raid defensive measures for the home front, including the blackout, theater and cinema closures, and the reduction of BBC programming to a single national wavelength. Throughout September, the government ordered the evacuation of more than 1 million mothers, infants, and schoolchildren from London and other urban centers to rural areas while 158,000 British Expeditionary Force (BEF) troops departed for France.[4] Following the escalating international crises of the late 1930s, the British public regarded the declaration of war as somewhat inevitable; however, the expected catastrophes of air raids, confusion, and civilian casualties failed to materialize.[5] As the fall and winter progressed, it was the blackout and other defensive measures, rather than German acts of aggression, that induced disruptions in routine, travel, and entertainment in Britain. During the period, which came to be known as the Phony War, the issue of morale remained at the forefront, less in order to motivate the BEF to fight or to combat panic on the home front than to mitigate boredom and frustration for all. As Nicholas observed, morale for the British at war involved "a tolerance of wartime conditions, a sense of commitment to the war effort, and a belief in ultimate victory."[6]

As anticipated by the BBC and government and military planners before the war, radio broadcasting played a central role in the United Kingdom's mobilization, with its ability to unite the nation, inform its people, and maintain morale—particularly for a population experiencing wartime displacement and inconvenience. While the BBC's role in providing information was easy to quantify by counting news bulletins and announcements, determining the BBC's success in maintaining good morale presented greater challenges. Music was regarded widely as a key component of the BBC's morale-boosting programming; however, there was significant disagreement over which music would best accomplish this task, especially given the lack of choice imposed by the single wavelength. Although the *Radio Times* scolded the "selfish music-lover" for not adapting to wartime conditions, which involved broadcasts of classical music jostling against light and popular programming, orchestral concerts moved to inconvenient morning and late night slots, and shortened classical broadcasts, numerous listeners and professional critics articulated their sense that the BBC was neglecting good music—a defining aspect of its mission, both traditionally and in "a war in defense of civilization."[7] Scott Goddard observed that "lovers of café music, light music, variety music...got what they wanted. But these were evil times for the rest of us...a serious lack of spiritual sustenance of the kind that music can offer, the kind that a nation at war needs as much as it does guns or butter."[8]

As registered by the complaints of classical music proponents and the cautious observations of popular music critics, the BBC demonstrated a fresh—if still circumscribed—commitment to popular and light programming during the early months of the war. The broadcasting of popular music fell under the rubric of morale maintenance, one of the BBC's major wartime goals. In July 1939, the BBC Board of Governors stated, "In war the Board...consider that it will be important to continue to provide as much entertainment and diversion as possible."[9] Bright radio entertainment, including dance music, helped to relieve stress and bring cheer for civilians and members of the BEF. As described in chapter 1, the BBC had acknowledged the relaxing possibilities offered by good dance music in the 1920s. During the late 1930s, it began to embrace brighter programs and more lavish dance music programming, motivated by competition from commercial stations on the Continent, the findings of the Listener Research Department, and the departure of the founding director-general, Sir John Reith, in 1938.

With the arrival of war, bright dance music was now justified as morale building. Unlike serious music, however, the BBC could not justify its broadcast along the lines of intrinsic musical merit, or "spiritual sustenance." Rather, the moments of pleasure, relaxation, and escape that light entertainment provided "strengthen[] us to face the grimmer tasks," as the *Listener* explained.[10] There was another, more practical side to the BBC's embrace of light programming: it recognized the importance of keeping British listeners tuned in to its wavelengths. While during the 1930s it had faced competition from commercial broadcasters, it now faced the threat of enemy broadcasters, most famously, Lord Haw-Haw, the British traitor William Joyce, who broadcast nightly from Radio Hamburg. During the long blackout winter, he attracted a significant audience among civilians and forces (around 30 percent), who found his "audacious naughtiness" entertaining. The BBC responded by scheduling popular entertainment shows after the 9:00 p.m. news to compete directly with Haw-Haw.[11] Programming more light entertainment overall would also help inspire loyalty to the BBC among British listeners.

Despite the rhetoric about a shift in priorities, the BBC's wartime embrace of popular music programming did not emerge as a fully formed policy. Indeed, its popular broadcasts were criticized for being insufficient, poorly planned, and haphazardly executed. In the first weeks of the war, advocates for popular programming were as unhappy with the BBC as those for serious music. The *Daily Mirror*'s "Cassandra" asked:

Have they smashed all their dance records? And where is comrade Arthur Askey and his ribald but enchanting crew [the cast of the popular show *Band Waggon*]? . . . We've got to keep our spirits up, so why not let us have the stuff we like. Or is there some deep military reason why the playing of the "Lambeth Walk" would endanger the country?[12]

The BBC appeared to have succeeded in its wartime aim of uniting the nation across divisions of taste—through a shared displeasure with its service.

Nevertheless, by late October, popular music critics began to note improvements in the BBC's offerings. While some changes, like live dance music and Outside Broadcasts (OBs), revived a semblance of the prewar status quo, others, like Sunday afternoon dance-band concerts, represented a shift toward more popular Sabbath broadcasting. Even more important was the January 1940 introduction of the Forces Programme, which served British troops and provided a lighter alternative to the Home Service. The Forces Programme was significant not only as the forerunner of the postwar Light Programme but also because it represented the BBC's attempts to conceptualize a special audience (male soldiers), acknowledge background listening, and program to serve both.

The question of repertory remained pressing throughout the Phony War. Dancing boomed in popularity, and British songwriters poured out a string of jingoistic numbers, but sentimental songs were also popular, a disturbing trend for those who regarded them as escapist: Where was the marching song that would emerge as the current war's answer to "It's a Long Way to Tipperary"? they wondered. Part of the challenge was that jingoism and marching songs did not suit the Phony War's "strange state of suspended animation."[13] More frustrating still, opportunities remained limited for British songwriters, since many of the most popular songs were American and imports, such as "Beer Barrel Polka," ignored the war as a topic.

With the reduction of the BBC to a single wavelength, the question of which musicians and songs were gaining access to the airwaves became increasingly contentious for the music press, Musicians' Union, popular music publishers, and listeners. Variety Department staff regarded good-quality programming as their primary objective, but many in the popular music industry argued the BBC should prioritize fair representation among publishers' catalogs. In early 1940, the issue came to a head in a song-plugging scandal. The "evil" of song plugging, which for years had beleaguered the BBC in its relations with bandleaders and music publishers, highlighted the uneasy relations between the Corporation's roles as public interest broadcaster, commercial music gatekeeper, and unofficial, unwilling, and underresourced regulator of an unruly industry. The demands of providing morale-boosting programming and preserving the domestic entertainment industry under the exigencies of war rendered the problem still more intractable. Overall, the period of the Phony War highlighted many concerns that remained critical for the BBC throughout the war: the challenges of determining whether popular music best achieved its morale-building ends through its inherent content or in meeting listener demand, the BBC's role as gatekeeper for an industry rendered more vulnerable in war, the importance of defining the audience—or audiences—for popular music, and the difficulties of providing a satisfactory wartime service for a public and press that were free to criticize the BBC's every move.

Broadcasting Frustration: The Phony War

In its transition to a wartime service that met the demands of national security, the BBC faced and surmounted a series of challenging "tests," as a self-congratulatory issue of the *Radio Times* reflected.[14] On Friday afternoon, September 1, the BBC converted its service to a single program to prevent its transmitter signals from being used as targeting devices by enemy aircraft, eliminating all regional programming—even the important London regional service—in the process. The BBC also canceled television service for the duration, and in order to relieve congestion on Post Office telephone lines and comply with censorship requirements, it halted OBs. It allowed no one—not even an instrumental musician—to broadcast until vetted by the Ministry of Information (MOI) Radio Relations Division, a process that involved providing the ministry with each performer's "family history, connections, and moral character."[15] Finally, to preserve broadcasting in the event of London air raids, the BBC dispersed its London-based production departments to remote locations around the country. The demanding technical and organizational maneuvers were carried out against the backdrop of the blackout and transportation restrictions, prompting the *Radio Times* to declare, "Broadcasting has carried on. From seven in the morning until after midnight, there is always something on the air.... in fact, broadcasting remains one of the most normal things in an abnormal world."[16]

While the BBC regarded the continuation of broadcasting as a significant accomplishment, its critics were more concerned with what they heard *in* the broadcasts, which, from the standpoint of listeners, were deeply flawed.[17] The different perspectives of broadcasters and listeners highlighted the tension between meeting the demands of security—that some incarnation of radio service survive no matter the circumstances—and morale, which required the provision of appealing, diverting, and even inspiring programming. The *Radio Times* remonstrated, "The BBC prepared for the worst, and the worst, mercifully, has not happened yet....anybody can say 'Why on earth didn't the BBC carry on as before?' We should like to remind them that nobody knew beforehand quite how things would work out."[18]

Of course, the BBC had addressed the importance of morale-boosting programming in both its prewar planning and its public rhetoric early in the war. The two most pressing goals, according to the *Listener*, were to provide news and light entertainment that would afford "relief and relaxation" to the public.[19] During the first weeks of war, the Corporation certainly succeeded in providing information, in quantity if not quality. It increased news bulletins from five to ten per day and provided an hour of official announcements daily while cabinet ministers and civil servants gave dozens of pep talks and King George VI made a "reassuring and moving" address on September 3.[20]

The matter of light entertainment was more challenging, however, since the BBC faced restrictions in performers and other resources, necessitated by security demands, at the same time that public attention to its offerings swelled. With the blackout in place and theaters, nightclubs, and music halls closed, "people who never before listened to radio entertainments" turned to their radios for the first time.[21] In their thirst for news, reassurance, and entertainment, many listened to the BBC's single wavelength almost constantly, a practice that—though understandable in the crisis—contrasted with the Corporation's traditional address to listeners who selected their programs carefully in advance. Between the news bulletins and information, they heard the entertainment that the BBC had prepared for the emergency: hundreds of gramophone records organized into recitals that lasted from ten minutes to an hour; scores of theater organ broadcasts by Sandy Macpherson, the BBC's resident theater organist; five to nine variety programs daily, utilizing a single variety orchestra and a twenty-two-member repertory company; and an equivalent number of programs by the Music Department, provided by a pool of players organized into several newly named light music combinations, with an occasional performance by the BBC Symphony Orchestra.[22]

The overall effect was tedium. By Sunday, September 17, the press abandoned its tone of understanding and began to attack the BBC in earnest, attacks that continued in the House of Commons on September 28.[23] Critics and MPs condemned the decline in reception quality, the loss of an alternative program, and the dreary, repetitious studio entertainment that had replaced OBs of sporting events and West End dance bands.[24] The unimaginative programming and presentation were particularly troubling because they were supposed to boost the morale of a worried nation that had little recourse for diversion. Most significantly, the press and Parliament criticized the extensive use of gramophone records in a medium that had featured live performance almost exclusively. Both Compton Mackenzie, the editor of *Gramophone*, and Collie Knox, the radio critic for the *Daily Mail*, argued that the problem resided not in the fact that gramophone recordings were used but in their poor selection and dull presentation. "Instead of...making up showmanship programmes...it falls back on the

Savoy-hill method of 'putting on a gramophone record' and leaving it at that," wrote Knox.[25] Ironically, the dullness the BBC's offerings influenced a spike in record sales among consumers: *Electrical Trading and Radio Marketing* urged its readers to "cash-in on the gramophone revival," noting that turnover in the first two months of the war had doubled 1938 sales figures.[26]

With its resident theater organist, variety repertory company, and light music pool, the BBC Home Service did provide some live light and popular entertainment during the early weeks of the war. Arguably, the most important performer was Macpherson, a Canadian who had played for ten years at the Empire Cinema in Leicester Square until he succeeded Reginald Foort as BBC theater organist in November 1938.[27] Macpherson logged heroic hours on air during the early weeks of the war, broadcasting six days a week and up to four times daily, leading one listener to wonder whether "you keep Sandy Macpherson chained up in the dungeons of the BBC."[28]

The warm personality and approachable repertory of Sandy (as he was known to many) earned him a dedicated following among listeners, with his fan mail averaging a thousand letters per week.[29] Macpherson offered a blend of light classical arrangements, such as Camille Saint-Saëns's "The Swan"; Franz Lehár and Rudolf Friml operetta selections; current hits, such as selections from *Snow White and the Seven Dwarfs*; and popular medleys, often arranged by Macpherson himself.[30] In his own broadcasts, and in those of other theater organists, whose programs he was responsible for vetting, Macpherson emphasized light and popular arrangements to the exclusion of serious classical repertory or "any item...which can by any stroke of imagination be labeled 'organ' music."[31] Macpherson's on-air persona also helped attract his appreciative following. The *Radio Times* described his personality as displaying "dignity without ostentation, a wit that is dry and never caustic, and a cordial friendliness" while a family wrote, "[His] quiet voice is very reassuring at a time when our ears are on the alert for warning sirens."[32] Sandy's audience responded with an outpouring of letters and gifts; in a Christmas letter published in the *Radio Times*, he thanked his listeners for "the flowers, mufflers, handkerchiefs, cigarettes, fruit, and pots of jam you've sent me."[33]

While the main criticism leveled at Macpherson was his ubiquity on the air, the BBC's other provisions for live entertainment gained far less favor, with many listeners in a September 26 Listener Research survey criticizing their "scrappiness."[34] The professional critics were more scathing. Knox described Variety's offerings as "puerility run riot. No scripts are written, and producers are confronted with artists...and are told to get up a show in the studio," the results of which Mackenzie compared to "fourth-rate village treats."[35] The disappointing offerings of the Music and Variety pools, relayed from their secret locations outside London, were especially galling because wartime theater closings and the cancellation of commercial broadcasting on the Continent had brought mass unemployment to musicians, actors, and variety artistes. "[The BBC] could have had galaxies of talent at a minimum cost for the asking," Knox lamented. By the time the MOI finally began to clear performers for broadcast, the theaters had reopened. Even worse, the Corporation itself had canceled all contracts with performers at the war's onset to meet its relocation needs and MOI requirements, leaving "more than 9000 artists" out of work without compensation.[36]

At first, the situation for dance music and jazz at the BBC was grim. While the Corporation had made emergency provisions for light music, variety, and drama and even evacuated the BBC Symphony Orchestra, it had made no provisions for a dance band.[37] Concerned about the criticism that might be engendered if it continued broadcasting American bands during a period of widespread unemployment for British musicians, the BBC also canceled the swing-oriented *America Dances*.[38] Instead, the much-maligned records programs became vehicles for the greater infiltration of swing into BBC programs. The BBC, observed Edgar Jackson in *Gramophone*, broadcast more swing records in the first month of the war than in the previous six months.[39]

In late September, the BBC began to address the dearth of live dance music, although the demands of wartime broadcasting complicated its provision. Since security restrictions blocked dance bands from broadcasting from its London studios, all bands that the Corporation booked had to travel to Bristol (known by the code name "Exbury"), which cost them in time and money. One of the BBC's solutions was to engage a resident dance orchestra, reviving a policy from its early days—and echoing the BBC's early wartime policy of sending select pools of performers to its remote production sites.[40] The *Sunday Mail* announced enthusiastically that one of Jack Hylton's bands, under the directorship of Billy Ternent, would be the new resident band.[41] Giving relief to the overburdened Variety Orchestra and the reduced and reallocated Television Orchestra, Ternent's band supplied music for Variety productions, including the perennial favorite *Band Waggon*, which the BBC had revived on September 16.[42] With these commitments, however, the band gave few broadcasts of straight dance music, requiring the BBC to find yet another band.[43]

Rather than instituting an indefinite contract with a single band, the BBC adopted a "weekly house band" scheme (later known as the Band of the Week), which permitted a more diverse representation of "name" bands. In the scheme, bands came to Bristol for a week or two at a time and broadcast eight to nine sessions throughout the week.[44] It was inaugurated with Hylton's residency during the week of September 24 and continued in October with Billy Cotton's band for two weeks, followed by a week each for Jack Payne, Jack Jackson, and Henry Hall.[45] Most of the weekly house bands during the early months of the scheme were populist favorites. Payne and Hall had made their names as past BBC Dance Orchestra leaders while Cotton and Hylton were fixtures on the commercial Radio Normandie in the *Kraft Cheese Show* and *Rinso Radio Revue*, respectively.[46] All four leaders directed popular "stage" bands as well. "Detector" wrote approvingly, "It makes it nearer worthwhile for a band to obtain and rehearse up the sort of arrangements which are excellent for broadcasting, but for which a use cannot always be found in the other work a dance band normally has to undertake."[47] The matter of special broadcasting arrangements would soon become far more controversial, however, as Bristol became a hothouse for the song publishing and entertainment industries.

The most significant indication of what the *Daily Mirror* proclaimed as "Brighter Radio Again" was the return of OBs, inaugurated by an October 11 concert by Gracie Fields, compèred by the director of Variety John Watt, and relayed from "somewhere in England" (i.e., Bristol).[48] Fields, whose performances throughout the 1930s in

FIGURE 2.1 "Gracie Fields entertaining at a Service Men's Garden Party." (Photo by Walter Sanders/Time Life Pictures/Getty Images)

variety and film were characterized by her plucky persona, warbling soprano, and working-class Lancashire accent, was at the apex of her popularity (figure 2.1). Getting her to perform was a significant coup for the BBC, both because of her widespread appeal and because she was ill. The *Daily Express* praised "Our Gracie's" determination to make the broadcast (and the difficult five-hour train journey through the blackout) in defiance of her doctor's orders.[49]

Accompanied by a chorus and a thirty-piece orchestra led by Louis Levy, Fields struck the participatory, cheerful, and stalwart tone that came to characterize representations of the People's War. Explaining, "I want to take people out of the war," she sang "Over the Rainbow" from the recent American film *The Wizard of Oz* and several old favorites, rather than newly composed war songs.[50] Fields did not entirely avoid topicality, however. To her famous comic number, "The Greatest Aspidistra," which described the outsized fortunes of the ubiquitous houseplant crossed with an acorn, she added the "riotous" line: "He [her brother Joe]'s going to string old Hitler on the very highest bough of the biggest aspidistra."[51] Her rendition of the depression-era anthem "Wish Me Luck as You Wave Me Goodbye" took on fresh meaning as the live audience of soldiers and other war workers "broke the bonds of restraint and began to shout and cheer as they joined in the song" (sound example 2.1).[52]◐ The broadcast earned a favorable mention in Parliament during a debate concerning "brighter radio" and plaudits in the press. Jonah Barrington of the *Daily Express* raved: "(a) Easily the greatest broadcast of the war. (b) Easily the finest broadcast of [Fields's] career....I felt all along—what a leader, what a Winston Churchill No. 2, what a backbone straightener, what a tonic for those blackout blues."[53]

For dance music enthusiasts, the twice-weekly resumption of late night dance music OBs, which had been a fixture throughout the 1930s, provided a sustained tonic for the blackout blues. From October, listeners and critics welcomed the opportunity to hear famous leaders and their bands, including Geraldo from the Savoy Hotel and Harry Roy from the Café Anglais.[54] The wartime OBs of dance music from the West End continued their prewar role of bringing the sophisticated music of exclusive establishments to the wider public. Only about 4,000 people could patronize the expensive restaurants where the best dance bands played, according to Count Ramon Vargas, who apparently was a member of this elite set. In the short-lived weekly *Band Wagon*, he speculated that, in the strained atmosphere of the blackout, "the wealthy are suffering from nerves. They want to get out on the floor and dance."[55]

Roy certainly catered to this need in a Saturday, October 21, OB with his recently re-formed band. While Roy's musicianship was not taken very seriously by musicians or jazz enthusiasts, he was popular with the public for his "King of Hot-cha" persona and often-risqué novelty numbers.[56] In his first wartime broadcast, Roy played up-to-date commercial swing imported from America alongside the new crop of British war songs, contrasting with Fields's unwarlike repertory. The program included the newly composed "Adolf" (with a second verse of Roy's own invention), the increasingly inevitable "Beer Barrel Polka," and recent Glenn Miller hits, including "Bugle Call Rag," which Roy had adopted as his signature tune.[57] At first glance, Roy's swing repertory suggested that the clientele of the Café Anglais were engaging in the jitterbug; however, with the restaurant's long, narrow floor, the 700 patrons most likely engaged in rhythm or "crush" dancing, a common adaptation of the quickstep, which featured a tighter embrace for couples and shorter steps suited to crowded conditions. It was a useful skill, as West End clubs and hotels began to enjoy capacity attendance.[58]

By the middle of October, nightlife had returned to London in establishments catering to all classes, ushering in greater opportunities for dance bands not only on the air but also in live performance. Ray Sonin argued in *Melody Maker* that the September dance band drought had actually benefited the bands, for "the public are beginning to miss them instead of being wearied by them."[59] For dance halls with their middle- and working-class patrons, Mass-Observation found that the blackout, which discouraged a wide range of leisure activities, barely affected attendance.[60] In December, *Melody Maker* concluded, "The war-time craze for dancing and first-class musical entertainment is bringing halcyon days back to the West End of London. Not since the palmiest era of Jazz prosperity has London's night life resounded to the strains of so many ace dance bands."[61]

Despite Roy's Miller-inspired repertory, few up-tempo swing numbers were popular in the early months of the war—with the exception of "Beer Barrel Polka," a brisk number that some performers chose to play in swing style. It was a pop—even a populist—hit in Britain, topping the list suggested by *Daily Herald* readers as "community songs for members of the Services."[62] "Tommy has taken [it] to his bosom," the *Daily Mail* observed.[63] The song became iconic of the British war effort in documentaries like Humphrey Jennings's *Listen to Britain* (1942); however, it was hardly a native product. The Czech songwriter Jaromír Vejvoda published it originally in 1934, and it became an international hit when it was published with English lyrics in New York earlier in 1939.[64] With Noel Gay's "Run, Rabbit, Run" and other prewar songs that remained popular during the war's early months, "Beer Barrel Polka" entered into a mass-mediated oral tradition of popular broadcasts and sing-alongs.

In contrast to their prewar repertories, which had already found favor with the public, music publishers faced significant obstacles in disseminating new songs during the early weeks of the war. Live broadcasting, which had come to play a central role in song promotion, was severely reduced, and live outlets, like variety theaters, were closed. The situation was complicated further by the public mood of waiting and frustration. In September, however, the crack songwriting team of Jimmy Kennedy and Michael Carr set a new tone with the cheeky fast foxtrot "We're Gonna Hang Out the Washing on the Siegfried Line" (referring to the series of defenses and fortifications along Germany's western frontier). Mass-Observation identified it as the first "smash hit" of the war, suggesting two reasons for the song's success. First, its inclusive use of first-person plural appealed to civilians, who could share in the pronouncements of the optimistic soldier-narrator. Second, in its anticipation of an easy victory over Germany, it voiced "the wish of ordinary people to get a bit rougher" at a point when governmental policy "remained exceedingly polite, logical and unbellicose."[65]

The tone of war songs remained largely "bright and cheerful" into October, according to *Melody Maker*, but "opinion ... is divided as to whether to cater for the civilian or the soldier—whose ideas of a good war song differ considerably." While soldiers preferred prewar songs, because of their topical remove from the conflict and comforting familiarity, jingoistic numbers like Ross Parker and Hugh Charles's march "There'll Always Be an England," which sold 200,000 copies by mid-November, appealed to civilians.[66] Parker explained, "I'm glad to see it is a smash hit because it proves ... that the man-in-the-street still appreciates his country and what it stands for. It means more to me and Hughie than a hundred comedy songs about the war."[67] Nevertheless, many war songs were comic: Art Noel and Don Pelosi's "Kiss Me Goodnight, Sergeant Major" featured a drunken private requesting that his superior "be a mother to me" and tuck him into bed while Annette Mills's "Adolf" informed the dictator that he had "bitten off much more than he could chew." The BBC was ambivalent about songs like "Adolf," however: "We do not ban jokes at the expense of the Nazi regime, but we do ban bad jokes, too frequent use of such material and, above all, mere vulgar abuse of individuals," explained J. Wellington, the assistant controller of programs.[68] In October, *Melody Maker* concluded, "The BBC has now, we believe, put its foot down against songs about Hitler."[69]

By mid-November, according to Mass-Observation, "7 of the leading publishers [had] produced 25 war tunes."[70] The new war songs were nationalistic not only in their topics but also in their mode of production, which was exclusively British. The American policy of neutrality forbade Tin Pan Alley from publishing war songs and broadcasters from airing them, although the British songs gained a North American outlet through Canadian publishers.[71] Inspired by this default monopoly, Mass-Observation predicted that the war would curb American influence in British popular music. The situation was short-lived, however, for the production of jingoistic numbers peaked in October; in November, 49 percent of releases were "plain love songs" from America and Britain while only 43 percent were war songs. According to Mass-Observation, the topics of love and longing were "likely to find an even larger place, for blackout, evacuation, [and] conscription increase frustration, separation, and insecurity." It listed nine titles alone on the theme of a soldier's separation from home, the most lasting of which was Parker and Charles's "We'll Meet Again," which became closely associated with the singer Vera Lynn.[72] The song combined the first-person plural, which had been so successful in more jingoistic numbers, with romantic longing and an insistent faith in the couple's eventual reunion. It was also unabashedly sentimental, a mood that bewildered critics who called for more bracing wartime fare.

Both jingoistic and sentimental war songs found critics among BBC listeners. "Blue Note" declared in *Band Wagon*, "I suppose we must have our bellyful of pseudo-patriotism, and I wouldn't mind that if these war-time melodies were, in fact, melodies."[73] Certainly, many jingoistic songs were characterized by simple melodies, short phrases, and repetition. Nevertheless, sentimental numbers, which followed models established before the war, attracted far more antipathy. One corporal begged, "Please, *please*, put an end to those dreadful songs which keep drumming into us the inevitable parting from our wives, our mothers, and our sweethearts."[74] The theme of separation was not limited to romantic relationships. Gaby Rogers and Harry Phillips's chromatically tinged "Goodnight Children Everywhere" was based upon the sign-off of the BBC *Children's Hour* announcer Derek McCulloch and was inscribed, "With a tender thought to all evacuated children."[75] A recording of the song by Joe Loss and his band featured a pseudo–music box introduction and a maudlin dialogue between the vocalists Chick Henderson and Shirley Lenner, impersonating a child (sound example 2.2).[76] ◐ In December, "Detector" deplored the quality of broadcast dance music, castigating the BBC for its willful ignorance and neglect of the genre. He wrote:

> Dance music has got into the rut where everyone follows everyone else in a parade of stereotyped nitwiticism unconcealed by its veneer of slickness....the war has made it more obvious by being the instigation of a run of tunes which, if possible, are more trite and reek more nauseatingly of cloying sentiment than ever before.[77]

Another popular subgenre that for its critics embodied the debased commercialism of the music publishers was "swung classics." Largely an American product, their borrowing of well-known classical works in the public domain reflected both a playful aesthetic and a means to avoid paying royalties to the American Society of Composers, Authors, and Publishers.[78] Swung classics had their British advocates, many of whom described them as a gateway to better things. In a letter to the *Radio Times*, one listener couched her approval in terms of the BBC's policy of uplift: "Thanks to 'Our Love' and

'Moon Love' for introducing me to Tchaikovsky—in fact thanks to the whole BBC for all my worldly knowledge."[79] Their critics could be scathing, however:

> This war is bad enough, but when one of man's most valuable compensations—music—is pilfered, robbed, and dressed up in the disreputable garb of "Tin Pan Alley," things are going from worse to worst. Let us have our music "decontaminated," to coin a modern phrase, from the notorious and intoxicated jitterbugs, of the world of cooing crooners and screaming saxophones.[80]

In 1942, the BBC would come to classify swung classics and sentimental songs as a serious problem, but for the moment, maintaining a balance of programs on its single wavelength that could please a diverse range of tastes was of greater concern. Dance music was a critical element in this endeavor.

Balancing the needs of multiple audiences was difficult, especially since listeners, the press, and the music industry liberally exercised their freedom to criticize the BBC. The first challenge was allotting hours of representation to the three main musical genres: classical, light, and popular. In the first Music Policy statement of the war, Adrian Boult, the director of music, evaluated the "typical" schedule of week 48 (December 3–9).[81] Twenty-one hours were devoted to light music, and twenty-six were given to serious music, which the *Radio Times* classical music critic defended as "surely a very fair representation. It is more than a fifth of the whole week!"[82] In the same week, popular music was scheduled for a little over half of this time—thirteen and a half hours, including five hours and fifteen minutes of straight dance music and three hours and twenty-five minutes of theater organs.[83] The *Daily Mirror*'s Bernard Buckham protested this distribution: "A large amount of time is devoted to music of the academic type, which can only interest a fraction of the listening public."[84] A Mass-Observation study of musical tastes "in a South London borough" supported Buckham's assertions. Seventy-six percent of middle-class respondents and even larger percentages of working-class men (84 percent) and women (86 percent) reported liking dance music. A nearly inverse number of respondents described classical music as their favorite type. While a significant number of middle-class respondents reported an enthusiasm for classical music, Hughes reminded readers that the middle class constituted less than a quarter of the total population.[85] Thus, the BBC was devoting significant time and resources to music favored by only 10 to 15 percent of the population, albeit a portion that tended to be proactive in advocating for its preferences.

Like the sudden close quarters that set off both cross-class encounters and tensions between evacuees and hosts, the BBC's single program, with its juxtaposition of contrasting genres, exposed listeners to a broader array of programming—with all its potential to irritate—than many had encountered before. The Music Department aimed to mitigate the effect by offering high-quality, shorter programs of "great classics" that would appeal to "an infinitely wider audience" whose only choice was now to switch off or listen.[86] By December, however, it became clear that the battle was less over how *much* of a given musical genre was broadcast throughout the programming week and more over *when* it was broadcast, particularly in regard to the prime evening hours.

Wednesday and Sunday evening symphony concerts constituted the "backbone" of Music Department offerings, which filled fourteen evening hours each week (nine hours devoted to serious music and five to light music).[87] In contrast, the BBC scheduled only five hours and twenty-five minutes of popular music after 6:00 p.m.—mostly in the form of late night dance music.[88] *Band Wagon* complained, "Bands go to Bristol for a week to broadcast at, say, 9 o'clock in the morning and twelvish at night. Very seldom do they get their full advertised time in the evening."[89]

Despite the partisan stance of dance and classical music enthusiasts, many listeners had catholic tastes. Mass-Observation reported that a significant percentage of its respondents liked "all types" of music while large majorities of those who preferred classical, light music, and jazz also appreciated dance music.[90] One of the most successful ways of pleasing the broad audience that was receptive to dance music was by cultivating the dance music entertainment programs that had been so successful before the war. The BBC achieved a major coup in this regard when it contracted Henry Hall to produce and perform in a series of his prewar favorite, *Guest Night*, during the winter.[91] The program, which featured visiting stars along with Hall's band, ran throughout the war and beyond.[92]

It was, however, Fields in her Christmas broadcast who again proved herself to be the entertainer best able to unite the nation over the airwaves. Mackenzie opined, "Her vitality is…so essentially English as to provide an assurance of this country's health."[93] Relayed from an Entertainments National Service Association (ENSA) concert for the troops "somewhere in France," her performance was heard by 67.5 percent of the audience, the largest recorded to date.[94] As in her October broadcast, she largely avoided the war as a topic, featuring Gounod's "Ave Maria" along with popular numbers like "F. D. R. Jones." Nevertheless, she also sang the sentimental war song "Goodnight Children Everywhere," which the "publicity-ace" (i.e., song plugger) Felix Mendelssohn had "crossed the channel" to deliver.[95] Fields's bravura performance was not enough to defuse criticism of the BBC, however. *Band Wagon* complained that the BBC's Christmas broadcasts took "the 'Christmas cake' for dreariness. Apart from the special news items; the King's Speech; and Gracie's magnificent performance, the BBC served up the most miserable day's programme ever. Why they deserted the dance fans I shall never understand."[96] The imaginary community that the single wavelength brought together was not a unified whole; rather, it was a collection of competing constituencies. Fortunately, the BBC's introduction of a new service for the forces in the new year helped address more of its listeners' demands.

A Service for the Troops

For military authorities and the BBC, the state of morale in the BEF as it entered a winter of stalemate was a matter of serious concern: soldiers were separated from their families, and they were bored. Entertainment was critical to maintaining good morale. "A dance band contains everything that a soldier needs," wrote the popular bandleader Joe Loss, upon his return from entertaining the troops in France. "It gives him lightness, brightness and noise…rhythm to exhilarate him…friendliness from hearing the tunes that

FIGURE 2.2   Joe Loss and His Band. (Programme Listings, *Radio Times* [24 May 1940]: 37)

he knows and loves so well (figure 2.2).[97] Performers touring under the auspices of ENSA, like Loss and Fields, helped address the need, but radio sets, which proliferated among the troops, provided a steadier and more accessible diet of news and entertainment.[98] Radio would help ensure "the contentment and morale of the troops."[99]

Throughout the fall, the BBC endeavored to convince the Air Ministry to allow it to mount an alternative program that would address the BEF. It finally gained permission in early December to offer special programming on an experimental basis from January 7. By the end of the month, the Forces Programme was deemed a success, and it was expanded on February 18.[100] The new program provided a much-needed alternative to the Home Service, offering a wider array of light and popular programming, for both civilian and forces listeners. Nevertheless, it addressed male soldiers primarily, and it helped define them as a new audience with specific listening needs. The BBC conceptualized soldiers as listening in groups and even inattentively, a far cry from the tired businessman listening at leisure in the privacy of his home, the traditional object of the BBC's address. These circumstances not only affected existing programming categories but also led to the development of new types. Throughout, Listener Research helped justify the new service, and its implementation coincided with the continued expansion of the department's scope and publicity for its efforts.

While the BBC was pushing to implement the Forces Programme, the BEF, along with many civilians, listened to Fécamp, Radio International, a commercial radio station based in France. *Band Wagon* described it as "offering plenty of light relief for knob-turners" and noted, "The fact that much of the programme material is sponsored by English advertisers is a major factor for dance musicians, particularly when it is remembered that jazz [i.e., popular dance music] is playing a substantial part in these daily offerings."[101] Fécamp broadcast top British artistes, like the variety star George Formby and the pianist Charlie Kunz, and its magazine, *Happy Listening*, was free to BEF units. Its popularity raised three major concerns for the BBC and military authorities, adding impetus to the drive to establish a BBC program for the forces. First, as with other transmitters, enemy aircraft could use its signal for orientation, but unlike the BBC, there were no clear protocols for closing it down in the event of an air raid. Second, it was not exclusively an English-language station but "also broadcast propaganda in several languages," including German, which worried British authorities. Finally, like Radio Luxembourg, which had closed down upon the declaration of war, it represented the threat of commercial competition. By the time that the BBC's experimental alternative commenced on January 7, the French command closed Fécamp, citing security concerns.[102] Although it never competed directly with the Forces Programme, the station did influence the BBC's decision to shape its new BEF service as a light alternative to the Home Service.

The most controversial aspect of the Forces Programme was its embrace of light Sunday programming. The Corporation's Sunday policy had already loosened on the Home Service during the early months of the war, with the occasional jazz record and the start in October of Sunday afternoon "popular" concerts (a staple in live performance), featuring bandleaders like Hylton and Geraldo.[103] In December, the BBC Board of Governors agreed to permit dance music, sport, and some variety on Forces Programme Sundays.[104] Although the Lord's Day Observance Society protested, Listener Research found that it was "very much in the minority" while listeners under thirty, a group increasingly involved in war service, welcomed the new policy.[105] "Sunday programmes have progressed a lot since those dreary days under Sir John Reith," wrote Bernard Buckham in the *Daily Mirror*, after the new policy had been in force a few weeks.[106] Others were less impressed. "Detector" complained that the Forces' first Sunday broadcast on January 7 was, barring a lively half-hour broadcast by Fields for the navy, "innocent enough for a Sunday School."[107] Meanwhile, Godfrey Adams, recently named as the new director of the BBC's Programme Planning Department, emphasized the need to strictly enforce the Sabbath ban the Home Service. The decision, he acknowledged, represented a "retract[ion] . . . on the light entertainment front," but it also helped distinguish the two services more clearly.[108]

During the experimental weeks, it was easy to distinguish between the two services on weeknight evenings, from 6:00 p.m. to 12:15 a.m., when the Forces Programme aired. While the Home Service featured programming that required concentrated listening, such as long talks, symphony concerts, and plays, the Forces Programme offered "dance music, theatre organ, Variety, light music, or sporting broadcasts instead."[109] For example, in the week of January 14, the Forces offered boxing and snooker commentary opposite the BBC Orchestra; an OB from the Mayfair Hotel by the Ambrose band, which fans had clamored to hear on air through the early months of the war, opposite selections from J. S. Bach's *Well-Tempered Clavier*; and Macpherson at the BBC theater organ opposite a recital of (classical) French organ music.[110] Indeed, during the week of January 14, the Forces Programme broadcast only eighty minutes of serious music, and talks and serious plays seldom found their way into its schedule.

The program aired a number of OBs by top dance bands, including those led by Loss at the Astoria, George Melachrino at the Café de Paris, and Sydney Lipton at Grosvenor House, but it also offered a significant amount of light music performed by salon orchestras, military bands, small combinations, and novelty groups (such as Troise and His Mandoliers). Light music maintained its high ratio in the early months of the program; during a "typical" week in May, for example, light music constituted more than half of all music offered, popular music constituted 36 percent, and classical music constituted less than 3 percent.[111]

Variety and dance music production shows were much less in evidence on the Forces Programme, except as concurrent broadcasts from the Home Service, which constituted more than half of its offerings. The concurrent broadcasts consisted primarily of late night dance music, news bulletins, and variety, such as *Monday Night at Eight*, *Itma*, *Henry Hall's Guest Night*, and *Garrison Theatre*. Variety shows were expensive to produce, but they had the largest potential audience (70 percent) of any BBC programming, so offering them concurrently made sense in terms of both audience and finance.[112] Concurrent broadcasts, gramophone recitals, and theater organs all helped contain the costs of the new service: in its early months, the BBC spent an average of only sixty-five pounds per hour on original material.[113] Although inexpensive, well-presented gramophone programs could be popular. *These You Have Loved*, a program featuring light classical recordings and comméred by the secretary-turned-producer Doris Arnold, was transplanted from its peacetime roots in 1938 to the Forces Programme, where it ran as a recurring series throughout the war.[114] Soldiers responded to her repertory of familiar works like Jean Sibelius's *Finlandia* and Mendelssohn's "On Wings of Song," as well as to her personality. The *Radio Times* reported, "The troops have loved [her broadcasts]—and any number of portraits of Doris have been given places of honour in billets in France and elsewhere."[115]

As a light alternative, the Forces Programme did much to build goodwill toward the BBC among listeners. Reflecting on the BBC's overall improvements since the early months of the war, the critic, composer, and erstwhile bandleader Spike Hughes reflected, "Perhaps for the first time in its history the BBC has put its finger on the Pulse of Public Opinion."[116] In May 1941, Listener Research demonstrated that the introduction of the Forces Programme had brought about a "phenomenal" two-thirds reduction in the BBC's "dissatisfaction percentage."[117] The light character of the new program, as well as the wavelength choice that it reintroduced, certainly contributed to the change. This was accompanied by greater publicity for the BBC's work in audience research, which demonstrated its interest in understanding listeners and their tastes. In April, for example, the *Radio Times* published "Finding Out What You Listen To," which detailed the breadth and technical sophistication of the Listener Research Department's daily surveys of civilians.[118] The experimental phase of the new program was accompanied by an energetic effort to study the forces' tastes, with the appointment of Major Richard Longland as the BBC's liaison officer with the BEF and a well-publicized (and well-regarded) trip by Director-General Ogilvie to France.[119] Although "there was never any formal attempt to use listener research to guide or shape BBC policy," Nicholas asserted, "it is hard to escape the conclusion that the Listener Research

Department made a difference.... In wartime, broadcasting had a completely new task: to keep its listeners, and to keep them happy, and [Listener Research] was essential to the fulfillment of both these tasks."[120]

Listener Research played a key role in helping to define the new audience of forces listeners. When it announced the expansion of the Forces Programme to twelve hours per day from February 18, the *Radio Times* explained, "The BBC has been conducting a systematic inquiry into what kind of programmes are most likely to satisfy those for whom the service is intended."[121] Their listening needs reflected changes wrought by war: "The listeners in the Forces are not new listeners, but they are a special section of the old listening public transferred to new and peculiar surroundings. Bodies of men need an approach different from that most suitable for the family circle."[122] Although less than a year before the BBC had found that more differences in listener tastes were attributable to age than to gender (the role of which was negligible), it now defined forces listeners through the lens of masculinity, as embodied by the brave, youthful, and physically tough "soldier-hero."[123] The soldier-hero archetype also influenced the focus in the public imagination (and in BBC publicity) on the BEF in France, despite the fact that the majority of troops were stationed within Britain in "small isolated A.A. [antiaircraft] posts 'living in unrelieved contact with an unchanging group' or concentrated in bigger units in small towns 'with only the most limited recreational opportunities.'" In a study on the troops for internal purposes, BBC researchers

FIGURE 2.3 The Forces Programme was designed for soldiers, listening in groups. Its novel reach into "dug-outs, messes, and canteens" did not extend to the parade ground, however. (Jack Dunkley, "What the Wartime Listener Thinks," *Radio Times* [26 April 1940]: 9)

FIGURE 2.4 The Home Service was still directed to an attentive domestic audience, listening around a "radio hearth." (Advertisement for Murphy sets, *Radio Times* [10 May 1940]: 2)

described them as strikingly "homogeneous" in their youth, literacy, and intelligence, sharing a "sense of fellowship," and possessing a "passionate interest in home and home interests."[124]

For the BBC, the most salient characteristic of the new audience was its tendency to listen "in groups in billets, dug-outs, messes, and canteens."[125] As the *Radio Times* explained, "The picture that the programme planners have in mind is of at least half-a-dozen men grouped round one loudspeaker rather than of a single listener sitting in solitary concentration by his own fireside." The BBC continued its address to male listeners, but it replaced the attentive, middle-class man at the radio hearth with the soldier-hero listening in fellowship with his peers. Another key characteristic of forces listeners for the BBC was that it could not expect them to listen with full attention, necessitating light programs "that do not suffer unduly by interruption, either by conversation or by the call of duty"—indeed, the kind of programmes that may be enhanced by communal enjoyment and a running exchange of comment. (figures 2.3 and 2.4).[126] Unlike "tap" listeners, whom the Corporation had scolded for their use of the radio as background to housework or conversation, the inattention of forces listeners was cast along lines of necessity and heroism: programming needed to support male bonding and accommodate "the call of duty" (figure 2.5).

During the experimental weeks of the Forces Programme, the BBC drew upon existing program types to serve the special needs of the new audience. In a *Radio Times* article, the producer Charles Brewer described the importance of news bulletins for RAF listeners (they were "the only programmes during which all conversation stops") and the popularity of variety, light music, well-presented dance music, and, "naturally" for manly men, sport.[127] The Forces Programme continued the Home Service practice

FIGURE 2.5 Domestic listeners who used background music frivolously were scolded for "careless listening." (Advertisement for Mullard radio valves and sets, *Radio Times* [23 July 1943]: 20)

of airing OBs of camp concerts for or by the forces, with titles like *Private Smith Entertains*. Variety for the troops took familiar forms of entertainment and repurposed them along patriotic themes, drawing a nation of civilian and forces listeners into the communal environment of a camp concert "somewhere in England." In camp concert OBs, the appearances of big stars like Fields heightened the sense of occasion; when amateurs from the services performed, they enhanced a sense of wartime egalitarianism (and also saved the Corporation money), although their too frequent use eventually opened the BBC to criticism.[128] The expansion of the Forces broadcasting day permitted greater representation for live jazz and swing music, appreciation for which was regarded as the special terrain of young men. In March, the Forces Programme broadcast the final hour of the second annual Jazz Jamboree from the State Theatre in Kilburn, with the popular disc jockey Christopher Stone as compère.[129] The same month also witnessed the return of *America Dances*, with broadcasts by Bob Crosby and Louis Prima.[130]

The Forces Programme soon launched a new form of entertainment programming that addressed the needs of forces listeners more directly: the messages program. Introduced in February 1940 by Sandy Macpherson, the messages program re-

FIGURE 2.6 Sandy Macpherson, the BBC theater organist, with his correspondence for *Sandy's Half-Hour*. ("The Human Story behind *Sandy's Half-Hour*," *Radio Times* [5 April 1940]: 10)

sponded to soldiers' "passionate interest in home."[131] In essence, it was a request program: servicemen as well as their mothers, wives, or sweethearts could write Sandy with a request for a tune and a message to a loved one, who would then be notified before the program aired. The concept struck an emotional nerve with listeners. Macpherson, already a popular broadcaster, began receiving 5,000 letters per week with requests like the one in a letter he shared with a reporter from the *Star*: "I want you please to play 'I Remember.' This song in my mind is a beautiful song which makes me think of my wife and my family. I have a baby girl who is seven weeks old, and I have not yet had the pleasure of seeing her" (figure 2.6).[132] Framed by Macpherson's waltz-time signature tune "I'll Play to You," the songs in *Sandy's Half Hour* featured titles and lyrics that ran the gamut of romantic and familial love as expressed in popular song.[133] Although they were performed instrumentally, the repertory, drawn from standards (e.g., Rodgers's "Blue Moon"), operetta, and parlor song (e.g., Carrie Jacobs Bond's "A Perfect Day") of the past thirty years, along with current war-themed hits (e.g., "Goodnight Children Everywhere" and "We'll Meet Again"), was familiar to a wide audience.[134] To further the personal touch already established by songs expressing intimate sentiments and his warm voice, Macpherson soon began to invite some of "the womenfolk" and children into the studio to give their messages themselves.[135] Macpherson's program and the many shows that soon adopted its format provided a comforting "life-line" between forces listeners and their families at home, building an on-air community of families and sweethearts separated by war.[136]

Sandy's Half Hour dramatized the central paradox of the Forces Programme: while it was conceptualized by the BBC and listeners as a service addressing the forces, its success also depended upon civilian listeners, for whom it functioned as an important alternative to the Home Service. Although its community embraced both groups, analysis of its success and prescriptions for its future direction were articulated by the BBC, critics, and civilian listeners through the needs of the troops. In the months after June 1940, when the BEF retreated to British soil, such individuals would have the option of listening to serious offerings on the Home Service, but even then, programming on the Forces was discussed in terms of the soldier-hero. Despite such rhetoric, however, more civilians than soldiers listened to the program, and by 1943 its audience was 50 percent larger than that of the Home Service.[137]

Certainly, Hughes was correct in affirming that at the beginning of 1940, the BBC had "put its finger on the Pulse of Public Opinion."[138] This was critical, given the close relationship established between pleasing listeners and boosting morale, a key aspect of the BBC's wartime mission. The Forces Programme helped the BBC to provide a broader spectrum of programming to its diverse audiences and to create the perception of choice for its critics while it also demonstrated the Corporation's patriotic consideration of the BEF in France. With its light music, variety, and dance music shows, it became the main source of light entertainment regarded as morale boosting. Nevertheless, access to the airwaves remained limited for dance bands, fueling rumors of song plugging and opening the BBC to renewed criticism.

Trouble in Bristol: The "Evil" of Song Plugging

"Bristol is the hub of the musical world," declared *Band Wagon* in February 1940 of the city that housed the BBC's wartime headquarters for variety, music, religious, and schools broadcasting.[139] Given the symbiosis between the BBC and the music industry, it was impossible for the identity of Bristol, which during the previous fall had been known as "Exbury," to remain secret. In addition to BBC staff, variety performers, and dance musicians, the exodus to Bristol soon included song pluggers, representing the interests of competing music publishing houses. As discussed in chapter 1, the BBC had reached a stalemate in its prewar attempt to end song plugging, resolving that it could only vet programs for a balanced representation of publishers. Under war conditions, however, the practice mushroomed. "People still talk of those months of broadcasting in Bristol as the wild hey-day of the plug racket," the bandleader Victor Silvester recalled.[140] In early 1940, the prevalence of song plugging ignited a scandal that highlighted the uneasy relations between the BBC and the music industry in wartime.

The BBC's wartime adaptations contributed to a rise in song plugging, which was manifested on the air by the annoying overplaying of new songs. While the constriction of hours devoted to popular music in the BBC's schedule increased the sway of those who broadcast, Bristol's location a half day's journey from London by train concentrated radio performers in a small geographic area, making them easy targets for the pluggers encamped there.[141] The BBC's popular Band of the Week scheme allowed individual bands to dominate dance music broadcasting for a week at a time; bands could earn £200 to £300 in plug money during their resident week in Bristol.[142] Meanwhile, the war heightened the stakes in discourse around song plugging: it lowered program quality, which in turn harmed morale. Critics cast it as unpatriotic profiteering: American firms could afford the steep costs of "the 'ether auction'" while British publishers could not, retarding the broadcast of British songs and diverting "thousands of pounds to the United States in royalties."[143]

In February, *Melody Maker* launched a four-month crusade against the virulent "scandal" of song plugging at the BBC, faulting the Corporation for paying inadequate broadcasting fees to bands, which necessitated their acceptance of plug money.[144] Given the weekly's complicated allegiances to the publishers who advertised in its pages, the dance profession it championed, and popular music and jazz enthusiasts who constituted much of its readership, the BBC was a frequent, safe, and sometimes deserving target of criticism. While the BBC's response to *Melody Maker*'s campaign was outwardly cool, internally its staff were worried and worked quietly to improve their vetting process, which had been disrupted by wartime relocations, in order to rein in the undue repetition of songs.[145] Nevertheless, the flow of plug money was difficult to stem. In May, prompted by *Melody Maker*'s campaign, Alfred Edwards, MP, raised a supplementary question in Parliament for Sir John Reith, the minister of information and former BBC director general, on the plugging problem. Reith responded:

I know that the BBC has been trying to eliminate this evil of song plugging. I know that the items in dance band programmes were, and are, chosen on their merits, but I know that the BBC finds an extraordinary difficulty in getting the cooperation of all concerned. They have been doing what they can and hope to minimise the evil.[146]

Given Reith's strict Presbyterianism, his use of the term "evil" went beyond mere rhetoric. Evil was sin, a state from which individuals could only be rescued by the grace of God.[147] Technically legal, plugging was worse than a mere annoyance or unpleasant commercial practice. It was sinful, greedy behavior, endemic to the worldly business of popular music, and it diminished the ability of radio to function as a force for good. As such, plugging and its worst effects should be minimized, although Reith and the Corporation recognized the impossibility of eradicating it. The BBC's internal bulletin, which notified staff of the parliamentary question and instructed them against publicity on the matter, framed the ultimate solution in terms of individual spiritual struggle: "Until the publishers and dance band leaders are prepared to adopt and observe a self-denying ordinance, all that the BBC can effectively do is to ensure so far as practicable that its programmes are not adversely affected."[148]

Melody Maker's antiplugging campaign focused on music business practices and BBC policy, rather than on specific repertory, a safe position, given its relationships with publishers and bandleaders. For many observers, however, the question of plugging was tied closely to musical nationalism. The turn to sentimental and escapist topics in late 1939 continued, allowing American songs like "Over the Rainbow" to dominate the airwaves, cinemas, and even gramophone shop windows.[149] The music publisher Lawrence Wright accused the BBC of being "chronic offenders" in ignoring British songs: "They play endless American records and plug foreign tunes out of all proportion to their merits. They should favour British songs."[150] Frustration with the limited representation of British songs would flare up repeatedly throughout the war, but the BBC resisted setting quotas in its careful balancing act of supporting British music and identity while also promoting quality.

The dominance of escapist topics also worried the MOI and others, who craved more stirring national songs, in the mold of Ivor Novello's First World War classic, "Keep the Home Fires Burning."[151] Lady Reading, the founder of the Women's Voluntary Service, suggested to Reith the desirability of encouraging the regular production of "really attractive national songs," a suggestion that Reith delegated to the BBC at the highest level, in a letter sent to Director-General Ogilvie in February.[152] Variety and Music Department staff were quick to point out the flaws in the idea of a BBC-sponsored contest (not least of which was inadequate staffing) and also pointed to the complexities of commissioning songs, particularly popular songs. The MOI was insistent, however, and a number of unsatisfactory and forgettable numbers were finally screened (and apparently rejected) in late August.[153]

Despite all of their difficulties in regulating song plugging, BBC Variety staff understood what the MOI did not: public taste and the popular music industry existed in an uneasy relationship that, notwithstanding the prevalence of song plugging (itself a form of commercial propaganda), resisted top-down interventions. Song plugging highlighted the messier, more obviously commercial nature of popular music, in contrast to the uplifting, spiritual, and noncommercial discourse surrounding the BBC's broadcasting of classical music. While a growing consensus agreed that popular music was doing something to boost morale, the songs of the new war were thematically different than those that lived on in popular memory from the Great War. Jingoism, or even uplifting national songs, had faded quickly during the winter of 1940, and a very different mood—of longing, escapism, and sentimentality—had come to dominate popular song as broadcast over the BBC.

Conclusion

Frivolous or not, the *Melody Maker* campaign drew attention to the challenges of broadcasting under wartime conditions. The disruptions and relocations faced by the people of Britain plagued the BBC as well. The evacuation to Bristol amplified the problems of plugging, but it also raised difficulties of expense and availability for dance bands and other performers who made the trip to "Exbury." Nevertheless, as a force of national unity and morale, listeners expected the BBC to rise above the fray of limited OBs, staff shortages, and the challenges of reorganization and reduced wavelengths. When these obstacles affected its program output, particularly in the early weeks of the war, the press quickly attacked the Corporation for failing in its duty to provide relief and cheer—not just news—for the nation's people.

Despite the missteps of the early weeks of the war, the BBC worked to brighten its broadcasting to please the general public, if not its audience for serious music. The Forces Programme represented the beginning of the BBC's efforts to reach special wartime demographics, a goal that also signified continuity with the BBC's tradition of broadcasting to many specific audiences rather than following in the American model of aiming at a single mass audience. The erosion of its Sunday policy signaled the BBC's recognition of the strategic necessity to avoid driving British listeners to seek lighter programming from Continental—and even enemy—sources. Meanwhile, the BBC's attempts to provide good live dance music over its wavelengths, particularly the Forces Programme, demonstrated the Corporation's view that good dance music was a key component of morale maintenance.

The song-plugging controversy suggested, however, that the BBC's attitude toward dance music was still ambivalent. Certainly, most of the criticism came from outside the Corporation in a campaign spurred on by a crusading paper. The BBC's defensive response—both external and internal—indicates, however, that song plugging could not be ignored as a minor threat. Due to its commercial nature, dance music had to be carefully policed or the "evil" influence of song plugging would corrode program quality from within. Concern with song plugging recurred periodically throughout the war, but the impulse to vet dance music programs broadened to include the crop of sentimental songs that seemed a side effect of war. As early as the fall of 1939, some listeners worried about their effect upon morale in the forces and among civilians—and these concerns would blossom in 1942. In the meantime, however, the concerns and controversies of the Phony War were quickly eclipsed. The spring of 1940 brought events that were far more serious than hanky-panky in Bristol. Germany went on the offensive, France fell, and Britain was suddenly isolated. As the nation embarked upon massive production drives and a German invasion seemed imminent, the BBC looked to new ways to promote morale and national unity. The next chapter examines the role of dance music in these efforts.

MUSIC WHILE YOU WORK: DISCIPLINE, DANCE MUSIC,

AND WORKERS IN WARTIME

IN 1943, WYNFORD Reynolds described the dramatic effect of music on factory workers "somewhere in England" the morning after an air raid:

> I observed the tired, drawn faces, the wearied droop of shoulders, the glances at empty seats and felt that the very air was filled with the nervous tension of the past night.
>
> Suddenly the loud-speakers came to life—a voice was heard "calling all workers"—and then followed the rousing strains of a march familiar to millions of people in this war and the last—"Colonel Bogey."
>
> Like a trumpet call to action, the martial melody echoed through the shop, and then I witnessed a transformation scene—tired faces breaking into smiles, the squaring of bent shoulders, chins uplifted, and suddenly voices, singing voices, that from a murmur swelled into a roar as with heads raised in defiance those factory workers shouted: "AND THE SAME TO YOU!"[1]

The materials upon which the transformation acted were the workers' anonymous bodies: faces, shoulders, chins, and heads. An announcer's voice and a familiar march triggered the transformation via the loudspeaker; however, it was the workers' sung and shouted response that signaled their renewed collective resolve.

Although powerful, the transformation was not unique. Rather, it represented the effects of the BBC program *Music While You Work* (*MWYW*) in factories throughout Britain, combining the wartime ideals of good morale and national unity. Reynolds's anecdote gave the human side of statistics that demonstrated the program's positive effect on industrial output. The program united ideologies of music as a force of cultural and moral uplift; research in industrial efficiency that focused on workers' bodies, psychology, and welfare; and the conviction that, in a state of total war, the contributions of every citizen mattered. As the program developed beyond its roots in the production drives of summer 1940, it reflected the growing concerns of the nation's leaders with the "problem" of the wartime factory workforce: conscripted young women engaged in "diluted" (simplified and more monotonous) labor. Women's apathetic and unruly bodies could slow production, detract from the nation's war effort, and even, as one wartime study warned, threaten "the health of all democracy."[2]

Music was a powerful tool in the project of disciplining workers' bodies. Though its ability to speed the rate of production and raise output was debatable, it was prized for its tonic qualities: it raised workers' moods, energy levels, and morale. At the same time that music acted on the bodies of workers, the demands of *MWYW* acted upon music. Reynolds and other producers studied musical repertories and used performances not on their own terms as "art" or entertainment but for their effect on production, their audibility, and their impact on worker morale. While the Music Department represented "serious" music as a spiritual force complete in itself, *MWYW* harnessed "lower" musics, drawn from popular dance and light classical repertories. Because BBC policy favored live music and suitable recordings were few, most programs were broadcast live (85 percent in the first year alone); the bodies of musicians laboring in the studio mirrored the laboring bodies of their auditors.

In addition to wartime ideologies of morale and total effort, *MWYW* existed in relation to concerns that emerged during the 1930s: the application of American innovations like the assembly line in British industry, the science of demography that had been honed in advertising agencies, and the anthropological studies of British life conducted by the left-leaning Mass-Observation. These concerns relate to what Susan Leigh Foster and Dorinda Outram have identified as a broad shift in the 1930s and 1940s to considering the body as a site for historical, anthropological, and social psychological inquiry. The parallel rise of fascism was no coincidence: the new work focused upon the body as a "transparent container" for cultural meanings, an entity acted upon by powerful external political and social forces.[3] Even in the democratic societies of Allied nations, the individual body was regarded as under siege by commercial, American-style, lowest-common-denominator mass culture.[4] In this light, it is tempting to interpret *MWYW* as using Americanized popular music to coerce the efforts of British assembly-line workers, ironically melding mass culture and dehumanizing technologies in a struggle against a fascist regime, which itself was manipulating the masses.

Two "escape routes" complicate the exclusive location of *MWYW* in discourses of social control, however. First, the Soviet Union, especially with its heroic resistance to Germany's June 1941 invasion, represented an alternate vision of vigorous cooperation for the British.[5] In his novel *Daylight on Saturday* (1943), J. B. Priestley portrayed workers who admired Soviet collectivism, which according to wartime propaganda, existed without the coercion of mass politics or mass culture. Even more, the denizens of Priestley's war factory yearned nostalgically for "the great mad months after Dunkirk, when the country came alive at last and worked in a glorious frenzy...saving the world—and its own soul."[6] Termed Britain's "finest hour" by Winston Churchill, the evacuation of 338,226 Allied troops at Dunkirk between May 29 and June 3, 1940, registered hope where all might have been lost. It had a remarkable effect on workers' commitment to the war effort: "Latecoming and absenteeism practically vanished; phenomenally long hours were worked; productivity soared."[7] The BBC introduced *MWYW* on June 23, 1940, three weeks after Dunkirk, as a direct response to the production drives: it intended the program to demonstrate its regard for workers as a crucial population in the war effort and to improve their morale. *MWYW* symbolized, and even helped workers to embody, the collective, democratic resolve of the nation.

The second escape route from interpreting the program only in terms of social control follows the possibilities of a modern "listening body," which interacted with musical sound in new ways. The interwar period in Britain witnessed an expansion of leisure for all classes accompanied by new opportunities for hearing music live, mediated, and mechanically reproduced. Dancing became a respectable mass leisure pursuit, with popular dance music carrying strong bodily associations. Meanwhile, via the gramophone and the radio, listeners at home had unprecedented opportunities to listen repeatedly, hear distant performers, and modulate the degree of attention with which they listened.[8] The BBC embraced the possibilities of repeated and distant listening, but it discouraged all but fully attentive, informed listening. Background, or "tap," listening was more complex than its detractors believed it to be, especially as improvements in sound reproduction technology allowed greater spatial and physical flexibility for listeners.

MWYW referenced flexible modes of listening and the bodily mechanics of leisure for factory workers. It did not simply create passive listening bodies that were more amenable to workplace discipline: workers sang, hummed, or whistled along. Moreover, the program drew a large and appreciative home audience. Throughout the war, *MWYW* moved toward favoring light music over dance music until it became a brand name for a distinctive light musical style. By the end of the war, more than 8 million workers, and still more people at home, regularly heard the program, which continued to air until 1967.[9]

Although *MWYW* was popular with home audiences, the BBC focused almost exclusively on workers listening in factories, continuing the Corporation's traditional disregard for housewives as a special audience.[10] Its producers collaborated with Robert Silvey, who headed BBC Listener Research, to make four extensive studies of *MWYW* and its reception in factories. Dealing with the practical considerations of broadcasting, they explored which musical styles, arrangements, and performances were most effective for factory audiences, whom they categorized according to gender, age, and skill. Examining *MWYW*'s early years during the Second World War provides a window into industrial music; ideologies of gender, class, musical value, and discipline; and the ways in which the BBC harnessed music and musicians for total war.

Industrial Bodies

The Second World War, with its modern weaponry and emphasis on industrial production, signaled a crisis in the relation between humans and technology.[11] Those invested in music, including musicians, critics, and the BBC, advocated for music as an essential palliative to the dehumanizing aspects of warfare, whether they emphasized music as a transcendent spiritual value in a war for civilization, a soothing escape from the anxieties of the Blitz, or dancing, with its "primitive" roots, as a natural release from the tensions of war. Despite the scientific demonstrations of the effectiveness of industrial music for a workforce unaccustomed to mechanization, it was music's cultural value that made *MWYW* so appealing to factory managers, government authorities, and the BBC.

The interest in industrial music, which reached a peak during the war, evolved out of industrial psychology, as part of the effort to correct the dehumanizing aspects of scientific management. Frederick Taylor, an American engineer, developed scientific management during the 1890s with the aim of increasing industrial efficiency. Analyzing the movements of the best workers, Taylor aimed to replace "wrong or slow-working methods" with "rational ones," and he advocated for rationalizing management structures according to a hierarchical military model.[12] He welcomed the "modern subdivision of labor" in which men with good minds were promoted while the unskilled laborer's "lower mental calibre renders him more fit...to stand the monotony of repetition."[13] Taylor's rationalized motions were further simplified by Henry Ford's assembly line, which was introduced around 1915. Labor unions opposed the dehumanizing effects of scientific management: the system deprived workers of control over their workplace, "caused irritability and fatigue," and even led output to decline in quantity and quality.[14]

Music played an important role in industrial psychology's attempts to remedy the effects of mass production on the relations between workers and their environment, coworkers, and management. In the mid-nineteenth century, industrialists treated music as an extracurricular enrichment, but the 1930s brought a new scientific approach to listening bodies: researchers tested the effects of music heard *while* workers went about their tasks.[15] In a landmark study published by Britain's Medical Research Council in 1937, Wyatt and Langdon found that music heard on gramophone records counteracted boredom and poor output in repetitive work better than when workers talked, sang, or varied their form of activity.[16] They suggested that music affected production in a manner that went beyond the Hawthorne effect, in which the mere perception that managements were attempting to improve working conditions increased workers' output, by directly improving a worker's state of mind. At the BBC, an institution that promoted music as culturally uplifting, Wyatt and Langdon's study helped motivate the wartime creation of *MWYW*.

In his preliminary report, "Music in Factories," Neil Hutchison, a member of the BBC Programme Planning Department, highlighted music's ability to increase productivity. The impact of music on workers' emotional and mental states was harder to quantify than its effect on production, but managements reported that music made workers more cheerful and, in the summer, less "tired mentally at the end of the day." More insidiously, music diminished "chatter" among workers, which helped improve the quality of their work, and "many managements" used it to replace breaks, for it appeared to be "equally beneficial and not so unsettling to the rhythm of work." Music was less effective and even counterproductive for workers engaging in tasks involving concentration, "whether typewriter or lathe"; for managements and workers, it carried strong associations with unskilled labor, a population that expanded during the war.[17]

While Taylor's vision of scientific management depended upon viewing low-status immigrant laborers as malleable, "stupid and…phlegmatic," Britain's wartime work-force was far less amenable to factory discipline.[18] The growing presence of conscripted women was a subject of special concern for managers, who feared their inexperience, and labor unions, which feared that the dilution of skilled work would ultimately lower wages for all. According to Rose, "the Government began registering women for war service" in April 1941, and their conscription commenced in December of that year.[19] By the war's end, 37 percent of women in factories were employed at munitions plants run by the Ministry of Supply, where morale was notoriously low.[20] Many conscripts came from rural backgrounds and had never before been required "to work to a strict timetable": dawdling and absenteeism were significant problems.[21] Managements re-garded unruly behaviors, such as conversation and lengthy bathroom breaks, as char-acteristically feminine.

In its fascinating study, *War Factory*, Mass-Observation addressed the question of *why* the new workforce was so problematic. Recognizing the importance of a "worm's eye" (i.e., experiential) perspective, Mass-Observation sent Celia Fremlin, a "highly trained and experienced Cambridge graduate, married, one child," to observe a war factory (at the bequest of its management), posing as an ordinary conscript.[22] Fremlin provided sensitive descriptions of the factory environment and the women with whom she worked and addressed directly the nature of labor on an assembly line: "To my surprise, I found that the boredom is far less than people imagine. In fact, for at any rate the first couple of hours, the work is definitely pleasant, rather like knitting in a fairly plain pattern." As the day progressed, however, the steady pace and windowless room began to take their toll: "At about three o'clock one gets the feeling that the time will *never* pass….A bewildering sense of helplessness comes over one….Between three and five in the afternoon more slacking and idling goes on than one would have thought possible in a wartime factory."[23]

Although the work was not mentally or physically taxing, the repetitive labor of the assembly line sapped workers' morale, affecting their bodily performance. For the Brit-ish in the Second World War, morale did not necessarily connote optimism but, rather, "a tolerance of wartime conditions" and "a sense of commitment to the war effort."[24] It was morale in this sense that suffered when workers engaged for long hours in monotonous factory labor:

> Paradoxical as it may seem, life in a twelve-hours-a-day war factory makes one feel further removed from the war than one could in any other type of life. It is hard for anyone who has not tried it, to realise the curious, almost exhilarating sense of the slipping away of all responsibilities that comes over people after a few days in this sort of work….All personal and social claims and responsibili-ties have vanished; and, in these lower grades of work, no alternative responsibil-ity for the work itself emerges.[25]

The BBC and managements considered women workers, most of whom were employed in repetitive, low-skilled work, to be especially receptive to the benefits of *MWYW*. The program brought the imagined community of radio—bolstered by a wartime sense of national unity—directly to workers engaged in monotonous tasks that required them to behave like automatons, separated from their communities by geography and long hours. Industrial managers came to view *MWYW* as a palliative for disorderly behavior by female workers, crediting the program with improving morale, reducing overlong breaks, and discouraging talking on the assembly line. Meanwhile, a BBC employee, who herself was conscripted for (skilled) factory labor, reported, "Those on more monotonous jobs were most evident in the demand for more music."[26] The ways in which *MWYW* came to have its powerful effect reflect the changing ways that its producers theorized factory audiences, how they listened, and the music that would serve them best.

Mechanized Music

The early history of *MWYW* situated it as the musical corollary to the post-Dunkirk production drives. The press welcomed the program as an important contribution to the nation's war effort, with glowing accounts of the benefits of industrial music. The *Daily Mail* described the first program:

> Factory workers in Britain's great war drive hummed and sang at loom and lathe yesterday to music broadcast...by the BBC....Dudley Beaven played marches, fox-trots, musical comedy selections, and old and new song hits on the BBC theatre organ. "We hope it will help you keep up the pace," said the announcer.[27]

BBC Programme Planning inserted *MWYW* into the schedule twice daily at 10:30–11:00 a.m. and 3:00–3:30 p.m. The program would "emphasise the drive towards production," "please workers involved in the war effort," and "relieve the tedium of work in...factories and shops." In contrast to the BBC's usual approach to music programming, *MWYW* did not represent music as justified in itself; rather, its music had to be "rhythmical," "non vocal," and uninterrupted by announcements.[28] Even entertainment value, which was generally attributed to dance bands and theater organs, became a means to support the larger project of increasing industrial production.

In the early weeks, the program featured a variety of ensembles, ranging from the BBC Symphony Orchestra to theater organists, all expressing musical solidarity with the production drives and factory workers. The BBC soon realized, however, that the program required closer oversight than simply instructing ensembles to play "rhythmical" repertory. The unacceptable Geiger and His Orchestra, with their program of ethnic melodies, popular songs, and a Johann Strauss waltz, sounded thin, paused frequently between items "during which they tuned up interminably," and played pieces that varied in "tempo and feeling."[29] By the end of the first week, producers resolved to treat the program's music in the most utilitarian manner possible. The usual pauses of live performance were to be excised for the sake of industry; musicians would churn out a steady half hour of music, mirroring the labor of their listeners on the assembly line. In essence, the program's music was "mechanized," with implications of dehumanization, industrialized modernity, and mass culture. Like the systems of factory discipline that transformed workers into docile bodies, *MWYW* subjected music to a "mechanics of power" in order to render it useful to the war effort.[30]

Central to the program's design was the idea that factory workers should audit it *while they worked*. Its producers distinguished it carefully from morale-boosting entertainment programs like *Workers' Playtime*, which was broadcast weekly during the "optimum" lunch break. "[Factory music] should form a background, so that listening becomes almost sub-conscious," the producer Hutchison declared.[31] Excising all but the introductory announcements was critical to the project, for speech drew attention to new songs, conveyed the personalities of bandleaders and announcers, and was inaudible when heard over many factory sound systems (some factories even complained that it could be confused with air raid warnings). Rather than envisioning listeners moving between different modalities of interaction with the music they heard, Hutchison argued that listeners should engage in a singular mode of listening, however monotonous their tasks. A program designed for background listening represented a radical shift from long-standing BBC policy, which discouraged "tap" listening; it was also a logical extension of the recognition institutionalized in the Forces Programme that although special wartime populations (i.e., soldiers) could not listen with full attention, they still deserved programming to serve their needs.

MWYW drew its programming from both the Music and Variety Departments, and Denis Wright, a Music Department assistant who worked with brass and military bands, soon joined Hutchison in an "advisory capacity." The producers took into careful account the needs and preferences of listeners, which were collected from surveys made in cooperation with BBC Listener Research and from investigating "at first hand the conditions of reception."[32] Unsurprisingly, dance music, the genre associated most closely with mechanical reproduction and the modern masses, became the program's central component when a study by the Industrial Health Research Board showed it to be the overwhelming favorite among factory workers—at least according to their managers.[33] The popular products of mass culture (and apparent mass demand) became a tool in the industrial machine for the defense of the British nation, rendering workers' bodies "as an arena where the sovereignty of a mass politics [and] a mass culture was made manifest."[34]

With his Music Department background of viewing popular tastes with suspicion and considering "good" music to be an end in itself, Wright soon became disillusioned by the demands of broadcasting music to factories: "In order to make these programmes as effective as possible, we shall have to be far more ruthless in destroying artistic value." "Artistic subtlety" was irrelevant, for performers needed to use a "moderately-loud to loud power" throughout.[35] The humanizing dynamic nuances valued by "serious" musicians had no place in *MWYW*. Hutchison cautioned against "artistic value" in tempo (i.e., rubato, etc.), for "the aim is to produce something which is rhythmically monotonous and repetitive."[36] The program, Wright believed, required a "strong two-in-a-bar swing"; the foxtrots, quicksteps, and marches required by these parameters would be best supplied by dance bands, cinema organs, gramophone records, and light orchestras with the occasional use of military or brass bands. There was "no place" in the program for the BBC Symphony Orchestra: indeed, workers' preferences and the producers' requirements removed most Music Department ensembles from *MWYW*.[37]

On July 22, Wright issued detailed guidelines to all performers and program builders to advance the aim of providing energizing, unobtrusive music for factory workers. He concluded:

> It may be heavy-going for your band, and they may feel quite exhausted at the end of half-an-hour, BUT you've no idea how exhilarating the *right* sort of music is to the jaded workers who listen to you.
>
> These programmes are purely utilitarian; they do not need much contrast either in style or dynamics (*never* any quiet playing, as the noise of machines just obliterates the music) nor need you think about the needs of the ordinary listeners during these half-hours, but just try to make the period one of unrelieved BRIGHTNESS and CHEERINESS.[38]

Wright's directive presented a challenge to bandleaders and performers. *MWYW* was an exhausting program to play, with guidelines that severely restricted the repertories of most groups and allowed for few pauses. Members of the BBC Military Band resisted the program as "tiring...depressing and inartistic," but for musicians outside the BBC it was a key point of access to national audiences.[39] The qualities that had helped the BBC's Music Department define music as a spiritual force (rubato and subtle dynamics) were excised while the most exciting (tangos and hot jazz) and most personal (dreamy numbers and sentimental vocals) elements of popular music were banned. The humane quality of musical interest was replaced by low, "mass-produced" repertories, performed by live musicians as if by machines. Musicians had entered the industrial apparatus as what the historian Sigfried Giedion called "lever[s] of the machine," "follow[ing] the rhythm of the mechanical system [that] is unnatural to man."[40] Rather than challenging or engaging audiences, music was adjusted to serve the tastes of young people, listening inattentively, while they worked in noisy factories.

The post-Dunkirk production drives, with their emphasis on a voluntary, collective effort to defend democracy, complicated the hierarchies of music, listening, and listeners. In the interests of spurring on war workers, more than 140 different ensembles and individuals performed on the program in its first year, covering the full spectrum of musical genres and evoking the diversity of those united by the war effort. "Calling All Workers," the program's signature tune, reinforced the connection, for as the *Radio Times* related, the composer Eric Coates was inspired when his wife suggested, "Why don't you write a workers' march? After all, we are all workers, from Cabinet Ministers to roadsweepers" (sound example 3.1).[41]● Every worker played a crucial role; every musical number served a patriotic purpose. Although Wright and Hutchison soon removed serious music from the program, lesser music demonstrated its usefulness and supported the greater good. As *MWYW* matured, "low" music was lavished with the most careful scientific study, the greatest concern for clear reproduction, and the closest attention to detailed planning of any program broadcast by the BBC during the war.

Such detailed attention also functioned as a tool of discipline, although the producers' control over *MWYW* was incomplete: performers and other staff regularly ignored and violated its guidelines. By the end of 1940, Hutchison departed the program, taking his industry contacts, while Wright became progressively frustrated with the program and his lack of authority over Variety Department performers (dance bands and theater organists), who constituted the bulk of *MWYW*'s offerings.[42] With the energy of the production drives spent and the nation battered by the Blitz—yet still free—the paradigm of mechanized music as a means to raising production was losing cachet.

Medicinal Music

In early 1941, the *Radio Times* printed a criticism of *MWYW* by a frequent factory visitor: "The programme has become 'Music while you sleep.' Oh, the soporific sameness of the daily, dreary, tuneless monotone of trashy music…crammed into this non-stop half-hour!"[43] Godfrey Adams, the director of Programme Planning, also had begun to question the project, requesting Listener Research to provide "any evidence…about the effectiveness of these programmes."[44] The reports were favorable, but Wright soon left for Scotland with the BBC Military Band. Programme Planning recognized that *MWYW* required a producer who could "keep a lively contact" with industry and scrutinize the fourteen weekly programs "in this most important war work of the Corporation."[45] On May 5, 1941, Wynford Reynolds assumed the job.[46] A "well-known band-leader," according to the *Radio Times*, he led orchestras and small ensembles, and broadcast regularly in BBC light music programs, including *MWYW*.[47] Experienced in providing music for leisure entertainment, Reynolds turned to factory music with a crusader's zeal.

Reynolds envisioned a more holistic role for music in industry than had Wright or Hutchison and aimed to "gain new disciples from the vast majority who had not realized the possibilities of 'Doctor Music.'" In a *Radio Times* article, marking the one-year anniversary of *MWYW*, he described the current war's "difficult conditions" with its demand for "more machines—more shells—and still more!" The benefit of working to music was a matter of "solid fact": it relieved boredom, cheered workers, reduced illness rates, and increased output. Reynolds concluded, "Music is a spiritual power that can be translated into a dynamic force, and that force is being directed towards one great and certain goal—Victory!"[48] Rather than reduce music (and workers) to a mechanism of industry, harnessed for total war, music for Reynolds maintained its spiritual properties and became a panacea for industrial ills; it humanized labor, inoculated workers against poor morale, and boosted production as a result. Reynolds's more humane stance coincided with the growing presence of women in industry, where they had become objects of special concern.

"Doctor Music" was a humanizing force, but it also required careful study and administration. Unlike Wright, Reynolds had the authority to administer the program effectively, and he supervised it closely—one of his first requests was for a radio set in his office with which to monitor the program.[49] He also set out, in collaboration with BBC Listener Research, to diagnose the program's effectiveness in factories. Their collaborative studies not only produced useful data on music and listeners but also educated the public, policy makers, and factory managements on the benefits of industrial music.

The first major study occurred during the week of July 6, 1941, when fourteen contrasting programs of dance bands, light orchestras, brass and military bands, theater organs, and records were broadcast. Employers were surveyed on "audibility, rhythm, enjoyment of workers and effect on output" of the different material.[50] Rich in demographic detail, the study also served as the centerpiece for a major publicity campaign on the benefits of *MWYW*. Reynolds broadcast announcements inviting employers to apply for questionnaires, solicited BBC staff for their views on the program, and held a press conference with Silvey on June 18.[51] According to a BBC observer, the reporters seemed to feel that the case for the program had been rather "pumped up" and that the detailed nature of the study was "a little finicky"; however, "after a certain caution ... the idea seemed to be accepted favourably." Still, one perceptive journalist queried, "Why aren't the workers' representatives ... to be consulted equally with the bosses?"[52] The question underlined the paternalistic assumption that managements could speak for workers.

Despite such criticisms, the appeals to the press provided the desired result: a cuttings book maintained by Reynolds preserved sixty-six articles from the period leading up to the experimental week that mostly celebrated music's impact on industrial output.[53] The *News Review* offered a vivid prose picture:

> Visiting a laundry, an investigator of the National Institute of Industrial Psychology saw collars and shirts cleaned at *panzer* speed to the sound of martial music. Supervisors described operatives' output as "astonishing, even alarming."
>
> Packingpeas in a Sheffield factory, girls worked at double speed when regaled by jazz and dance bands.[54]

On July 7, the *Manchester Evening News* declared, "When you tune in your radio this week to 'Music While You Work' you will be listening to one of the most significant experiments ever carried out in industrial welfare."[55]

Listener Research released its full report on the experimental week in October. The study's 140 surveys represented 52,000 workers, three-quarters of whom worked in women-only shops. At least 57.4 percent of the surveys represented workers doing "wholly or mainly repetitive" tasks, and no respondent reported using *MWYW* during rest periods exclusively.[56] In other words, the program was reaching the population of workers who were of greatest concern to authorities (women) and those for whom music was considered most beneficial (those doing monotonous tasks) in the intended manner (while people worked).

The survey provided extensive data on how different repertories, instrumentation, and performance sounded in factories—and how workers experienced them. Reynolds used the data to shift *MWYW*'s emphasis from rhythmic to familiar music, observing "in one factory there may be thousands of different work rhythms, and in most cases the operators . . . cannot adapt their tasks to a musical rhythm."[57] By necessity, music was not a mechanistic response to industrial work or mere background; rather, "workers definitely prefer tunes that they know and the most popular programme is one which enables them to join in by humming or whistling."[58] These aims were best served by familiar music, including hit numbers, like "Amapola," which Victor Silvester and His Ballroom Orchestra, Geraldo's dance band, the theater organist Jack Dowle, and George Scott-Wood and His Grand Accordion Band all played during the experimental week. Reynolds issued a new requirement based on this finding: twenty minutes— two-thirds—of each program should be familiar to listeners. Like Wright, he identified several technical challenges in broadcasting music to factories: performers needed to play with a constant tone level, further leveled by engineers, and arrangements had to feature a clear and prominent melody. Reynolds concluded that dance bands, such as Silvester's and Scott-Wood's, favoring simple arrangements of familiar, popular repertory produced the best music for factories.

Reynolds issued two directives on rhythm, one for dance bands and theater organs and the other for light orchestras, military bands, and brass bands, since the latter group could not "supply the same ideal of rhythm." "A jig or quickstep tempo" was most suitable for dance bands and theater organs; light orchestras, military bands, and brass bands could compensate for their rhythmic deficiencies by maintaining "a cheerful, bright and lilting spirit" and performing familiar "selections from Musical Comedy and Light Opera," as the Black Dyke Mills Brass Band had done when it included Rossini's *Tancredi* overture in its well-received "experimental" airing. Viennese waltzes and other selections that changed tempo abruptly, which Wright had banned, were acceptable if they fulfilled the requirements of familiarity, clear melody, and cheerful tempo.[59] The overriding criterion of familiarity allowed a greater variety of musical styles.

Although *MWYW* featured familiar, popular music, it was still utilitarian and could not be replicated by any novice with a gramophone; to remain effective, it had to be administered by experts. Reynolds's expertise was based in "constant research": he maintained a card index of all *MWYW* broadcasts with comments from factory managements, visited factories, and researched all available literature on the topic (figure 3.1).[60] In factories across the country, as he encountered the internal music programming that supplemented *MWYW* airings, Reynolds worried that "managements are overlooking the fact that output is the primary consideration and that workers' requests may often run contrary to this main objective." He cautioned managers against indulging their employees by "acceding to requests . . . for longer periods of music, special vocal items and the playing of records of classical music."[61] Music could retain its tonic effects only if the correct music was applied in small doses, totaling no more than 2.5 hours per day.[62] Managements needed "proper guidance" in "using efficient apparatus," planning musical programs, and choosing "responsible subordinates" to administer industrial music. The government's influential Committee on Industrial Publicity became concerned that "actual harm was caused by the prevailing ignorance of the essential requirements" and recommended that Reynolds create an informational "General Directive."[63]

FIGURE 3.1 Wynford Reynolds, the *Music While You Work* organizer, visits a factory. ("BBC Picture Gallery," *Radio Times* [6 November 1942]: 4)

Drawing upon his research, Reynolds identified seven distinct ways that *MWYW* aided production. Rather than considering quantifiable output, or even addressing worker efficiency in a direct manner, he focused on the actions, bodies, and psyches of workers, particularly if they were female. Reynolds distributed the list of benefits widely and included it in his June 1942 "General Directive," accompanied by management comments (some of which are bracketed and interpolated into the following list), detailing each point:

1. Boosting the tired worker.
2. Acting as a mental tonic.

["Music is a mental stimulant. It has a humanising effect which helps counteract the evil effects of the mechanisation of workers. This, indirectly, is a decided benefit to production."]

3. Relieving boredom, especially that caused by repetitive work.
4. Increasing happiness and improving health.

["Our female workers leave at the end of the day much fresher and brighter."]

5. Minimizing conversation.

["The introduction of music has undoubtedly helped production if only by eliminating a considerable amount of the talking that takes place between the girls."]

6. Relieving nervous strain.

["Music is of great value as a means of relieving nervous strain amongst workers after blitzing."]

7. Cutting down absenteeism.

["Before the introduction of music female workers used to wander off to the cloakrooms towards the end of the day and were absent for 15 to 20 minutes. Since the introduction of music this practice has ceased."][64]

The focus upon *MWYW*'s disciplinary and medical benefits to workers was tied to concerns surrounding newly conscripted women. Although the research had neither focused on, nor detected, appreciable differences in the musical tastes of male and female workers, managements were anxious about female conscripts (figure 3.2).[65] In addition to the usual improvements in discipline, Reynolds presented the program as offering an impressive range of physical and mental benefits.

Despite the promises of health and happiness for workers, the program's utility for creating docile bodies remained. Emphasizing that *MWYW* pushed workers to achieve greater output was impolitic in a period of tension between management and labor groups, each blaming the other for low productivity.[66] Echoing Reynolds's medicalized vocabulary, an executive with the General Electric Company, questioned the wisdom of listing "boosting the tired worker" as the first of music's advantages: "I feel that in this

FIGURE 3.2 Women in a munitions factory working to *Music While You Work*. ("Third Anniversary of *Music While You Work*," *Radio Times* [18 June 1943]: 1)

way you tend to classify music as a nervous-exitant [sic]....As you say yourself...the real value of music lies in its general tonic properties of keeping the workers contented and alert, and thus indirectly increasing the production rate without affecting fatigue."[67] Improved productivity was the ultimate benefit of factory music, but music would not achieve this end by encouraging unnatural and unsustainable speed. It was inappropriate for industrial music to manipulate employees into working harder; rather, it lifted their moods, relieved their "acute state of boredom" in monotonous tasks, and raised their morale. It was as a mental tonic that music sustained output.

Describing music on the program as a mental tonic was not merely rhetorical: it was a convincing "scientific" argument for why MWYW was beneficial to workers, production, and the war effort, which moved beyond the patriotic justifications of the post-Dunkirk production drives. It helped extend the program's reach, both in the broadcasting schedule and in factories. In 1942, Reynolds collaborated with groups including the Industrial Welfare Society, the Committee on Industrial Publicity, and Parliament to push the BBC to institute a third daily broadcast for night shift workers.[68] The BBC finally agreed to an evening broadcast (or, rather, a rebroadcast recording of an earlier, live MWYW program), which commenced on August 2, 1942. "Night work notoriously exacts a higher degree of nervous strain which even half-an-hour of music can do much to ease," explained the Radio Times.[69]

With his educational "General Directive" and the support of the Committee on Industrial Publicity, Reynolds worked to expand the number of factories taking MWYW.[70] According to a May 1942 Mass-Observation report, only 20 percent of factories had radio installations.[71] This was an improvement over the 800 factories that had had the equipment when the program began, but it was still a minority.[72] Reynolds needed the Ministry of Supply to reclassify factory sound equipment, which had been lumped into the domestic category, as an unrestricted good. Official recognition of the usefulness of music to industry was also critical if MWYW was to reach employees at the 12,000 to 15,000 government-controlled factories, only a fraction of which took the service. Royal Ordnance (munitions) factories were a particularly difficult case:

> It is considered to be too dangerous to have a background of music as the concentration of the workers might be affected. Our findings do not support this theory and it seems that a valuable aid to war time production is not being made available to the majority of Government factories owning to a certain lack of knowledge and co-ordination in the Ministries.[73]

By 1943, Reynolds's efforts to reclassify factory sound equipment had succeeded, and the Royal Ordnance factories were finally "wired for reception."[74] The benefits of "Doctor Music" would reach new populations of female conscripts, supporting morale and discipline in notoriously demoralized locations. The program's success with all parties was signaled in medicinal terms: According to the Liverpool Evening Express: "Employees, no less than employers welcome the music. It has gripped them like a drug. Almost the first question asked by new hands when engaged is: 'Have you got music?'"[75]

Disciplined Music

In January 1942, the controller of programs promoted Reynolds to the rank of organizer and reclassified *MWYW* as a section, an unusual status for an individual program. The title carried power: Reynolds now controlled all live and recorded allocations for the program, which remained an important source of income and broadcast exposure for ensembles that met his requirements. Until the end of the war, he continued his project of "constant study," refining classifications of listeners and the program's ensemble, repertory, and stylistic requirements.[76] Reynolds used taxonomies to rationalize the program's offerings, subjecting music and musicians to ever-stricter control.

Improving discipline for *MWYW* answered broader BBC concerns with popular music and its impact on civilian and forces morale. The year 1942 witnessed military setbacks for the Allies, with Rommel's forces pummeling the British Eighth Army in North Africa and the Germans continuing their Soviet offensive. Traditionalists blamed the Forces Programme and its "flabby," sentimental dance music, which they considered a poor substitute for military marches, for demoralizing listeners.[77] The BBC Music Policy of 1942 responded by extending Music Department scrutiny to Variety Department offerings. It reaffirmed hierarchical understandings of musical genre, value, and administration. Great music was an "ultimate value, indeed a justification of life" while other music could "enrich leisure hours with entertainment."[78] "Lower forms," however, required close supervision: in July, the new Dance Music Policy Committee began to vet song lyrics, styles, and singers in order to encourage and enforce more "virile" dance music.[79]

Reynolds had to negotiate carefully his administration of a program that, however patronizingly, aimed to please women factory workers with dance music at a time when the BBC was obsessed with effeminacy in music and encouraged virility as a matter of policy. He soon reassessed the value of light music and increased its representation in the program, justifying his decision with new musical criteria and refined classifications of workers and their tastes. Meanwhile, Reynolds sharpened the distinction between the categories of light and dance music and subjected dance music repertories and ensembles to closer regulation: taxonomy served as a disciplinary tool.

Like dance music, light music suffered from effeminacy problems at the beginning of 1942, but unlike dance music, it was located in the Music Department, positioned higher in the BBC's musical hierarchy, and proved ultimately redeemable. Between April and December 1942, the Music Department and Programme Planning Department worked to cure light music of "a certain lack of virility." The root of the problem lay in the fact that small ensembles playing transcriptions had come to dominate light music offerings; a Programme Planning report described their unmanly qualities:

> The sounds they produce are generally thin and listless, and their programmes consist mainly of abbreviated, emasculated versions of music originally written for a full orchestra, or dainty little pieces written for teashop ensembles. Favourite subjects are fireflies, goblins, fairies and flowers. Particularly flowers.[80]

Fred Hartley, the light music supervisor (and well-regarded bandleader and composer), set out to correct the problems by using more large orchestras and specialty ensembles, such as gypsy orchestras and mandolin bands, and fewer small ensembles of undifferentiated character. He also vetted program materials for robustness and eliminated thirteen unsatisfactory combinations, concluding, "Certainly all the conductors and leaders are kept much more on their toes."[81] With pressure from Hartley and Reynolds himself, light music combinations very likely sounded better by the end of 1942.

The 1942 *MWYW* study by Listener Research and Reynolds paralleled the effort in light music to scrutinize performances given by individual ensembles. It examined ensembles appearing regularly on the program, seventeen of which were booked by the Variety Department (large dance bands and "novelty and small" dance bands) and eleven by the Music Department. Reynolds used the study to open a dialogue with bandleaders on ways to improve their contributions to the program, suggesting changes in instrumentation, repertory, and tempos. For example, a violin was added to the New Organolians to relieve the "monotony of tone from the Hammond organ," and the Casino Orchestra, a light ensemble, was steered away from "a complicated arrangement of 'Lambeth Walk'" and Johann Strauss II's technically demanding "Tritsch-Tratsch Polka." Some ensembles, including Mendelssohn's Hawaiian Serenaders, which was described as "too dreamy—no clarity and crispness," and two undistinguished dance bands, fared so poorly that they were not booked again.[82]

Initiated with little publicity, the study also helped Reynolds rethink his audience and which ensembles best fulfilled *MWYW*'s requirements. The scope was extensive: between March and September, twenty-one firms representing 74,000 workers completed questionnaires about each Wednesday afternoon program. The most surprising finding was that large light orchestras, military bands, and brass bands earned high ratings, often outperforming dance bands. On the Music Department side, only small light ensembles fared poorly, partly because small string ensembles reproduced feebly in noisy shop environments. Although Reynolds had maintained in his 1941 directives on rhythm that light orchestras, military bands, and brass bands could not "supply the same ideal of rhythm" that dance bands could provide, light orchestras rated higher than their dance band counterparts in "style of playing," which had replaced the previous year's "rhythm" category.[83] Overall, survey respondents received with equal approval the contrasting repertories of dance bands and light orchestras.

If familiarity was the key to the 1941 study, variety was the theme of the 1942 study. The timbres featured in both Variety and Music novelty ensembles, such as the xylophone in Jack Simpson's Sextet, accordions in Eric Winstone's dance band, and Troise and His Banjoliers, sounded clear in noisy environments, and "they gave a variety in tone colour that broke away from the monotony of saxophone combinations [i.e., dance bands]."[84] Survey respondents were tired of hearing a steady stream of dance bands, and light orchestras provided relief. One respondent described a light orchestra as "very Satisfactory after twice daily dance music" while another reported that DeWolfe and His Orchestra, whose airing included Brahms's Hungarian Dance no. 5 and Friml's "Indian Love Call," were "enjoyed by all departments.... Those who usually prefer more modern music give the opinion that it was very good for a change."[85] Reynolds concluded, "While dance music is the most popular there is an ever-constant danger of irritating the worker by the over repetition of the 'plug' tune of the moment."[86] In the next two years, as the BBC slashed its funding for dance bands, both in response to a perceived decline in popularity and as a cost-saving measure, Reynolds adapted by increasing the proportion of light music in *MWYW*.[87]

The newfound appreciation for light music ensembles was conveyed in surveys that finally represented the opinions of workers: both managements and workers' representatives at the twenty-one participating firms completed each week's approximately fifty questionnaires.[88] Unfortunately, the surviving documentation did not record how the surveys obtained workers' opinions, the number surveyed, or *which* workers were consulted. Since women workers were rarely permitted to join labor unions and tended to have lower status overall, the "workers representatives" who filled out the surveys were most likely older, unionized men. Thus, while the 1942 survey represented workers' voices where the 1941 survey did not, it favored the workers who were least sympathetic to dance music. Indeed, brass and military bands, like the Band of H.M. Royal Marines and the Sunderland Constabulary Band, favored by older, male workers, enjoyed unusually high rankings in 1942.

Based on the new findings, Reynolds used occupation, age, and gender to describe two distinct groups of listeners: older, male workers in heavy industry versus younger, female workers doing monotonous tasks in light industry. The former preferred "a 'heavier' type of programme—music of a more robust nature played by military bands, brass bands, or large light orchestras" while the latter wanted dance music.[89] Managements might be more concerned with "problem" female workers, but they could not entirely ignore the contributions—and tastes—of skilled and experienced older male workers.

Young, female workers still needed to be served, but they could not be overindulged. Even as managements worked to render docile the bodies of female conscripts, Reynolds subjected dance music to stricter regulation. In April 1943, he issued the first set of "Instructions for Dance Bands, Light Orchestras, Military and Brass Bands," which listed prohibited—and accepted—repertory for the program. Unlike in previous guidelines on repertory and style, Reynolds created specific parameters of acceptability for *MWYW*, and he did not hesitate to "ban completely" entire categories of dance music.[90] Because they emphasized rhythm over melody, he banned all rumbas and thirty-seven other songs, including Count Basie's "One O'Clock Jump" and "Deep in the Heart of Texas," the chorus of which elicited claps (or bangs) from listening workers.[91] Ten numbers were "too lethargic," including the 1939 hit "Deep Purple," and were banned along with thirty-four "modern slow waltzes," including the popular "Anniversary Waltz."[92] Over the next two years, Reynolds issued a series of updates that listed not only release dates but items banned entirely or indefinitely, including "In the Blue of the Evening" and "Say a Prayer for the Boys over There."[93] His language of banning and index of forbidden songs echoed the work of the Dance Music Policy Committee.

In June 1943, Reynolds sought to tighten control over *MWYW* performances by requesting that engineers and producers remind bandleaders of the program's guidelines during rehearsals. "Unnecessarily slow tempi," for instance, were "a prevalent fault" that needed "constant correction." "'Hot' or 'stunt' choruses" required more drastic treatment: "Witness Hargraves on 22nd April playing 'Yankee Doodle Boy' and Joe Loss on 21st May playing 'In the Mood.' The stunt effects in these items should have been ruthlessly 'cut' on the spot."[94] In matters of balance, engineers were to avoid too much bass and percussion (they "gave the effect in a factory of a machine gun, which was both irritating and distracting to workers"), emphasize the melody by improving internal balance and having some instrumentalists stand up, and discourage the "shrill and screechy" registers of violins and clarinets.[95] The once-popular cinema organ fared especially poorly in the area of sound reproduction: it sounded "woolly," "booming," and generally unpleasant when amplified in factory settings, particularly in noisy shops, and from 1942, it was largely excluded from the program.[96] Sound quality also depended upon the receiving conditions in factories, which were often "far from satisfactory," so Reynolds continued his efforts to educate factory managements through personal visits and publicity.[97]

Reynolds also regulated the proportion of dance music heard in *MWYW* and reinforced the taxonomic distinctions between light and dance music. In fall 1942, Reynolds prohibited most light music organizations from including dance music in their programs; for those permitted to present mixed programs, he limited dance music to a maximum of ten minutes.[98] In July 1943, he clamped down on song plugging by requiring dance bands to include at least "ten minutes [of] music more than two years old."[99] Time limits, however, did not prevent song plugging, for some bandleaders "crammed" as many songs as possible into their allotted period. A year later, Reynolds extended his regulations to individual numbers: dance bands could play no more than eight numbers in the twenty minutes in which they were allowed to perform current hits; variety orchestras were limited to six titles within their ten-minute period.[100] With his lists of banned numbers, time limits, and regulations on tempi, balance, and stunt playing in performance, Reynolds minimized the opportunities for performers to evade *MWYW* guidelines. Although dance music was still important to the program, its utility depended upon careful discipline.

In March 1944, Reynolds responded to a BBC-wide crackdown on song plugging by refining his previous classification of the factory audience and its tastes. He added a third term to the binary division of the audience: the middle-aged, who preferred "a mixture of light music and the latest dance music." Reynolds wrote, "I think that in general...there is always an audience who likes a 'mixed bag' of musical items. Also some combinations, such as music-hall orchestras and rhythmic novelty outfits are at their happiest when playing mixed programmes."[101] The new category of ensemble— the "variety" combination—included groups like the Coventry Hippodrome Orchestra, which had excelled in the 1941 study. Reynolds's tertiary categories averted a crisis of inadequate taxonomies and maintained the special status of *MWYW*. By reserving the right to classify ensembles for the program according to his own criteria, he mitigated the effects of policies created by a BBC that was increasingly hostile to dance bands.

As Reynolds refined his control over the program's content, he continued to observe the effectiveness of *MWYW* in factories, contacting more than 422 companies by June 1946.[102] In December 1944, he reported that factories perceived *MWYW* as maintaining a satisfying balance of dance and light music, that workers indeed preferred familiar, singable numbers, and that his efforts to eliminate song plugging had succeeded, for there were "no complaints, as of old, about the duplication of items." In sum, "Our programmes... were said to be a model of what 'Music While You Work' should be."[103] Reynolds also learned of evidence that demonstrated the program's impact upon quality of work. An engineering firm reported that the two hours in which *MWYW* broadcast (10–11 a.m. and 3–4 p.m.) had the lowest accident rates over a nine-month period. A Royal Ordnance factory manager supported music in explosives departments because "accidents usually occurred through carelessness engendered by boredom, and music would provide an excellent antidote to such boredom."[104] The project of disciplining workers' bodies into docile instruments of production depended upon attending not only to their actions but also to their mental and emotional states. *MWYW*'s closely regulated programs were ideal for the task.

Humanizing Music: Leisure and Home Life

The central justification for *MWYW* was that it improved factory worker morale and discipline, thus increasing industrial output. Through careful study and oversight, Hutchison, Wright, and Reynolds transformed entertaining music into a tool of war. The revolutionary nature of the program, however, lay not in its repertory but in its insistence that it should serve as background. Despite interwar developments in leisure and technology, through which background music entered the everyday lives of the middle and lower classes, the BBC had continued to insist upon the ideal of a physically passive, mentally focused listener. Even in war, the *Radio Times* warned, "Music while you work—at home or factory, with or without quotation marks—is an admirable tonic, but like most tonics can be taken to excess."[105] Overuse of music strained the nerves, wasted electricity, wore out radio valves, and increased unnecessary noise; its effect became negative, even unpatriotic. The BBC insisted that it took extensive research, careful oversight, and musical expertise to administer the potentially dangerous "drug" of background music, ignoring the evidence that most of the public had been happily self-medicating for years.

Industry, with its hierarchies, timetables, and rationalized approach to labor, proved a far more appealing environment to investigate the effects of *MWYW* on workers' listening bodies than the home. At home, listeners' bodies were not subject to industrial discipline; they were relatively autonomous in their actions and could choose to work—or not—as they listened to the program. Researchers also had to rely on home listeners to account for their own behaviors and listening habits without recourse to the "objective" descriptions of industrial managers. Although Listener Research had at its disposal a variety of means for obtaining quantitative and qualitative information on the public's listening habits, *MWYW*'s producers actively ignored home listeners. At the beginning of Reynolds's 1941 study, the *Radio Times* insisted, "If you *are* able to listen to it at home, remember you are only harmlessly eavesdropping on somebody else's programme. To be quite blunt, the BBC doesn't worry whether you people at home enjoy 'Music While You Work' or not."[106] "You people at home" implicated housewives, whom programmers excluded from consideration, even as women in *MWYW*'s factory audience became objects of concern.

The home audience for the program was significant from the beginning: in 1940, 10 percent of the adult population listened to the program, although only 5.6 percent, at most, could listen in factories.[107] Bandleaders who played for the program were certainly aware that many in their audience were not auditing their broadcasts in factory shops—and might judge harshly their unconventional performances—necessitating Wright and Hutchison's injunction against considering "the needs of the ordinary listeners."[108] A similar distinction spurred the early limitations on light music (before it had been "remasculated"): Geiger and His Orchestra were dismissed as "a reasonable background for an afternoon chat over teacups, but totally inadequate midst the rattle of a machine shop."[109] Background music for a factory had to be distinguished from the music that accompanied ladylike leisure activities.

Many housewives, however, used the program to accompany labor, as BBC Listener Research learned when it gathered data on home listeners in the program's first year. After receiving several spontaneous comments in its daily surveys, the department requested qualitative information on *MWYW* listening practices from local correspondents, volunteers who wrote regular reports on their own and their community's responses to BBC programming. Silvey noted, "The replies reveal that the programme is highly popular for home listening, particularly among housewives who like to hear it while *they* work."[110] In an April 1941 study of home listening, *MWYW* had the highest ratings of all morning music sessions, in both the number of listeners and the "quality of…enjoyment": it gave "a great deal of pleasure as a background session" and was "ideal for its purpose."[111] By 1942, 90 percent of "keen" women listeners who stayed at home during the day tuned in to the program at least occasionally.[112] For housewives, background music played a vital role in humanizing household labor. In response to a critic of background listening, one woman argued, "If Mr. Buckham had had a reasonable experience of the kitchen sink, he would appreciate how vital our background music can be, occupying our minds and raising us above ash in the saucers and unscrapable potatoes."[113] Clearly, a double standard, rooted in divisions of public and private space, existed when the BBC scolded women who listened while they worked at home for abusing music while it treated music for female conscripts as a matter of national concern.

In addition to accompanying labor in the home, *MWYW* provided leisure entertainment: Listener Research reported that the program's listening figures were "at their highest for the night and week-end sessions, when comparatively few listeners are at work."[114] Even as the BBC decreased its dance music programming, arguing that "only one type [of program], Dance Music, has shown a steady decline in popularity, with a corresponding increase in unpopularity," *MWYW* still enjoyed a large following, with audiences as large as 22.7 percent for the evening broadcast.[115] The program not only offered a pleasant musical background but also gave listeners an opportunity to hear dance bands in a purely instrumental mode.

The efforts of *MWYW*'s producers to create music suited to factory listening created, as a side effect, a distinct popular musical aesthetic. Seton Margrave, the radio critic for the *Daily Mail*, praised the results of the 1941 study, along with its criteria of familiarity, clear melody, and lilting rhythm in music performed without the interruption of "syrupy blather," linking them to a populist British aesthetic:

> Here for the first time by expression of popular wish is a plan for popular music. It hits hard at our more ostentatious orchestras. . . . the people of Britain are looking for what is simple and honest, well known, and well loved. When bands that try to be clever will try to be good they will qualify for "MWYW," and the band that appears most often in "MWYW" will be the band of the year.[116]

Margrave listed the strict-tempo bandleader Silvester, the Coventry Hippodrome Orchestra with its mixture of light and dance music, and working men's brass bands like Black Dyke Mills as leaders in such a popularity contest. His choices corresponded to the bands that ranked highest in the 1941 study.[117] This was popular music that eschewed sentiment, hot playing, and Americanization. It consolidated a People's War sensibility that bridged the domestic and factory fronts, depicted in one advertisement by photographs juxtaposing male factory workers with a housewife and her tea set.[118]

The circuits between labor and leisure, home and factory also extended the leisure associations of dance and light music into the factory. Strict-tempo dance music referenced the palais, where social dancers moved according to the voluntary disciplines of choreography. Theater organs, despite their uneven history with the program, recalled the popular activity of cinema going. Light music, often dismissed as the music of "tea shop ensembles," called to mind the leisurely world of dining out in the daytime. Such frivolous activities were gendered as feminine and located within the realm of modern mass culture, but *MWYW* evoked them with serious aims: bringing accessible, popular music into a work environment helped to encourage docile bodies. It also relaxed the regimented atmosphere of the factory: workers might pause to learn the words or simply to remember an enjoyable evening. *MWYW* rendered audible the changes wrought in the war: the penetration of women into factories and the unskilled, increasingly mechanized character of many jobs. When Alfred Cleeton, a foreman in Priestley's novel, observed a young woman and two young men bobbing along to *MWYW*, he decided that the factory had become

> something between a dance hall, a chapel bazaar, a glorified café and the Y.M.C.A., plus a lot of electric power and half a million quid's worth of machine tools, and they were turning out planes as if they were mousetraps. If some of the old lot he'd served time with, when engineering shops were engineering shops . . . came back now and saw this carry-on, they'd run screaming for whiskey.[119]

Conclusion

Popular with workers and home listeners alike, *MWYW* helped support the co-operative spirit so important to national unity and morale during the People's War. Of course, it could be seen as reinforcing the state authority of conscription and the industrial discipline of assembly-line work, and indeed from Hutchison's "black-coated" (i.e., nonmanual) workers to Priestley's Cleeton, the resistance to background music aligned with a proud assertion of the skilled nature of one's work.[120] Nevertheless, a great deal of war work was repetitive, unskilled, and alienating. The young women who so concerned Mass-Observation registered their apathy by removing their bodies through absenteeism and the bodily practices of slacking (including "doing their hair, talking, [and] eating the cakes and sandwiches they have brought for dinner and tea"). Mass-Observation worried that such attitudes and the lack of "positive citizenship" among youth would contribute little to a better postwar society unless a stronger sense of cohesion developed.[121] *MWYW* played a crucial role not only in rendering war work more bearable but also in promoting a sense of unity among listeners.

Even late in the war, as the program became a reliable source of light background music, the BBC reasserted its connections with the war effort. When in 1944 the General Forces Programme replaced the domestic Forces Programme, the announcement "Calling All Workers" was changed to "Calling All Forces and Workers," establishing "a link between the fighters on both fronts—the soldier and the factory worker—thus strengthening the bond of unity between our forces on land and sea."[122] Although most soldiers, like most listeners on the home front, used *MWYW* as a background for leisure, Reynolds related the dramatic use of the program when the crew of a disabled tank, "surrounded by mines, enemy mortars and snipers," sang along to the program as they waited for rescue.[123]

While the program evoked the unity required by the war effort, it also helped listeners enact the practices of community. Echoing music's leisure role in dance halls, homes, and sing-alongs, *MWYW* foregrounded the practices of interactive, group listening in the space of the factory, which involved formal and informal negotiations of shared space and different tastes. *MWYW*'s imagined community extended beyond individual factories and homes, creating links not only among listeners but also between listeners and musicians, for, as the BBC argued, "the 'liveness' of 'Music While You Work' has enabled the producer to turn out the ideal 'inattentive listening.'"[124] Listeners, however, did not regard the program as mere background; they engaged with its music as pleasurable in itself, in addition to regarding it as a companion to leisure and work.

In a war against fascism, *MWYW* had complex goals and effects. While designed as a disciplinary tool, its music also referenced leisure and complex modes of musical and social interaction. It created a communal, humanized space, improving the quality of life for workers in homes and factories, while it acknowledged subversively the dullness of a great deal of work. With music's multivalent qualities, *MWYW* helped open a different space (however ill-articulated) for individual bodies, working in dehumanizing conditions. As the elated Rosie yelled to Cleeton, "It's only the tune they're playing. I think it's lovely. It makes me think—oh—of I don't know what."[125]

4

BETWEEN BLITZKRIEG AND CALL-UP: *BBC DANCING CLUB*,

MASCULINITY, AND THE DANCE BAND SCHEME

IN ITS 1940 Christmas issue, *Melody Maker* asked, "For over a hundred nights bombs have rained down upon London.... Yet throughout this nerve-wracking time, London has never lacked music.... How has this—one more instance of the ability of the British to 'take it'—been achieved?" By way of answer, the weekly published a firsthand account by Harry Parry, who led the Radio Rhythm Club Sextet and the band at the Coconut Club in the West End. Parry explained:

> It's not so bad when you're actually on the stand. It's only when you stop playing, and your mind returns to its surroundings, that you become aware of the banging and whistling overhead. But somehow, even when...I find myself staggering a little as the floor rocks from a nearby explosion, the lights and the people dancing—and, above all, the music of a really sympathetic group of players— seem to relegate the danger and inhumanity of it all to a secondary consideration.[1]

In early September, at the beginning of the London Blitz, Parry and his band survived a direct hit on the club at which they were then playing, but grueling routine, not terror, soon came to define their days. Parry's main challenge was getting to work, which involved walking more than seven miles through the blackout from his home in Streetham to the Coconut Club while avoiding bomb craters, shrapnel, and the occasional bomb. When work ended at 5:00 a.m., he slept at the club for about three hours and then proceeded to study wireless telegraphy from 9:30 a.m. to 4 p.m. in preparation for joining the Merchant Navy as a radio officer.[2] ("I see nothing of my wife these days except on Sunday," Parry observed.) *Melody Maker* concluded, "His adventures...are typical of those experienced by the hundreds of other musicians who have been—and still are—'on active service' in London and other 'blitzed' towns."[3]

Parry's experiences were indeed representative of the challenges civilian dance musicians faced during the Blitz, which was at its height from late August 1940 until the spring of 1941. Unless forced to evacuate, musicians played for dancers and other patrons during the nightly raids while contending off the bandstand with transportation difficulties, equipment shortages, and nonexistent compensation when their contracts were canceled because of air raids. Broadcasting bands faced their own array of troubles: the shutdown of transmitters in response to raids could lead to the cancellation or abrupt truncation of programs while air raid warnings could interrupt rehearsals and balance tests.[4]

Throughout the Blitz, *Melody Maker* provided guidance to its readership on survival in the changing landscape of wartime entertainment with articles like "If Your Band Is 'Blitzed...'"[5] In addition, to the extent it could do so without revealing strategic information, it chronicled the dramas, disasters, and everyday bravery of the dance music profession during the period. While this certainly involved reporting on name leaders, like Parry, it also involved celebrating the matter-of-fact heroism with which "ordinary semipros and section players—went about their work."[6] For example, in publishing the account of a direct hit on a dance hall by the semipro Don Ralfe, the editor interjected, "It will be noticed that he doesn't think it worth while mentioning that the Blitz was on, and that he somehow managed to get through it to the dance hall," and asserted, "This Is the Spirit of the Musicians of Britain."[7]

Melody Maker's coverage not only reinforced a sense of unity for a profession facing significant hardship but also sutured dance musicians into national narratives of the Blitz. Central to the Blitz narrative was the concept of "carrying on" with everyday life in the face of attack; war films and the press depicted Londoners and other British civilians as "self sacrificing, relentlessly cheerful, and inherently tolerant."[8] Within this framework, it was no surprise that Parry ignored the bombs in order to focus on making music at the Coconut Grove, that Ralfe and his bandmates helped evacuate patrons to a "nearby shelter" before running back into the burning dance hall to save their instruments, or that they recounted their unsettling experiences with an air of sangfroid. This stoic, even cheerful, fortitude was one of the "myths" of the Blitz. According to Angus Calder, such concepts were rooted in propaganda, but they were soon accepted by British citizens as the standard for behavior during the Blitz and thus achieved truthfulness.[9]

Dance music, as the Musicians' Union, *Melody Maker*, and others insisted, played a critical role in London's, and the nation's, ability to "take it." It boosted morale in a multitude of ways. Dancing provided a physical release from stress and energized sleep-deprived bodies. Even listening to dance music and other popular entertainment offered a momentary escape from the daily rigors of wartime life and provided a mental tonic. The continued operation of dance halls and clubs along with the ongoing broadcast of dance music reinforced the sense that the Luftwaffe had not managed to entirely disrupt daily life and its pleasures.[10] However, dance music's everyday qualities and its associations with leisure worked against the public's appreciation for the labor involved in its provision—and, more critically, the BBC's recognition of the degree to which conscription would threaten the profession. *Melody Maker* observed, "The public...is apt to take dance musicians for granted. They are regarded as rhythmic robots in evening dress. But they are men—and fine men, too, for the work that they are now doing so uncomplainingly is national service of the highest order."[11]

Although others in the press upheld the value of dance music to the nation's morale, *Melody Maker*'s position in support of the manliness and national service contributions of dance *musicians* was a lonely one.[12] (There were women's bands, too; however, women dance instrumentalists were treated as exceptional, proving the profession's masculine norms.)[13] From January 1940, it responded when other newspapers, particularly the widely read *Daily Express*, attacked civilian dance musicians (and, later, members of forces dance bands) as unpatriotic and cowardly.[14] The catalyst for the debate was the call-up for military service, which expanded during 1940 until it included all fit men under thirty-five who were not in reserve occupations regarded as essential to the war effort, such as mining, farming, and merchant shipping. The call-up highlighted questions of masculinity and the value ascribed to different categories of men's labor. Rose argued, "In WWII hegemonic masculinity was unstable, not in small measure because its successful enactment...depended upon being visibly a member of the fighting forces."[15] Men not in the forces could access hegemonic representations through embracing physical toughness and everyday heroism; indeed, contemporary propaganda upheld the contributions of firefighters, working-class men in reserve occupations, and other skilled, manual workers. The voluntary Home Guard played a critical role in this regard for older men and young men serving on the home front in less visible ways, particularly because its members wore military uniforms, which represented a man's commitment to the war effort in a visible manner.[16]

Dance music was a difficult profession to value within the framework of a wartime British masculinity built upon physical fitness, temperate emotions, and sacrifice. Music in British (and, more specifically, English) culture had historically been regarded as a foreign occupation: as scholars including Richard Leppert and Cyril Ehrlich have argued, there was a long tradition of questioning the masculinity and Britishness of professional musicians.[17] This was even more the case in the field of popular music, for its style and repertory carried strong associations with American, Jewish, and black identities—all regarded as alien in interwar and wartime Britain. Indeed, many top bandleaders—including Bert Ambrose, Geraldo, Joe Loss, and Harry Roy—and dance musicians were Jewish (often, born of immigrant parents) and managed to thrive in the profession while negotiating the period's unofficial, but pervasive, anti-Semitism.[18] The problem of regarding the Britishness of musicians as suspect became particularly fraught when Italy entered the war in June 1940, and the BBC began banning the broadcast of "enemy alien" composers and songwriters and significantly limited the broadcasting of performers of those ethnicities.[19] Meanwhile, the dance profession's state of defensiveness about the masculinity of its enterprise contributed to a sometimes-hostile environment for women instrumentalists and bandleaders who dared to compete directly with men.

Another factor that contributed to the undervaluing of dance musicians' contributions to the war effort was that dance music was ephemeral and regarded by many as a trivial enterprise. Unlike most reserve occupations, dance musicians did not produce tangible goods, food, or raw materials; moreover, the nation's need for entertainment was difficult to quantify while judgments as to what constituted high-quality and appropriate entertainment were subject to debate. In response to these attitudes, the Musicians' Union argued for dance music's morale-boosting contributions to the war effort and its status as a skilled trade (like plumbing) that, if it could not be classified as a reserve occupation, should at least be subject to individual deferments and special enlistments in the forces. Unfortunately, its critics—and more to the point, the Ministry of Labour—continued to regard dance music as inessential and as a field that required few full-time practitioners.

The final problem for the dance music profession was that its practitioners were almost entirely young men under thirty, the individuals most targeted by the call-up. When they performed, dance bands offered a spectacle of able-bodied, young men engaging in what many considered to be a frivolous pursuit. Their snappy uniforms or evening dress, smart grooming, and well-drilled manner represented a travesty of military discipline. Even forces dance bands and moonlighting servicemen and firefighters did not escape criticism as being soft, intemperate, and insufficiently committed to the war effort. In the *Daily Express*, Paul Holt wrote, "As the couples revolved to *Amapola* or *It's Always You* in the West End restaurant or munitions towns last night they glanced, maybe, at the band, and noticed how many young men of military age there were handling the fiddle, lipping the saxophone, stroking the keys."[20] Holt also questioned the appropriateness of dancing at such a serious time, but it was the musicians—not the dancers—whom he portrayed as deviant. As registered by *Melody Maker*'s outraged response, Holt's charges of dodging stung, particularly for a profession reeling from the loss to the call-up of more than 80 percent of its players.

The BBC as an institution certainly did not share Holt's hostility toward dance musicians; it recognized the importance of good dance music, and while Variety Department and other staff frowned on practices like song plugging, they had good working relations with most bandleaders. Nevertheless, during the critical first year of the war—and the call-up—the Corporation failed to recognize that it would be nearly impossible to continue to provide high-quality and varied dance music if it continued its laissez-faire approach to booking bands. It was only in early 1941 that the Variety Department and Overseas Service, led by Cecil Madden of the Empire Entertainments Unit, instituted their wartime Dance Band Scheme, under which the BBC engaged two of the largest, most stable, and best remaining civilian dance bands in long-term contracts as house bands, essentially subsidizing them and ensuring their survival. The BBC's new house bandleaders were Jack Payne, the director of the first BBC Dance Orchestra, and Geraldo, from the Savoy Hotel. Remaining in place until early 1944, the scheme guaranteed the sustained availability of high-quality broadcasting bands and eventually defined the stylistic poles of British and American dance music through the personalities of Payne and Geraldo, respectively. Despite the usefulness of the scheme in maintaining a supply of good-quality dance music, there continued to be difficulties in offering a diverse representation of it. Listeners wanted an element of novelty as well as familiarity: dealing with "rationed" dance music was as challenging for the BBC as a monotonous supply of potatoes and cabbage was for wartime cooks.

The other key challenge of the period for the BBC was in striking a suitable balance of entertainment and other programming. With each grim turn in the war, the BBC fretted about how to achieve a tone in popular music broadcasting that would best serve the broad range of listener tastes and susceptibilities. In the fearful summer of 1940, through the winter of the Blitz, and into the extended rationing and calling up of women in 1941, the claims for dance music's benefits to morale continued to be tested, even as the provision of high-quality dance music became more difficult. In July 1941, the BBC instituted the long-running *BBC Dancing Club*, which featured Victor Silvester, the bandleader who arguably made the most successful case for the value of dance music to the war effort. A decorated veteran of the First World War, ballroom dance champion, and popular recording artist, Silvester offered dance instruction and his own brand of strict-tempo dance music. Although most musicians dismissed his broadcasts as monotonous, they were extraordinarily popular among listeners. With his advocacy for physical fitness, discipline, and accessibility, Silvester offered a model of dancing and dance music that accorded with notions of hegemonic wartime masculinity.

Understandings of wartime masculinity, no less than the Blitz, helped shape the fortunes and the hardships of both dance musicians and the Corporation—not to mention members of the forces, war workers, and other civilians who turned to dance music and dancing for entertainment, escape, and relief. While the field of dance music included a few leaders who did not broadcast frequently, most notably Joe Loss, who bridged swing and strict-tempo styles in his recordings and live performances, the BBC managed to put under contract three key civilian bandleaders, Geraldo, Silvester, and Payne, who came to define British dance music during the war, in no small part because of their broadcasts. Broadcasting also helped catapult service dance bands, especially the RAF Squadronaires, to national stardom while also promoting the notion that playing dance music could be an expression of patriotic masculinity. Throughout this grim period on the home front, the BBC continued to play a critical role in defining the quality, style, and wartime role of dance music in Britain.

Music, Morale, and the Blitz: Broadcasting Dance Music for a Nation in Crisis

"Every time a news bulletin is switched on the listener opens the door to something new and potentially unpleasant," asserted an August 1940 Listener Research report on broadcasting policy and the "average listener."[21] During the preceding spring and summer this was a frequent experience for the, on average, 13 million listeners who heard the 1:00 p.m. news bulletin, the listenership of which spiked with every crisis.[22] The grim news of Dunkirk stimulated a spirited discussion among listeners and within the BBC on the place of radio entertainment in wartime. F. H. Shera, a *Listener* music critic, noted the new insistence of letters opposed to popular music, exemplified by one correspondent's objections to the juxtaposition of "crooning, jazz, swing music, and other noxious noises" with the news.[23] Basil Nicolls, the BBC controller of Programmes, agreed. On June 4, he issued a directive on reducing "the trivial and the frivolous" at serious times, which involved separating "grave news" from "light entertainment" and avoiding the broadcast of "frivolity" simultaneously on the Home and Forces wavelengths.[24]

Nevertheless, Nicolls also recognized that "recreational programs" held value for listeners in difficult times.[25] As "A Smiler" wrote to the *Radio Times*, "Some of us are leading difficult lives, filled with hard work from dawn to dark, and a few minutes of leisure spent listening to comic relief sends us back to work with a grin and a fresh relay of strength."[26] The problem for the BBC lay in the diversity of opinions on what constituted appropriate recreational listening, which ranged from "Beethoven sonatas" to "jazz and theatre organs" to nothing but "religious services and war news." The *Radio Times* explained, "It has to try its hardest to please most [listeners] most of the time."[27] Listener Research soon found that the BBC was successful in this aim, despite the spate of letters complaining of excessive lightheartedness: the crisis had simply "sharpened" the preexisting likes and dislikes of a vocal minority.[28]

The BBC, critics, and social observers understood dance music in terms of escapism. Although serious music and drama might also distract listeners from their circumstances, "highbrow" programming was never considered escapist. The *Listener* clarified this distinction early in the war: "There are plenty of anodynes at hand.... They pass the time and help one to forget reality, but they do nothing more. Their value is negative; that of great literature ... and great music is positive. These offer not merely temporary escape but permanent strengthening and underpinning."[29] For those already critical of popular music and concerned about the war's progress, however, the problems of escapism soon took on more concrete ramifications. "A middle-class housewife" explained, "I have heard it said that the troops were too busy listening to Gracie Fields during the winter, when they should have been preparing to face the enemy."[30] At its worst, escapism distracted soldiers and other citizens from their responsibilities. This view transformed sentimental popular music from mere anodyne to scapegoat, and it spread with each military setback until it peaked in the 1942 ban on "slushy" songs.

During the "strange summer" of 1940, romantic, escapist themes in popular song returned to their prewar dominance.[31] They replaced war-themed songs, which had flopped by March: humor, jingoism, and march time were out of step with Britain's defensive position. According to Mass-Observation, the hits of the summer derived from three main sources: revivals, films, and the United States—all of which ignored the war. There was a "tendency on the wireless to revert to past successes," which nostalgically evoked prewar times. For example, Geraldo performed Irving Berlin's playfully romantic "I'm Putting All My Eggs in One Basket" (1936) and "I've Got My Love to Keep Me Warm" (1937) in his late night broadcast on July 24. In Mass-Observation's list of nineteen current hits, ten originated in the United States, including Mack David's swung classic "On the Isle of May," which freely deployed the lyrical staples "love" and "June."

Most of the American songs were linked to film musicals and had already been plugged heavily on air, including "Over the Rainbow" (*The Wizard of Oz*), "When You Wish upon a Star" (*Pinocchio*), and "It's a Hap-Hap-Happy Day" (*Gulliver's Travels*).[32]

In late August, two weeks after "the air battle of Britain began in earnest" but before the Luftwaffe commenced regular raids on London and other urban centers, Listener Research turned its attention to how the BBC could best sustain morale in the coming winter. In one intriguing summary, it explained why "colour"—a term that, with its potential for diversion and reassurance, closely resembled escapism—would be so important during "the coming winter." Color was "perhaps the greatest lack in the work-day life of an industrial society," and popular music could provide it in a variety of ways: as background, it could help "keep up the people's spirits"; in request shows, it could unite communities "vicariously" in pleasure; and in entertainment programs, it offered familiarity, an important commodity in wartime when "the context of ordinary lives is either threatened or actually changing rapidly."[33] As color, popular music was critical to maintaining the morale of civilians as well as the forces, who would be spending the winter in rural camps "in conditions that they hate" with "absolutely nothing to do."[34]

The escapist benefits of dance music were linked closely with the act of dancing. In early May, army authorities supported a series of regimental nights at dance halls to promote morale among the public and the forces.[35] Despite air raids, dancing remained a popular activity throughout the summer. In seaside resort towns and in areas outside of London, dance halls were packed, with dancers concentrating on the "popular four dances, waltz, quickstep, foxtrot, tango."[36]

While dancing flourished, however, civilian bands were entering a state of crisis. The call-up, which expanded throughout 1940, "play[ed] havoc" with bands at all levels of the industry: personnel were unpredictable and difficult to replace, costly orchestrations were rendered useless when key players left, and extra rehearsals to acclimate new players increased overhead.[37] Beginning in July 1940, *Melody Maker* began almost weekly to report the enlistment of musicians who belonged to major "name" bands in the capital as well as regional bands.[38] While a few bandleaders managed to quietly obtain service deferments for "key men," the Ministry of Labour regularly dismissed Musicians' Union pleas for more extensive deferrals.[39] In August, Charles Bohm of the Musicians' Union estimated that at least 7,000 of the nation's 11,000 instrumentalists would be registered by the end of 1940, asking in exasperation: "Do the public think they ought to do without popular music...for the duration?"[40]

The decimation of the profession's ranks by the call-up soon affected broadcast dance music. As early as April 1940, "Eavesdropper" complained, "I have heard bands on the air lately cracking, splitting and gurgling, with wrong notes by the handful, playing in a way that would disgrace the lowest-place entrant in any *Melody Maker* Dance Band Contest."[41] The BBC, however, was slow to act. In early 1942, Douglas Lawrence, who oversaw dance bands for the Variety Department in London, asserted

I think it was pretty obvious right at the commencement of the war that dance bands, who in the main employ only spirited young men, would suffer as the call-up proceeded, but due to the apparent lack of interest in dance music in the Corporation, this matter of attempting some form of reservation was overlooked as compared with the reservation of certain straight musicians for the Overseas programmes.[42]

While the BBC dallied, the Royal Air Force (RAF) and other branches of the forces indicated in early 1940 that they would consider the skills of musicians who enlisted, moving, in effect, to reserve the best dance musicians for themselves.[43] In March, seven of Ambrose's best musicians joined the RAF en masse, forming the core of the Squadronaires, the first of the elite service dance bands, which also included the Sky-rockets (No. 1 Balloon Centre Dance Orchestra), the Royal Army Ordnance Corps Blue Rockets, and the Blue Mariners.[44] In all, more than 500 Musicians' Union members, including many of Britain's finest dance musicians, played in official service dance bands during the war.[45] The elite forces bands set a high standard that few of the struggling civilian bands could meet: they rehearsed extensively, and their freedom from commercial constraints enabled them to play more adventurous repertory:

> They are not told what to play, or how to play it; they are not asked to lay *à la* Victor Silvester or *à la* Duke Ellington. They do not have to bother about song-plugging; they can play old tunes, Dixieland tunes, "swing" tunes.... In fact, if it weren't for the war, their job would be a Dance Musicians' Utopia.[46]

By early 1941, *Melody Maker*'s "Detector" declared the Squadronaires to be the finest dance band in Britain.[47] The BBC was eager to air the Squadronaires and other top service bands, with their strong musicianship and implicit patriotism, and it engaged them frequently from late 1940. The bands' first obligations were to the military, however, not the Corporation.

Thus, the Corporation remained dependent upon civilian bands for most of its dance music, particularly for the Band of the Week scheme, which was supposed to provide good-quality music at an affordable cost.[48] Unfortunately, a week's broadcasting brutally exposed a band's weaknesses, and the Band of the Week system began to offer a painful index of the declining quality of civilian dance bands. Personnel problems caused by call-up played a significant role in poor on-air performances, but the "Bristol Blues" of acoustically inferior churches, plugging necessitated by inadequate fees and an expensive week away from London, and a grueling broadcast and rehearsal schedule all took their toll. Worse still, top-rank bandleaders, like Geraldo and Ambrose, declined Band of the Week contracts in Bristol because of their London commitments.[49] In August, the BBC finally moved the Band of the Week back to London and grudgingly agreed that contracted bands could take other engagements.[50]

The Band of the Week arrived in London a week before the Luftwaffe raided London's West End and the German air offensive was transformed into the Blitzkrieg. At first, it seemed that even air raids would not disrupt the capital's nightlife. Proclaiming that "LONDON'S WEST-END CONTINUES TO SPARKLE BEHIND BLACK-OUT CURTAINS," *Melody Maker* described dance bands performing marathon sessions at major restaurants and hotels to keep audiences "safe and happy" until the all-clear sounded.[51] During the early weeks of the London Blitz, dance halls and restaurants stayed open—and busy: "The general policy seems to be 'business entirely as usual,' until bombs or guns are heard, when patrons and the band go down to the shelters."[52]

By the third week of September, however, the previously stalwart West End began to close down, as air raids became a nightly affair. Dance halls, theaters, clubs, and restaurants that depended on late night crowds soon found their business harmed by air raid warnings (which tended to sound just as performances were about to begin), the unreliability of transportation for patrons, the dangers of falling shrapnel from British antiaircraft defenses, and temporary closures necessitated by unexploded bombs.[53] In London, most theaters closed down entirely; theaters in other areas adopted earlier schedules, and matinees grew in popularity.[54] Dance halls in the London area remained open, with the Mecca circuit maintaining that dancing was "the safest of amusements" during air raids since, unlike theaters, the spacious, single-level, and well-lit palais allowed for easy evacuation.[55] Underground clubs also remained open, with some, such as the cocktail bar at Landsdowne House (known as "The Farm"), declared as official shelters.[56] This created another set of problems, for shelter seekers would queue up to enter the clubs for free after the air raid warnings sounded, driving away the paying clientele.[57]

With theater and cinema closures, the blackout, and air raids keeping many citizens at home, millions turned to the BBC for entertainment, as they had the previous fall. This time, the BBC was better prepared. Rather than canceling programs wholesale, it followed a "day-by-day policy regarding air raids—transmissions from studios or outside venues being dictated by circumstances existing at the time."[58] *Melody Maker* reported that Eddie Carroll was the first bandleader to broadcast through an air raid, in an OB from the Hammersmith Palais de Danse for *London after Dark*, a series that was relayed to North America: "With fine irony, one of the numbers featured was *A Nightingale Sang in Berkeley Square*," a song that described a quiet London night, transformed by love.[59] For studio productions, the BBC depended upon prerecording, especially in the case of large variety shows, like *Band Waggon* and *Garrison Theatre*, which it revived for the fall in response to popular demand, and the new hit *Hi Gang!*, which featured the Americans Vic Oliver, Bebe Daniels, and Ben Lyon, and an outstanding band led by Jay Wilbur.[60] For live broadcasting, it used "special underground centres" where performers could stay the night rather than venture home through the Blitz.[61]

While the BBC gained approval for its logistical approach to broadcasting through the Blitz, the question of how air raids affected listening was a more contentious issue. A *Melody Maker* records reviewer related that auditing new releases in his cellar during air raids "certainly helped to take my mind off the ominous *crumps* going on around me," but BBC Listener Research found that most listeners in raided areas focused on the news while their listening to other types of programs declined because of stress, earlier bedtimes, and poor reception.[62] As they became accustomed to raids, many listeners craved "short, light items," especially popular music, which required low levels of concentration.[63] They reverted quickly to their "normal listening habits" when heavy raids ceased.[64]

The BBC responded by producing "snappier, shorter programmes" that would last a half hour or less.[65] The issue of poor reception during nighttime hours, which left many listeners no alternative but to turn off their sets, proved more difficult to address.[66] Atmospheric changes related to the season and time of day were partly responsible for the problem, but the other cause was the war precaution of closing down the local transmitter when enemy aircraft were nearby and transmitting the program via a different station.[67] More frustrating still, the BBC tended to interrupt the more popular Forces Programme before it would cancel the Home Service, at least according to "Detector."[68] Poor reception aggravated listeners, leading to a sharp decline in listener satisfaction during September and October.[69] Fortunately, the problem abated in March 1941, when the BBC made a series of wavelength changes that greatly improved reception of the Forces Programme.[70]

In early November 1940, *Melody Maker* announced that, despite the Blitz, nightclubs were reopening and London's West End was returning to normal.[71] Nevertheless, the Blitzkrieg continued, and "entertainment centres" did not escape unscathed. The BBC sustained a direct hit in October when a bomb hit Broadcasting House, killing seven staff members; in December, a land mine exploded near the building.[72] Several of London's landmark variety theaters—the Holborn Empire, London Coliseum, Finsbury Park Empire, and Stratford Empire—suffered attacks as well.[73] In Manchester, *Melody Maker* reported that, due to air raids, "What would have been a record Christmas from a dancing point of view became a record in cancellations."[74] Responding to numerous queries, the weekly instructed readers on government compensation for air raid losses: "tools of trade" (damaged instruments or music), which were difficult to replace under wartime rationing, were subject to limited compensation in the short term with full compensation a possibility only after the war.[75] No wonder so many musicians' Blitz accounts included terrifying trips back into bombed buildings, where they risked life and limb to retrieve instruments, uniforms, gramophone records, and sheet music.[76]

Several well-known musicians were injured or killed in the Blitz. *Melody Maker* duly reported the mid-April death of Al Bowlly, the famous crooner, when a bomb fell outside his home, but it devoted even more coverage to the death of Ken "Snakehips" Johnson on March 8, 1941.[77] The death of a well-known bandleader in the Blitz was certainly news, but even more significantly, Johnson had been killed "in action"— while he and his West Indian Dance Orchestra were performing—in a direct hit on the Café de Paris, an underground and supposedly bombproof restaurant.[78] Within a few weeks of Johnson's death, fans began to write to the BBC, requesting a memorial program.[79] Apparently, the BBC did not share their regard for Johnson's importance: although it aired a tribute program on June 26 for Bowlly, it failed to broadcast a tribute to Johnson until September 3, in an installment of *Radio Rhythm Club*.[80]

During the difficult winter of 1941, the BBC found itself embroiled in a controversy at the intersection of politics, music, and freedom of expression when it banned from broadcast signatories of the People's Convention, along with those who were "known publicly to hold pacifist views." A number of bandleaders, including Sydney Lipton, Lew Stone, Phil Cardew, and Ben Frankel, had joined the communist-backed group in urging "a people's peace that gets rid of the causes of war." The BBC Board of Governors determined not to book them for broadcast unless they renounced their connection to the convention.[81] When the ban was finally lifted in mid-March, Churchill observed in Parliament that "musical and dramatic performances" were not tied to "political acts and opinions":

> If [Sir Hugh Robertson, the conductor of the Glasgow Orpheus Choir and a paci-fist,] were allowed to broadcast it would be in his capacity as a musician or in a musical performance and would have no relation to his political or conscientious view, but I think we should have to retain a certain amount of power in the selection of music. (Laughter.) A very spirited rendering of "Deutschland Uber [sic] Alles" could hardly be allowed. (Laughter.)[82]

Melody Maker, which had protested the ban as undemocratic and irrelevant to a musician's "entertainment value," welcomed the decision, but the *Musical Times*'s "Feste," who had supported the ban, wrote, "If I were one of these gullible people…I'd rather feel myself a martyr for The Cause than to be told…that I don't really matter so long as I behave myself and stick to my job as an entertainer."[83]

While the BBC overlooked the political views of British performers for the rest of the war, it would remain less sanguine about the music itself. Indeed, Churchill's comments on retaining power over musical selections proved prescient, given the extensive vetting that the Dance Music Policy Committee began to exercise over popular songs and their performers in 1942. In the meantime, however, the BBC still faced enormous challenges in filling nearly thirty dance music sessions a week for its Home, Forces, and Overseas programs. Most listeners wanted dance music, and the Corporation regarded it as beneficial to morale, but in late 1940 with the call-up and the decline of civilian bands, providing *good-quality* dance music, at an affordable price, had become a serious problem.

The Dance Band Scheme

During the fall of 1940, with both the Blitz and the call-up threatening the survival of civilian bands, the BBC faced the task of filling its schedule from a far more circumscribed pool of "name" dance bands than it had the year before. Throughout the fall, it signed fewer leaders to longer contracts, until in early 1941, prodded by Madden, it offered first Payne and then Geraldo indefinite contracts as "house bands." The Dance Band Scheme, as it came to be known, provided for most of the BBC's dance music needs at a bargain rate while helping to improve the quality of broadcast dance music, since it allowed the contracted bands to maintain relatively stable personnel. Steadily modified through negotiations between the leaders, Variety staff, and Overseas producers, the scheme remained in place until early 1944. During that period, Payne and Geraldo played a central role in defining the sound of dance music on the wartime BBC.

The Dance Band Scheme evolved from the Band of the Week. Soon after the Band of the Week returned to London, the BBC began extending its bulk-buying approach to fill more of its dance music needs. In October 1940, Nicolls proposed instituting a second Band of the Week, an idea that the director of Variety John Watt and his assistant director, Pat Hillyard, greeted with enthusiasm. A second Band of the Week offered several advantages over the nine ad hoc bookings that it would replace. First, the nine shows would cost £275 rather than £450 at ad hoc rates, a savings of £175. Second, the band would be better rehearsed, since the BBC could schedule regular rehearsals as part of the week's contract. Third, the system enabled bands to be booked on a lengthier rotation (every ten weeks rather than every six), giving listeners the sense of greater variety. Finally, the Variety Department determined that two of the second band's airings would be "high-spot" programs, which could be produced at a bargain rate.[84]

Geraldo, who had recently left the Savoy for a lucrative variety tour, only to have his plans limited by air raids, inaugurated the scheme on November 4 with a six-week residency at the BBC's London studios, during which he reprised his prewar productions, *Dancing Through* and *Romance in Rhythm*.[85] The contract, which was extended to twelve weeks, was a coup, since the BBC had only once lured Geraldo to Bristol. Geraldo was on his way to becoming one of the most popular bandleaders of the war and was regarded in the Variety Department as a creative, conscientious leader with one of the best remaining civilian bands.[86] Critics praised his precision, excellent brass section, and conducting. "I think Gerry's success lies in an infinite capacity for taking pains. His band always sounds rehearsed-to-the-minute and polished-to-the-last-demi-semiquaver. Other leaders, please copy!" stated *Melody Maker*'s "Eavesdropper" while no less a critic than Leonard Feather wrote, "I have seldom met a band-leader with such a diversity of activities and ideas; without a logical, orderly mind he would never get through so much work."[87] At the end of 1940, thanks in part to his popular *Dancing Through* series, "a non-stop pageant of popular music during the past twenty years," respondents to a Listener Research bandleader popularity poll ranked Geraldo second only to the long-standing favorite, Henry Hall, who had been broadcasting his hit *Guest Night* for nearly a year.[88]

The prospect of working with Geraldo and gaining access to more live dance music appealed strongly to Madden, the "intelligent and energetic" head of the Empire (later Overseas) Entertainments Unit (EEU), which had been established in April 1940.[89] Madden cut an elegant and cosmopolitan figure at the BBC. Born in Morocco, where his father was a diplomat, he had been involved with the theater in Spain and Paris; in 1933, he joined the Corporation, where from 1936, he was a producer in the experimental medium of television.[90] During the war, Madden developed scores of innovative programs at the EEU, which produced entertainment for the rapidly expanding Overseas Service. Although the Overseas Service, which included the global Empire Service as well as the European, Latin-American, and Near Eastern Services, was concerned primarily with news broadcasting in dozens of languages, it also offered variety and music to foreign and colonial listeners, as well as British troops stationed abroad.[91] Madden's leadership at the EEU was characterized by his shrewd ability to obtain the services of top dance bands and star performers on a limited budget in a Corporation that was often indifferent or hostile to popular entertainment. Unsurprisingly, then, the Band of the Week contract with Geraldo had not yet gone into effect when the Overseas Service, at Madden's urging, asserted its claim for one of his nine weekly sessions, arguing "that the band of the week should be engaged by the BBC as a whole," not only the Variety Department.[92] Anticipating his Unit's imminent move to the underground Criterion Theatre, which would provide blitz-proof office, studio, and sleeping space, Madden was pleased when he learned of Variety's consent, but he was soon negotiating for more live dance music sessions.[93]

Madden later recalled, "To ensure Best Music in Wartime I created a scheme to put Geraldo & Jack Payne under contract plus one alternating other band to ensure variety of styles."[94] Although Madden exaggerated the single-handedness of his role, he was the first within the Corporation to outline the scheme in a complete form, and his intense commitment to live dance music for Overseas broadcasting helped make it a reality. In late December, Madden informed A. H. Brown, the Variety booking manager, that Overseas could use another six dance band engagements a week. Brown soon concluded that, providing Variety was willing to cooperate by using the same band for two or three additional sessions, a dance band could be booked on an indefinite contract for half the equivalent ad hoc rate, a significant savings.[95] Madden was particularly interested in hiring Payne, a seasoned broadcaster with experience going back to his days leading the first BBC Dance Orchestra, who relied upon meticulous planning, a stopwatch, and an exact sense of tempo to give perfectly timed performances.[96]

In early January 1941, *Melody Maker* announced that Payne had signed a long-term contract with the BBC.[97] For the economical rate of £250 a week, Payne provided three broadcasts for the domestic Home Service and Forces Programme and three for the Overseas Service and agreed to be available on a first-call basis for the BBC six days a week. Since £250 alone could not support a band, Payne reserved his Sundays so that he could accept lucrative Sunday concert engagements.[98] His band consisted of eighteen players (expanding to twenty-five for "Concert Orchestra" performances) and three singers: Georgina; the youthful Bruce Trent; and Anne Shelton, who had recently begun her rise to fame.[99] Payne also featured the solo work of his wife, the pianist, arranger, and violinist Peggy Cochrane, and the keyboardist Arthur Young.[100] In addition to straight dance music programs, Payne and his band aired in special production series, including *Moods Modernistic* and *Our Kind of Music*. *Moods Modernistic* included a high proportion of current plug numbers (both ballads, like the sentimental "I Don't Want to Cry Anymore" sung by Trent, and swing numbers, like "Bugle Call Rag"), which leavened Payne's light classical selections, such as Massenet's Elegy, featuring Cochrane.[101] Beginning with "The [Arthur] Young Idea," *Our Kind of Music* featured the works of a different "modern English rhythmic" composer each week.[102] Although "Detector" gave a lukewarm appraisal of the band's first weeks, noting the "too overdone" arrangements and weak brass section, he reported its marked improvement a month later.[103]

Meanwhile, Watt became concerned about the fate of Geraldo's band as it reached the end of its twelve-week broadcasting run. He was unstinting in his praise for the band and unequivocal about the BBC's role in guaranteeing its survival:

There is no doubt whatever that Geraldo's band is the best band on the air today, and his performance and general versatility and slickness are very great assets in London. I am anxious that this band should not...be broken up....To keep a band of this excellence together and permanently employed is a good thing for the Corporation as a whole, as we therefore get the best band available cheaper than we otherwise would, and keep up a high standard both on Home and Overseas when most other bands are deteriorating.[104]

Madden was sympathetic to Watt's desire to preserve Geraldo's band, particularly when it involved continuing his service at a bargain rate, but he also wanted to maintain diversity in his dance music sessions. He responded by outlining the Dance Band Scheme, with its balance of stability and variety.[105]

On March 31, after several weeks of negotiations, the scheme went into effect. With the Bands of the Week, it supplied thirty-four of the BBC's dance music sessions each week (table 4.1). Payne's indefinite contract and the new agreement with Geraldo formed the scheme's foundation. The BBC's contract with Geraldo specified that he and his seventeen-member band would broadcast nine programs weekly from London at the rate of £300 a week.[106] His nine sessions were split between the domestic wavelengths (Home and Forces) and the Overseas Service at a ratio of three to six and six to three in alternate weeks; Payne's now seven sessions were divided in a similar manner at a ratio of three to four. Meanwhile, the BBC continued to engage two Bands of the Week. One band continued to broadcast from London for a week or more at a time, with its nine sessions split between Overseas and the domestic wavelengths to

TABLE 4.1 Allocations of bands according to the Dance Band Scheme and Band of the Week ("Dance Bands," BBC ICM from Variety Booking Manager, to PC Ex., March 28, 1941, BBC WAC R27/21)

	Overseas Service	Domestic wavelengths Home Service and Forces Programme
Week of March 31, 1941	Payne (4 sessions) Geraldo (3 sessions) Band of the Week (London): Ambrose (6 sessions)	Payne (3 sessions) Geraldo (6 sessions) Band of the Week (London): Ambrose (3 sessions) Band of the Week (Weston): Joe Loss (9 sessions)
Week of April 6, 1941	Payne (3 sessions) Geraldo (6 sessions) Band of the Week (London): Ambrose (3 sessions)	Payne (4 sessions) Geraldo (3 sessions) Band of the Week (London): Ambrose (6 sessions) Band of the Week (Weston): Billy Cotton (9 sessions)

complement Geraldo. The other band, which broadcast only on the Home and Forces wavelengths, aired in two-week stints from Weston-super-Mare, a location deemed safer from attack than Bristol.[107]

Although the scheme carried the flavor of clockwork, it managed to sustain for broadcast dance music a degree of variety, quality, affordability—and even reassuring familiarity—in a difficult climate. The Bands of the Week, plus a number of ad hoc bookings (particularly for *Music While You Work [MWYW]*), provided a steady supply of novelty while Payne and Geraldo alternated frequently enough between the domestic wavelengths and Overseas Service to remain fresh. Payne and Geraldo themselves offered a range of styles, both individually and in their occupation of opposing stylistic poles, which by 1942 Madden cast as British and American, respectively. Payne, with an orchestra that included strings and upper woodwinds, offered a blend of straight dance music, comedy numbers, and light classics while Geraldo, a polished showman, embraced newer trends like swing and Latin music.[108]

The bandleaders' contrasting recordings of Noel Gay's "Let the People Sing" from C. B. Cochrane's February 1940 revue, *Lights Up!*, demonstrated their stylistic differences.[109] Payne's recording treated the song to one of his characteristic concert arrangements, with prominent strings and every measure touched by a shifting kaleidoscope of instrumental color, articulation, texture, and intensity. The recording had "Jack Payne's personality etched in every groove. Strong, powerful, aggressive, dominant—sort of 'This is the way I play this tune—and if you don't like it you know what you can do.' First class stage-band playing," wrote *Melody Maker* (sound example 4.1).[110] In contrast, Geraldo's recording inhabited the world of foxtrot sides, with the full-voiced Cyril Grantham and male chorus limited to the central verse and chorus. Geraldo's more restrained arrangement allows the often-swinging rhythmic assuredness of the band, the triple-tonguing, technical accomplishment of the trumpets, and some clever countermelodies to move into the foreground of the listener's awareness (sound example 4.2).[111]

In a period when dance musicians and bandleaders were easy targets for charges of unmanliness and shirking, Payne and Geraldo negotiated distinct personas that upheld their patriotism and masculinity. Payne, the elder of the two men, recalled his service in the First World War and emphasized his band's contributions in the present war at military camps, charity dances, and hospitals. He also cultivated an image of temperate masculinity, asserting, "Running a dance band these days is a serious, dignified business" (figure 4.1). In a 1941 interview, "Dance Bands Do a Good War Job," Payne explained, "The wartime usefulness of popular bands is not to throw listeners back on their emotions, but to keep them cheerful"; to promote this wartime virtue, he favored lively 6/8 marches over sentimental songs and regarded the "queer antics of jazz" as out of step with the public mood.[112] His policy of middlebrow variety appealed to mainstream listeners, who appreciated having "their particular tastes catered for," but dance enthusiasts deplored his pretentious concert arrangements and patronizing attitude to the token swing numbers that he did feature.[113] "Jack's band...never really swings a phrase, even by accident," observed "Corny," *Melody Maker*'s commercial records reviewer.[114] Nevertheless, Payne ranked fourth in a BBC survey of dance band

FIGURE 4.1 The bandleader Jack Payne: "Running a dance band these days is a serious, dignified business." (Photo by Evening Standard/Getty Images)

popularity, with 51.5 percent of respondents declaring that they would make a point to listen to his broadcasts.[115]

In contrast to Payne's old-guard respectability, Geraldo represented the ambitious future. One Columbia Records advertisement described him as "polished and stream-lined," adjectives that could be applied to both his music and his "fastidious" appearance, if not his voice, which had "a distinct trace of his native Cockney accent" (figure 4.2).[116] Geraldo was born in 1904 as Gerald Bright, the son of a master tailor in North London. With his twin brother, Sidney, who went on to play in his band, he studied piano at the Royal Academy of Music; by his early twenties, he led hotel bands in the Blackpool area, but in 1929, he disbanded and traveled abroad. According to his colorful and highly dubious account, he went to Brazil to study coffee planting but became fascinated with the "native" tango.[117] Upon his return to London, he formed a flamboyantly costumed Gaucho Tango Orchestra (becoming known as Geraldo along the way), which was hired by the Savoy Hotel in 1930.[118] Throughout the decade, Geraldo expanded the scope of his Savoy bandleading and became an active and imaginative broadcaster on the BBC.

Geraldo's adaptability, which during the war included an openness to swing, made him a solid favorite with young listeners in war service. His innovations included

FIGURE 4.2 The bandleader Geraldo: modern, dapper, and "polished-to-the-last-demi-semiquaver." (Cover, *Radio Times* [27 December 1940]: 1)

forming a swing septette-within-a-band and hiring top players, such as the outstanding swing-oriented trombonist Ted Heath.[119] Geraldo appealed to a far broader audience than swing enthusiasts, however. While he tended to avoid the light classics favored by Payne, he programmed a wide range of new and old popular songs, such as "Stormy Weather" and "Ain't Misbehavin'" in the "reminiscent programme" *Tunes We Shall Never Forget*, which attracted an impressive 22.8 percent of the listening audience.[120] Part of Geraldo's wide appeal resided in his singers' varied styles: the outstanding interpreter Dorothy Carless, the crooner Len Camber, and the comedy singer (and drummer) Jackie Hunter. He also valued good showmanship, aiming not only to appeal to music lovers but also to "interest the hundreds of people who are out to get entertainment and relaxation from their sets."[121]

Geraldo's masculinity and patriotism were anchored by his utter commitment to entertaining the forces. Peter Noble, his wartime biographer, explained, "His whole organisation is today geared up, as it were, for war production." Geraldo and his band made weekly visits to isolated camps throughout Britain, and he developed overseas broadcasts around the request letters sent in by the troops.[122] His embrace of swing and newer styles of dance music certainly earned him his following in the forces, but so did his cheery appeals for their input, in which he observed, "I think the greatest kick I get out of my job these days is when we are broadcasting to you fellows."[123] Unlike Payne, whose pompous announcing irritated many, Geraldo seemed to have mastered radio's intimate and potentially informal address, aided by his less refined accent.

With their appeal to two large, overlapping segments of the public, Geraldo's and Payne's regular airings pleased a broad audience; however, the institution of two house bands strained relations between the BBC and the dance music profession as a whole. Hillyard noted, "There is a very strong feeling amongst band leaders generally with regard to our contract bands, which they feel tend to have a monopoly of broadcasting." He regarded the six ad hoc sessions that were available each week to be a political necessity, both for external relations with bandleaders and even within the Corporation for producers who wanted to use noncontract bands.[124] *MWYW* proved to be another important source of employment, but it could not accommodate the full range of civilian bands, particularly those that featured swing.[125] Stone and his Stonecrackers, for example, gave "a brilliant swing programme with an 'all-star' pick-up band" in early October; however, as an outraged "Detector" reported, the BBC informed Stone that, although his broadcast was "very good," it would be a year before his "turn [came] round again."[126]

The Dance Band Scheme was the BBC's answer to the forces "reserving" dance musicians in the Squadronaires and other top service bands. As an institution expected to support the civilian dance music profession while also maintaining quality, the BBC faced a difficult balancing act of supporting its scheme while not alienating other bandleaders. Although in the fall of 1941 it became increasingly difficult to fully utilize each week's contract band sessions, the persistence of the system testified to its value to Overseas and Home variety producers.[127] A key aspect of the scheme's survival was the excellence and stylistic range offered by the two leaders, Payne and Geraldo. Both bandleaders brought a strong work ethic, precision, and polished showmanship to their work for the BBC, and they brought their semiofficial status to bear in other areas of their work, particularly in their commitment to entertaining soldiers and war workers. Nevertheless, neither Payne nor Geraldo topped dance band popularity polls in 1942 and 1943. That honor went to the strict-tempo ballroom phenom, Victor Silvester.

BBC Dancing Club, Manliness, and Victor Silvester

In his 1958 memoir, *Dancing Is My Life*, Silvester described the genesis for his long-running radio (and then television) series, *BBC Dancing Club*:

> In March 1941 Mike Meehan, . . . then assistant director of BBC Variety, asked me to meet him. He said he wanted to talk about a new sort of BBC programme. "Victor," he explained, "there are thousands of Service men and girls stationed at camps and gun sites miles from anywhere. It occurred to me that if you gave dancing lessons on the air it would help them to pass the time."[128]

The "new sort of programme," *BBC Dancing Club*, premiered on Wednesday, July 30, 1941, on the Forces Programme. That summer, the war had taken another serious turn: Germany had invaded Russia, and on the home front clothing rationing had begun and conscription was extended to women up to age thirty-one and men up to age forty-six. *Dancing Club's* fixed 8:00 p.m. time slot signaled the BBC's regard for its importance and determination that it would succeed. Indeed, its audience figures soon expanded from a very respectable 14.5 percent for the first broadcast to impressive numbers of more than 20 percent.[129] The program's formula did not at first glance carry the hallmarks of wartime success. Unlike *Itma*'s oddball humor, the intimate warmth of *Sincerely Yours—Vera Lynn*, or J. B. Priestley's homey *Postscripts*, *Dancing Club* seemed—and according to its detractors, was—dull.[130] Lasting forty minutes in all (it was expanded to an hour from October 28, 1942), it began with ten minutes of dance instruction, given by Silvester, followed by thirty minutes of strict-tempo dance music, which was characterized by its "good solid beat" and unembellished, nonvocal presentation of the melody, played by his Ballroom Dance Orchestra.[131] Nevertheless, *BBC Dancing Club*, Victor Silvester, and even the program's music embodied wartime values of temperate British masculinity, sensible recreation, and community in a manner that resonated for civilian and forces during the most difficult years of the war.

At first glance, it seems counterintuitive that a bandleader and dance instructor could embody hegemonic British wartime masculinity. While social dancing for women during the interwar years embodied modern freedoms, male ballroom dancers who achieved celebrity status had to distance themselves from the figures of the effete lounge lizard and racialized, lower-class gigolo. The route lay in balancing restrained Victorian notions of manliness and newer understandings of masculinity, which tapped into the energizing possibilities of primitive aggression and sexuality.[132] Silvester adeptly negotiated these codes in his publicity to locate himself within hegemonic masculinity. He highlighted his military service during the First World War (as a child soldier) and characterized his start as a professional dance partner, following 1919 his demobilization, as serendipity.[133] After winning the first World Dancing Championship three years later at age twenty-two, he moved quickly to prominence in the profession, opening a dancing school with his wife, Dorothy; collaborating with other ballroom teachers in the Ballroom Section of the Imperial Society of Teachers of Dance to shape the English style of ballroom dance; and, in 1927, publishing his classic manual, *Modern Ballroom Dancing*.[134] In his approach to the English style, Silvester forged powerful connections between naturalness, discipline, and British masculinity, and he packaged it as an accessible modern commodity for a mass audience. He applied these values to music when in 1935, frustrated with the unmetronomic approach of most dance band recordings, he began to record strict-tempo dance music for Parlophone.[135] The series was a success, and in 1937, Silvester began broadcasting on the BBC.[136] Silvester's career as a bandleader flourished during the war: he closed his school, toured Mecca dance halls with his band, and broadcast frequently, especially on *MWYW*.[137]

Silvester was the ideal host for *BBC Dancing Club* not only because of his fame as a dance instructor and popularity as a bandleader but also because as an athletic, "well-built six-footer," who enjoyed football, he embodied the wartime value of physical fitness.[138] With others in the profession, Silvester promoted dance both as a tonic for both manual and "brain" workers to help them sustain "maximum effort" and as "a healthy recreation for all."[139] Given the influx of beginners who were "handicapped by not knowing how to dance," however, the ballroom dance profession soon recognized the need for easy, accessible instruction.[140] *BBC Dancing Club* addressed both the

DANCING CLUB

Victor Silvester, well-known band-leader and dance expert, writes of his new series, 'BBC Dancing Club'. It starts in the Forces programme on Wednesday.

IN response to many requests from listeners the BBC Dancing Club has come into being. The idea at the back of it is two-fold—first, to provide half-an-hour's music that is ideal for dancing at a time of the evening when most listeners are able to take advantage of it, and second to give ten minutes of dancing instruction to the many people who wish to learn how to dance.

GENTLEMAN   LADY

This diagram shows the quarter turns of the Quick-step. Keep it by you, because Silvester will refer to it in his broadcast on Wednesday evening.

The Club will be on the air at 8 p.m. every Wednesday evening for the next four months, and perhaps longer, so you can be sure of getting music that you can dance to at the same time regularly each week. This will give listeners a chance to make their plans accordingly.

I shall devote the first few minutes of each broadcast to giving instruction in the most important figures used in ballroom dancing today. All these figures are standardised, which means that they never change. They have evolved and developed through practice and experience, and have been found to be the most natural and rhythmic forms of movement to music in tempo.

There are still numerous people who hesitate about learning how to dance. They seem to imagine they will have to learn masses of intricate steps which are popular one year and out of date the next. Nothing could be further from the truth. The main feature of modern ballroom dancing is that it is based on natural movement. The fundamental principle is ' the

walk ', and once you can walk well and rhythmically to music, with good balance and movement, you are more than half way to being a good dancer. Anyone can learn, and it is never too late to start.

Ballroom dancing is the most popular pastime in the world. It is enjoyed by every class of the community, in all weathers and climates, hot or cold, wet or fine. It helps people to take their minds off their troubles and worries, and gives them a chance of stepping forth into a gay, colourful atmosphere. That, as any mind doctor will tell you, is a mental tonic.

Fitness, Too

As an exercise, dancing is one of the best forms of recreation you could have, and it will give you physical grace and fitness besides the pleasure you derive from it. As a social exercise, too, I should be inclined to put it in a class by itself—the ballroom provides intense common interest set to music, friendship in rhythm.

In the running of the BBC Dancing Club I shall be ably assisted by producer David Miller. We shall do all that we can to cater for the non-dancing, as well as for the dancing, public. ' How can we interest the former ? ' you may ask. Well, after the brief dancing lesson, there will be thirty minutes of non-vocal rhythmic melody played by my Ballroom Orchestra, and this I hope will be 'easy on the ear', even to those who profess to dislike modern dance music !

So David Miller and I hope that you will join the BBC Dancing Club, and be with us on the air every Wednesday at 8 p.m.

FIGURE 4.3 An article by Victor Silvester on the first airing of *BBC Dancing Club*, accompanied by a diagram of the quickstep. (Victor Silvester, "Dancing Club," *Radio Times* [25 July 1941]: 3)

need for accessible ballroom dance lesson and the sizable audience for "easy on the ears" dance music.[141] The *Radio Times* printed diagrams to accompany the program each week, underscoring its pedagogical aims (figure 4.3). In its first twelve weeks on the air, Silvester gave three lessons each on the four standard dances: the quickstep, waltz, tango, and foxtrot. During the ensuing months, he continued to explore the standard dances but also addressed other trends. In November 1941, for example, he offered two lessons on the rumba, which had grown in popularity since 1940, following Edmundo Ros's introduction of a new ballroom version of the dance.[142]

Silvester and *Dancing Club*'s producer and compère, David Miller, worked to keep the lessons short, to avoid alienating nondancers, but also "explicit" for listeners who were

FIGURE 4.4 In the studio during a broadcast of *BBC Dancing Club*. (Copyright © BBC)

trying to learn. In one surviving recording, an early lesson on the natural turn in the waltz, Silvester offered a few general comments and then called out the steps for men and women, which he encouraged listeners to transcribe. Then, inviting listeners to try the steps with music, he called out, "Feet together, everyone. All ready. Now. [Piano accompaniment begins.] Forward. Side. Close. Backward. Side. Close."[143] Many listeners regarded the instructions as helpful. In a poll of forces listeners, nearly 90 percent agreed that the program was "very helpful" or "fairly helpful" to those interested in dancing; however, "some thought that the instructions were useful to those who could dance but of little use to beginners."[144]

Dancing Club went beyond instruction to unite listeners and boost their morale. The use of the word "club" in the title was no accident; through Silvester's on-air instruction, dancing offered the hope of harmony for one's body and the nation. Dancing, he contended, was "a social exercise.... [T]he ballroom provides intense common interest set to music, friendship in rhythm."[145] Appealing democratically across social classes, dancing also supported the nation's morale. "It helps people to take their minds off their troubles and worries, and gives them a chance of stepping forth into a gay, colourful atmosphere," Silvester explained.[146] To achieve "colour," the element Listener Research had argued radio was so well equipped to bring to everyday listeners, Silvester and Miller brought live (and audible) dancers into the studio, aiming "to create an illusion of a gay, glittering ballroom crowded with happy couples enjoying themselves. We wanted to bring a little glamour into the drab war-time lives of listeners" (figure 4.4).[147]

While learning to dance could certainly help listeners access a new, more colorful world, even background listening to *Dancing Club* brought pleasure to the domestic spaces and military canteens where it was heard. In a survey of forces listeners, Listener Research observed, "A very large number of reports said that the instruction period was ignored but that the straight dance music was enjoyed."[148] Silvester's aim was to please rather than challenge listeners: "I hope [it] will be 'easy on the ear,' even to those who profess to dislike modern dance music!"[149] Not surprisingly, this approach became subject to intense derision among musicians and dance music enthusiasts, with "Detector," for example, offering "ten shillings for the best letter...on: Why I don't like Victor Silvester's Strict Tempo Dance Band."[150] Nevertheless, Silvester appealed strongly to the large audience that asked for "no more than a pleasing melody plus a nice rhythmic 'pom, pom, pom.'"[151] In early 1942, he ranked first in a Listener Research survey of bandleader popularity among the forces, and in 1943, the civilian-oriented *Sunday Pictorial*'s "What Listeners Want" radio poll ranked him first again.[152]

More than the musically ambitious and experimental bandleaders, like Payne and Geraldo with their concert arrangements and forays into swing, Silvester on *BBC Dancing Club* and *MWYW* embodied the populist value of musical accessibility—appropriate to the ethos of a unified "People's War." Part of Silvester's appeal in 1941 was certainly the fact that his programs were nonvocal in an environment in which hostilities toward crooners and dance band vocalists had increased markedly.[153] With his disciplined approach to tempo, Silvester also avoided the slow, sentimental style demanded of wartime ballads and the charges of dragging leveled at many British dance bands. During 1942, as BBC policy turned against sentimentality and male crooners, who were regarded as emasculating and demoralizing, Silvester came to embody disciplined, hegemonic masculinity, and the populist, cheerful qualities of dance music that were regarded as crucial to morale. Silvester's upstanding Britishness and the approachable repertory of *BBC Dancing Club* also stood in contrast to the racial other, embodied in the swing and hot jazz featured in another on-air community, *Radio Rhythm Club*, the subject of the next chapter.

Conclusion

In November 1940, the producer Philip Brown detailed the "care, time, and trouble" that were devoted to dance band broadcasts in an article for *Radio Times* readers, countering the widespread impression that such programming was uninvolved. Brown described the bandleader's careful planning of repertory and performing forces; the extensive rehearsals, one of "at least four hours" a few days before and a balance test on the morning of a broadcast; the expertise of the program engineer, who had to understand dance music and control "as many as four microphones"; and the responsibilities of the producer in coordinating the entire operation. He concluded:

> When the red light goes out...the band-leader usually walks into the listening cubicle and says to the producer: "How was it?"—whereupon the producer may suggest that a cup of tea in the canteen wouldn't be a bad idea. And so they

adjourn, and over "the cup that cheers" they...try[] to see where they can make the next [broadcast] even better.[154]

In his account, Brown revealed the negotiations, time, and hard work that went into programs that the *Radio Times* listed simply with the name of the bandleader and the phrase "and his band." He humanized the work of producers, engineers, and bandleaders, whom—with dance musicians—"the public...[was] apt to take...for granted."[155] Meanwhile, Brown's description reassured listeners of the BBC's and the bandleaders' commitment to improvement at a moment when civilian bands were in crisis and BBC dance music was struggling. His account showed the everyday complexities of dance music broadcasting that underlay the structural and contextual issues addressed in this chapter.

Brown's article gently intervened in wartime discourses that cast dance musicians as unmanly shirkers. Before male dance musicians could avail themselves of the strategies employed by men in reserve occupations, who "emphasized their manly skill, strength, endurance...fashioning themselves as worker-heroes who were as important to the nation as soldier-heroes," they first had to establish that playing dance music in wartime was indeed work and that it was necessary.[156] Behind-the-scenes accounts and stories of performing through the Blitz reinforced dance music's status as work; its status as a morale booster proved its utility. The value of dance music as a masculine morale builder was most easily established by describing its appeal to the troops, whose tastes were understood implicitly as manly. Thus, Geraldo and Payne registered their commitment to the war effort by touring and broadcasting for the forces. Silvester, who had already spent decades establishing a manly British image that balanced elegance and popular appeal, asserted the physical and mental benefits of dancing—or simply listening—to *BBC Dancing Club*.

As the BBC became more conscious of the importance of dance music to the war effort, it increasingly treated it as worthy of special support and careful study. By 1941, a wide variety of music fell under the BBC's rubric of "dance music." While it included a number of service bands, which often boasted excellent players and carried intrinsic patriotic appeal, most of the BBC's dance music programming involved the civilian name bands that were so disrupted by the war. The new Dance Band Scheme ensured that the BBC would have, with the contrasting styles that Payne and Geraldo brought to the air, a variety of good-quality dance music at a bargain rate, although the Corporation still faced the challenges of maintaining good relations with uncontracted civilian bands and of establishing precisely what popular music best supported the nation's morale.

5

RADIO RHYTHM CLUB: RACE, AUTHENTICITY, AND THE BRITISH

SWING BOOM

RADIO RHYTHM CLUB *(RRC)* first aired on June 8, 1940, only a few days after the re-treat from Dunkirk. For the remainder of the war, the half-hour program was the weekly "must hear" radio event for Britain's jazz and swing enthusiasts. "Eavesdrop-per," the *Melody Maker*'s radio critic, observed, "The BBC Rhythm Club is the final and ultimate gesture—a sort of non-aggression pact between Swing and officialdom, and everybody is happy."[1] Indeed, fans and critics regarded the BBC's introduction of *RRC* as materially and symbolically important: it signaled a shift in policy in a way that previous jazz records series and transatlantic relays had not. Why was this so? First, an ongoing series signaled the BBC's recognition that the audience for jazz and swing deserved to be served in a sustained and specialized manner. Second, with its informa-tive gramophone records recitals, jam sessions, talks, and guest appearances by profes-sional musicians and critics, the program's format followed the model established since 1933 by rhythm clubs throughout the United Kingdom. Guided by the sympa-thetic and knowledgeable producer, Charles Chilton, the subculture of those who took jazz seriously had finally found a foothold on the national airwaves.

The appearance of *RRC* a few months after the Forces Programme was established was no coincidence, for press and social survey organizations envisioned jazz and swing enthusiasts to be young, male, and of diverse class backgrounds: on the surface, they resembled soldiers. Mass-Observation published figures in *Band Wagon* demon-strating that 24 percent of middle-class men and 19 percent of working-class men liked swing while of their female counterparts, only 2 and 9 percent, respectively, enjoyed the music.[2] B. M. Lytton-Edwards made the connection even more clearly in *Melody Maker*, citing the case of a London store that specialized in hot records where 60 percent of the orders came from servicemen: "The young soldiers of to-day are drawn from the ranks of the 20-year-olds—and who knows better than they the fascination of dance tempo, and the exhilaration it can bring?"[3] *RRC*'s on-air discussions and convivial atmosphere responded directly to the BBC's own studies of forces programming needs, which emphasized communal listening practices and the potential demand for educational, yet entertaining, talks.[4]

RRC represented a masculine counterpart to *Music While You Work*, the other key music program established in June 1940, for which young women came to be regarded as the primary audience. Although the latter series emerged out of the post-Dunkirk production drives while the former was intended to entertain bored servicemen, both series aired on the Forces Programme, and both were directed to audiences involved in critical wartime service. Nevertheless, the two programs constructed their audiences in radically different terms. *Music While You Work* was designed to discipline workers' bodies while humanizing their labor, its producers sought to perfect the art of programming for inattentive listening, and its dance and light music repertory was mainstream, familiar, and approachable. *RRC*, in contrast, addressed its listeners as connoisseurs (or connoisseurs-in-training), demanded careful, engaged listening, and frequently aired challenging repertory. The contrasts between the programs mapped with disconcerting ease onto gendered dichotomies that privileged the masculine, the mind, and connoisseurship while devaluing the feminine, the body, and mass culture. Indeed, despite its progressive content and format, *RRC* accorded neatly with the BBC's traditional address to a mentally attentive, physically relaxed, and education-minded male listener.

The masculine tone of *RRC* was not merely an abstract construction: it was established by the featured voices and topics. Out of 211 wartime broadcasts, only 2 featured women as guest experts or announcers, when Mary Lytton and Bettie Edwards (the writing team known as B. M. Lytton-Edwards) gave gramophone recitals on Miff Mole in September 1940 and Red Nichols in February 1941. The dominance of male voices in *RRC* contrasts markedly with the rest of the BBC's entertainment broadcasting, particularly for the troops, for during the war, women made significant inroads into the BBC's announcing ranks as Variety Department and Overseas Service commères. By 1945, the BBC regarded "a male voice [as] essential" for the program's announcing.[5]

RRC's exclusion of women extended to its records recital subjects and performers: no woman was ever featured as the primary topic of a gramophone recital, and women figured rarely as live musicians. The exception was a handful of "girl" singers, most notably the well-regarded Doreen Villiers, who performed with the house band, and the pianist Clare Deniz, who played on the program three times in 1943 with Cyril Blake's and Bertie King's bands. Despite their limited representation on-air, women did belong to rhythm clubs, and as Bill Elliott, the founder of the No. 1 Rhythm Club, explained, they were "equally as keen as any of the males."[6] Given the gendering of jazz knowledge as masculine, however, women enthusiasts were often subject to attack, as when one reader wrote to *Melody Maker*, "Swing is a man's hobby, so leave it alone girls, and stick to your knitting," a comment that generated four weeks of outraged protests from other readers.[7]

"Eavesdropper" celebrated the disputatious nature of jazz and swing discourse, which filled the letters and opinion columns of *Melody Maker* and smaller, independent jazz publications, rhythm club meetings, and sometimes even *RRC*: "Swing fans are a voluble race, and it is the dogmatic 'I-don't-think-you're-right-and-I-am-entitled-to-my-opinion' attitude that gives vigour and piquancy to the whole subject," he wrote.[8] One of the most controversial issues was the relative merits of jazz and swing. The points of contention in the British jazz versus swing debate resembled those of the American scene.[9] In broad terms, swing was criticized for being commercial, mechanistically slick, and inauthentically white, although it could more positively be construed as progressive, modern, and technically advanced. Golden age jazz was criticized as corny, crude, and out-of-date, although its advocates argued for its authentic Negro character, emotional affect, and status as "real" improvised jazz. As Chilton put it in a 1943 "Information Bureau" session, "The lovers of Negroid style are…using the old term jazz in its original meaning.…Swing is a term applied to the popular music which is a cheap imitation of that produced by Negro combinations."[10]

A critical difference between the British and American debates was that British advocates of both sides knew their heroes through records only. With touring U.S. bands barred in the country from 1935, live swing (and jazz) fell largely outside of British experience, with the exception of American shortwave broadcasts, the occasional transatlantic relay, and the token swing numbers featured by British dance bands. In this climate, record collecting played a vital role in jazz fandom, and given the expense and uneven availability of imported records and British releases, it required knowledge and resourcefulness. During the war, shellac rationing, U-boat attacks on shipping, and the American Federation of Musicians' recording ban further limited the availability of gramophone records. Small wonder that as American enthusiasts reached Britain as GIs, they regarded British fans as denizens of a jazz Galapagos. *Metronome* observed, "They [*Melody Maker*'s writers] have heard scarcely of any of the great US jazz musicians who have come up in the last five or ten years.…Because of this, and because there are all too few great British jazzmen…many of Britain's jazz writers seek refuge in the glories of the past."[11]

Nevertheless, British rhythm club culture was not devoid of live performance. Many clubs included jam sessions, featuring guest artists or in-house amateurs, in their programs. Sometimes, though, jam sessions exacerbated tensions between swing and jazz advocates—and the generations. In November 1940, for example, an anonymous rhythm club secretary complained of the infiltration of jitterbugs into his club and the accompanying exodus of "sincere" members. Unlike "the true jazz fans" who appreciated "the Chicagoans," Duke Ellington, and Fletcher Henderson, the jitterbugs had the poor taste to declare Gene Krupa's "Tuxedo Junction" "terrific" and Glenn Miller's "In the Mood" to be "solid."[12]

Fulfilling the claim that "membership of the club will be extended to all who listen," *RRC* served both the "true jazz fan" with informative records recitals and pleased the "jitterbug" with jam sessions and, from October 1940, a regularly appearing house band, Harry Parry's RRC Sextet.[13] Chilton's feat was impressive given the territoriality of BBC departments: he was a gramophone producer running a series that included live music, the usual province of Variety. It was only in early 1943, when *RRC* had become a well-established and popular program, with 92 percent of forces listeners reporting that they liked it, that Variety asserted its stake in the program.[14] *Melody Maker* reported that a "battle royal" ensued behind the scenes, which resulted in the Gramophone Department maintaining control of the program it had created but agreeing to book live bands through Variety.[15] At the program's inception, however, jazz was still regarded ambivalently within the Corporation: "I don't think the BBC quite approved of [*RRC*], 'too jazzy, old boy,'" Chilton's supervisor, Leslie Perowne, later recalled.[16]

RRC provided an on-air community for rhythm club members, particularly those in their teens and twenties who were disproportionately affected by the displacements of war, but it also brought swing and jazz to a mass audience. Parry, the house bandleader who also became producer when Chilton left the BBC in February 1941 to serve in the RAF, rose quickly to wartime fame. By late 1941, he and his band were being mobbed at concerts, and in early 1943 they placed third in the mainstream *Sunday Pictorial*'s band popularity poll.[17] Once the narrow terrain of swing enthusiasts, the press hailed Parry as "the first band leader to arrange swing music for the layman *and* to get the layman to listen to it and enjoy it."[18] On a smaller scale, *RRC* helped build interest in Golden Age jazz. It featured records recitals by key collectors, including Elliott and Rex Harris, who advocated for the reissue of classic titles, a practice that the gramophone companies increasingly embraced.

RRC also opened a space for British jazz musicians and critics to argue, discuss, and grapple performatively with jazz authenticity, particularly in regard to national and racial identities. It had long been axiomatic for British jazz fans that any British efforts in jazz performance were imitative, inferior to the American original, and ultimately inauthentic. Nevertheless, throughout the war, a number of ambitious and creative British musicians, including Parry, George Shearing, and Lauderic Caton, performed on *RRC*, which helped them build careers outside the commercial dance bands. It provided a public space for musicians to perform and embody music that they had learned largely through their study of American recordings. In addition, nearly forty non-BBC critics, enthusiasts, and musicians spoke, gave records recitals, and debated on the program. Their focus on recordings made more than 3,000 miles away certainly carried risks of "abstraction...manipulation and misinterpretation," but like the musicians who performed the music, the records recitalists also engaged passionately and performatively with cultural production of the American (and often African American) Other.[19] *RRC* opened the scope of the dialogue in Britain beyond that of any rhythm club, a timely development, given the United States' entry into the war.[20]

Finally, *RRC* provided an important space on the BBC's domestic service for the serious examination and dissemination of black cultural production, as well as the musical performances and voices of black musicians. Although there were in Britain as many as 8,000 black British residents, hundreds of West Indian war workers and soldiers, and, by 1944, 100,000 African American GIs, serious discussion of race and racism on the home front was limited on the BBC.[21] Race was an inescapable theme in jazz discourse, however, and while primitivist assumptions were endemic, there were also voices that insisted on the artistry, work ethic, and originality of black musicians and even those that advanced antiracist ideologies. At the BBC, whose representations of black musicality ranged from the sophisticated cabaret stylings of Adelaide Hall and "Hutch" (Leslie A. Hutchinson) to the radio blackface of the *Kentucky Minstrels*, *RRC* provided an important space for black British musicians: the BBC's tardy tribute to the bandleader Ken Johnson, who had been killed when a bomb hit the Café de Paris, took place on the program; it aired expert talks by the songwriter Spencer Williams; and it featured bands led by Cyril Blake and others. Moreover, *RRC* offered early and sustained examples of interracial music-making: Parry's sextet included from the start the guitarist Joe Deniz, who was announced enthusiastically as "coloured," and other black musicians, most notably the well-regarded trumpeter Dave Wilkins, cycled through as well.

Reflecting the wartime disruptions and displacements of its audience, *RRC* was not a static entity: the producers, house bands, and contributors shifted periodically, and the BBC "rested" the program twice, from May to June 1943 and from June 1944 to February 1945. *RRC* only briefly stemmed jazz enthusiasts' frustrations with the BBC; certainly, as the Russians learned to their disadvantage when Germany invaded their borders in June 1941, nonaggression pacts were fragile creations. Nevertheless, *RRC* permitted jazz and swing enthusiasts to infiltrate the corridors and airwaves of "officialdom," it opened a performative space for engagement with racial and national "others," and it gave representation to both hegemonic and subversive wartime masculinities.

Jam Sessions and Jitterbugs: The Wartime Swing Boom

In November 1941, *Melody Maker* described the frenzied responses of a Cardiff audience to a Sunday concert given by Harry Parry's RRC Sextet. Fans jitterbugged in the aisles; an enthusiastic "young fellow...jumped on to the stage in an attempt to congratulate the boys" and had to be wrapped in a curtain and carried out by the stagehands; and the audience mobbed the band on its return to the station, delaying the train's departure and causing the guitarist Lauderic Caton to miss the train (and thus a *RRC* taping) entirely. "It was amazing," reported an eyewitness. "I can only liken it to the stories I have read of similar things happening in America, but which have never before, to my knowledge, happened here."[22]

Like the enthusiastic audiences that greeted Benny Goodman and his band at the Palomar Ballroom in 1935, the fervent response of Parry's Welsh fans signaled a shift in swing's cultural status, from minority taste to mainstream vogue. Similar to the beginning of the American swing era, the British swing boom of late 1941 and 1942 was more an "economic and cultural" than a musical revolution. It witnessed the coalescence of a distinct youth audience, who embraced the thrill of swinging four-to-the-bar rhythm, improvised solos, and blues harmonies, which had originated in African American bands; venerated the "bandleader-as-celebrity"; and adopted new, American-derived dance movements, rejecting "the ordinary staid...English style" as "*completely inadequate* in relation with [swing]."[23] The emergence of a youth audience for swing coincided with official recognition of young people, aged sixteen and seventeen, as an underserved group, too old for school and too young for war service. The December 22, 1941, Registration of Boys and Girls Order encouraged youth to join organizations like the Girl Guides or Air Training Corps, in which, it was hoped, they would learn the habits of constructive citizenship rather than simply attending dance halls, cinemas—or swing concerts.[24] Obviously, the authorities failed to appreciate the group identity forged by joining rhythm and fan clubs, reading *Melody Maker*, amateur and semiprofessional music-making, or keen jitterbugging.

Unlike the American case, in which big bands constituted the center of the swing industry, small bands led the British swing boom. This was hardly surprising in wartime, given the reach of the call-up and the shrinking size of most dance bands, but there were other factors at work. In Britain, live swing performance first thrived in small-group jam sessions held in rhythm clubs and small dives. Large dance halls, with the notable exceptions of London's Paramount and Astoria palais de danse, tended to discourage jitterbugging. Most name bands eschewed swing or gave it only token representation, regarding it as a specialized taste, beyond the ken of their West End clientele, BBC listeners (and administrators), and variety audiences—not to mention the commercial interests of music publishers and gramophone companies. *RRC* played a critical role in transforming swing into an economically viable enterprise in Britain by bringing approachable, small-group swing before a mass audience on a regular basis and by building up Parry's celebrity. It also promoted the concept that jam sessions and amateur performance were integral to British swing culture—ideas that bore fruit in two large public jam session in late 1941/early 1942 and in an efflorescence of small amateur, semipro, and professional bands toward the end of the war. As the *Radio Times* reflected in the wake of Parry's Cardiff concert, "When the RRC first started, it could be said to be almost of an experimental nature, for swing had then got little hold upon the country. The experiment has been thoroughly justified."[25]

Of course, swing was not unknown in Britain before 1941. Early in the war, the *Dancing Times* reported disapprovingly on the incursions of jitterbuggers into the ballrooms, and Glenn Miller's "In the Mood" was a hit in the summer of 1940 (the published sheet music included instructions for dancing the jitterbug).[26] Nevertheless, the market for hot, American-style swing was minuscule. Most British dance bandleaders regarded swing as a subgenre of dance music—"something you turn on and off with a tap"—rather than a style demanding a thoroughgoing shift in approach.[27] The results of this attitude were audible in a hit recording of "In the Mood" by Joe Loss, who in January 1940 became the first British bandleader to record the number; while the arrangement followed Miller's note for note (including the solos), the playing, particularly in the syncopated brass riff, had a stiff, rushed quality (sound example 5.1).[28] ◐ Other bandleaders ignored swing. "The general public don't want to hear it," Harry Leader claimed.[29]

Although swing was regarded as a taste particular to young men, it had a limited presence on air during the first six months of the Forces Programme. Barring a few notable exceptions—a peppering of gramophone programs, including the short-lived series *Kings of Jazz* by Chilton; a broadcast by Hatchette's Swingtet featuring Stephane

Grappelli; and a brief revival of *America Dances*—swing enthusiasts began to complain of a drought.[30] *RRC*'s nascence in June 1940 soon helped change the optics—and the reality—of the situation. An important aspect of the shift was that Chilton, the series' twenty-two-year-old producer, was regarded as a peer by other enthusiasts, despite his seven years with the jazz-averse Corporation: he attended the No. 1 Rhythm Club, read *Melody Maker*, and even played "a peculiar guitar" with a small band (figure 5.1).[31]

With his compèring and a diversity of guests, Chilton quickly established a relaxed, welcoming atmosphere on *RRC* that distinguished it from other BBC programming. This quality was evident in Chilton's introduction to one program that survives in an off-air recording:

> Hello, Rhythm Club. Well, this afternoon we have a Collectors' Corner....the other day I bumped into Bill Elliott, who told me he had a collection of records just over from America issued by the Blue Note company, which were just the last word. So I went down to his flat and heard them. And now the Collectors' Corner is entirely Bill Elliott, and here he is.[32]

In less than a minute, Chilton brilliantly established his credentials—he was friendly enough with Elliott to be invited casually to his home—and set an inclusive tone with his friendly greeting, colloquialisms, repetition, and behind-the-scenes narrative. Chilton's air of "pleasant informality" was also conveyed by his Cockney accent, which

FIGURE 5.1 Charles Chilton, producer and founder of *Radio Rhythm Club*, playing the guitar while stationed with the RAF at Cranwell (c. 1941). (Courtesy of Mr. Charles and Mrs. Penny Chilton)

reflected his London working-class background and stood in marked contrast to the Standard English required of BBC announcers.[33] More important for *RRC*'s target audience, he could pronounce jazz names correctly, employ jazz terminology properly, and speak respectfully about the music, in contrast to many BBC announcers, who displayed their ignorance of and disregard for jazz with mispronunciations and patronizing comments.[34]

While expertise was lacking within the Corporation, there existed plenty outside of it. During the series' first eight months, Chilton brought a wide range of critics and musicians onto the program, fostering a polyvocality unusual in Gramophone Department programs. Indeed, only seven of thirty-nine broadcasts featured Chilton giving a solo gramophone recital. Chilton invited critics like Jackson and Leonard Hibbs to speak, but even more strikingly, he featured numerous talks by musicians, who illustrated their points by playing records and their own instruments. Among others, George Shearing discussed the blues and the piano in jazz, and the trumpeter Frenchie Sartell reminisced about Jack and Charlie Teagarden. Chilton also featured a diversity of live and recorded swing broadcasts. During the first summer of the program, he rebroadcast transatlantic relays by Teddy Wilson's band and Louis Prima's and featured Stephane Grappelli and his band. In the fall of 1940, Parry became a regular guest, and that winter, Chilton twice featured the drummer Phil Watts and His Dixieland Seven, which included in its lineup Sartell and the popular swing trombonist Ted Heath, playing swing hits like the riff-based "Woodchoppers Ball" and jam session standards like "Honeysuckle Rose."[35] The diversity of formats, guests, and repertory was impressive, but Chilton's arguably most ambitious show was a studio jam session. Its appearance during the first month of the series indicated its significance; certainly, it generated the largest response of any airing in *RRC*'s first eight months.

A jam session was the musical extension of the casual, yet expert, atmosphere that Chilton cultivated in *RRC*. In 1942, Hugues Panassié explained, "A 'jam session' is a reunion of musicians, outside of their regular work, at which they play the music they enjoy with complete liberty.... [In the jam session] jazz music is returned to its natural state and is delivered of all preparations and artifice."[36] During the late 1930s and early 1940s, jam sessions became public performance events, shifting the dynamics of risk taking and community building while offering enthusiasts the prospect of jazz in its "natural state." In the United States, public, admissions-charging jam sessions emerged from private initiatives, such as the 1936 sessions at the Famous Door; in Britain, however, the BBC led the way, a role that was congruent with its anticommercial status if not its ambivalence toward jazz.[37] It first broadcast two sessions in 1937, but two expensive jam session relays from New York in November 1938 and January 1939, featuring famous American performers, were the most influential for *RRC*.[38]

On radio, the success of a broadcast jam session depended upon the producer's ability to translate a live and ostensibly private performance into an intelligible, appealing broadcast for home listeners, as was demonstrated in the contrasting critical fortunes of the American jam session relays. Several factors helped make the 1938 relay a fiasco: bad atmospherics, too many musicians, sloppy playing, and a champagne-fueled party atmosphere. Alistair Cooke's compèring conveyed anxious confusion rather than relaxed spontaneity, especially because he so frequently spoke over the musicians.[39] In contrast, a controlled studio environment, a small group of musicians, and a limited audience contributed to "Detector's" glowing review of the 1939 jam session: "In place of...last November's gin party we had on this occasion music that was as captivating in its artistry as it was thrilling in its swing."[40] This time, Cooke's running commentary drew listeners into the gathering: he identified players as they soloed, described their actions, and explained the proceedings for the uninitiated. "A band like that may say, 'Play another one, Chu,'" he said as Chu Berry began a second chorus in "Boogie Woogie Blues." By moving back into the studio and emphasizing small-group intimacy, the second jam session appealed to radio listeners as participants, rather than interlopers. Cooke's straightforward compèring and the generally sympathetic musicianship operated effectively within the medium's intimate mass address to render the proceedings comprehensible to a home listening audience.

RRC's first jam session on June 29, 1940, built upon these precedents. Chilton brought an audience into the studio and featured eight musicians, a relatively small number, in the 28.5-minute broadcast, which was organized in cooperation with London's No. 1 Rhythm Club: the audience was drawn from the club's membership, and several of the musicians played in jam sessions at its Sunday afternoon meetings. Chilton wisely chose to approximate the club's atmosphere in the studio, rather than making an outside broadcast, with all its expense and potential chaos. At the start of the broadcast, Chilton drew the radio audience into the proceedings by introducing Elliott. Then, Chilton turned the announcing over to the well-liked dance band compère David Miller, a choice that echoed Cooke's role in the American relays. This proved to be the broadcast's first misstep, for as "Eavesdropper" reported, Miller's tone "varied between bewilderment and flippancy." The second misstep was the playing: "The musicians...didn't pull together. They didn't get that vital, spontaneous spark, and not one of them felt what the next man was doing or was going to do." Instead of energizing the players or conveying the thrill of the event to home listeners, the studio audience helped register the session's failure. "I've heard a No. 1 Rhythm Club audience in full cry when the music was to their liking," "Eavesdropper" wrote, "but their applause on Saturday was like the genteel clapping that greets the fall of a wicket at Lord's."[41]

Beginning with a promising, 7.5-minute "Honeysuckle Rose," the musicians tackled a handful of jam session chestnuts. Several listeners blamed the rhythm section for the ensemble's problems. Carlo Krahmer, a small-group drummer and No. 1 Rhythm Club regular, lacked "lift" and drowned out the soloists while the bassist Russ Allen was barely audible. Although George Shearing earned praise for his solo improvising, especially in "China Boy," he lacked "solidity" as a rhythm player. The session's other problem was a "lack of originality," the perennial weakness of British jazz playing. (Grappelli, who had arrived recently from France, was exempted from this critique.) According to one listener, "By listening to the musicians...one could almost tell what hot records they owned." Nevertheless, several *Melody Maker* correspondents were more sanguine about the session and its implications for British jazz: "[The broadcast] proved conclusively that European musicians can imbibe the spirit and vitality of an art whose home is 3000 miles away." Indeed, many of the front-line players earned at least limited praise. Among others, the little-known clarinetist Parry was widely praised for his ideas and "fluid" execution.[42]

Despite criticism that the session had translated poorly over the air, Chilton did not give up on jam sessions or live small-group swing for *RRC*; indeed, he broadcast another jam session, which he compèred himself, the following month. He did change his tactics, however. Rather than again attempting to render for radio the casual atmosphere of the No. 1 Rhythm Club jam sessions, he opted to present comparatively established small combos that played improvised, jam session–inspired music. Chilton's timing was excellent, for his decision coincided with a wartime efflorescence of small-group swing. As small American combinations, notably the bassist John Kirby's Sextet from the Onyx Club and Goodman's Sextet, became familiar to British listeners through recordings and transatlantic relays, they inspired a growing (and often interracial) cohort of British musicians, who honed their skills as improvisers at a range of jam sessions. Meanwhile, with the call-up's constriction on the availability of musicians, good civilian players were not forced to play exclusively for a single bandleader and could participate in a wider range of music-making. Finally, smaller, jam-style groups were more flexible than big dance bands in adapting to personnel changes, they were cheaper to run, and they could inspire a deeper investment from their players. The difficulty was that their repertory challenged mainstream audiences.

By engaging small combos, Chilton could continue to feature live, jam session–style playing on *RRC* while avoiding the organizational hassle and risks—a chaotic atmosphere, an ensemble that failed to gel, and an alienating experience for listeners—of broadcasting a true jam session. The most important group for the program was the St. Regis Quintet, whose members aired in the July jam session and appeared subsequently in a variety of permutations. Its members included Parry and Shearing, who had played in the first *RRC* jam session. The *Radio Times* explained:

> Most of these boys have often been heard broadcasting with other bands, but for the last two or three months they have been playing together at the St. Regis Restaurant in Mayfair. They are expert in providing smooth, sophisticated dance music, but in this jam session we may expect them to let themselves go, and as all five are virtuosos of their instruments, Rhythm Club fans may expect something really worthwhile. Listen particularly for George Shearing, the blind pianist, who at the age of twenty has been acclaimed as the best swing pianist in Britain today.[43]

Shearing was undoubtedly the star of the group during its early months. He had learned jazz by studying the "recordings of Earl Hines, Fats Waller, Teddy Wilson, Meade Lux Lewis and Art Tatum."[44] In July 1939, Feather hailed Shearing as "England's first master of that peculiar phase of piano-playing known as the 'boogie woogie.'"[45] Given the regularity with which he was designated a "blind pianist," blindness certainly played a role in Shearing's celebrity. Not only was visual disability coupled romantically with musical genius, but during the war, it protected him from charges of shirking as he advanced his career as a soloist and small-group player.

Parry was, by some accounts, the founder of the St. Regis Quintet; in any event, he soon became its leader and, through his involvement with *RRC*, a swing celebrity.[46] Before he began bandleading, he had a varied and peripatetic career as a sideman: starting out as a saxophonist and scat singer, he played with more than a dozen bands as he moved from Llandudno in Wales to London. His contemporary biographer, Peter Noble, identified a consistent thread that ran through his eight-year career leading up to his *RRC* work: Parry "was a real swing-music martyr," who "refused to play waltzes" or "play in a quiet 'tea-room manner.'"[47] In 1939, he formed his first seven-piece band at the Coconut Grove, where he was resident through the early months of the war; in May 1940, he began leading the St. Regis Quintet.[48] "This was a complete revolution," Noble claimed, "for up to that time no out-and-out jazz band had ever been offered a big-time engagement in a West End restaurant or hotel."[49]

On October 25, 1940, Parry debuted as leader and arranger of *RRC*'s new house band, the Radio Rhythm Club (RRC) Sextet (figure 5.2). Asked how the "virtually unknown" Parry became the resident bandleader, Chilton recalled that he had gotten "permission to form a band of some kind" for the program, and when he learned of the group from Shearing, he and Perowne went to hear the band at the St. Regis by way of an informal audition.[50] Parry was already a semiregular guest on *RRC*, playing in the two summer jam sessions and leading two small-group airings in September.[51] Parry's group, as Fletcher announced, was modeled after Benny Goodman's sextet, whose records reached Britain in February 1940.[52] Like the famous American clarinetist, Parry included a vibraphonist and guitarist in his lineup: "the vibraphone ace" Roy Marsh and Joe Deniz, who also played with Ken Johnson's West Indian Dance Orchestra and frequently jammed at the No. 1 Rhythm Club.[53]

FIGURE 5.2 Harry Parry, leader of the Radio Rhythm Club Sextet, in 1947. (Copyright © BBC)

The presence of Deniz in the original lineup (and that of other black British musicians who played in the sextet over the next few years) meant that Parry also followed Goodman's much-publicized model of integration. This may have been familiar for the hip attendees of the No. 1 Rhythm Club, where black and white musicians jammed together, but it was highly remarkable for most BBC listeners. For Fletcher, who admitted to knowing "nothing about swing," the presence of Deniz, "who hails from the West Indies and is the only coloured player in the ensemble," was noteworthy. (Deniz was actually born in Cardiff's diverse Tiger Bay district.) By implication, his exotic background added authenticity to the group's performance of "music in the American Negro style."[54]

More knowledgeable critics soon acclaimed the improvisatory skills and musicianship of the RRC Sextet. "Detector," for example, described it as "the best swing outfit on the air these days. As an ensemble it plays with an ease and relaxation which are an end in themselves. As soloists the boys not only have plenty to say, but know how to say it."[55] The final proof of the sextet's exceptional status was its recording contract with Parlophone. Parry and his players were the first British musicians to be featured in the label's celebrated "Rhythm-Style" series. In his review of the first disc, Jackson observed, "British boys *can* hold their own with the Americans when it comes to getting the real thing in improvised jazz on to the wax."[56]

By taking on Parry's sextet as house band, Chilton had succeeded in obtaining reliably high-quality jam-style swing for *RRC*; he had also inadvertently found his replacement. In early 1941, Chilton went into the RAF to serve as a wireless operator/air gunner, "wondering what the hell I was going to do with *RRC*."[57] For Perowne, Parry was the logical choice to take over as producer, given his status as resident bandleader and prior experience in broadcasting, as well as the amiable working relationship that they were developing.[58] Given Parry's busy schedule during the period, Perowne's support was important: in addition to his *RRC* duties, Parry continued regular nightclub work at the Coconut Grove and spent his days doing war work, building ship engines in a London factory.[59] He gave his first broadcast as host, a review of the month's swing releases, on March 7, 1941, and also continued to broadcast frequently on the program with his sextet. For more than two years, from its October 1940 debut until February 1943, the RRC Sextet broadcast at least monthly, making it one of the most regularly heard bands on the BBC.

Parry's band was one of the most distinctive ensembles on air in terms of repertory, style, and instrumentation; through regular appearances, it soon came to epitomize the increasingly popular *RRC*. Examining fourteen of the sextet's thirty-five solo broadcasts, a few matters become clear. First, extended jamming on a single number was rare. In programs that lasted twenty-five minutes (thirty minutes from mid-1942), Parry usually included seven or eight numbers, averaging around 3.5 minutes per tune—approximately the same length as a commercial 78-rpm side. Second, in addition to the augmentations that Parry made to his "sextet's" membership, he also regularly featured vocalists and guest instrumentalists in his broadcasts. The inclusion of guest soloists, including the trumpeter Johnny Claes, the trombonist George Chisholm, and Grappelli, helped address "Detector's" early critique that the sextet's instrumentation, which included only one melody instrument, tended "to make all the numbers sound too much alike."[60] Featuring vocalists, particularly Villiers and her replacement, Rita Marlow, increased the sextet's mainstream appeal. Villiers also gained the cognoscenti's approval for her individuality and mastery of "jazz language": "At last we have a girl who compares favourably with the better American coloured singers," "Detector" sighed.[61]

Finally, the RRC Sextet featured repertory rooted in contemporary American swing and jam session standards, eschewing the commercial ballads that dominated in dance band broadcasts. Nearly every program included a blues, whether a standard composition like W. C. Handy's "St. Louis Blues" or a jam-based piece. While the Sextet regularly aired hit swing numbers associated with leading American bands, including Basie's "Jumping at the Woodside," Goodman's "Jersey Bounce," Shaw's "Softly as in a Morning Sunrise," and Miller's "Kalamazoo," it also played new compositions by its members, most notably Parry's relaxed, minor-mode signature tune, "Champagne." Its repertory was most dominated, however, by numbers that were becoming jazz standards, having been adopted or revived by small American combinations, as well as the Quintette of the Hot Club of France: "Tea for Two," "Lady Be Good," "Honeysuckle Rose," and others.[62]

On *RRC*, the sextet's diet of attractive swing, jazz vocal numbers, and approachable jamming proved to be highly appealing to listeners, who sent increasing quantities of fan mail.[63] Record sales, performances, and most of all, the enthusiastic mass response of his fans registered Parry's growing celebrity. In the fall of 1941, the RRC Sextet was mobbed by fans when it played a series of Sunday concerts, and that winter it was signed for a theater tour.[64] Parry's popularity carried over to *RRC*, whether the sextet was playing or not. Listener Research reported that the program's average monthly audience had grown steadily during the first half of 1941, from 6.2 percent in January to 10.1 percent in May, and subsequent figures ranged as high as 15 percent.[65] These were excellent numbers for a program that still lacked a regular time slot.

As producer, Parry focused more than Chilton on contemporary swing. In addition to programs on classic players like Sidney Bechet and Bix Beiderbecke, he programmed gramophone recitals on Shaw, Goodman, and Will Bradley, a bandleader who help popularize boogie-woogie. He featured a range of British soloists and small groups in addition to his own sextet: Watt's Dixieland Seven, Cyril Blake's well-regarded Jig's Club Band, and a promising new band led by Claes. Parry also produced two ambitious amateur features, which aimed "to illustrate the widespread interest in swing music on the part of amateur combinations."[66] Although the participants revealed "more ambition than talent," and "Detector" dismissed the airings as flops, the enthusiastic response to the broadcasts (both of which attracted record audiences) registered swing's significant following among young fans, who were eager to participate not only as listeners but also as players.[67]

The three professional jam sessions that Parry organized for *RRC* during 1941 fared far better. Featuring jam session and small-group regulars, the broadcasts suggested the musical and even commercial viability of British swing. The July 9 session led "Detector" to conclude that some British musicians, particularly the alto saxophonist

Harry Hayes (of Geraldo's band), had begun to find "their own souls" and express themselves with originality in jazz.[68] A second session, broadcast on September 22, was prerecorded before a live studio audience. The intense competition for tickets and flood of discussion in *Melody Maker*, which greeted the airing as an "oasis in the desert" of wartime broadcasting, demonstrated the appetite for public jam sessions among youthful swing fans.[69] This was confirmed when BBC Listener Research found that the December 22 jam session had attracted a "large" forces audience and earned an A-minus rating for popularity.[70]

Parry's *RRC* jam sessions helped inspire two landmark events: the November 16, 1941, *Melody Maker*–HMV Public Jam Session and the January 25, 1942, Cavendish Swing Concert at the London Coliseum. Their mass scale and personnel confirmed the centrality of *RRC* to British swing culture: thousands of fans applied for tickets; RRC Sextet members and guests figured prominently in the proceedings; and in January 1942, *RRC* dedicated a show to recordings from the *MM*-HMV session (both commercial releases and a few unissued "special recordings") while the BBC opted to carry a portion of the Cavendish concert.[71] The *MM*-HMV Public Jam Session was an expansive affair: 1,000 intent enthusiasts crowded into the Abbey Road Studio No. 1, listening for more than five hours to three different eight-piece groups, led by the clarinetists Frank Weir, who with his New Style Rhythm played "tasteful...'commercial' melodic-swing"; Carl Barriteau, a well-regarded Johnson band alumnus; and Parry (figure 5.3) (sound example 5.2).[72]◑ *Melody Maker* explained that the selection committee had favored "up-and-coming youngsters" over more famous players, although nearly half of the participants had appeared on *RRC*.[73]

In contrast to the rapt audience and expertly selected players of the *MM*-HMV session, the Cavendish Swing Concert registered swing as a powerful youth phenomenon. "Swing fervour reached a new high level in this country...when 2500 eager, enthusiastic, foot-stomping and wildly applauding fans packed the London Coliseum to capacity," exclaimed *Melody Maker* (figure 5.4).[74] The concert's "gimmick" was that *Melody Maker* readers voted on which musicians would be invited; more than 36,000 responded. Current and past RRC Sextet members so dominated the winners' list—with Parry himself attracting one-third of the votes—that the regular band was asked to play in the concert "as a change from the many Jam Sessions taking place during the afternoon."[75] Although a wide range of performers were involved, the BBC focused in its thirty-five-minute broadcast from the afternoon-long concert on known quantities: the RRC Sextet, a small group jamming on "Crazy Rhythm," and an appearance by the famous, Louis Armstrong-inspired trumpeter Nat Gonella.[76] One (female) listener complained, "The *wrong* part was broadcast; most of the time allotted being taken up by Harry Parry and his Sextet. Granted they were...excellent; but we hear them on every RRC broadcast."[77] The Cavendish Swing Concert not only operated as a referendum on Parry's status as Britain's leading swing celebrity but also demonstrated the synergies of broadcasting, recording, and live appearances that had led to the leader's fame and the attendant boom in swing.

Of course, broader popularity for swing also meant that an increasing proportion of its audience was less knowledgeable, inspiring ambivalence for its critics and longtime

FIGURE 5.3 Photo-collage from the November 16, 1941, *Melody Maker*–HMV Jam Session. "(1) Frank Weir with Andre Goersh, Leslie Hutchinson and Woolfe Phillips in action. (2) (l. to r.) Kenny Baker, Bobby Midgley, Jaap Sajet, Tommy Bromley and Leslie Hutchinson. (3) Autograph-hunters scramble round one of the stars. (4) Len Lewberry and Frank Weir listen critically. (5) Carl Barriteau with Buddy Featherstonhaugh, Kenny Baker and Lad Busby. (6) George Elrick in the audience; the seven-year-old Kid Krupa, Victor Feldman is two seats away. (7) Christopher Stone enjoys the show. (8) Maurice Burman, framed by Frank Weir. (9) Geraldo listens. (10) David Miller 'conducts' Carl Barriteau (Aubrey Franks is just behind). (11) Eric Winstone (right) chats to Joe and Frank Deniz. (12) (l. to r.) Wally Moody, Bill Elliott, Edgar Jackson and Harry Parry." ("Jam Session," *Melody Maker* [22 November 1941]: 4–5)

FIGURE 5.4 Photo-collage from the January 25, 1942, Cavendish Swing Concert at the London Coliseum. "(1) Harry Parry leading his Radio Rhythm Club Sextet during the broadcast. (2) Reed Aces—Freddy Garner (left) and Buddy Featherstonhaugh—go to town, with Frank Weir (on right) behind them. (3) Brass Aces—Nat Gonella (on right), with Johnny Claes and Wolfe Phillips. (4) Rhythm Aces—Guitarist Frank Deniz and Drummer Bobby Midgley. (5) George Shearing snapped during his solo performance. (6) Carl Barriteau leads Gardner, Featherstonhaugh and (half hidden) Dave Wilkins. (7) Dave Wilkins takes a solo. The others in the picture are Joe Deniz (guitar), Featherstonhaugh, Weir and Gardner. (8) Compère David Miller introduces seven-year-old Victor Feldman, whose amazing performance on drums was one of the highspots of the show. (9) Drum Aces—Bobby Richards (left) and Clinton Maxwell.... (10) From the Royal Netherlands Navy, Jaap Sajet comes along to do his stuff on bass. Bobby Midgley and George Shearing are also in the picture. (11) L./Cpl. Nat Gonella goes to town at the mike while David Miller watches. (12) Autograph hunters invade the Coliseum stage door." ("Your Swing Concert," *Melody Maker* [31 January 1942]: 3)

enthusiasts. At the Cavendish Concert, *Melody Maker*'s reviewer registered just how far the public jam session had come from the rhythm club: "It must be remarked ... how very undiscriminating parts of this audience appeared to be. ... one had the impression that had something really shockingly corny been put over, parts of this audience would still have been just as generous with their approval."[78] Mainstream bandleaders took notice of the new audience for swing. A month after the Cavendish Concert, Geraldo formed his own swing club, which featured a variety of small groups and semiprofessional combinations, while Payne, who had stated his disapproval for most swing, signed Grappelli to his band.[79] In May 1942, Spike Hughes observed, "Until 'swing' became the vogue your fashionable bandleader had no use for anything remotely 'hot' in dance music. But once he saw a chance of cashing in on the 'novelty' of 'swing' and making money out of it—why, 'swing' almost became a national duty."[80]

As *Melody Maker*'s critics looked askance at undiscerning swing fans and dance bandleaders who "cashed in," they also became increasingly disappointed in Parry as a bandleader. In August 1941, "Detector" had published a detailed critique of Parry as a producer and identified a "serious shortcoming" of his sextet: "When you've heard it play one tune you've heard it play them all. It has just one set style."[81] A year later, Jackson observed, "The record [I Can't Dance/Rock It Out] is the usual Harry Parry 'popular' swing; which means that while nothing happens which one could describe as inspired, at least the music is bright."[82] If Parry had lost his edge, he still remained popular. Indeed, early in 1943 Parry's sextet placed third in the mainstream *Sunday Pictorial*'s band popularity poll.[83]

Parry's popularity began to work against him at the BBC, which had a history of dismissing house bands that became too entrenched. The direct cause for Parry's discharge, however, was Chilton's new post as an RAF radio communication instructor, which allowed him to resume producing *RRC*. In December 1942, *Melody Maker* announced that the BBC had asked Parry to step down as producer at the end of the year.[84] After Chilton took over in January 1943, Parry and the RRC Sextet broadcast twice more on the program, which was then "rested" during April and May. Upon its resumption in June, Buddy Featherstonehaugh and a sextet of RAF musicians replaced Parry's Sextet as resident band.[85] *Melody Maker* reflected, "Undoubtedly the programme is a very big success, for no small part of which Harry's own personality, his Sextet, and his appreciation of what the rank-and-file swing fan (if not always the jazz fan) likes to listen to are responsible."[86]

In late 1943, Chilton shifted the program's format to a focus on records recitals covering historical topics, especially Golden Age jazz, rather than live performance, which he argued, turned *RRC* into "just 'another' type of popular entertainment—all puffed up, with no inside."[87] Rather than reneging on his original commitment to diverse programming, Chilton's repudiation of live swing on *RRC* registered the degree to which Britain's swing and jazz landscape had changed during the three years it had been on the air: small bands, jam sessions, and swing clubs had proliferated while large dance orchestras, like the Squadronaires and Geraldo's, had absorbed swing idioms. *RRC* arguably had been so successful at building an audience for small-group swing that it had jeopardized its distinctiveness in the BBC schedule. Indeed, between 1943 and 1945, the Corporation booked numerous swing combos: Claes, Grappelli, Barri-teau, Parry, and Weir all led airings outside of *RRC*.

The most striking sign that swing had joined the mainstream was when the ball-room dance profession, which had frowned on jitterbugging since the beginning of the war, finally embraced a modified form of the dance, the jive. In late 1943, Josephine Bradley, a doyenne of English-style ballroom, introduced the jive at the Hammersmith Palais de Danse, where jitterbugging had been banned. She discussed the new dance in the *Dancing Times* and recorded several discs for Decca with her Jive Rhythm Band, composed of leading session players.[88] Not to be outdone, Silvester also recorded a series of jive records, published the manual *This Is Jive* (1944), and expressed his inten-tion to devote a programme of *BBC Dancing Club* to the dance.[89] The jive's adoption by the strict-tempo authorities demonstrated the degree to which swing had penetrated Britain's wartime culture, particularly for young fans, in no small part because of Harry Parry and *RRC*. As will be discussed, their engagement with swing also involved an engagement with racial difference.

"Obviously Coloured": Race, Representation, and Performance

In 1942, the *Radio Times* variety columnist C. Gordon Glover wrote:

> There are still people who imagine jazz bands to be groups of gibbering Negroes howling through out-of-tune saxophones, biffing at banjos, and hitting out hap-hazardly at appliances loaded with cowbells and tin cans. But there is an increas-ing body of serious-minded persons ... who study and understand the whole rich history of this full-blooded and deeply sincere thing, called "Jazz."[90]

Whether it was rejected or embraced, jazz was linked closely in British thought with African American identities, and it was often regarded through a lens of racism and xenophobia. Indeed, the attitude that jazz was immoral, primitive, and alien had played a major role in the BBC's refusal to broadcast it until the late 1930s. *RRC* not only rep-resented a significant shift in the BBC's attitude toward the music but also served as an important site where black cultural production was taken seriously.

During the Second World War, the BBC's representation of black people and culture on its domestic wavelengths, the Home Service and Forces Programme, was complex and often contradictory. Overwhelmingly, its Variety and Music Department broad-casts situated Negroes, whether Americans, West Indians, or British, as Other to a white British audience. "What is it about Negro voices that gives so many people a peculiar delight?" asked the *Radio Times* in 1943. "Is it perhaps the blend of richness of tone with simplicity of expression? Is it their unusual gift for sounding as if they en-joyed it? Or is it something appealing about the songs they prefer to sing...?"[91] Much of the non-jazz black music heard on the BBC followed a folkloric vein: spirituals, calypso, and several African American musicians, like Josh White, who had been cham-pioned by the folk music revivalist Alan Lomax.[92] Although the BBC's presentation of black music and performers tended to be depoliticized and exoticizing, the very act of including such cultural production in its programming helped to legitimize it. The BBC also used its power of exclusion when it refused to promote the segregationist policies and "colour-bar propaganda" that accompanied the American military to Britain.[93]

Nevertheless, the BBC's practices of exclusion and inclusion frequently advanced more racist representations of black individuals and culture. In its tradition of avoiding controversial topics, the BBC tended to shun discussions of racism, whether at home or abroad.[94] Meanwhile, *Radio Times* writers frequently drew upon offensive racial stereotypes when introducing black artists, such as when Glover described Blake and his band: "jolly as sandboys, black as your hat, making rhythms as only Negroes make it for dancing as only Negroes can dance."[95] Most strikingly, the serious programming of black folk music and jazz aired alongside the nostalgic "fun" of the *Kentucky Minstrels*, with their "blacked-up faces" and "twanging banjos," which ran on Monday nights throughout the war.[96]

RRC's approach to black cultural production set it apart in several ways from the minstrelsy, folklorism, and limited political discussion that characterized black representation on the BBC's domestic services. First, it not only took African American jazz musicians seriously, it valorized them. Many of the program's records recitalists celebrated the authenticity, creativity, and noncommercialism of black music from the past and present. Their approach defined jazz repertories in terms of originality and seriousness similar to those applied to the classical music valued by the BBC, although their stance was characterized less as a bid for legitimacy than by hipness, with its attendant oppositional and primitivist tendencies. Second, the program provided a space for African American and black British musicians to reach a national audience as experts, composers, and virtuosi. This was particularly important given the BBC's wartime aim "to reflect the richness of Britain's regional, social and cultural diversity" in its programming, which nonetheless tended to exclude racialized minorities.[97] *RRC* presented black British musicians as *British* rather than alien. Finally, *RRC* grappled with the historic, cultural, and stylistic complexities of black cultural production to a greater degree than other BBC programs, exposing its listeners to debates about the relative contributions of black and white American performers to the development of jazz, and juxtaposed these discussions with regular examples of interracial musicmaking. While the conversation could easily veer into essentialism, the possibility for antiracist practice remained open as well.

Although black cultural production was a significant focus for *RRC*, nearly all the experts and critics who contributed to the program were white. Many of these contributors, including Jackson, Denis Preston, Max Jones, and Albert McCarthy, had distinguished themselves in other venues as strong advocates for jazz produced by black musicians, and they brought their opinions onto the air. In contrast to the restrained announcing style cultivated within the BBC, they tended to be more effusive in their enthusiasm, a tendency that earned the censure of critics. "Detector" scolded Preston for providing only "glorification blurbs" in a talk on Armstrong as a singer while the *Daily Mail*'s Seton Margrave complained of the un-British "syrupy blather" that characterized *RRC* as a whole.[98] The passionate engagement of these critics with African American jazz demands closer attention, given its contrast to the ignorance, fascination, and sometimes discrimination that most white Britons brought to their encounters with black soldiers, war workers, and civilians.

Preston, who served unofficially as *RRC*'s producer from April 1945, was a striking case in his intense engagement with black music, bohemianism, and antiracist attitudes. Dubbed the "Highbrow of Swing" by the BBC soon after his first records recital in May 1941, he broadcast more than nineteen times during the war on the program (only Chilton and Parry appeared more often). In his scripts he focused primarily on African American musicians and early jazz; his topics included Ellington, Armstrong's Hot Five, the clarinetist Jimmy Noone, and Scott Joplin. A prolific critic, he was an early contributor to McCarthy and Jones's *Jazz Music* (1942–53), a periodical with a strong editorial focus upon "the superiority of black musicians," the limitations of commercial swing, and the problems of American racism.[99] (After the war, Preston went on to become a record producer and a staunch proponent of black British calypsonians and jazz musicians; he also engaged in antiracist activism, campaigning successfully, for example, to remove *Little Black Sambo* from schools.)[100] Chilton recalled Preston's bohemian style—he "had a beard and wore sandals and was a vegetarian"— and attitude: to avoid military service "he bought books on psychology and cultivated all the symptoms that he was psychologically unsuited."[101] The nonconformist stance that Preston and other jazz enthusiasts adopted through black music resonated with Ingrid Monson's discussion of hipness, a term that was emerging in the United States at the same time. Although these affinities might form the basis for antiracist coalitions, they more often worked to subject black male musicians to a romantic, primitivist gaze that undervalued their discipline, intellect, and respectability.[102]

In Britain, the primitivist regard for jazz was compounded by its exotic origins in America, a country that, prior to the massive influx of American soldiers during the latter half of the war, was known largely secondhand through Hollywood films. As one RAF sergeant commented to BBC Listener Research, "There is a tendency in this country to still regard the States as a sort of backwoods country with Red Indians and Cowboys, and so forth— or alternatively as a land of millionaires, glamour girls, and precocious child prodigies."[103] In contrast to the vague, Hollywood-inspired conceptions about America in the broader population, British rhythm club participants went to great trouble to build their understanding of jazz and its cultural context. Because of the limited availability of records and books (and, for many, funds to buy them), rhythm clubs served an important pedagogical function, allowing members to pool their recordings and knowledge.

Despite its serious-mindedness, however, British jazz discourse was still infused by racial essentialism. One striking, though characteristic, example was a transcript of the No. 1 Rhythm Club reviewing the month's new swing records that *Melody Maker* printed in December 1939. After dismissing (the not incidentally white) Krupa's and Tommy Dorsey's latest discs, the group turned to Louis Jordan and His Tympany Five playing "Flat Ace" and "Keep a Knockin'." On the way to their verdict, "Both Sides Swell," they addressed the topic of race in jazz:

BILL ELLIOTT: This is the nearest to real jazz we have had to-night.
PAT MACNAMARA: And obviously coloured.

THE CHAIRMAN [JACKSON]: I take it you mean that as a compliment. If so, do you think that coloured jazz is on the whole better than white?

The discussants proceeded to enumerate how black bands differed from—and often excelled over—white bands, advancing a familiar series of positive descriptors that were nonetheless rooted in primitivist discourse. Recordings by black jazz musicians had "atmosphere" (i.e., "the suggestion of sincerity and enjoyment") and "a more genuine sense of rhythm." More specifically, Jordan's record displayed spontaneity, excellent soloing, a strong sense of swing, and a manly "boldness."[104]

For the reviewers and many British enthusiasts, authenticity in jazz—signified by rhythmic and timbral complexity, original improvisation, noncommercialism, and even naturalized, emotional "sincerity"—was rooted in African American identity and virile masculinity. While admiring, such constructions not only reinforced primitivist stereotypes but also participated in a long tradition of white men identifying with black musicians as a means to claiming a more assertive, freer masculinity for themselves.[105] This gendered and raced exchange became clearer in the case of white exceptions that did (or did not) prove the rule. When the group turned its attention to Shaw's latest disc, Elliott observed, "It's the one white band that has guts."[106] The concerns about inadequacy and inauthenticity in American white bands multiplied when British jazz enthusiasts considered British bands. In an extreme iteration of this perspective, R. D. Ramsey contended, "Jazz is not the music of the white man; to him it is but a fashion, a craze, to be interpreted for mercenary purposes....British Jazz never was. It never will be."[107]

Because British identity was linked inextricably to whiteness, black British musicians "assumed the mantle of being American," according to the guitarist Frank Deniz. This carried the advantage of being perceived more readily by audiences as authentic: Deniz observed, "Being coloured was an asset...they thought I was the greatest player in the world."[108] Nevertheless, black British musicians also faced the burden of being inscribed within the same primitivist discourse as African Americans. These were complex waters to navigate. At the beginning of the war, the black British musician who had the greatest success at attaining both mainstream recognition and subcultural prestige was the bandleader Ken "Snakehips" Johnson. Born into the professional class of British Guiana, Johnson attended public school in Britain but abandoned university to pursue a career in stage dance. He reached Harlem in 1935, where he refined his tap dancing and, according to Val Wilmer, "learnt to wind his hips in the suggestive manner that his nickname implied."[109]

When he returned to Britain in 1936, he set about creating a band on the model of entertainer-bandleaders like Cab Calloway, skillfully negotiating British expectations for an all-black band. Johnson delegated the task of rehearsing the group while he focused on showmanship, incorporating his own dance routines and choreographing the players' movements—something rarely done by British bands. Johnson was determined to take on not only the strong visual impact of African American show bands, but also their swinging repertory (figure 5.5).[110] It was this determination that earned him the admiration of swing fans, despite the constraints of playing for musically

FIGURE 5.5 The bandleader Ken Johnson. (Programme Listings, *Radio Times* [23 February 1940])

conservative West End audiences. *Band Wagon*, for example, applauded Johnson's determination to "sell swing to the 'swells'" when he began his residency at the Café de Paris in October 1939.[111] Enthusiasts celebrated the band's "American sound, which you could then liken with the records you'd hear. He was playing the same numbers as Count Basie…or Tommy Dorsey."[112] Johnson's charisma was his greatest asset, however. His business manager, Leon Cassel-Gerald, recalled, "Ken Johnson may not have been a great musician personally, but he had the gift of imparting his terrific enthusiasm for swing music to those who were."[113]

Given his growing prominence and his staunch advocacy for swing, Johnson's March 8, 1941, death in a direct hit on the Café de Paris was a serious blow for British swing fans. For three weeks, *Melody Maker* devoted extensive coverage to the loss of "England's swing king," along with the death of his tenor saxophonist, Dave Williams, the sufferings endured by his musicians, and worries about the fate of his band.[114] "Who can take his place?" asked the bandleader Van Phillips.[115] The BBC was slower to acknowledge the significance of Johnson's death. A week after *Melody Maker* had devoted most of its front page to the news, the *Radio Times* offered "a belated word of regret for Ken Johnson."[116] His fans must have flooded the weekly with tributes because the next week it published three, which not only expressed regret but advocated for a special program to memorialize Johnson himself.[117] Nevertheless, it was four more months (during which the BBC broadcast a tribute for Al Bowlly, who had been killed in an air raid a month after Johnson) before the editors announced that a program was in preparation. By August, frustrated fans asked *Melody Maker* to intercede with the BBC on their behalf.[118]

Johnson's memorial finally aired in *RRC* at 10:00 p.m., Wednesday, September 3, 1941, nearly six months after his death. The broadcast drew a listenership of 15.3 percent, an unusually large audience for late nights on the Forces Programme and the biggest audience that the program had attracted to date.[119] Perowne's tribute earned raves from "Detector," who praised his engaging presentation of Johnson's life and his playing of off-air recordings from the bandleader's last broadcast.[120] The program publicly acknowledged Johnson's importance and the loss that his fans and associates had experienced. One soldier wrote, "Thank you, Harry Parry, for the 'Radio Rhythm Club' programme on the late Ken Johnson.... The final words of Leslie Perowne touched me deeply—'Goodnight Rhythm Club, goodbye Ken.'"[121]

The grateful response begs the question: Why did the BBC delay broadcasting a tribute to Johnson for so long, given the strong demand from listeners, many of whom were in the forces, which the BBC regarded as a priority audience? In the Corporation's defense, Johnson was a relative newcomer as a name bandleader, having broadcast regularly only from 1938. Moreover, with no recording contract, Johnson and his band had recorded only a handful of discs, of which only a few featured swing.[122] Perowne's ability to create an effective tribute even with a shortage of commercial recordings, the powerful reaction from fans, and the BBC's speedier move to commemorate Bowlly render these explanations unsatisfactory, however. A more convincing explanation was rooted in the BBC's politics of inclusion and exclusion as it pursued its wartime mandate of representing the nation to itself. Johnson's race rendered his death less worthy of mainstream acknowledgment, as registered by the delay in producing his tribute and by the fact that it aired in the localized space of *RRC*. A clue to this oversight lies in the *Radio Times*'s assertion that Johnson "was very proud of the fact that his band—which suffered heavily by the same bomb—though all coloured, was all-British, too."[123] For the BBC and for many white British citizens, reconciling Johnson's race and nationality as belonging to the same category (and entitling him to equal respect) was deeply challenging. To its credit, the BBC offered two more remembrances to Johnson in February 1942, when it aired a records recital by Perowne and a performance by Johnson's briefly reunited band, organized by David Miller and led by Barriteau.[124]

The Café de Paris bombing had a devastating effect on the members of Johnson's close-knit band, many of whom were injured and traumatized by the attack. While fans hoped publicly that the band would stay intact, its players scattered to other ensembles; it was not until 1944 that another all-black British band (composed primarily of Johnson band alumni) formed to play swing-dominated repertory, under the auspices of Ambrose's management and leadership of the trumpeter Leslie "Jiver" Hutchinson. In 1941, however, "the other leaders came on them like vultures," recognizing an "opportunity to secure a better sense of swing for their" performances. Hutchinson, for example, spent three years with Geraldo.[125] With the diaspora of Johnson's players, several major British bands were suddenly integrated. Although this would have been an arresting sight for most West End patrons, rhythm fans had become accustomed to mixed-race music-making. Parry's Sextet had been integrated from the start, as was Tom Bromley's outstanding sextet, which played for "Making Your Own Swing," a *RRC* subseries that ran for most of 1943.[126] If Johnson's tragic death made integrated dance bands possible, *RRC* did much to make this prospect relatively unremarkable. Indeed, integrated bands garnered favorable responses from swing fans, and many bandleaders treated the presence of black performers as authenticating spectacle.

While black musicians brought the flavor of swing authenticity to mainstream bands and integrated small bands pleased their hip listeners, British swing fans continued to place a premium upon all-black or mostly black ensembles, particularly small combos. *RRC* helped raise the profile of a handful of these groups, most notably those led by the trumpeter Cyril Blake and the guitarist Lauderic Caton. Parry featured Blake's Jig's Club Band, playing "The New Lowdown," "Cottontail," and "Well, All Right," on *RRC* in February 1942.[127] The airing coincided with the highly anticipated release of the Parlophone discs, made in a live "stunt" recording session (organized, like the *MM*-HMV session, by Wally Moody of EMI) at Jig's Club, which served an Afro-Caribbean clientele but had also become a destination for white jazz enthusiasts.[128] Godbolt recalled, "Palefaces from the suburbs, immersed in the historical and racial background of jazz, came to Jig's naively believing that they were entering the approximation of one of the lower level Harlem 'joints.'"[129] Parlophone aimed to capture both the atmosphere, which so titillated enthusiasts' primitivist imaginations, and the band's "rough and ready" playing (sound example 5.3).[130] ❂ The discs rendered Blake's music accessible to rhythm fans unable to venture into a Soho nightclub, let alone a Harlem dive; this aim was furthered by the *RRC* broadcast, which also circumvented the BBC's policy against outside broadcasts from vice-ridden "bottle party premises," like Jig's Club.[131]

Blake and Caton returned to *RRC* in March and August 1943, following Chilton's resumption of his duties as producer. Rather than being featured as part of an exotic "gin mill," however, they were now participating in a preservationist project. Chilton had turned *RRC* in a more historical direction, and their "Negro Orchestra" (an iteration of the Jig's Club band) contributed a live element to the project. They performed two programs of "Negro Spirituals and Folk Songs"; as the specification "Negro" implied, their racial identity did much to bolster the authority of their work. "Detector" was especially impressed by their second broadcast, in which they played "Shortenin' Bread," "John Henry," "St. James Infirmary," the spiritual "Don't Be Discouraged," and an extemporized blues. He suggested that the performances offered "yet another clue to that still incompletely solved problem, the origin of jazz," observing, "I am prepared to accept these interpretations as authentic," and praising the group's "swell" playing and Caton's arrangements for their reproduction of "genuine old-time naivety."[132] The African American songwriter Spencer Williams, who had composed the famous "Basin Street Blues," served a similar authenticating role as a speaker on *RRC*. In 1944, he spoke once at the end of a tribute to Fats Waller, whom Williams had known well, and in two installments called "Reminiscences of a Jazzman," which explored New Orleans and Chicago jazz.[133] Williams's legendary status, "naïve, almost halting way of speaking," and racial (and national) identity bolstered his—and *RRC*'s—authority.[134]

Despite such noteworthy inclusions, the overwhelming balance of British musicians featured live on *RRC* were white. Parry's integrated house band was fronted by a white musician-celebrity while Featherstonhaugh's Sextet, which broadcast twelve times as house band between 1943 and 1944, was an all-white ensemble. Of the remaining small British bands and soloists who appeared on *RRC*, thirteen out of eighteen were white. The case was very different for records broadcasts, however.

A significant number of *RRC*'s records recitals celebrated the central role of African Americans in jazz. Of the fifty records programs that focused upon a specific artist or band, as indicated in the *Radio Times*, twenty-six featured black musicians. If programs on topics like the Chicagoans (a school of white musicians including Dave Tough, Bud Freeman, and Eddie Condon), spirituals, or Harlem were included, the numbers grew to thirty-seven out of sixty-five programs. The bias in favor of African American musicians became more pronounced upon closer examination, however. Given the producers' mission of educating listeners about jazz and its history, it is probably not surprising that most of the records programs addressed historical topics; their relative importance can be gauged by the number of times they recurred. Bix Beiderbecke, Sidney Bechet, and the blues (a jazz version of the three Bs), each with three programs dedicated to them, topped the hierarchy. With two programs apiece, King Oliver, Armstrong, and Ellington, along with the white Miff Mole, Red Nichols, and the Original Dixieland Jazz Band, were next in the pantheon. From this point, numerous musicians and topics were featured once, with possibly another shared appearance. A fairly predictable list of white players, including Jack Teagarden, Pee Wee Russell, and Muggsy Spanier, fell into this category. The list of African American players was striking in its breadth, however, including Johnny Dodds, Benny Carter, W. C. Handy, J. C. Higganbotham, and Earl Hines. In all, 60 percent (thirty-one out of fifty-two) of *RRC* records recitals on historical topics focused upon African Americans, revealing the position of Preston and other recitalists that black musicians had contributed far more to the development of jazz than white players, an outlook contested by many British enthusiasts. The nearly equal distribution of records recitals demonstrated Chilton and Parry's commitment to airing different, even conflicting, perspectives on *RRC*.

Throughout the war, *RRC* helped ensure black cultural production, and black British musicians, a place on the national airwaves. More critically, it treated black music and musicians seriously, as original, creative, and culturally important. Although proto-hipster discourses, with their attendant "romantic version of racism," certainly helped frame the program's discussion of "Negro" identity and creativity, threads of antiracist and integrationist discourse (and, more important, practice) also ran through *RRC*.[135] It not only regularly featured black and white British musicians playing together but also presented a historical and cultural framework for jazz that admitted for complexity, multiple perspectives, and the roles of both black and white musicians.

Conclusion

In April 1945, *Melody Maker* printed an anecdote from Jimmy Bunting, who had been invalided out of the RAF, involving the late conductor and Promenade Concerts founder Sir Henry Wood.[136] Bunting had splurged on a first-class rail ticket and settled down to read the latest copy of *Melody Maker* when Sir Henry and his wife entered the car and sat down opposite him.

> I had the *Melody Maker* open in front of me...but over the top I was watching Sir Henry, whom, of course, I recognised. He was leaning forward, reading the front pages of the "MM" and the more he read the more disgusted-looking he became. Finally he could stand it no longer. I could see from his face that he had to say something to suggest what he thought about swing, jazz, the people who wrote

about it, and the people who read about it, and he leaned forward and tapped the paper irately, with his forefinger. "Young man," he thundered, "are you entitled to travel first class?"[137]

Bunting's expectations were reasonable. While rhythm club enthusiasts spent the war squabbling internally over the relative merits of jazz and swing, black and white, they united to respond to critics outside of their community, who attacked jazz and swing indiscriminately, often without distinguishing "authentic" forms from commercial dance music. Commentators on the popular BBC *Brains Trust*, particularly Drs. Malcolm Sargent and C. E. M. Joad, were some of the worst offenders in this regard, infuriating fans, critics, and bandleaders.[138] *RRC* aired several programs in which classical and light musicians debated the merits of jazz with its defenders, such as a well-received debate between Wynford Reynolds and Jackson in December 1942.[139]

The often colorful assaults on jazz yielded some entertaining broadcasts, but they also pointed to deeper issues, most notably the fact that jazz and swing enthusiasts' claims to space, whether in a first-class railway coach or on the air, was far from settled. Indeed, this was a key reason behind the vehement response of fans like the Warworkers Rhythm Club, which wrote to the *Islington Gazette*:

> We read with disgust Mr GG Sheffield's article on jazz. Perhaps it has not occurred to Mr. Sheffield that he is utterly selfish in his views. Does Mr. Sheffield not realise that if jazz programmes were eliminated from the BBC, thousands of our troops and workers, who do understand and appreciate jazz, would be deprived of one of their favourite programmes? Just as Mr. Sheffield finds jazz boring, so we find classics and the music he classes as art. But we don't ask for them to be omitted from the BBC programmes....We, too, hold a wireless license.[140]

Jazz enthusiasts regarded curmudgeonly attacks on jazz as attacks on themselves, a particularly galling situation given their active role in war service.

While the BBC's decision to broadcast *RRC* for most of the war granted powerful external validation for young war workers, youth, and their tastes, the program also built an imaginary community among fans, particularly those who had embraced swing through the appeal of Parry's music and his celebrity. *RRC* was striking in its breadth, both in its formats and in the range of opinions that it aired. Its producers made significant efforts to appeal to a wide range of fans, to expand their horizons, and to respond to criticism from the rhythm club community. The program's jam sessions and policy of discussion, openness, and even argumentation offered a compelling example of democracy in action. Even more powerfully, *RRC* presented British citizens working actively to make sense of a foreign culture, and it engaged deeply and celebrated the music of an oppressed class—African Americans and black British citizens. For its diverse audience of soldiers, war workers, invalided ex-servicemen, conscientious objectors, and bohemians, *RRC* stood as a potent example of "what we are fighting for."

6

SINCERELY YOURS: THE TROUBLE WITH SENTIMENTALITY

AND THE BAN ON CROONERS

IN MARCH 1942, the *Daily Telegraph* published a letter, criticizing the "crooners and sloppy sentimental rubbish inflicted by the BBC on its listeners," from a retired lieutenant colonel and Victoria's Cross holder. He concluded, "The sickly and maudlin programmes are largely responsible for the half-hearted attitude of so many people towards the war and its seriousness generally."[1] It is hard to imagine who in Britain would have underestimated the seriousness of the war. In North Africa, British and German forces were at a standstill after Rommel's Afrikakorps, in a series of surprise January offensives, had retaken most of Libya, leaving only Tobruk. Britain could expect no help from the Soviet Union because the Russians were repelling a German invasion on the Eastern Front. The Americans had finally entered the war, after Japan's December 1941 attack on Pearl Harbor, but the gain of an ally was offset by Japanese advances, which resulted in the fall of Hong Kong, Rangoon, and Singapore. Meanwhile, the Battle of the Atlantic, in which German U-boats attacked the shipping that sustained the British Isles, was reaching its peak.[2]

Many commentators worried publicly about the mettle of British forces. Their concerns were reinforced in early 1942 by two humiliating mass surrenders, the largest of the war. In Singapore on February 15, "80,000 Australian, British and Indian troops [surrendered] to an inferior number of Japanese," and on June 22 Tobruk fell to the Germans, resulting in the capture of 35,000 British, South African, and Indian soldiers. Meanwhile, as the Eighth Army command prepared for the contingency of being driven out of Egypt, desertions increased to the degree that "some senior officers" requested (unsuccessfully) the reinstitution of the death penalty for the offense.[3] Surrender, desertion, and defeat all worked to undermine the belief, particularly on the part of veterans, that Britain's forces possessed the "bravery, courage, physical strength and endurance" of the soldier-hero—and the wherewithal to win the war.[4]

One of the easiest scapegoats for such problems was popular music, particularly the sentimental songs and crooners broadcast by the BBC Forces Programme.[5] Although many members of the forces were located too far abroad to hear the service or, if stationed in Great Britain, could also access the Home Service, broadcasting over the Forces wavelength was still endowed with the stamp of institutional approval as "the stuff to give the troops."[6] There already existed a gap in taste between those who had fought in the First World War and preferred its "rousing songs" and "real voices" over the sentiment and crooners favored by the troops.[7] The military setbacks of 1941 and 1942 lent new vigor to those who condemned crooners as debilitating and depressing, deplored "swung" classics (i.e., popular songs based upon classical melodies) for corrupting the essence of great works, and accused the BBC of belittling the intellect of the forces and undercutting their morale with "flabby and spineless...entertainments." Such criticism became a regular theme in the press, and in July, Vernon Bartlett in the House of Commons lambasted the "sentimental and sloppy muck that goes on hour after hour on the Forces' programme."[8]

In March, Basil Nicolls, the controller of Programmes, identified what he believed to be the root of "much of the rather wild criticism of the Forces Programme": *Sincerely Yours—Vera Lynn*.[9] The program, which adopted the format of "a letter to the men of the Forces...in words and music," had run in two six-week installments during November and December 1941 and again in February and March 1942.[10] Signing Vera Lynn for the first series had been a coup for the show's producer, Howard Thomas. Lynn had become established early in the war as a top solo artist in recording, variety, and broadcasting, and by the spring of 1941 she was voted the No. 1 Sweetheart to the Forces.[11] As befitted a performer of her stature (and to accommodate her busy performing schedule at London variety theaters), the series was scheduled for 9:30 p.m. on Sunday evenings, after the news and the *Postscript*—a prime place in the schedule.

Sincerely Yours was unabashed in its embrace of sentimentality. In promoting the series, the BBC's *Programme Parade* celebrated both its inclusion of "plenty of sentiment" and its ascent "into the exclusive top rank of radio shows with an audience of more than 20% of the radio public."[12] Its tone was rooted in Lynn's persona, for the singer was known as a specialist in the intimate, heartfelt delivery of sentimental songs—most famously, "Yours" and "We'll Meet Again."[13] Thomas extended the theme of sentimental hominess into Lynn's spoken dialogue, which communicated "news from home" and celebrated the "peace and calm" of married life, the fidelity of wives and sweethearts on the home front, and the joys of parenthood.[14] The program's high point was the announcement to a distant serviceman of the arrival of an "expected baby," until so many individuals called the BBC "with news of babies" that they overwhelmed the staff and the feature was canceled (figure 6.1).[15] Nevertheless, Lynn continued to sing a lullaby, such as "Baby Mine" from *Dumbo*, nearly every week.[16] *Sincerely Yours* represented a triumph in its evocation of feminine, domestic space and ability to turn the wartime experiences of longing for an absent beloved into a communal experience.

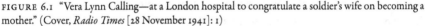

FIGURE 6.1 "Vera Lynn Calling—at a London hospital to congratulate a soldier's wife on becoming a mother." (Cover, *Radio Times* [28 November 1941]: 1)

It was her ability to envoice over the mass medium of radio the longings felt by so many of her listeners that made Lynn emblematic of British experience during the Second World War, but it was also these qualities that made her a symbol of "flabby amusement" at the BBC in early 1942. For listeners who believed that marches, robust singing, and uplifting classical music were the proper entertainment for fighting men, Lynn's heartfelt vocalizing and the program's celebration of sentimental femininity was anathema. Moreover, sentiments like those of Buddy DeSylva's "Wishing," the signature tune for *Sincerely Yours*, which promised that "if you wish long enough, wish strong enough...wishing will make it so," seemed unrealistic and even inappropriate after the grim Sunday evening news program. Despite, or likely because of, the depressing war news, the program had wide appeal, however. It seemed "to have reached the hearts of even the most hard-baked anti-sentimentalist," "Detector" observed.[17] In March 1942, Nicolls acknowledged the BBC's quandary: "There is no doubt whatever, of course, that the programme is solidly popular with the ordinary rank and file of the Forces. On the other hand, it does not do us any good to have a reputation for 'flabby amusement.'"[18]

The problem of reconciling the attacks on "sickly and maudlin programmes" with their popularity lay at the heart of the BBC's decision to craft a new Dance Music Policy in early 1942, affecting the fate not only of *Sincerely Yours* but also that of all popular singers, dance bands, and theater organs at the Corporation. Indeed, 1942 was a turning point in the BBC's wartime approach to popular music. During the early years of the war, the BBC had struggled to develop popular music programming that would please, reassure, and cheer large swaths of the public, particularly listeners engaged in war service. From 1942 onward, the Corporation worked to reconcile such crowd-pleasing efforts with its traditional status as a mouthpiece for British national identity and cultural uplift.

There was a significant obstacle to the laudable aim of providing popular music programming that was "as good of [its] kind as possible."[19] Determining what constituted "the best" in repertory and style for popular music was a subjective enterprise, as the BBC learned to its chagrin when its July 1942 announcement that it would ban crooning by men, overly sentimental performances by female vocalists, and swung classics precipitated a heated debate in the nation's press. Those who deplored crooners and sentimentality were pleased, but many young listeners, especially men in the forces, rejected the development as undemocratic and out of step with modern, American-influenced tastes. The difficult task of enforcing the ban fell to the newly created Dance Music Policy Committee (DMPC). Its members, drawn from high-ranking staff in the Music, Variety, and Programme Planning Departments, had to delineate the limits of acceptability in terms of decency, sentiment, and offensiveness to religious and "allied" susceptibilities. Recognizing that censoring song lyrics could have only limited effectiveness, they began in 1943 to secretly audition nearly every popular singer who broadcast, banning those whom they deemed insufficiently robust.

The BBC's decision to monitor its popular music programming more closely took place in the context of a significant reorganization within the Corporation. When Director-General Ogilvie, who had led the BBC through the first years of the war, resigned on January 27, 1942, he was succeeded by joint directors-general, Sir Cecil Graves and Robert Foot. Foot oversaw an overhaul of the Corporation's structure and finances while Graves focused on the programming side, a critical task, since Listener Research detected a "severe slump" in listener satisfaction in 1942. Throughout 1942 and 1943, the Variety and Music Departments scrutinized their music programming, led by the eminent composer, conductor, and "towering ex-Grenadier Guardsman" Arthur Bliss.[20] Bliss, who became the Music Department's director in April 1942, worked to extend Music's oversight to dance bands and cinema organs, which Variety administered. Although not entirely hostile, he regarded popular music as at best diverting and at worst morally suspect, a perspective reflected in the BBC's Music Policy of 1942, which helped shape both the "crooner ban" (i.e., the new Dance Music Policy) and the DMPC. The "crooner ban" represented an effort to codify the borders of acceptability in terms of sexuality, gender, class, and emotional expression, for a nation at war. Ultimately, the protests against the ban revealed how contested understandings of good wartime citizenship truly were.

"Quite Divorced from the Reality of the Times": The Problem of Sentimental Songs and Crooners

In February 1942, Mass-Observation listed the month's most popular songs, all of which featured slow tempos, sentimental lyrics, and an affinity for crooners: two American imports, "Yours" and "I Don't Want to Set the World on Fire"; Jimmy

Kennedy's "homey, English tune," "St. Mary's in the Twilight"; and Hugh Charles's "Russian Rose," whose exoticized addressee wept "where the river Volga flows." "Most of the songs people are singing to-day aren't anything to do with the war," Mass-Observation explained. "They are dream, rhapsody, escape stuff.... But many of them started out from the war situations in which we are living, and somehow soften the pain or strain."[21] While Mass-Observation regarded the trend as ultimately supportive to morale, others perceived it as a demoralizing threat, casting sentimental songs and their singers as pathological rather than therapeutic. Citing *Sincerely Yours*, Cecil Madden, the head of the BBC's Empire Entertainments Unit (EEU), wrote, "The type of song being written and sung by [Lynn] has a drugging effect on troops, but drugs are bad for one. It will have the opposite effect to making any of them 'fighting mad' and rather turn them to 'wishing it could be all over and done with.'"[22]

Against the backdrop of major surrenders, a consensus emerged within the BBC that sentimental songs and crooning were a serious problem, undermining its wartime mission of boosting the nation's morale.[23] Of course, the assessment of sentimentality as demoralizing, along with the decision to engage in explicit—and publicized—censorship did not arise fully formed. The "crooner ban" emerged out of the BBC's sense in early 1942 that dance music broadcasting was in trouble: song plugging was again rampant, the quality of performance was suffering (despite the Dance Band Scheme), and the popular song repertory was insufficiently robust.[24] Within a fortnight of each other, two staff members, the Variety Department's Douglas Lawrence and Madden, each offered substantial assessments of the situation, which helped shape the 1942 Music Policy and the Dance Music Policy that followed from it. Both men offered solutions to the problems, but Madden's proved more influential.

For Lawrence, the problems of "dreary" dance music and song plugging were linked. Bandleaders and the BBC both preferred "bright tempo numbers"; however, cheerful numbers "from a commercial angle [we]re not so popular as the sentimental 'slushy' slow rhythm type."[25] Most purchasers of popular songs preferred slow, sentimental numbers, which were easy to play. Popular publishers, dependent upon mass sales of cheap sheet music, catered to this "'song' public" and paid bandleaders to plug such lowest-common-denominator songs on the radio.[26] The solution, according to Lawrence, was to increase the BBC's inadequate broadcasting fees. This would empower bandleaders to honor their own tastes rather than pandering to the masses and accepting plug money. "Paying just that little bit more," he argued, "would...enable us to direct that bright waltzes, marches and cheerful numbers of every kind were played in place of the 'dreary jazz sophistications' of which at least 85% of dance music and plug numbers is composed."[27] Unfortunately, the additional funds were simply not available at the cash-strapped Corporation.[28]

Two weeks later, Madden offered a different solution, which he had already put into practice at the EEU: close scrutiny of all programs and a willingness to be firm with bandleaders, singers, and music publishers. Madden enjoyed two advantages in implementing his reforms: the EEU production facilities were centralized, and he did not have to worry about song plugging, since publishers ignored the Overseas Service wavelengths. His reforms involved promoting robustness and discouraging sentimentality in presentation, singers, and repertory. For example, the EEU had not broadcast the controversial (if popular) *Sincerely Yours* because of its "sloppy and rather insincere talking presentation." Instead, it offered Lynn and similar singers to the troops overseas in "straightforward" programs that featured singing but no speaking, a strategy that reduced sentimentality to respectable levels. While the presentation of sentimental female singers could be finessed to render them suitable, Madden prohibited the broadcasting of male crooners, observing, "Male crooners are quite divorced from the reality of the times." He admitted that "baritones of the vigorous rollicking sort," like Payne's Bruce Trent, or the rare "robust" tenor could be acceptable, providing they sang appropriate repertory.[29]

Madden's reforms also involved convincing bandleaders to select more "stirring" songs and to play them in an appropriate manner. He appealed directly to the two house bandleaders for help. Geraldo regarded the push for more robust programs as "mere squeamishness," but Payne, who was no friend to sentimentality, worked "to stiffen his programmes with marches and so on." Madden also booked small, "swingy" bands, which had risen to popularity in *RRC*, for they were "fast and stimulating and never ... sloppy." Finally, when persuasion failed, coercion succeeded: Madden forbade the singing of "sloppy" (i.e., sentimental) numbers, such as "Baby Mine." Ultimately, he argued, the solution lay in forcing publishers to produce more stirring songs—and this could only happen if the domestic wavelengths joined Overseas in "dropping male crooners and becoming more robust generally."[30] The 1942 Music Policy adopted Madden's seemingly straightforward solution when it advocated "exclud[ing] 'crooning,'" banning "unsuitable songs," and encouraging "better and more virile lyrics," cementing the links between sentimental repertory, popular music publishers, and the much-abused figure of the crooner.[31]

With her prominence in *Sincerely Yours*, Lynn became a lightning rod for much of this criticism, but she was also regarded as a people's entertainer. Wartime profiles celebrated her working-class background, the fact that she still lived near her mother in Barking (in London's East End), and her sweet, unsophisticated manner.[32] In May 1941, the *Radio Times* published "an appreciation by a middle-aged listener," who attributed Lynn's appeal to her intimate address, her reassuringly feminine manner, and her sincerity: "The words of her songs may have been so much sentimental twaddle. But she treated them with as much tenderness as though they were precious old folk songs ... something that she believed in and assumed that her audience believed in too."[33] Although he positioned Lynn as conveying comfort to her listeners *despite* the "twaddle" of her songs, the care that she invested in selecting and performing her repertory suggested that she sincerely endorsed the words she sang.

Lynn's status as icon—and exception—in the crooning debate spared her from the condescension and hostility directed at the much larger class of dance-band crooners. Although top singers made excellent wages, many earned less than their instrumentalist colleagues, and they were often regarded as peripheral to the dance music profession for reasons that included their feminized roles and associations with amateurism. They were also responsible for the most commercially charged job in the band: delivering song lyrics. Although "Detector" argued that their critics were "too greatly influenced by the songs most…long-suffering dance band crooners are forced to put over the air," the equation between the "ultra-sob ballad" and the "nauseatingly fulsome" dance-band singer was pervasive.[34]

As the presence of crooners expanded on air throughout 1941, a groundswell of criticism registered many listeners' visceral annoyance with their vocal timbre, alleged insincerity, and depressing affect. Much of the problem was rooted in overexposure: A. A. Thomson, the Radio Times humor columnist, who frequently ridiculed crooners and popular song lyrics, imagined himself as the new "Controller of Crooning," who would ration the practice.[35] Even as the complaint letters poured in, Listener Research confirmed their popularity, especially with the forces. In one study, 70 out of 103 forces correspondents confirmed that the men in their units appreciated crooning in morning programs, like the weekly Bing Crosby feature, while 84 reported that the American crooner was popular or "extremely popular." "He is the best thing in radio, with Mr. Churchill," one respondent wrote.[36]

The naming of Crosby in the same breath as the prime minister, renowned for his rousing speeches, was somewhat ironic, given the BBC's decision a year later to ban crooners as part of a policy to "encourage a more virile and robust output of dance music to accord more closely with the present spirit of the country."[37] Indeed, the day after Nicolls charged his assistant controller of Programmes, R. J. F. Howgill, with forming a committee to draft "a realistic, practical, working [dance music] policy," Listener Research reported on a wide-ranging survey of units in the Army Northern Command.[38] The responses were characterized by "general satisfaction" with the status quo and the absence of "any demand for a tougher broadcast diet in the Forces Programme."[39] Meanwhile, the most appreciative audience for the wavelength tended to be civilian, working-class, and female. Mass-Observation's Tom Harrisson observed, "The Forces nowadays is really the housewives' programme, and might well be renamed. It is tap listening for the home."[40] In pursuing its new Dance Music Policy, then, the BBC was embarking upon a course that heeded a vocal minority while ignoring majority opinion.

Nevertheless, Howgill's committee had several reasons for ignoring the preferences of the majority. First, powerful voices continued to condemn sentimentality and crooning, a view supported on the committee by Bliss and other Music Department representatives, who were committed to giving the forces what they regarded as "only the best music."[41] Lawrence, Madden, and others on the Variety side likewise regarded too much sentimentality as poor programming. Finally, as the committee worked, from early May until June 3, the British army retreated from Burma, and Rommel began the series of offenses that resulted in the fall of Tobruk on June 21.[42] The forces (and civilians) seemed desperately to require invigorating entertainment. "The times are unusual, they demand realistic reactions; there is a desperate War on, and the War news is much graver now. What was suitable then may be less suitable today," an unsigned BBC document noted.[43]

The pungent language and urgency with which Howgill's committee and others framed crooning as antithetical to the nation in wartime deserves a closer look. For their critics, crooners embodied poor wartime citizenship. At a time when both men and women were conscripted for war service, the *Musical Times* assumed "the physical unfitness of these young men and women, because it is inconceivable that their 'vocal' occupations are of the reserved type."[44] Male and female crooners also represented inappropriate wartime gender roles. Under his curmudgeonly guise as "Mike," Spike Hughes wrote:

> I could devote my column every week to the…shocking, ridiculous, tearful out-pouring not only of whining little girls whose voices are so full of pseudo-emotional breaks that I wonder whether their mothers know they're out; but also of (apparently) grown men who protest with tears and broken hearts that their dreams of love have gone.[45]

Crooners' excessive emotionality raised fears of indecency for women and unmanliness for men. Even the relationship between crooner and microphone carried the suggestion of sexual perversion for Payne, who condemned "people who woo and kiss the microphone."[46]

As will be explored more fully in the next chapter, women's sexuality was regarded with ambivalence during the war. Hughes's description of female crooners as "whining little girls," who stayed out too late, referenced the figure of the "good time girl," who was deplored for her promiscuity, selfishness, and irresponsibility.[47] Nevertheless, female crooners' romantic repertories, glamour, and reassuring femininity could bolster morale in the forces if properly channeled. Howgill's committee asserted, "Performance by women singers will be controlled to the extent that an insincere and over-sentimental style will not be allowed."[48] The qualification of sincerity was a critical distinction; it meant that Lynn's popular brand of earnestness was acceptable, but that her cannier imitators could be censored. Similarly, recognizing the popularity of sentimental songs with the forces, the committee classified "*sincerely* sentimental numbers" (italics added) as acceptable.[49]

While the potential unruliness of female crooners could be controlled, the committee agreed from the start on the necessity of "eliminating" male crooners.[50] Crooning was difficult to define, but the 1942 Music Policy had described it as "sub-tone, falsetto, and other modes of effeminate singing."[51] Ultimately, the committee replaced the ambiguous term "crooner" with a more encompassing phrase: "any form of anaemic or debilitated vocal performance by male singers."[52] In other words, the BBC's new Dance Music Policy characterized crooners as weak, unmanly, and depressing, traits that echoed their external critics, who described them as "effeminate creatures," "sufferers from acute melancholia," and "girlish."[53] These characteristics were antithetical to wartime hegemonic masculinity, which celebrated physical toughness, bravery, and the task of protecting women and the nation.[54]

Although the connection between effeminacy and homosexuality "did not correlate" as "inevitably" as it did in later decades, the vitriol heaped upon crooners was certainly rooted in homophobia. In contrast to the circumscribed tolerance that "discreet" (i.e., closeted) homosexuals might enjoy, the figure of the effeminate queer, defined more through "fairy" mannerisms and overt emotionality than sexuality, was regarded alternately with humor and hostility. Critics derided crooners as unmanly and demoralizing with language derived from such ridicule. Nevertheless, the BBC's descriptions of crooning as debilitated echoed the medicalized language that had arisen around homosexuality when Sigmund Freud's translated writings on sexuality reached Britain during the 1920s and 1930s.[55] In wartime Britain, both queerness and overt homosexuality carried the threat of pollution; tolerating its presence could itself be construed as dangerously "effete."[56]

As Rose argues, hegemonic masculinity tended to be defined in negative terms, which suggests why the press and the BBC devoted so much attention to describing "the" male crooner and explaining what was so objectionable about him.[57] Nevertheless, the BBC's new Dance Music Policy also offered a more positive evocation of hegemonic masculinity in its call for "a more virile and robust output." No program better embodied this aim than *I Am John Citizen*. The short-lived series featured Charles Dorning, an aircraft factory draftsman, singing with a "leather-lunged choir" and Debroy Somers's band.[58] It was, according to Dorning, "a programme of man's music. No crooners need apply."[59] The nearly self-parodying formula fell flat with many listeners: "You are wrong, John Citizen; we ordinary folk want not the boomings and bangings of martial airs or tub-thumping tunes, but the quieter deeps of music that restore the tired mind and remind us of the essential goodness in man."[60] If overtly robust entertainment was a failure, it still remained to be seen how the ban on sentimentality and crooning would be received.

Battle Lines: The Ban's Announcement

The BBC rolled out its new Dance Music Policy with military precision. On July 21, 1942, the recently established DMPC communicated the new policy to BBC staff, publishers, bandleaders, and the press.[61] The press release stated the terms of the ban in unequivocal language:

1. To exclude any form of anaemic or debilitated vocal performance by male singers.
2. To exclude an insincere and over-sentimental style of performance by women singers.
3. To exclude numbers which are slushy in sentiment or contain innuendo or other matter considered to be offensive from the point of view of good taste and of religious or Allied susceptibilities.
4. To exclude numbers, with or without lyrics, which are based on tunes borrowed from standard classical works.[62]

Two days after the ban's announcement, the *Radio Times* reinforced the BBC's position: the ban would guarantee better programs, and it represented a response to popular demand for "something more virile, more robust."[63] Rather than dictating tastes, the BBC was responding democratically to its listeners. At first, it seemed, the public and the press agreed. Of the thirty-eight clippings from July 22 to 31, preserved by the BBC, only seven items were critical. Meanwhile, more than 200 letters in appreciation of the new policy poured into the BBC, with only a handful protesting it.[64]

Support for the policy was not universal, however, and in late July several arguments emerged against it. The most obvious critique was that the ban did not truly reflect public opinion. Writing in the *Sunday Dispatch*, Lynn used statistics to support her claim that men in the forces as well as their "wives and sweethearts" valued sentiment: "During my two series of 'Sincerely Yours' broadcasts, I received letters from the boys in the Forces at the rate of 1,000 a week. By the end I had received 18,000 and they have been coming in ever since."[65] Certainly, Lynn's thousand letters a week outnumbered the 200 that the BBC received in support of the ban. Other critics argued that the BBC had misjudged what *sort* of virile entertainment the public required. They framed their discussion through several dichotomies: elitism versus populism, the past versus modernity, and Britishness versus Americanness. The *Star* decried the BBC's embrace of "robust and virile" programming as regressive cultural policy while in August, "Detector" argued that the BBC was promoting an old-fashioned, unpopular version of vigor, casting American music as up-to-date and vital, not effete or dangerously foreign.[66]

Whether viewed favorably or not, crooners and sentimental songs were generally regarded in Britain as American products. Some supporters of the ban welcomed it in nationalistic terms: the *Western Telegraph* imagined that John Bull was more likely to belt out a sea chantey than to croon, and Payne argued, "There is ample virile English music to be found without having to resort to American songs which are more often than not of a slushy character."[67] The British were also encountering more U.S. citizens, in the person of American GIs, whose numbers in Britain had grown between May and July, from 36,644 to 82,249.[68] For the GIs, the ban confirmed their stereotypes about British elitism and an autocratic BBC. Edward Kirby, the army officer in charge of radio for Americans stationed in Britain, recalled his outrage: "This edict was imposed upon millions of Yanks who had left a country much of whose popular musical literature was based on [swung classics]," and it also deprived them of the "sentimental songs" that they favored.[69]

Some British critics likewise regarded the ban as high-handed, perceiving it as a return to Reithian paternalism. Many of their misgivings involved the BBC's unwillingness to divulge the DMPC's membership, for the prospect of an anonymous committee making secret decisions smacked of authoritarianism. Seton Margrave of the *Daily Mail*, who was otherwise sympathetic to the new policy, made it his duty to reveal the names of the committee, which was chaired by Howgill and included Bliss, Madden, and the director of Variety, John Watt.[70] The critiques of Lynn and others notwithstanding, most observers initially welcomed the policy as a timely response to the public mood, following Tobruk's fall. However, the response had been limited: most bandleaders and music publishers were guarded in their comments while most listeners remained silent. This situation would change once the DMPC began enforcing the ban.

The Slush Committee or the "Slash" Committee? Song Vetting and Controversy

On July 31, the DMPC held its first meeting to vet songs, reviewing roughly a hundred numbers. It passed "Blues in the Night," "Anniversary Waltz," "Skylark," and many other songs, but it banned twenty-five. Although the minutes did not specify the grounds on which the committee banned (or passed) a particular song, it is possible in most cases to extrapolate its reasoning. Continuing the BBC's traditional ban on indecent songs, the DMPC rejected Glenn Miller's hit "Moonlight Cocktail," which offered a mixological recipe for romance, and the playfully suggestive swing number "Four or Five Times."[71] Under the new Dance Music Policy, the committee banned five swung classics, including "So Deep Is the Night," based on Chopin's E Major Etude , op. 10, no. 3 (known popularly as *Tristesse*), and it rejected "Comrade" (a "dance band 'Tribute to Russia'") as offensive to "Allied susceptibilities." Thirteen songs fell into the policy's more subjective, and potentially controversial, "slushy in sentiment" category. Thus, the DMPC rejected the sentimental, child-themed number "Good Night, Daddy," along with several songs that dealt with romantic separation, including the hits "Miss You" and "Singing Sands of Alamosa." It labeled a few songs as "special cases," which passed with special provisos. For example, the committee required that the publisher Francis, Day and Hunter change the directive of "plaintive" for "Long before You Came Along" and warned that "Say a Little Prayer" was only "to be sung straight."[72] In all cases, barring swung classics, bands could perform the excluded numbers instrumentally: it was sentimental *lyrics* that were objectionable.[73]

The July 31 meeting, which lasted an "arduous" 3.5 hours, transformed the BBC's broad statements against slush into a series of discreet acts of censorship that carried material consequences for BBC producers, bandleaders, singers, music publishers, songwriters, and other participants in the popular music industry.[74] By taking action, the BBC hoped to transform what listeners heard over the wireless and eventually what the public would demand from its entertainment. Instead, the committee's rulings catalyzed energetic opposition to the policy from publishers and the, until now, silent mass of listeners who appreciated sentiment.

The first concerted act of resistance occurred a week after the July 31 meeting, when music publishers received letters informing them of the banned songs. Frederick Day of Francis, Day and Hunter (publishers of the banned "Good Night, Daddy" and "Song of Hope") and the chairman of the Music Publishers' Association (MPA) declared, "The BBC apparently want to ban from popular music faith, hope, and charity. We resent their negative attitude."[75] His statement represented an attempt to wrest the moral (and morale) high ground from the BBC. The publishers conveyed several criticisms of the new policy to the press: the BBC's presentation style was more at fault than the songs themselves, songs on similar themes (e.g., "Roses of Picardy") had been popular in the last war, and the BBC was banning already popular numbers, like the week's third-best-selling song, "Miss You." Worst of all, the DMPC had failed to adequately explain on what grounds the songs were banned.[76] On August 11, the MPA resolved to send a deputation to the Corporation to discuss the new policy.[77] As the MPA announced to the press, it wanted the BBC to elucidate the difference between slush and healthy sentiment.[78]

Others soon adopted the publishers' framing of the ban: the BBC was being dictatorial, and it had failed to define its grounds for censorship. Several newspapers took up the question, "What Is a 'Slushy' Song?"[79] The London *Times* suggested that slush was an impossibly subjective concept—and that sentimentality seemed harmless to troop morale, if camp concerts given by the soldiers themselves were any guide.[80] Indeed, a number of voices emerged, extolling sentimentality as beneficial to morale and questioning the BBC's judgment. Clearly, the BBC had a budding public relations problem. Unlike previous conflicts over song plugging, in which both the BBC and the publishers had lost standing, credibility in the conflict over slush depended upon which party had better judged the public's mood.

On August 26, Bliss, Watt, Howgill, and Lawrence of the DMPC met with the MPA delegation, headed by Day. "After the [publishers'] steam had been let off," the two contingents entered into more substantive negotiations, primarily around how the DMPC defined slush. Although the group arrived at some "clarification" through the discussion of specific songs, the BBC's representatives maintained that they would not, or could not, provide a watertight definition of slush. To soften the blow, they agreed to an appeals process for the publishers. The two groups announced the compromise in a joint press release, promising to meet further "to decide where sentiment ends and sentimentality begins."[81] *Melody Maker* recognized that the Corporation had emerged with the upper hand: the DMPC retained the final say in whether songs were banned and avoided having to define slush.[82]

Although the BBC had won the battle with the publishers, it was encountering problems in the fight for public opinion. In early September, *Melody Maker* declared that the policy had finally generated "a public protest sufficiently strong and widespread to put even anyone so self-satisfied as is the BBC off its stroke."[83] It had taken a few weeks for opposition to build because, as BBC Listener Research explained, younger and poorer listeners, the groups most opposed to the ban, were also those least likely to write to the BBC.[84] Indeed, in response to *Melody Maker* efforts to inspire a letter-writing campaign, readers described their frustrations with friends who believed that writing to the BBC was a useless exercise.[85] Despite such barriers, BBC Listener Research reported on August 22 that the number of letters opposing the ban had increased while the number of letters supporting it had fallen. By the fourth week of the ban, critical letters outnumbered appreciative letters four to one, a ratio that continued to grow.[86] The question remained: In a people's war, did popular demand constitute sufficient grounds for reclassifying slush as a public good? Tom Harrisson encapsulated the quandary: while hearing slush on the radio reminded better-educated listeners "that there are a lot of people in this country who are still living at a slightly retarded level of cultural awareness," it still served "a human need" for comfort, "which is not always being filled by older agencies, out of touch with the modern world."[87]

Whether scourge or comfort, slush did not disappear overnight from the airwaves, and many writers complained throughout the fall about on-air violations of the ban.[88] In response, Watt commissioned the producer Gordon Crier to implement the antislush policy in Variety programs and to "tighten up" their spoken presentations while the DMPC continued to elucidate for music publishers what it considered unacceptable (and exemplary) in popular song.[89] For example, it advised the publisher Irwin Dash that "'star peek-a-booing' are not the sort of thing we want," although it passed the song, Hugh Charles's "Where the Waters Are Blue."[90] Many British songwriters responded by writing heartier numbers, such as Noel Gay's "We Mustn't Miss the Last Bus Home," a comic song about fuel economy.[91] Few of these songs were critical or popular successes, however.

The BBC also promoted crowd-pleasing genres that were already robust. In October, programmers expanded Silvester's popular *BBC Dancing Club* to an hour. "Corny" observed, "It may be the most perfect example of corn that has ever been conceived, but it has a bright, exhilarating character."[92] Exhilaration also came in the form of American swing numbers, which continued to enter the mainstream dance-band repertory, along with series like *Tea and Trumpets*, which paired the swing trumpeter Johnny Claes with the brass band legend Harry Mortimer.[93] Finally, the BBC aired more Latin music, played by the well-regarded specialist Edmundo Ros and even Geraldo, who broadcast the feature *South American Way*.[94]

Given the interlocking economies of popular music in Britain, the new Dance Music Policy also affected gramophone and film companies. The ban on slush had coincided with a sharp reduction in record production, brought about by shellac shortages.[95] Since they could issue only a handful of discs each month, gramophone companies needed their products to be best sellers, and, like publishers, they depended upon radio to generate hits. British film companies likewise depended upon the BBC's support, if their songs were to be published and recorded.[96] Thus, in November 1942, the songwriting team Val Guest and Manning Sherwin submitted all the songs for *King Arthur Was a Gentleman* for vetting by the DMPC before the film's release, and they "concentrated on a virile score" for *Miss London Ltd*.[97] Although the BBC had claimed that the ban would apply only to radio, new British songs needed to pass its censors if they were to be commercially viable.

The situation was different for American songs, particularly those featured in Hollywood films. During the war, approximately 80 percent of feature-length films shown in Britain came from the United States. For British music publishers, Hollywood films functioned as lavish commercials, with their slick production and famous singer-actors like Bing Crosby and Judy Garland; moreover, American film songs—many written by top songwriters like Irving Berlin and Cole Porter—arrived with their hit status already established. Cinema going was a popular wartime activity, and many patrons (particularly if they were young and female) saw films—and heard their songs—more than once.[98] A successful Hollywood film could become a juggernaut, and during the fall of 1942, songs from American films, most notably *Holiday Inn*, were prominent in publishers' lists, on air, and in gramophone catalogs.

In December 1942, the MPA asserted that the ban was unfair to British songs, charging that the BBC tended to pass songs already successful in America. Howgill denied that the DMPC discriminated against British songs, but the mechanisms of the ban undoubtedly had a stultifying effect upon their production.[99] Meanwhile, the committee did seem to give the benefit of the doubt more often to American songs than British. For example, the committee finally passed the Crosby vehicle "Singing Sands of Alamosa" on the publisher's second appeal while its concession that it would "give special and sympathetic consideration to a case where banning might involve heavy financial loss" was first applied to the American hit "My Devotion."[100] Finally, when the DMPC presented the MPA with examples of outstanding recent songs, nearly all, such as Berlin's "White Christmas" from *Holiday Inn*, were American.[101]

Nevertheless, relations between the MPA and the DMPC were fairly cordial by the end of 1942. The *Star* reported with disgust that the two groups "got on very well" and that the BBC had not banned a single Christmas song: "What a waste of time it all is...in all their sittings since their inauguration...I believe they have banned fewer than a dozen."[102] The reporter had the figures wrong: the committee had considered 301 songs in the first six months of the ban (July 1942 through January 1943) and passed 258, 42 of which it approved only after extended consideration or with special provisions for performance. It upheld the ban on 43 songs (about 14 percent), despite appeals by the publishers. More important, the *Star* reporter overlooked the BBC's ultimate goal, which was to change the sort of songs that were written and published in Britain. Whether the DMPC accomplished this aim was debatable, however, for sentimentality remained popular. Meanwhile, all it took was a slow tempo or a crooner to transform an acceptable number into slush. As one publisher observed, "The BBC employs the bands. We publish the tunes. It is up to the BBC to control their own musicians."[103] In 1943, the DMPC attempted to do just that.

"Waxing Critical": The Problem of Performance

When it announced the BBC's new Dance Music Policy, the *Musical Times* observed, "The first two points...deal with performers. This is probably not mere chance: first things have been put first. Eliminate the 'debilitated vocal performances of male singers' and the over-sentimental women singers and most of the reform is done."[104] The interpretation proved incorrect, but throughout the fall many in the press agreed that, in order to combat slush, the DMPC *should* have been focusing on singers rather than songs. While the committee was cognizant of the need to address matters of performance, several factors contributed to the delay: crooning was pervasive, banning singers required delicate negotiations with bandleaders, and making and reviewing off-air recordings demanded more time and expense than song vetting.[105] Moreover, the high modernist notion that performers were conduits for compositional intentions, rather than shapers of musical meaning, translated at a practical level to the DMPC being more comfortable censoring musical texts than musical sound. "The committee rarely hears songs played. All members have the music script. All are experts in reading music," the *Star* reported.[106]

While the DMPC stalled, its critics claimed that the task of identifying crooners was easy: "a singer at the piano whose vocal method consists of a mixture of sobs, croaks and bleats (we have a specially popular performer in mind)," the *Musical Times* offered.[107] Almost certainly, the *Musical Times* was referring to the popular cabaret and variety artiste "Hutch" (Leslie A. Hutchinson), the first singer whom the DMPC secretly auditioned through the use of recordings. In September, Howgill alerted his committee of Listener Research's finding that nearly 25 percent of listeners "condemned [Hutch] strongly for the sentimentality of his songs, and called his act 'slush' of the worst type" (another 10 percent considered him "outstanding"). Quoting a listener who called Hutch "the King pin of slush," Howgill advocated banning the singer "unless he can change his methods."[108] For his critics, the Granada-born singer embodied the traits that they most loathed in crooners: his style was intimate and emotionally expressive while his persona combined charismatic sex appeal with racialized difference.

A protégé of Cole Porter's, Hutch was a fixture in exclusive London nightclubs, and he mixed with their high-society clientele, whose regard for his charm, elegance, and talent was nonetheless tainted by racism (e.g., he was "expected to enter by the tradesmen's entrance" for official events). Participating in the "gentlemanly decorum" characteristic of the period's queer subculture, the singer was also inscribed within discourses of the exotic, sexually available gigolo and primitivist understandings of virile black masculinity. Meanwhile, with his matinee-idol looks he became more broadly popular in variety, film, and on the BBC as "Britain's heart-throb of song."[109] Hutch's demonstrative performances could be understood comfortably within primitivist notions of black (and un-British) emotionality; however, his frankly romantic approach moved into riskier terrain, given the racist myths of black men's lust for white women.[110]

According to *Band Wagon*, Hutch was "a dramatic actor in song."[111] Since he often accompanied himself on the piano, he had greater latitude in tempo and interpretation than dance-band vocalists, and he used sudden tempo shifts, vibrato, portamento, and even a vocal "catch" to render lyrical content with a high degree of nuance (figure 6.2). These characteristics were apparent in Hutch's early 1942 recording of "That Lovely Weekend," which described a couple spending the husband's leave together.[112] In contrast to Dorothy Carless's recording with Geraldo, with its restrained emotion and emphasis on the elegant melodic line, and Vera Lynn's version, with its slow tempo, heartfelt pauses, and caressing delivery, Hutch delivered the lyrics as a series of short, extemporaneous phrases, employing accelerando for "You had to go, the time was so short, we both had so much to say" and slowing to explain with a catch, "Sorry I cried, but I just felt that way" (sound examples 6.1, 6.2, 6.3).[113] The narrator's "writing through my tears," the military associations of the addressee's "kit to be packed," and the publicity that emphasized the song's origin in a letter Moira Heath had written to her husband all underscored that this was a woman's song. Hutch's performance claimed it for emotionally honest (and, for critics, effeminate, possibly queer) men as well.

With the singer's overt emotionality and the animus against him documented by Listener Research, it is not surprising that the DMPC vetted Hutch. The committee did not support Howgill's inclination to ban the singer, however. The minutes of November 13 were laconic: "records heard: no ban."[114] It is likely that they decided Hutch, like Lynn, was too popular to censor under the new policy. Moreover, he was no untrained dance-band crooner: members like Madden would likely have pointed to his sophisticated résumé, reputation as a skilled song stylist, and even his powerful champions.

FIGURE 6.2 The singer Leslie Hutchinson ("Hutch") performing in a December 1944 broadcast: "Britain's heart-throb of song." (Copyright © BBC)

Two months later, the DMPC considered another matter of vocal performance: assigning songs to vocalists of the "appropriate" sex. As demonstrated by Hutch's recording of "That Lovely Weekend" and the numerous women who sang "Lilli Marlene," in which a male soldier addressed his (female) sweetheart, cross-gender performance was common during the period.[115] To twenty-first-century ears (and likely, some 1940s ears, too), such performance could sound queer, particularly in the case of love songs. The number that spurred the committee's objections, however, was the hit "Praise the Lord and Pass the Ammunition," by the American songwriter Frank Loesser. In January 1943, the DMPC forbade women from singing the number, which *Gramophone* described as "the battle cry of a padre who serves the guns."[116] Given that combat's masculine status was one of the most fundamental gender distinctions in wartime Britain, a woman singing a "battle cry" was highly transgressive. As women assumed traditionally male (noncombat) roles, reinforcing gender differences in entertainment helped assuage men's anxieties about future employment, romantic fidelity, and social continuity.[117] The committee extended its ruling to assert that singers of the appropriate sex should be encouraged for all songs, urging publishers to print alternate versions so that "appropriate" lyrics would be available to singers of both genders.[118]

According to critics, however, the ban on slush and crooners remained ineffectual. "Can it be maintained that there has been any appreciable reduction of these features...?" asked the *Musical Times* in early February. "We think not."[119] This changed on February 23, when the DMPC auditioned twenty-one singers via recordings, which had been made secretly during their broadcasts.[120] Given the DMPC's reticence about how it defined crooning, the lists of banned and passed singers in its minutes offer an important window into how it distinguished between acceptable singing and objectionable crooning. Interpreting the surviving documents is complicated, however, by the limited or nonexistent recording careers of most of the 136 singers whom the DMPC vetted (29 of them more than once) between February 1943 and August 1945. With wartime cutbacks in gramophone production, it was difficult for all but the most established singers to record.

In this context, the DMPC's rulings at its February 23 meeting are particularly revealing because a large number of the vetted singers had made commercial recordings. Moreover, they were strongly representative of what British listeners heard on air, since the committee auditioned vocalists belonging to Geraldo's, Payne's, and Ivy Benson's house bands, along with those affiliated with six other bands that had broadcast during the previous two weeks. The DMPC passed ten singers, including Payne's Carole Carr and "stalwart" Trent; and Geraldo's Doreen Villiers (late of Harry Parry's RRC Sextet) and Georgina (a recent addition, who had sung previously with Payne). The committee also banned four singers, most notably Geraldo's Len Camber, and ruled that a remaining seven vocalists were "to be heard again." This latter group included the youthful Beryl Davis, who had sung with Oscar Rabin's band and Hatchette's Swingtet before joining Geraldo.[121]

Three key elements distinguished the singers who failed the DMPC's audition process from those whom it deemed acceptable: their approach to breath support, use of "scooping" and portamento, and adoption of American accents. A singer's approach to breath support while at the microphone lay at the heart of the opposition that the BBC ban had established between "anaemic," "debilitated" vocalizing on one hand and robust singing on the other. As dance-band vocalists (and broadcasters!), all of the singers heard by the committee used microphones, but many also utilized the training and techniques they had acquired in unamplified stage performance, especially musical theater. The DMPC tended to pass singers—like Carr, with her full, mature tone; Georgina, with her thinner, "pretty" voice; and the baritone Trent—whose voices displayed their "legitimate" training. In other words, they sang with consistent diaphragmatic support, maintained an even tone between their chest and head voices, had good intonation, and used a constant and consistent vibrato (sound examples 6.4 and 6.5).[122] ◑

For the DMPC, a singer's use of expressive ornamentation, especially scooping and portamento, was the characteristic most likely to move him or her into the categories of crooning and oversentimentality. In "The Art of Singing in Decline," Edwin Evans described the roots of the "terrible disease" of crooning as "an emotional slither, a passionate *portamento*, the mildest form of which, rising to the note, is sometimes called scooping." The microphone aided the practice, since "so long as the sob was there, it did not matter much whether the voice was or not," and it allowed in the taint of commercialism, for the "sob" in a singer's voice—"really a *portamento* beyond cure or control— was a source of profit."[123] It was in these areas that Camber and Davis must have violated the DMPC's standards. Both singers employed the timbral shading, scooping ornamentation, and relaxed affect that the microphone enabled—and which American crooners like Crosby had cultivated so effectively. Although Camber and Davis crooned, their singing was hardly anemic: both vocalists had warm-toned voices, which were enriched by vibrato and moved supplely throughout their ranges—traits that indicated they still maintained diaphragmatic control. Nevertheless, they did not sound "legitimately" trained in the manner of Carr or Trent (sound examples 6.6 and 6.7).[124] Indeed, Davis had sung with dance and jazz bands since she was a teenager while press coverage of Camber, who had left his medical studies because of poor health, emphasized his amateur roots: he had auditioned for Geraldo "just for fun" (figure 6.3).[125]

There was one other area in which Davis and Camber likely offended the DMPC: their adoption of American accents. The practice of British singers modeling their phrasing, ornamentations, and even accents after American stars was widespread; indeed, in 1944 a *Radio Times* correspondent estimated that 80 percent of popular singers "have adopted Americanese as their singing language."[126] By 1943, with more Americans in the country and American songs in the repertory, the BBC became increasingly concerned with fostering British-style dance music and discouraging British musicians who imitated American styles.[127] While the DMPC did not specify its disapproval of Davis and Camber in this regard, it did note its objections to the "pseudo American accent" of Kay Yorston (who was passed nonetheless) and conveyed its concerns to Benson, her bandleader.[128]

FIGURE 6.3 The teenage "croonerette" Beryl Davis in 1940. (Photo by Picture Post/Hulton Archive/ Getty Images)

The DMPC went about enforcing its February 23 rulings cautiously. Tawny Nielson, the dance music supervisor, was instructed to inform only the bandleaders who employed the banned singers and BBC staff directly responsible for their contracts; the singers' identities were otherwise to be kept secret, even from the singers themselves.[129] These precautions helped guard against the damage that a ban could inflict both on a singer's career and on relations between the BBC and his or her bandleader. The DMPC must also have recognized that banning a well-liked singer might generate bad publicity. This certainly threatened to be the case with Camber, whom the forces had ranked second in popularity among male vocalists in a 1942 Listener Research survey.[130] Although the DMPC moved forward with its bans on other singers, it specified for Camber, "No action to be taken before next meeting."[131] In March, the committee permitted Camber to continue broadcasting as an ensemble singer, although his solo and duet performances were cut.[132] Impressively, all the affected parties cooperated, and the DMPC's new vigilance with singers remained secret.

The story broke on April 1, when the *Star* reported, "The famous Anti-Slush Committee has apparently tried, condemned and executed five alleged slushy crooners." The news that the BBC had banned five unnamed crooners in the bands of Maurice Winnick, Lou Preager, Harry Leader, and Geraldo generated a flurry of coverage.[133] In "Vocalists Are BBC Scapegoats Again!" *Melody Maker* presented comments from a coy Geraldo, who acknowledged only that he had been asked to "use [his] discretion" about the songs sung by "the person you mention" (i.e., Camber), and an outraged Winnick, stung by the DMPC's March 29 decision to uphold its ban on his singer, Doreen Stevens.[134] Winnick, who modeled his sweet, string-infused sound after Guy Lombardo's, did not divulge Stevens's identity; rather, he pulled all four of his singers from his ad hoc broadcast on April 9, giving his first fully instrumental airing in five years.[135] Clearly aggrieved, he explained to the *Daily Express*: "It is a reflection on my judgment on how a crooner should sing, and this after I have been broadcasting for the BBC for 13 years. I consider my judgment is fully equal to the BBC in this matter, if not better. Otherwise, I might just as well be keeping rabbits."[136] Winnick promised to withhold his vocalists from broadcasting until the "silly ban" was lifted.[137] In late May, the DMPC finally passed Stevens, although it stipulated that it would continue to monitor her singing.[138]

Winnick's protests drew attention to the BBC's new vigilance on crooners, which many listeners undoubtedly welcomed, but they also cast the DMPC's approach in unsavory terms. First, there was the problem of the committee's judgment. While admitting that many singers fell short of "the desired standard," critics of the ban questioned the committee's ability to recognize good dance-band singing.[139] "Detector" argued that only Watt and Nielson really understood dance music and related a "by no means impossible story" circulating in Archer Street (a center for dance musicians in London) that demonstrated the DMPC's ignorance.[140] Apparently, the staff member responsible for playing recordings at the committee meetings had slipped in one of her own Crosby records, on which the committee ruled, "No good at all; out."[141] True or apocryphal, the tale illustrated the profession's belief that the DMPC could neither recognize nor appreciate the performance of a vocalist considered one of the finest exponents of popular song. Meanwhile, the DMPC approved some dubious singers, including Billy Cotton's vocalist, Dolly Elsie, whom it rated highly.[142] Despite her clear diction, controlled tone, and steady vibrato, her singing could be expressionless and rhythmically square; she inspired little critical enthusiasm.[143]

Second, the *Star* accused the members of the DMPC of being unpatriotic spoilsports. At its March 29 meeting, the DMPC had auditioned three singers associated with the London Fire Force Band, a well-known voluntary service dance band, which rehearsed during off-duty hours and engaged in extensive charity work. The committee banned outright two firefighter-vocalists, Jack Harris and Bob Winette, along with Stella Ramon.[144] Their leader, Ordinary Fireman Eddie Franklyn, protested his confusion as to why his singers had been banned. In contrast to popular celebrations of firemen as masculine and brave, the *Star* observed, "Firemen, it seems, are not virile enough for the BBC when they sing."[145]

Finally, there was the problem of the DMPC's enforcement of the ban, which the *Star* compared to the secrecy of the "German High Command."[146] *Melody Maker* charged that the committee's lack of transparency encouraged rumormongering, a freighted claim given propaganda that cast the practice as unpatriotic. The DMPC failed to contact banned singers directly, refused to explain its reasons for a ban, and informed ad hoc bandleaders that a singer was banned only after they submitted their programs.[147] Such practices had a crushing effect upon up-and-coming singers, since bandleaders were loath to hire vocalists whose broadcasting status was uncertain.[148] When a ban was actually imposed, it ended careers for all but the most prominent singers. With the exception of the swing bandleader Harry Parry and Doris Knight, who sang briefly with Benson, few of the thirty vocalists whom the committee banned (22 percent of all singers vetted during the war) recorded or gained more than a passing mention in the contemporary press. Meanwhile, the committee's secrecy left a vacuum of information, which external observers filled with speculation.

One of the most virulent rumors in circulation during the spring of 1943 was that Camber had been banned. The DMPC had censored the singer in its first meeting, but both Geraldo and the BBC were tight-lipped about the situation, and Camber's name appeared nowhere in the press. His fans, however, must have noticed his reduced presence on air and deduced his identity when the press revealed Geraldo as the employer of one of the banned singers. In late April, the BBC received at least five letters and two petitions protesting Camber's ban and urging his reinstatement.[149] Although Howgill suggested a bland response to the letters, the DMPC did take Camber's popularity into consideration when it resolved to re-audition the singer, and in late May it lifted the ban, citing Camber's "great improvement."[150] While listener pressure and public opinion certainly influenced the committee's decision, Geraldo's canny diplomacy also played a role in the singer's return to solo performance on the air. With his long-term contract, the bandleader had little to gain from a Winnick-style attack on the Corporation.

By the summer, most of the uproar over the banning of singers had subsided. The DMPC had begun permitting banned singers to re-audition after three months, an action that did much to assuage bandleaders' frustration. (It also maintained a policy of re-auditioning any "passed" singers who declined in quality.)[151] Re-auditioning saved popular singers, like Camber, from being removed permanently from the air while also maintaining the threat of a ban, however temporary, to discourage overly sentimental repertory and interpretation. Director-General Foot recognized the success of this approach when, in October 1943, he attended a DMPC meeting and "expressed his appreciation of the work done by the Committee, saying that it was now being reflected in the BBC's output, and stressing the importance of such work."[152] With a few well-publicized exceptions, the DMPC's work became a matter of routine, operating below public awareness up to and beyond the end of the war.

Although the majority of the more than 136 singers vetted by the DMPC were eventually approved, only 47 passed without caveat on the first audition. The committee placed special conditions on many of the singers it passed: fourteen-year-old Helen Mack, who sang with Lew Stone, was forbidden from singing "Nain, Nain" while Payne's Nadia Dore was limited to Latin numbers. The DMPC passed thirteen singers, including Davis, only after multiple auditions; another eleven, like Camber, were initially banned but then passed in a subsequent audition. While in most cases the ban operated as a disciplinary mechanism, promoting "good taste," it cannot be forgotten that the DMPC banned permanently approximately one-fifth of all the singers it vetted, more than thirty individuals. In all but a handful of cases, it is impossible to judge whether these singers were genuinely incompetent or simply failed to accord with the committee's sensibilities, for few ever recorded.

Conclusion

In November 1943, the *South London Press* queried, "What happened to the BBC 'antislush' campaign? Hit of the moment is 'Say a Prayer for the Boys Over There,' which makes strong men burst out crying....And Vera Lynn's back, sobbing her heart out on Sunday nights."[153] On October 31, Lynn had returned to the Forces Programme for an eight-week series. Unlike *Sincerely Yours*, which had aired on Sundays directly after the news and the *Postscript*, an implicitly official spot, the new series *It's Time for Vera Lynn* was cushioned between the popular variety show *Happidrome* and "that attractive programme of light, soothing music," *Grand Hotel*.[154]

During the eighteen months since Howard Thomas had suggested "resting" the singer, Lynn had been busy—recording, touring in variety, starring in two feature films, and broadcasting for the BBC (especially in the Overseas Service) on an ad hoc basis.[155] Although Nicolls had attributed the early 1942 outcry against flabby entertainment to *Sincerely Yours*, Lynn, with other irreproachably sincere singers like Anne Shelton, was never auditioned by the DMPC. She was simply too popular to ban, a fact confirmed by the peak audience for her new series of 26.5 percent.[156] "Say what you will, there is none like her, whether she is singing into a microphone or sitting in an arm-chair saying that nothing much has happened to her really, save a film called *Rhythm Serenade*, and a weekly despatch of 500 pictures of her face to the Forces," observed Glover in the *Radio Times*.[157]

Between early 1942 and late 1943, the homey, sentimental repertory Lynn championed became more firmly inscribed into populist, People's War ideologies. When it announced the new series *For the Sentimental Soldier*, which featured old-fashioned ballads, the *Radio Times* remarked, "The taste in song of the British soldier has never much run to patriotism and the thrills of the battlefield....Rather, it is the choice always, and with good reason, towards the sentimental."[158] Such representations offered a distinctly British blend of the kindly everyman and the tough soldier-hero.[159] Defenders of sentiment and crooning also turned to People's War ideals of tolerance and democracy to support their case. One soldier explained, "We have an occasional concert (local talent) when these songs are sung—the real 'slushy' ones—and they go down pretty well, I can tell you. After all we blokes are all sentimentalists....We think there are too many pocket dictators in the entertainment sphere these days."[160]

Allied advances in the war also helped smooth the return of "healthy sentiment" to the airwaves. The second Battle of Alamein, in which General Montgomery and the British Eighth Army finally achieved victory in North Africa, had been won for more than a year, and Italy had surrendered, although German forces still held much of its territory. Meanwhile, the Germans had surrendered at Stalingrad and withdrawn from the Eastern Front. Much still remained to be done: heavy fighting continued in the Pacific, and despite the popular British bombing raids on Germany, the Nazis remained in control of "Fortress Europe." Military successes had dispelled concerns about the resolve of the forces; although worries about demoralizing sentiment continued to be voiced, they were not regarded with the same urgency as they had been in early 1942.

In early 1944, Bliss, a driving force behind the 1942 BBC Music Policy, the crooner ban, and the DMPC, left the BBC. The *Musical Times* noted the departure of a "good man" who had arrived with laudable goals, observing, "The Head of music now seems able neither to vet nor veto"—a victim of bureaucracy.[161] Certainly, Variety had regained a greater degree of control over dance music, permitting popular crooners like Lynn to air. Nonetheless, the DMPC continued to enforce a strict ban on swung classics, a priority for Bliss, and to scrutinize the BBC's popular music output. The committee played a key role in several challenges facing dance music at the BBC in the latter years of the war: navigating the alleged decline of dance music's popularity, preserving forces morale, and asserting a distinctly British approach to dance music in the face of American influence. Meanwhile, another backlash against BBC entertainment loomed, spurred by the new General Forces Programme, which exposed audiences on the home front to the programs—featuring girl crooners and swing!—that Madden's EEU had devised for the forces overseas.

7

CALLING THE BRITISH FORCES IN MALTA: BROADCASTING

FEMININITY ABROAD—AND AT HOME

ON OCTOBER 15, 1940, during the height of the London Blitz, a 500-pound bomb hit Broadcasting House, crashing in through a seventh-floor window and coming "to rest in the Music Library on the third floor," where after an hour it exploded. The direct hit killed seven BBC employees and destroyed a great deal of studio space.[1] Two weeks later, Cecil Madden and the BBC Empire Entertainments Unit (EEU) moved its operations into the newly requisitioned Criterion Theatre, which had the advantage of being underground. The "famous theatre" soon became the bustling center of overseas entertainment broadcasting.[2] Madden described the transformation: "The box office is closed. The theatre bar dispenses tea, and the boxes house apparatus."[3] The cloakroom became the office for the all-important messages programs, in which members of the forces and their families would send a song request and greeting over the air to their loved ones: staff used the white-tiled walls to track "the names and addresses" of messages senders, washing them off as their greetings were dispatched.[4] Those entertainers and BBC staff who broadcast late at night arrived each day before the Blitz began and bedded down in the boxes or balcony until they went on air.[5] The dressing rooms served as offices, with that of the "leading lady" going to Madden (figure 7.1). "Audiences still pack the theatre—overseas Forces in khaki and blue," *Parade*, a magazine for British troops in the Middle East, assured its readers, but the stage featured a range of broadcasters, from professional artistes to Commonwealth troops and British families broadcasting their messages in person.[6]

The repurposed theater was a busy, cosmopolitan place. *Parade* described a "kaleidoscope" of activity: a broadcast by a sophisticated dance band and "glamorous girl

FIGURE 7.1 "Cecil Madden and a secretary work in the star's dressing room of the [Criterion] theatre." (Charles Graves, "BBC Non-stop Variety for Empire Forces and Listeners," *London Calling* [17 February 1942]: 14)

crooner" followed one by "merry-eyed, stocky Canadians" and "breezy Australian seamen," who gathered around a microphone to sing "for the folks way back home"; meanwhile, "off stage...a West Indian pair of cross-talkers indulge[d] in a practice-round of negro-badinage" while Madden hurried about, giving orders and announcing programs.[7] The EEU's performers, visitors, and broadcasters reflected the diversity of the Empire, a challenging concept for the wartime BBC, which in its domestic and overseas broadcasting emphasized themes of democracy and "fellow struggle" with the Commonwealth (the term increasingly preferred over "Empire"), rather than imperial power relations.[8] (Indeed, by 1943, the EEU was known as the Overseas Entertainments Unit.)[9] Madden's unit produced a wide range of variety and dance music for Commonwealth, forces, and foreign audiences in the Americas, Africa, the Pacific, India, and the Middle East. As the Overseas Service expanded, the EEU's output grew as well: at its formation in April 1940, its "fifty to sixty programmes a week" included several rebroadcasts from the Forces Programme, but by the beginning of 1942 it had become a "a 24-hour-a-day service."[10]

Messages programs directly advanced the EEU's mission of linking "those at home and their men serving abroad," and they constituted a significant part of the unit's output—20 percent in 1941.[11] Although many of the series, like *Calling the West Indies*, helped maintain ties between Commonwealth troops and their communities at home, the messages programs that gained the most attention on the British home front were those directed to British troops stationed overseas. This attention reflected the separation experienced by many British families, the increasing focus from 1941 on the war in North Africa and the Mediterranean, and concerns with forces morale that peaked in early 1942.[12] While critics railed against demoralizing, "flabby entertainment" on the Forces Programme, which by 1942 was functioning more as a domestic alternative to the Home Service than as an exclusive service for the troops, Madden had been devising his own "anti flabby" formula for entertaining overseas forces and maintaining their ties to the homeland. The formula combined the proven effectiveness of the messages format with what a spate of early 1942 publicity described as "radio girl friends" for the forces:

> In an underground theatre in the heart of London, work the seven Girl Friends of the empire. Their names are known to every soldier who fights for us overseas, but England—strangely enough—has never heard of them.... The women of Britain owe a debt to these girls who, day by day, keep thoughts of home in the minds of a great army of men.[13]

The prominence of women at the EEU microphone reflected the wartime realities of the call-up: as men joined the forces, women moved into a wider array of occupations, including those that had traditionally been gendered masculine.[14] The end of 1942 represented a watershed moment in this respect at the BBC: there were fifteen women announcers in the Home Service and Forces Programme, where "a few years ago there were none"; Tawny Nielson, one of several women to join the Corporation's administrative ranks, was hired as dance music supervisor; and the BBC had replaced the increasingly unsatisfactory Band of the Week scheme with a fourth house band: Ivy Benson and Her Ladies' Dance Orchestra.[15] Madden anticipated the BBC's wartime promotion of women broadcasters and producers by more than a year, however, cannily embracing their propaganda potential for forces listening overseas. As he explained in March 1942, the EEU negotiated with bandleaders to "cut out" male singers and feature "bright girls" in order "to show the men [overseas] that the women are doing men's jobs these days."[16] While women's pursuit of nontraditional jobs tended to threaten civilian men, as demonstrated by the dance music profession's enraged response to Benson's plum BBC contract, the situation was different for troops stationed overseas. The EEU's representation of women in "men's jobs," with its "three girl producers," "nine girl commères," and "girl announcers for all entertainment programmes etc.," conveyed that people on the home front were fully committed to the war effort, a reassuring gesture for soldiers enduring hardship and danger for their country.[17]

The embodiment of total effort was only a small component of the propaganda value of Madden's "radio girl friends," however. Like the beloved theater organist Sandy Macpherson, women commères and singers of the EEU cultivated a friendly, personal manner on air. They acted as intermediaries, conveying messages and song requests between soldiers and loved ones at home, but on air and in their correspondence they also developed connections directly with their forces listeners. In letters, servicemen expressed both a sense of intimate connection and their communal interest in the "girl friends" they addressed. "We are all waiting anxiously to take you up on 'Howzabout a Date,'" wrote a member of the Middle East Forces to the singer Doreen Villiers, the star of *A Date for the Desert*.[18] While several male broadcasters, most notably Macpherson, also developed close bonds with overseas troops, women carried a special appeal for an overseas forces audience that broadcasters envisioned as male, heterosexual, lonely, and bored.

Madden used a number of terms (e.g., "girl friends" and "sweethearts") to describe the women vocalists and commères who broadcast to the troops, but his most telling phrase was "pin-up personality."[19] During the war, the term "pinup" came into use to describe both the glamorous women and the images of them that were believed to bolster military morale.[20] The unthreatening, innocent sexuality represented by the pinup contrasted starkly with the realities of wartime sex and romance faced by troops stationed abroad. Venereal disease was a real risk for the sexually active—and many soldiers did pursue casual or paid sex, a fact that British military officials acknowledged when they established "official VD Centres" in Cairo's red-light district, for example.[21] Double standards aside, a major strain on the morale of troops, whose postings overseas could last for years, was the fear that their wives and sweethearts were unfaithful.[22] Neither fickle nor diseased, the idealized image of the pinup represented "what men were fighting for" and reinforced the heterosexual masculinity of their consumers.[23] As women pursuing successful careers in broadcasting and performance, the EEU's women announcers and singers certainly enjoyed greater agency than the term "pin-up personality" implied; nonetheless, their on-air personas offered a similarly reassuring, idealized version of sexuality.

The work of the BBC's radio girl friends was part of a broader phenomenon that Marilyn Hegarty called "patriotic sexuality," in which "magazines, movies, posters, and other media covertly and overtly urged wartime women to provide sexualized support for the military in various types of public and private entertainment."[24] In this environment, as Pat Kirkham explained, women's physical attractiveness and "beauty culture," which "had previously been matters of individual pleasure and pride now became patriotic issues central to the war effort."[25] The wartime embrace of feminine glamour offered a reassuring vision of social continuity: even as women engaged in men's work, they still looked—and acted—like women. Although in small doses patriotic sexuality reaffirmed traditional gender roles, it could also be a destabilizing force. First, it raised the specter of sexual deviance: "good time girls" who expressed their sexuality too freely could be accused of selfishness, immorality, and "amateur prostitution"—which undermined the war effort. Second, it coexisted uneasily with what Rose called "maternal femininity," which celebrated women's roles as caring mothers, faithful wives, and the embodiment of family, home, and nation.[26] One of the most striking accomplishments of the EEU's women broadcasters was their ability to balance patriotic sexuality with respectable, "maternal" femininity, combining glamorous "sex appeal" with cheery hominess.

The "radio girl friends" became emblems of Madden's innovative programming for the troops. Following the early broadcasts to Gibraltar, commèred by Joan Gilbert, who became known as the "Sweetheart of the Rock," the EEU produced several messages programs that promoted relationships between women broadcasters and forces stationed around the Mediterranean. Many featured popular vocalists: most famously, Anne Shelton sang in the long-running *Calling the British Forces in Malta*; Villiers sang in *A Date for the Desert*, which was directed to the Eighth and First Armies in North Africa; and Beryl Davis sang in *Appointment with Beryl* for the Ninth Army in the Middle East. The labor of building such personas continued off the air. Madden recalled:

> All the girls took a tremendous amount of trouble to answer those airgraphs and letters, with photos, and they soon became the most popular characters in the respective armies, far more so than the variety stars the Forces left behind them, who could not make the same positive contact on the air.[27]

Musical performance played a critical role in building a link between the "croonettes," as they were sometimes called, and their forces audiences. All were masters of the microphone, the nuances the technology enabled, and the intimacy it permitted between broadcaster and listener. Indeed, Lynn, who was recognized by 1942 as the most popular female singer with the forces overseas, never sang in a messages program (*Sincerely Yours*, which was structured in the form of a letter, aired only on the domestic Forces Programme); instead, from September 1940, she sang regularly in *Starlight*, which offered "an imaginative picture of a star in an intimate setting," accompanied only by a pianist. During the fifteen-minute program, Lynn sang five or six numbers, such as "We'll Meet Again" and "Only Forever," framed by her wistful theme song, "Wishing."[28] Her repertory was popular, romantic, and frequently nostalgic; like other EEU singers, her performances, unfolding in real time, enacted the emotions of separation, transforming them into a communal experience for wartime listeners.

While "radio girl friends" appealed to overseas forces, they found far less favor at home when the BBC instituted the General Forces Programme (GFP) in February 1944. The GFP represented an amalgam of the domestic Forces Programme and the General Overseas Service (GOS), which aired the EEU's productions. Representing the BBC's best ideas on broadcasting to fighting men, the GFP featured short, light programs, and it was dominated by the EEU's female announcers, producers, and singers. The BBC promoted the GFP to home audiences as a service that would tie them to their loved ones fighting abroad; however, it was a public relations disaster, with listeners and critics heaping particular abuse on its women announcers and singers. Many of their arguments echoed those advanced during the anticrooner attacks of two years earlier, spurring again a vigorous debate over what music was best for the troops.

By early 1944, the EEU's programs were airing around the globe, and women played a critical role in their production and performance. To address how women singers performed the labor of respectable, patriotic sexuality, this chapter will focus upon the wartime career of Shelton. Although she was young—aged only fifteen—when war was declared, Shelton began broadcasting in *Calling Malta* in July 1941; by 1943, *Gramophone* described her as the best English crooner on the air.[29] This chapter will also consider the backlash on the home front against the GFP and its women singers. Although the GFP was intended to serve as a lifeline between the home front and overseas forces, its early months did far more to highlight the rifts that existed between the military abroad and civilians at home.

"Sing a Song from London": Women Broadcasters, Patriotic Sexuality, and the Overseas Forces

In February 1943, Gilbert, the producer for *Hello Gibraltar*, visited "the Rock," a tiny, strategically important fortress on British territory overlooking the Strait of Gibraltar, the passage between the Mediterranean Sea and the Atlantic Ocean. Gibraltar's forces, who had been following her program for more than two years, greeted her enthusiastically. In her report, Gilbert described the challenges to morale on the Rock: servicemen were homesick for their families and had not enjoyed home leave in years, they longed "for feminine society," and they worried that their wives and sweethearts in Britain had forgotten them. Radio was one of the few sources of entertainment for enlisted men, who listened in barracks, canteens, and "isolated gunsites." Gilbert's findings affirmed the EEU's focus on messages programs and popular entertainment. Messages, even those directed to others, were universally appreciated; according to the officers, "Every man who received a message is a better man for ages afterwards, and spreads content to his fellows in a very definite and traceable manner." Gibraltar's forces overwhelmingly favored dance music, preferring Geraldo's band to Jack Payne's, crooners over straight singers, and female crooners (especially Shelton and Lynn) over male—except for Bing Crosby, who was "in a class by himself." "I came away with the strong impression that apart from a few News bulletins, Ann [*sic*] Shelton and Bing Crosby could more or less fill the entire radio bill between them," wrote Gilbert.[30]

A great deal changed between the first airing of *Hello Gibraltar*, during the winter of 1940–41, and Gilbert's 1943 visit to the garrison—the period of Shelton's career, and the EEU's, that this section will trace. First, the Middle East and Mediterranean went from being outposts far from the action to being a critical theater of war, with the Allies finally on the verge of triumph in North Africa after two years of difficult fighting. Second, as the number of British and Commonwealth troops in North Africa grew, the BBC expanded and improved its service for overseas forces. Following complaints by army authorities, the BBC in 1942 replaced a patchwork of offerings on the BBC's African and Eastern Transmissions with a dedicated service for the forces in North Africa and the Middle East.[31] Finally, Shelton had become a singer who rivaled Crosby and Lynn in popularity, largely as a result of the BBC's efforts to promote her to the forces.[32]

Shelton's first solo disc was released in September 1940 at the start of the London Blitz. *Melody Maker* praised the "blonde, blue-eyed Dulwich girl" for her singing, which was characterized by "self-possession and restraint that [was] extraordinary for one so young." With her distinctively low voice and a warm, lustrous tone, the singer sounded far more mature than her sixteen years. In contrast to other young singers, like Davis in her early recordings with Hatchette's Quintet, Shelton's technique appeared fully formed from her first release, "Fools Rush In."[33] Her rise was fast: she had joined Ambrose's band (where she replaced Lynn, who was embarking upon a solo career) only the previous May, remaining under the bandleader's management as she pursued a solo career.[34] With Davis and Villiers, Shelton led a cohort of teenage singers who under Madden's auspices were to become some of the most popular entertainers with the overseas forces during the war.

Madden worked vigorously during the winter of 1940–41 to expand the EEU's programming. In September, Lynn began to broadcast regularly in *Starlight*; in October *Sandy Calling*, a fortnightly messages program modeled after Macpherson's popular domestic *Sandy's Half-Hour*, began airing for the British forces in Egypt and the Middle East ("the desert outposts will be more Sandy than ever," the *Radio Times* observed); and *Hello Gibraltar*'s debut gained a rapturous reception, as registered by one telegram: "programme smash hit everyone wildly excited suggest extension immediately."[35]

Request programs were exceedingly popular. "It is not minutes of request programmes that we want, but days and weeks running from 1400 hrs to [2000] hrs daily with just breaks for the news," insisted thirteen members of the Royal Army Service Corps in the Middle East Forces.[36] In June 1941, the EEU introduced yet another messages program, *Calling the British Forces in Malta*, which featured Shelton singing requests. Only a few thousand British forces were stationed on the island, but the RAF aircraft based there provided reconnaissance for the Royal Navy and raided Axis supply ships. During the first four months of 1941, the Luftwaffe responded with intense bombing raids aimed at Malta's airfields, dockyards, and urban centers.[37] The attacks eased in May 1941, but between January and May 1942 they became so intense that Malta became "the most heavily bombed place on earth." Meanwhile, the Axis naval blockade, which lasted into 1943, meant that everyone on the island existed upon starvation rations.[38] The long-running *Calling Malta* served an important purpose: not only did it provide a weekly reminder that Malta was not forgotten but the program's messages filled the gaps in mail service caused by the blockade. In September 1942, one soldier wrote to the producer Alick Hayes:

> The weekly programmes to this island ... are still most eagerly awaited, bringing as they do a flood of sunshine into the lives of all of us. You may be interested to know that for some time we have been short of electricity, but that has not stopped us from listening-in; on the contrary, many of us have cycled several miles to listen to Anne, Ronnie, Nat and the Padre on battery radio.[39]

From June 1941 until July 1944, the half-hour program aired every Sunday night; it featured numerous musical selections and requests (not only from Malta) played by the versatile Nat Allen and His Octet, interspersed by a handful of regular features. Compèred by the Cockney comedian Ronald Shiner, who also read the messages, *Calling Malta* featured each week a different "hometown" and included "an effective" two-minute talk by the Reverend D. Bernard Clements (figure 7.2).[40] Between April 1942 and March 1943, it also presented "Home Made Music," which featured amateur

FIGURE 7.2 The cast for *Calling the British Forces in Malta*: (left to right) Alick Hayes, producer; the singer Anne Shelton; the Padre; and Ronnie Shiner, "the genial Cockney compère." (Charles Graves, "BBC Non-stop Variety for Empire Forces and Listeners," *London Calling* [17 February 1942]: 14)

musical performances and personal messages by families of forces serving on the island.[41] The program's three signature tunes furthered its homey, cheery qualities: Allen's band played instrumental versions of "Oranges and Lemons," a nursery song cataloging the church bells around the City of London, and the upbeat classic "Dinah," with Shelton joining in to sing "Let's Start the Show with a Smile."[42]

In May 1941, *Melody Maker* announced that Shelton had "soared to vocal stardom" during her year with Ambrose.[43] "She has personality, a voice and...she can do something much more than mouth numbers at a microphone," it gushed in a review of her appearance with the band at the Finsbury Park Empire.[44] Despite her success, Shelton maintained a wholesome, fun-loving public persona. "Charmingly unassuming, Ann [sic] has never been out alone, and goes everywhere with her brother Bill. Her hobbies are riding, rowing, swimming, and darts, and she has a 'crush' on the Navy," *Melody Maker* wrote.[45] Madden soon identified Shelton as a potential replacement at the EEU for Vera Lynn, who at "any time...might go into a show."[46]

Like Lynn, Shelton possessed a distinctive voice and a respectable, "girl next door" persona; however, she soon distinguished herself as a far more versatile performer. Reflecting the diversity of listener requests, Shelton's repertory in *Calling Malta* ranged from comedy numbers to nineteenth-century parlor songs, such as Henry Bishop's "Home Sweet Home," which she sang near the end of the program. Nevertheless, she did not neglect the sentimental repertory favored by Lynn and a large percentage of the forces. Among the numbers that Shelton performed multiple times in *Calling Malta* were "Only Forever," from the Bing Crosby–Mary Martin film *Rhythm on the River* (1940), which became something of a signature tune for her, and the Latin-style hit "Yours," which was closely associated with Lynn. In *Starlight*, Shelton sang more upbeat hits, like the swing number "Kiss the Boys Goodbye," and older songs, such as "Some of These Days," the signature tune of Sophie Tucker, with whom Shelton was sometimes compared ("but sweeter").[47] Shelton's mastery of sentimental pop and intriguing interpretations of numbers like "St. Louis Blues" reflected the contradictions embodied in her voice, which according to the commercial reviewer for *Melody Maker* "couple[d] the maturity of a woman of 40 (which she certainly isn't) with the freshness of a kid of 17 (which, in fact, she is!)" (sound examples 7.1 and 7.2).[48] ◐

Overseas forces listeners responded enthusiastically to Shelton's singing in *Calling Malta* and *Starlight*. Like critics in Britain, they appreciated her musicianship, but Shelton's unusually low voice, for which Allen's orchestra transposed standard arrangements down a fifth, proved to be a particular asset in shortwave broadcasting, which tended to favor lower instruments and voices.[49] Echoing the program's informal style, a private wrote on behalf of his platoon in Cairo to request a photograph and a song: "Yours is definitely the nicest voice we have ever heard, (We mean that, but don't get bashful)."[50] Other correspondents responded in a manner that demonstrated their sense of intimate, even erotic, connection with the voice of the new "pin-up personality." One captain wrote, "That voice of yours, really, well I can't say what it does to one but everything else goes into the background. Do you look like you sound? If you do you must be delicious."[51]

Shelton's "big following" with "all ranks" materialized quickly, and Hayes responded by increasing her contributions to *Calling Malta*: while early in the program she had sung only a few numbers each week, by early 1942 she was singing six to ten requests. The task of "building up" Shelton as the Forces' Favorite involved more than increasing her presence on the show, however: it was critical to balance Shelton's patriotic sexuality with respectability, given her youth and the BBC's sensibilities. Leaving nothing to chance, Hayes and Madden devoted "a great deal of time, trouble and the Corporation's money" to presenting Shelton "not only as the possessor of a lovely voice, but as a cheerful and cheery personality; in fact, as the sort of pleasant English girl whom a man serving overseas...would be glad to introduce to his wife or mother or sister or girl friend." From October 1941, all of Shelton's fan mail (with her permission) was sent to Listener Research for analysis and then went to Hayes, who wrote the replies, which Shelton signed. Her popularity, the research determined, was based upon her "lovely voice"; "friendly, cheerful personality," as conveyed in her scripted interactions with the comic Shiner; and varied repertory, which avoided oversentimentality.[52]

By early 1943, when C. F. Meehan took over producing *Calling Malta*, Shelton was its indisputable star. Meehan made several changes that transformed the homey program into a slicker, more up-to-date show: he discontinued the Padre's talk; replaced Shiner with a "hostess," Avis Scutt, one of the ubiquitous girl announcers of the EEU; changed the signature tune from the nostalgic "Oranges and Lemons" to an up-to-date Carmen Miranda number, "Brazilly Willy"; and replaced the "Home Made Music" segment with a celebrity guest feature. Two surviving scripts from 1944 demonstrate a greater emphasis on music: while the scripts conveyed a cheerful familiarity ("hello boys") on the part of Shelton and Scutt, they used an economy of words to introduce songs and give dedications.[53] *Calling Malta*'s musical formula remained consistent throughout its run: the requests were eclectic, Shelton remained as star singer, and Allen's outstanding

Octet continued to anchor the show. When Shelton and her management decided to leave the program in July 1944, she was so closely associated with it that, rather than continue the program with a new singer, the BBC canceled *Calling Malta* and replaced it with *Anne to You*, a big-budget show, featuring Shelton accompanied by Allen and a twenty-one-piece orchestra.[54] "'Calling Malta' [was] regarded by troops overseas as virtually an Anne Shelton show," Hayes explained.[55]

In April 1942, when Malta was enduring its heaviest air raids and with serious setbacks in the Desert War, Shelton appeared, posed glamorously at a BBC microphone, on the cover of *Parade*.[56] Amid serious concerns about the war's progress, the BBC promoted the morale-boosting work of the EEU's women announcers and singers, of which Shelton's *Parade* cover was only one component. For home audiences, the publicity praised the "girl friends'" role in extending a comforting "life-line" from home to the troops overseas. For the forces, it emphasized the pinup personalities' interest in their overseas listeners, with pictures of the women reading fan mail, and celebrated the availability of a full evening (7:30 p.m. to midnight) of BBC programming.[57] Despite the publicity claims, a report, which circulated in May through the BBC's Overseas Service, warned that BBC programs were "having an adverse effect on the morale of the troops." While at home critics accused the BBC of pandering to the troops with "flabby," lowest-common-denominator entertainment, the "Mid East Army authorities" complained that "there [wa]s too little Light Music and entertainment in the programmes," causing the troops to turn to "enemy stations" instead.[58]

A letter sent in June from an RAF squadron leader in the Western Desert gave more specific form to the threat: "our boys throughout the desert" were listening "nightly" to a thirty-minute program for the Afrikakorps, which opened with "a woman known to the troops as 'Marlene' singing a catchy little number" that was repeated "once or twice" more in the show.[59] The song was "Lili Marleen," and the singer was Lale Andersen, who had recorded Norbert Schultze's marchlike setting of Hans Leip's World War I text in August 1939. When the Nazis began broadcasting from Radio Belgrade, a high-power station that could be heard in North Africa and through much of Europe, Andersen's recording was one of the few available, and, with its bugle call introduction, it had struck the station director as excellent "close-down music." It soon "became a fixture on Radio Belgrade at 9.55 p.m.—the last record of the night." From late 1941, the song could be heard thirty times daily on German-controlled stations.[60]

Both the song and the singer fascinated British troops. A captain explained, "Perhaps you have not been away from the sound of a woman's voice for a year; for this voice was at once seductive and soothing, husky, intimate but mysteriously unattainable." The experience of listening to Andersen inspired for British troops a sense of connection to the singer; however, unlike the BBC's radio girl friends, her singing was inflected by the frisson of the exotic: "She put it over in a way we hadn't heard before with an accent lovably un-English."[61] Although the broadcasts seemed to have "little propaganda value" at the moment, they reinforced a sense of community, not only among British listeners but also with the Germans: "This broadcast...will possibly create a feeling that Germans who can produce such good music, etc. cannot be such bad chaps after all," the squadron leader wrote. He linked the song's role in humanizing the enemy with stories that the Germans treated their captives well: both encouraged surrender, a significant fear given Singapore's recent fall.[62]

The BBC responded with alacrity to the criticisms of its service by military authorities in the Middle East, taking comprehensive steps to render its programs more appealing and accessible to overseas troops. On June 14, 1942, the BBC introduced "a continuous programme of music or entertainment" especially for the Middle Eastern forces that ran each evening from 7:30 to 10:00 p.m. on a dedicated wavelength (forces programming also continued on the African Transmission). In addition to messages programs, listeners could hear big-name variety and dance band "production" shows, including *Henry Hall's Guest Night*, *Tommy Handley's Half Hour*, and *Anzac Hour* with Geraldo's full concert orchestra and his battery of singers (including Davis and Villiers).[63] Over the next year, the BBC continued to expand the service, improve its continuity (although wartime demands on transmitters meant that it still moved between different wavelengths), and develop appealing content. By the summer of 1943, the GOS, as it came to be called, was extended to include India, expanded to twelve hours daily, and acquired a mandate as an English-only service aimed primarily at the forces, distinguishing it from other regional overseas transmissions.[64] Charged with filling the service's expanding hours with programs that would keep forces overseas tuned in to the BBC rather than enemy stations while contending with wartime budgetary constraints, Madden declared, "We are giving the boys the best material we can, and what the boys ask for they will have—if we can get it for them."[65]

Madden and other BBC staff also worked to combat the lure of "Lili Marleen" more directly. During July 1942, a few weeks after the BBC's first round of improvements to its service for overseas troops, the squadron leader's letter circulated among the BBC staff. In the wake of Tobruk's disastrous fall to the Afrikakorps, they gave serious consideration to his suggestion that the BBC air a program that could compete directly with the Germans' broadcast. Their deliberations gained further urgency in August when the BBC Monitoring Service reported that Nazi stations had begun broadcasting an English version of the song—most likely an adaptation by the British defector Norman Baille-Stewart, which Andersen had recorded in June. Although its text was innocuous, the English-language "Lili Marlene" signaled that British forces had entered the sights of Nazi radio propaganda; the intelligence was forwarded up to the director-general's office.[66] With his "radio girl friends" formula well established, Madden had strong opinions about how best to respond:

> If you really want to counteract the Marlene idea for sex-starved troops, give us a time every day at the same time and let us put on a Glamour programme with say Four girls, with plenty of songs and kidding (well written scripts), say a Blonde, a Brunette, and a Redhead—and an American girl too, for the USA troops in the Middle East. Plenty of songs, Records, all sorts of changes. How's about it?[67]

However the performers' hair color would have been transmitted over radio, it was clear that Madden identified patriotic sexuality, fun, and feminine intimacy as the best way to woo British forces back to the BBC and away from the temptations of Andersen's voice.

Madden's brainstorm was pared down considerably by the time that *Introducing Anne* debuted on the evening of Sunday, October 4, 1942. Given her popularity with troops around the Mediterranean, Shelton was the obvious choice for the program. Featuring the singer in an intimate, solo presentation echoed the format of *Sincerely Yours*, and the live, carefully produced program represented a direct, yet characteristically BBC, answer to the Nazi's repetition of Andersen's recording. The program aired simultaneously over the Forces Programme and the Overseas Service, creating a real-time link between listeners at home and abroad. Because it aired domestically, *Introducing Anne* fell under Variety Department auspices, rather than Madden's EEU, and one of Variety's staff, David Miller, produced it. Miller was a clear choice for the job: he was one of the best-known dance music producers, with credits including Victor Silvester's *BBC Dancing Club*, and he had worked with Shelton before.

Miller failed to consult with Hayes, Shelton's producer in *Calling Malta*, however, and Shelton's persona in *Introducing Anne* contrasted strikingly with what Madden called her "natural tomboy personality" in the Malta show.[68] She sang more current pop songs, and her repertory, although tempered by comedy numbers, was more sentimental. The most striking contrast was that Shelton read all of the script's continuity talk. Hayes was dismayed by the changes that Miller had wrought: "I cannot but feel that fifteen months' hard work looks like being wrecked....Anne Shelton was represented speaking platitudinous sentimentalese with a pseudo American accent. Her voice was as good as ever, but I feel the choice of songs was rather over sentimental."[69] Indeed, Miller's early scripts did tend to garrulousness, as when "Anne" observed in one tortured transition from the sentimental hit "Only You" to Raymond Scott's comic "Huckleberry Duck":

> You know, planning a little programme like this isn't so easy as it might seem. I feel that one wants a little of everything and perhaps a little more of some things than others—but what are the things we want a little more of? Well, I just wouldn't be sure, but I *am* sure that we can always do with a little real light-heartedness.[70]

Not only did the script lack a "motive," according to "Detector," but Shelton was not as effective in her delivery as Lynn in *Sincerely Yours*, "to which 'Introducing Anne' is an obvious sequel."[71] For Madden, the problem went deeper: Shelton was being cast as "another Vera Lynn" rather than building upon her cheery Malta persona.[72] The EEU had striven to present singers like Shelton to the overseas forces by emphasizing an atmosphere of friendliness, reassurance, and respectable sex appeal while limiting sentimentality; Miller's production ignored that work.

The script for *Introducing Anne* may have been weak, but its music was another matter. In increasingly enthusiastic reviews, "Detector" heaped praises upon Shelton as a singer and upon Stanley Black, who arranged the program's music and led its band, the Ambrose Players. The thirteen-piece ensemble included several respected jazz players, including Carl Barriteau in the reed section and Tom Bromley on bass.[73] After the November 1 broadcast, "Detector" raved, "Programme reached its supreme moment in the swing version of...'After You've Gone.' Brilliant solos just tumbled over one another in a riot of swing at its best. And as for Anne...well, she always is at her best in numbers of this calibre."[74] It was likely that Black arranged the program's signature tune, a "heavily and ornately orchestrated" version of "Lili Marlene," which "listeners would not be likely to recognize...distinctly and instantly as the German song."[75] Although numerous accounts have since stated that Shelton sang the song in *Introducing Anne*, the BBC's Programmes as Broadcast logs indicate clearly that she did not sing the signature tune; indeed, Tommie Connor's English-language version of the song, of which Shelton recorded a famous version in May 1944, was not yet written.[76] Howgill recommended a rather disingenuous response to queries about the signature tune: "Lili Marlene" was "being used deliberately because of its popularity with British troops in the Middle East," but the BBC possessed no copies of the lyrics or "gramophone records" of the song, although an English version was due to be published.[77] Certainly, the BBC could have arranged for Shelton to sing a version of the song if it had judged it appropriate. Instead, the decision to use a disguised instrumental version helped maintain the distinction between Shelton's wholesome, English "pin-up personality" and the mysterious temptress of the Nazi wavelengths.

Introducing Anne was much more of an introduction for home audiences than it was for overseas listeners. Its listenership did not have the exceptional numbers of *Sincerely Yours*, averaging instead around 12 percent. This was respectable for 9:40 p.m. on a Sunday night, and the BBC extended the program from six weeks to twelve.[78] Since BBC Listener Research did not have the same ability to survey the forces about their opinions, determining the size of its overseas forces audience was far more difficult—and understanding how it competed with the Germans' "Lili Marlene" was nearly impossible.

Although he lacked a comprehensive opinion survey, such as that employed domestically, Madden did make careful use of the information he did have: 1,200 letters a week from overseas forces that were filled with requests, suggestions, and avowals of fandom; 400 observers in the forces; and "guinea-pig panels" (i.e., focus groups) based in Cairo.[79] This material convinced Madden of the forces' continued appetite for dance music and women broadcasters. The EEU continued to introduce new messages programs: in December 1942, for example, Villiers debuted in *A Date for the Desert*, which was aimed at the now triumphant British Eighth Army as it pushed Rommel's forces out of Libya.[80] Home listeners who preferred dance music and variety envied such programming: "Good BBC Programmes? There *Are* Such Things! But Home Listeners NeverHear Them!" "Detector" declared.[81]

Madden staunchly promoted light entertainment for the troops, but he also recognized that such material had to be presented carefully. In late 1943, he warned EEU producers against insinuating that women at home were romantically involved with Allied troops; referring to leave, "which some men have not had for 9 or 10 years";

suggesting that people at home were "having a very gay time"; using racist language; or purveying "too much nostalgic sentiment."[82] The EEU's programs represented a lifeline, connecting troops overseas to Britain, but it was designed to filter out aspects of life on the home front that could harm morale. Performers like Shelton balanced the casual appeal of patriotic sexuality with respectability, but more important, they played a critical role as reassuring, feminine intermediaries between the overseas forces and the homeland. This approach continued to function effectively in the EEU's programming throughout 1943; however, the strength of the imaginary community forged by its lifeline would be tested with the introduction of the GFP in early 1944.

"Bridging the Distance": The General Forces Programme, Radio Girl Friends, and the Home Front

On February 27, 1944, the GFP went on the air. It incorporated programs from the domestically popular Forces Programme into the GOS to form a single service that would unite families at home with the forces abroad through the shared experience of listening. "It reduces the sharpness of separation; it is almost a telephone line from every home in Britain to every man abroad," claimed the *Sunday Dispatch*.[83] To introduce the GFP, the *Radio Times* described the letter that a signaler in the Central Mediterranean Force had sent to a BBC messages programme. Requesting " 'Every Night About This Time' for a girl called Joan in Croydon," he had concluded, "I hope I'm lucky enough to be listening when you do." "Why has the BBC decided that . . . its service for the troops overseas shall become the alternative programme in this country? Why, in the fifth year of war, make such a drastic change that will affect the habits of every home listener?" the *Radio Times* asked. "The reason is to be found in that letter. And it is the only reason. The BBC gets a great many letters of the kind. . . . through [them] all . . . there is a constant note, a common wish. It is to share their listening with the folks at home."[84]

The *Radio Times*, of course, was being somewhat disingenuous. According to Briggs, "The reduction of BBC general programmes from three to two liberated studio space and saved money"—an important consideration for an organization whose resources had been stretched in wartime and which anticipated no increase in income until after the war's conclusion.[85] Nevertheless, in its publicity the BBC emphasized the notion that the GFP would nurture a "spiritual link" between home and overseas forces. Reflecting upon a press conference at Broadcasting House, "Detector" observed, "Everyone present . . . seemed willing not only to give the BBC credit for honesty of motive, but at least to allow its new venture time to be thoroughly tested out.[86]

The press managed to withhold judgment on the GFP until March 7, when Earl Winterton, MP, raised the question in Parliament, "Are female crooners really necessary in the General Forces Programme of the BBC?" Impugning their benefit to forces' morale, he compared the singing of women crooners to "the caterwauling of an inebriated cockatoo."[87] Winterton's vivid words triggered a wave of criticism of the new program. Although Madden had built the EEU's entertainment policy for nearly three years upon the premise that women singers and announcers were uniquely equipped to boost the morale of overseas troops, they proved anathema to a vocal segment of the home audience. The controversy over women crooners on the GFP revived the debates about demoralizing sentimentality on the Forces Programme, which had raged two years earlier. This time, however, the wishes of the forces—and the sound of their request programs—remained at the center of the discussion: "Listen to the records demanded of the BBC by the Forces," the *Observer* instructed. "Slush...is shown to be as popular in the camp as ice-cream at the seaside. To cut crooning right out might be a mingling of Attic good taste with Spartan resolution. It would not be democratic."[88] Although the BBC had introduced the GFP as an instrument of national unity, the March 1944 debates about its radio girl friends demonstrated instead just how divided opinions were about wartime gender roles and how difficult it was to "bridge the distance" between differences of class, age, and musical taste. The People's War values of tolerance and shared sacrifice existed in tension with the democratic ideal of vigorous debate.

Hired by the BBC on September 1, 1943, W. J. Haley, the BBC's visionary new editor-in-chief, was to provide oversight for its entire output, taking on the role that Graves had played as joint director-general with Foot.[89] After a visit to the Italian front, Haley concluded that enabling the troops to hear the same programming as their families and friends in Britain would be a tremendous boost to morale. In December, he proposed that the Forces Programme be relayed to Italy, but by January he determined with Foot and the controller of engineering Sir Noel Ashbridge to replace the Forces Programme with the GOS instead. There would still be a link, but the overseas, not the domestic, service would be the unifying medium. The link was critical not only for troops already overseas but for those who would participate in the western European invasion, which Foot believed (correctly) to be imminent: the transition needed to be made quickly.[90]

From the first leaks about the new service in early January, the notion that the GFP would provide "a strong link between home and the boys" remained a key theme in the Corporation's publicity about the new program and in the generally receptive press.[91] *Melody Maker* praised the idea as the BBC's "brightest and most human idea...since goodness knows when," and Listener Research found that on the eve of the new service, a third of listeners favored change, a majority reserved judgment or were indifferent, and only 4 percent opposed it.[92] Given the popularity and familiarity of the Forces Programme, the public was strikingly receptive to change.

Much of the coverage focused upon the question of how the switch would affect listeners at home. Describing the "new" programming, Ernest Betts of the *Daily Express* portrayed an exotic world where "from 'dark' theatres in London's West End Arthur Askey, Anne Shelton...and Jack Payne have been transmitting secret sessions of entertainment to millions of men and women in the Forces throughout the Middle East" and an "Overseas programme, run by a handful of girls who have proved themselves expert in understanding what the soldier wants from his loudspeaker."[93] The press alerted listeners that they should expect frequent news bulletins and several new shows, including *Calling Malta* and *Hello Gibraltar*.[94] *Melody Maker* welcomed the changes as "stimulating to listeners, who have found the Forces programmes tending to get into a rut," but the syndicated radio critic Ronald Strode warned, "Many new features, strange…announcers, and new times for…familiar broadcasts will puzzle and intrigue listeners for a time. However, when the novelty wears off, I am afraid many home listeners will wish they could have the old Forces programme back again." In particular, Strode and others worried about the profusion of messages programs. Although in her visit to Gibraltar, Gilbert had noted the widespread appreciation of messages, even among those who were not the recipients, Strode doubted that nonrecipients would find much appeal in such programs.[95] Civilian concerns were ultimately irrelevant to a service designed specifically for the troops, however. "Will I like the changes?—That, madame and sir, is not the point. The programmes are designed to please tired, news-thirsty men in remote, hot, shell-scarred corners of the globe. Tastes of the Home listener don't count," wrote Jonah Barrington in the *Sunday Chronicle*.[96] With their opinions pointedly ignored, the question of whether the prospect of a "spiritual link" would be enough to win civilians over to the new service remained to be seen.

The early response when the GFP commenced airing on February 27 was muted. "I experienced no thrill from the big change-over," Betts wrote.[97] The *News Chronicle* described a generally positive response to the GFP's frequent news bulletins while its radio critic observed that *Calling Malta*, *Palestine Half-Hour*, and *Variety Band Box*, some of the request programs that had worried Strode, "were like most BBC variety shows apart from the messages which punctuated them."[98] By the end of the first week, Listener Research noted that 25 percent of listeners considered the GFP a poorer program than the Forces, but 56 percent believed it to be "as good as, if not better than, the Forces Programme."[99]

One of the most striking characteristics of the new service for home listeners was that it had "far more women announcers."[100] Women already played an important role in the Home and Forces Variety pool, but the GFP featured both women newsreaders and variety commères; moreover, in early March it halted the practice of bandleaders announcing their own broadcasts, replacing them by "women staff announcers."[101] There existed a tradition of criticizing women announcers, but their greater presence in the GFP sharpened the attacks. Women announcers were criticized as thin-voiced, patronizing, and insipid. Such comments invited a speedy defense: radio microphones were improperly modulated for higher voices, women spoke more clearly than men, and broad dismissals of women on air were misogynistic.[102] The most common arguments in favor of women announcers on the GFP cast them as normatively feminine, supporting men rather than replacing them: "There is a warmth in their voices, friendliness and anxiety to please, a note of sympathy.… I do not doubt that our soldiers, sailors and airmen, wherever they may be, will be cheered and strengthened by the voices of these women from home."[103] Recalling Madden's reason for using women in the first place—and the raison d'être for the GFP—women announcers, for many, belonged on the service because the forces wanted them there.

While women announcers were widely perceived as engaging in nontraditional war work, women crooners were far more normative: there was a long history of women singers in popular entertainment, and singing was regarded as a naturalized, feminized vocation. The difficulty was that crooning and sentimental popular song had been the object of official scrutiny at the BBC since 1942. Although it was an "insincere *and* over-sentimental style" (italics added) of singing by women that was banned, and Madden had worked to feature "bright girls" and limit nostalgic repertory in EEU programs, the unstable definitions of sentimentality, crooning, and slush—not to mention the ways they infused popular tastes and performance practice—made regulation difficult and second-guessing by the public commonplace.[104]

Winterton's March 7 question in Parliament about the necessity of having women crooners on the GFP drew upon familiar tropes about forces' morale, women's roles, and sentimental entertainment to create a scapegoat for the domestic audience's growing displeasure with the new service:

> They resemble no known American accent, and remind one of the caterwauling of an inebriated cockatoo. I cannot believe that all this wailing about lost babies can possibly have a good effect on the troops who are about to engage in a very serious pursuit in which their lives will be endangered.[105]

A week later, Winterton further explained his position in the *Evening Standard*. First, he opposed crooning on the grounds that it lowered standards. In a veiled gibe at Lynn, a born Cockney, he explained that, although he liked American accents and "adore[d] the genuine Cockney," the striving, "'refaned' Cockney" of the West End was repugnant and unsuited to the airwaves. Crooning's worst fault, however, was that its sentimental repertory, which dealt with "'canoodling—domestic canoodling if you like, but still canoodling," distracted the forces from "their grim task." Directly contradicting the central aim of the GFP, Winterton argued that the troops had to "forget ... domestic ties. They are out to kill or be killed. [War] is a tough, horrible, but necessary business."[106]

"Such rhetoric was too good 'copy' to be missed by the Press in general," "Detector" observed. The *Daily Express*, *Daily Telegraph*, and *Evening Standard* all covered the story extensively, and the BBC's press clippings files preserved thirty-six articles, letters, and opinion pieces that were published by newspapers around Britain during the two weeks that followed.[107] Although the earl revived much of the language that had been used to criticize crooners on the Forces Programme in 1942, the ensuing debate of March 1944 differed in two significant ways. First, although Winterton asserted that his "fan mail" following his speech had been overwhelmingly supportive of his position, nearly a third more of the press materials preserved by the BBC opposed his position than supported it.[108] This was especially noteworthy, given that in 1942, few had voiced their support for crooning until the BBC ban had been in effect for several weeks. Second, rather than focusing on the proscriptive questions of what music the troops *should* hear, both sides of the 1944 debate focused upon what they actually *wanted* to hear.

The most common argument advanced in favor of women crooners on the GFP was that they were what the troops wanted. When approached for comment, both Lynn and Shelton cited their voluminous mailbags as evidence of their popularity with the forces. "We have received 97 letters from Malta to-day. They prove that the boys are very grateful for the programmes," said Shelton's mother.[109] A handful of those who agreed with Winterton asserted that such a sampling method was flawed. "My own idea is that there are many...hundred thousands of members of the Forces who agree with Lord Winterton, but who do not write letters to the ladies mentioned," wrote one correspondent to the *Yorkshire Evening News*.[110] This was, however, a minority contention; most writers who participated in the March debate regarded anecdotal evidence and the composition of the GFP's request programs as adequate proof of the forces' tastes—as when George Stagg reported that the week's top requests for the gramophone program *Forces Favourites* were Crosby's "If I Had My Way," Lynn's "Kiss Me," and Shelton's "You'll Never Know."[111] The debate's primary focus upon the forces' wishes demonstrated how successful the BBC had been in convincing the public that the GFP belonged to the troops. As the radio critic Collie Knox wrote, "Lord Winterton...can refer to crooners as 'inebriated cockatoos' till his noble Lordship is puce with indignation. The Forces demand the crooners, and the croonerettes, and they like the songs they sing and the peculiar way they sing them....it is not for us at home to reason why."[112]

With the justification for crooning on the GFP resting upon popular opinion in the forces, fewer arguments were advanced that the GFP's "croonerettes" were inherently beneficial—or detrimental—to morale. More frequently, writers claimed that crooning had no effect whatsoever upon morale. "Isn't it a fact that our nation is noted for its splendid morale, and women crooners have been in vogue for some years now?" asked six sergeants.[113] Several writers illustrated the point by offering dramatic juxtapositions between the forces' valor and their slushy musical tastes. "Libya, Tripolitania and Tunisia were conquered to the tunes of lugubrious melodies, songs about babies bereft, mournful mammas, and other miseries," wrote H. W. Seaman in the *Sunday Chronicle and Sunday Referee*.[114] Seaman's claim represented a striking reversal of the contention, which had been commonplace two years earlier, that there was a causal link between sentimental songs and defeatism: clearly, arguments that crooning demoralized the troops were less convincing when they were victorious.

Nevertheless, opposition to the new service grew during the month. On March 27, BBC Listener Research reported "a very pronounced hardening of civilian opinion against the new policy." In three weeks, there had been a slight increase in the percentage of those surveyed who thought the GFP was worse than the Forces Programme and an equivalent reversal in those who thought it better; more significantly, nearly half of the public thought the BBC had made a mistake by replacing the Forces with the GFP.[115] The *Evening Chronicle* asserted that the BBC had made a "psychological mistake" in warning civilians that their opinions were superfluous while others questioned the fairness of the Corporation ignoring the desires of license-paying civilians.[116] Both for those who objected specifically to crooning and for those who protested the new service in more general terms, Winterton's vivid imagery of caterwauling cockatoos represented a service they perceived as noisy, unruly, and distressingly modern. Although, as will be discussed in chapter 8, the GFP significantly reduced its dance music output, many older listeners perceived the service as being dominated by swing, in addition to slush.[117]

BBC Listener Research soon determined that much of the public's frustration with the GFP was rooted in its short programs and frequent announcements, which disrupted the domestic tap listening habits that the Forces Programme had rewarded.[118] Many regular listeners to the Forces had come to expect "a continuous succession of cheerful programmes"; they left their sets permanently tuned to the wavelength, using it "mostly as a background to other activities."[119] Such listeners found the GFP to be "restless" and "profoundly unsatisfying...perpetually interrupted by changes of programme, station identification, and the like."[120] Indeed, some of the most stinging critiques of the GFP came from listeners who had "all day to listen."[121] Fortunately, the Home Service and its sustained format remained in place; listeners frustrated with the GFP turned to it to such an extent that its listenership, which had once lagged behind the Forces, soon outpaced that of the GFP.[122] The forces were far more receptive to the new service, however. A sailor explained, "We in the Forces can snatch only a few minutes' listening here and there. What seems like a jumble of bells and time signals to a continuous listener is a series of entertaining interludes to us."[123] Background listening in a domestic setting differed significantly from distracted listening in a crowded canteen.[124]

In the spring of 1944, the press pronounced the new service a "flop." Throughout the following year, however, the GFP's approval figures crept up until Listener Research reported in July 1945 that the public had come at last to regard GFP "with as much favour as the original Forces Programme."[125] That same month, the GFP ceased broadcasting domestically; it was replaced by the postwar Light Programme, with the GFP's director Norman Collins at the helm. As Collins insisted, the GFP was "radio in battledress": it was a wartime service that prioritized the needs of forces listeners, whose greatest desire was to remain in touch with their homes.[126] In this regard it succeeded. "Do you think," wrote a sergeant, "that [the lads] would switch off a show that comes all the way from the heart of the Empire?"[127]

Although some civilian listeners continued to complain, women singers and announcers remained a critical presence on the GFP throughout its life. Indeed, in the fall of 1944, the GFP introduced two new programs, starring Lynn and Shelton. *Thirty Minutes of Music in the Vera Lynn Manner* was Lynn's first lengthy series in a year while *Anne to You* filled the gap left by the cancellation of *Calling Malta*.[128] The features were significant for two reasons. First, they represented the BBC's commitment to pleasing the troops—and its willingness to regard them as a special audience that deserved service, an inclination that would bear fruit after the war. Second, the big budget shows featuring Lynn and Shelton signified the important role that the BBC continued to accord to women broadcasters. They projected the values of home and family to the forces overseas and even, in an environment of total war, to listeners on the home front. While the technology, the mass medium, and the professionalism were new, the impulse was not. As Seaman argued, "It is only for the last hundred years or so that the troops have been denied that sweet inspiration [of wives and sweethearts]. Now the BBC restores it, or as much of it as can be filtered through the ether."[129]

Conclusion

In the 1943 film *Rhythm Serenade*, Lynn played a role that drew upon her public persona during the war—that of a cheerful, ordinary "girl," Ann Martin, who contributes enthusiastically to the war effort and who possesses a distinctive, deeply moving voice. Ann falls in love with John, a navy radio operator who is suffering from what would now be labeled post-traumatic stress disorder and who carries a torch for the singer whose voice he encountered while enduring an air raid with a group of recently debarked survivors from a failed commando mission (his eyes were bandaged). Not realizing that Ann and the singer are the same, he confesses that he has idealized the singer, for when she sang, "one felt somehow as if fear could never touch us"; he accepts a new commission with the Merchant Navy before Ann can confess her identity. In the penultimate scene, John, whose oil tanker has been hit, wakes up at his desk, where he fell asleep after a night spent sending out a distress signal, and tunes in to the BBC. "This is London calling," he hears, followed by a familiar voice singing and giving an encouraging message to the forces, Merchant Navy, and war workers. Even before rescuers arrive, he smiles at the reassuring voice and at the realization that his idealized voice and beloved are the same.[130]

The powerful imagery of women's voices over the radio binding those serving overseas to the homeland was grounded in the experience of many. In her report on Gibraltar, Gilbert described the camaraderie messages could inspire: "If a man from Yorkshire gets a message, every other Yorkshireman shares in the feeling of 'a little bit of Yorkshire' on the air and feels at home."[131] Like the EEU's women producers, announcers, and singers, the "ordinary" women who delivered their messages negotiated the wartime expectations that they envoice a sense of home and connection while remaining silent about the difficulties of their daily lives. The litany of greetings on the GFP may have annoyed their critics, but they also registered the commonality of the wartime experiences of separation and longing.

While they embodied the maternal values of home and family, the EEU's "pin-up personalities" also cultivated an extra layer of glamour, reassurance, and sex appeal. Madden aimed to represent women doing men's jobs, but the performance of femininity that they offered to the troops involved a heavy dose of fantasy. Not everyone approved. One correspondent to the *Daily Telegraph* wrote, "Might one inquire what class of English womanhood the appalling songs which the 'Moaning Minnies' wail on the wireless are supposed to be written about? They certainly do not represent the busy and efficient housewife and mother, the smart ATS, Wren or Waaf, or the munition or canteen worker."[132] The regard for singing as an instinctive activity and the radio girl friends' cultivation of approachable glamour obscured their very real labor, both as professional broadcasters and entertainers and as women in the public sphere who had to negotiate the "complex border zone" of wartime femininity, sexuality, and citizenship.[133]

Aided by the airwaves, performers like Lynn and Shelton were masters at balancing the codes of patriotic sexuality and cheerful respectability. They also became some of the most iconic musicians of the war, embodying the values of the People's War.

Although Lynn and Shelton soared to the top of their profession, they remained in all their publicity (and, one suspects, in actuality) true to their families and grounded in the working- and middle-class milieus in which they grew up. As such, they were ideal broadcasters for a service intended to please other ranks as much as officers, not to mention the working class and youth who tended to favor the GFP. Winterton might have deplored the "refaned" Cockney, but as Lynn observed, "millions of Cockneys are fighting for us."[134] Although those opposed to crooning cast their singing as "doping our young people" and threatening the survival of "an intelligent electorate" for the postwar future, Lynn, Shelton, and the other croonerettes of the GFP "did their bit," according to Madden, "they were friendly, they had sex appeal, they filled a need."[135] In addition, they subtly gave voice to the differences of gender, class, and age that underlay the People's War ideologies of unitary national identity.[136]

8

"INVASION YEAR": AMERICANS IN BRITAIN,

AMERICANIZATION, AND THE DANCE MUSIC BACKLASH

ON AUGUST 27, 1944, two days after he had arrived in the United Kingdom and as V-1 flying bombs buzzed overhead, Bing Crosby participated in a taping of *Variety Band Box* at the Queensberry All-Service Club before a capacity audience of 4,900 people (figure 8.1).[1] Following its usual format, the show featured a range of British talent requested by the forces overseas, but the biggest star was Crosby, a last-minute addition.[2] Ray Sonin, *Melody Maker*'s editor, described the thrill of seeing the iconic American at first hand: "There he was...the one and only Bing Crosby....He bounded on to the stage, beaming, and stood there while the biggest reception ever accorded an artist in my memory thundered through the vast hall." Crosby sang "San Fernando Valley," "Long Ago and Far Away," and the audience request "Moonlight Becomes You." Sonin reflected on Crosby's universal appeal as an "amazingly relaxed...natural good guy": "Men and girls [*sic*] alike were completely captivated by him. Tough Commandos and burly sergeant-majors were among those who yelled out for him to sing 'White Christmas,' not hysterical girls."[3]

After the taping, Crosby returned to the stage for another half hour to sing, banter with the American comedian Joe DeRita, and—thanks to a brainwave of Cecil Madden, the show's producer—sing a duet with Anne Shelton. Crosby had never heard her sing, and, Sonin suggested, he was "startled" by the gusto of her reception. After she sang "I'll Get By," she "gagged around with Bing as if she'd been doing it all her life" (DeRita had "put her wise to certain standard gags"), and then Crosby invited Shelton to join him in a duet. In the recorded performance of Irving Berlin's "Easter Parade," Crosby improvised an accompaniment to Shelton in a manner assertive enough to have distracted a less assured performer, and when he took the melody, she responded in kind.

FIGURE 8.1 Bing Crosby at a rehearsal for *Variety Band Box* in August 1944. (Joe DeRita sits to the right.) (Copyright © BBC)

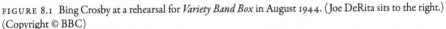

Sonin observed, "Anne didn't let the old country down. Far from it. Her voice blended beautifully with his, she copied his twiddley-bits against the melody, and it was really a terrific performance."[4]

In the months after D-Day, the arrival of American star performers and big-name service bands, particularly Glenn Miller's Army Air Force Band (which represented a significant exception to the Ministry of Labour ban on visiting U.S. bands), was a dream come true for dance music and jazz enthusiasts. British dance musicians availed themselves of every opportunity to learn from their transatlantic allies while fans tuned in to hear them on the BBC or, more often, the popular, jointly controlled Allied Expeditionary Forces Programme (AEFP). It was a heady time: the Allies were liberating the Continent, and American stars had arrived in "war-weary and war-torn" Britain "with a breath of peace-time atmosphere." Sonin concluded of Crosby's performance, "That evening did more for transatlantic relationship than a hundred speeches."[5]

While Winston Churchill's formulation of a "special relationship" between the United States and Great Britain in 1944 has influenced both policy and cultural imagination since the Cold War, it was hardly common sense during the Second World War.[6] For much of the war, the Soviet Union was a far more popular ally with the British: in a mid-1942 Gallup poll, 64 percent cited the USSR as their favorite ally while only

24 percent named the United States.[7] Much of the frustration with the United States early in the war was rooted in the perception that it was a wealthy, "self-centered nation" that was more forthcoming with words than with actions. The situation began to change with the beginning of the American lend-lease program, which "constituted about one-fifteenth of all food consumed in Britain in 1941," and the Americans' December 1941 entry into the war.[8] Still, the British remained ambivalent about the United States. Their concerns were rooted both in "an uncomfortable sense of dependence," according to Nicholas, and in a sense of distant kinship that made more apparent "certain defects of character," as Mass-Observation put it.[9]

The BBC had recognized even before the war that the broadcast of entertainment and educational programs could play a critical role in developing good Anglo-American relations. At the most basic level, radio communication spanned the physical distance between the two nations. In addition, radio with its intimate address could represent ordinary people and everyday life in a manner that countered the glamorized, stereotypical depictions of Hollywood film. Once the United States entered the war, the BBC established the Interdivisional Committee on Use of Radio in Anglo-American and Imperial Relations, recognizing that building "understanding and cooperation" between the two nations had become even more critical.[10] While sending British material to the United States would help, the creation of programming that would educate British listeners about "American ideals, the American way of life etc." served a dual purpose: it would combat distrust and ignorance at home, and it would please the Americans, who would then "cooperate to the limit with a constant exchange of publicists, radio material etc."[11]

The January 1942 arrival of the first contingent of 4,058 American troops in Britain increased the urgency of the situation. Anglo-American relations was no longer simply a matter of high policy and public opinion about a distant nation; rather, as the number of GIs stationed in the United Kingdom grew, it involved direct contact between British citizens and an occupying army. Following the model it had established for other visiting troops, the BBC requested and designed a range of American and American-style material to entertain the GIs, many of whom were stationed in isolated camps. While its offerings for Canadian, Indian, and other Commonwealth troops had consisted primarily of news, the most visible contribution from the American networks was popular music and variety, with the advertisements removed. By 1943, the BBC was featuring a significant proportion of American material, both in stand-alone shows and through "programme infiltration," in which programmers inserted "short contributions from across the Atlantic in[to] existing programmes."[12] American content provided a critical infusion of fresh ideas at little cost for a Variety Department suffering from personnel losses, insufficient funding, and creative exhaustion; it was also popular with British forces and many civilians.

The American authorities were not satisfied with the amount of American content available to the GIs over the BBC, however, and they agitated to establish the American Forces Network (AFN) on British soil, an infringement on the BBC's monopoly. Although the BBC strenuously opposed the move, the AFN went on the air in July 1943, in yet another manifestation of the exceptional treatment that the Americans required for their troops.[13] With the approach of 1944, "Invasion Year," the growing presence of American troops, from 279,171 in May 1943 to more than 1.67 million in May 1944, elicited predictable ambivalence from British civilians and forces, which was captured in the familiar phrase "over-paid, over-sexed, over-fed, and over here." British jazz and swing enthusiasts, however, were thrilled to discuss music with the Americans—although *Melody Maker* published numerous anecdotes that showed the average GI to be as ignorant about swing as most Britons. Meanwhile, the AFN's offerings of American variety and swing delighted those within range of the network's low-power transmitters, and the possibilities for developing commercial, American-style radio in postwar Britain became a recurrent theme in the press.

Within the BBC, the July 1943 commencement of the AFN served as a catalyst for those worried about Americanization, which they regarded as a threat to the survival of a distinctly British culture. In 1944, Haley, who in March succeeded Foot as director-general, began to limit American content in variety, but the process had already begun in the case of dance music. During 1943, the Dance Music Policy Committee (DMPC) discouraged popular vocalists from adopting American accents, and later in the year it began to regard the in-house bandleader Geraldo's "American style" approach as unacceptably derivative. Meanwhile, grappling with straitened finances and pointing to Listener Research findings that showed dance music to have decreased in popularity, the BBC Overseas Service moved to cut dance music programming. Against Madden's strenuous objections, the Dance Band Scheme, which, with its long-term house bands contracts, had provided economical, varied dance music to BBC for nearly three years, was shut down.[14] The BBC maintained its contract with Jack Payne, whom it had long characterized as "all-British," but it gave notice to Geraldo in January 1944. In addition to promoting British-style bands, the BBC publicized its efforts to feature more British songs on the air, a challenge, given the dominance of Tin Pan Alley and Hollywood.

Defining what constituted distinctively British dance music in a popular music field dominated by American repertories and styles was a challenge for the BBC, particularly since Geraldo and other bands popular with keen fans actively modeled themselves after the Americans. *Melody Maker*'s "Detector" and other critics vigorously contested the BBC's actions, contending that *good* dance music was still popular and criticizing the leaders, especially Payne and Victor Silvester, whom the Corporation promoted. Meanwhile, the BBC managed to collaborate with the Americans and Canadians in establishing and running the AEFP, a unified radio service for the Allied Expeditionary Forces (AEF). Featuring top American and British stars, the AEFP was popular with forces and civilians alike, and it remained on the air from D-Day until victory in Europe.

The Crosby-Shelton duet symbolized the future that the BBC was trying to avoid. While the British tended to cast the national character of the United States in terms of boisterous, cocky adolescence in contrast to the more grown-up Great Britain, the duet reversed the national roles.[15] The American Crosby was the established star while the British Shelton was the adolescent, feminine sidekick. That Shelton held her own against the old pro, Crosby, was a pleasant surprise, rather than an expectation. Those like Sonin, who had embraced American performers and American-style entertainment, praised Shelton's mastery of Crosby's idiom and celebrated the "transatlantic relationship" embodied in the duet. For those who were suspicious of Americanization, however, the duet represented the hybridization or even eclipse of British common culture; it could also be interpreted as foreshadowing the nations' respective political, economic, and military roles in the postwar world, an uncomfortable prospect for a beleaguered imperial power.

Over Here and on the Air: The AFN, Popular Music, and Americans in Britain before D-Day

"In practically every house which I visited the radio was tuned to the AFN Programme night after night," wrote William Beith to *Melody Maker*, describing his observations while doing "house-to-house" gas mask inspections in a Glasgow neighborhood during the winter of 1943–44. No more than 10 percent of the British population could receive the AFN, but "Detector" claimed that Beith's letter was typical: "Wherever the programme is audible, few listen to anything else."[16] For the British, the AFN represented the best that American radio could offer. The BBC's Maurice Gorham, who worked closely with American military broadcasters, reminisced:

> [It was] the ideal programme for British teen-agers, for...it consisted of all the top ranking band and comedy shows that American commercial radio could supply....The AFN thus brought listeners the best entertainment picked from four competing networks, with millions of advertisers' money behind it but without the advertisers' announcements...[it was] in fact a more or less continuous procession of swing music and gag shows.[17]

While the AFN offered popular American content in concentrated form, the BBC had aired increasing quantities of American variety and popular music since 1941. Many greeted the new shows with enthusiasm, but for others, both within the Corporation and without, the situation highlighted a crisis for British popular culture. "The BBC ideas department seems to have dried up," wrote the *Star*.[18] While the BBC had recognized variety and popular music as critical tools for building cultural understanding, Americanization itself represented a problem, not least because it revitalized discussions of postwar commercial radio. In this environment, lend-lease became a powerful metaphor, with its mingled connotations of cooperation and dependence. Following the establishment of the AFN, the BBC increasingly prioritized the need to equalize, or at least moderate, the flow of cultural influence across the Atlantic. It also worked to ease tensions brought on by the presence of American troops in Britain, one of the most difficult being the perception that, as a Nazi propaganda leaflet put it, "The Yanks are 'lend-leasing' your women."[19]

Two weeks after the arrival of the first food shipment under lend-lease, the BBC commenced broadcasting of *The Jack Benny Show*, which aired fortnightly from June 15, 1941.[20] The program was a canny choice for introducing British listeners to American radio, since Benny was already well known in the United Kingdom.[21] It was also a bargain: while each half-hour show cost $12,000 to produce and air, the BBC paid only £15 per program. The BBC soon added *The Bob Hope Show* and, during a hiatus in the shows between December 1941 and February 1942, aired weekly programs featuring top American swing bands on record, including Benny Goodman, Miller, Duke Ellington, and Artie Shaw.[22] Such programming served as subtle pro-American propaganda, and it was popular; according to BBC Listener Research, "there was a considerable appreciation of, and a desire for more, American variety programmes...and for more American music" among the forces.[23]

While cultivating goodwill toward America among the British remained important, attending to the needs of American GIs became critical as more American troops arrived in Britain. In February 1942, the BBC initiated discussions with the U.S. military about increasing its offerings for American GIs; it began airing *Command Performance* on April 27.[24] Produced by the U.S. War Department for overseas servicemen, *Command Performance* was "the best wartime program in America," according to *Time* magazine; GIs wrote in with their requests, and radio stars fulfilled them, with everyone "including the production staff" donating their time and talent. While some requests were for "bizarre" items, like "the sounds of birds chirping in one soldier's Indiana hometown," many were for musical numbers and performers.[25] The BBC regarded the show's "intelligibility" as "limited," but "Detector" was impressed: "You ought to hear these 'Command Performances.' They're great."[26]

In addition to such "lend-lease" content, the BBC also considered how its own content could please American GIs, who tended to regard its offerings as "lousy."[27] As Laurence Gilliam, the assistant director of features, gamely observed, "Generally speaking an ordinary American does not like British radio. It is going to be a very hard job to make him like it, but the attempt should be well worth making as it might result in the British listener liking British radio!"[28] Jazz programming represented one avenue for promoting Anglo-American goodwill, and *Radio Rhythm Club (RRC)* figured prominently in a list of "programmes likely to be of interest to USA troops in this country."[29] The BBC also featured amateur bands from the American forces. In October 1942, it devoted most of its broadcast from the annual Jazz Jamboree to a Band of the U.S. Army Engineers, and in *Doughboys Entertain* it featured an "American Forces Swing Band" in a remote broadcast from Northern Ireland.[30] Being American did not automatically raise the level of amateur swing performance, however. "Perhaps I expected too much....But even so, faulty intonation and a drummer who didn't even keep time were hardly to be expected from Americans," wrote "Detector" of the latter performance.[31]

Unfortunately, Gilliam's August 1942 statement coincided with the implementation of the BBC's ban on slushy songs and crooners. For the BBC and British elites, sentimentality was an object for censure; however, the Americans embraced it. It was likely no coincidence that the American generals Marshall and Eisenhower began to "vigorously" assert the need for the U.S. Armed Forces Radio Service (AFRS) in Britain during July 1942, the month that the ban was announced.[32] Unsurprisingly, the BBC tried to block governmental approval for AFRS broadcasting in Britain.[33] Not only would American forces radio violate the BBC's monopoly but it would undermine Anglo-American cooperation. "The American Army authorities are anxious to have everything over here of their own...their own food, their own sports kit to play their own games, and so forth....If, now, they have their own broadcasting transmitters, this separatism will be carried a stage further," the BBC's director of Programme Planning Godfrey Adams contended.[34] Indeed, the controversies about the AFRS followed closely upon frictions that had arisen around the American Red Cross (ARC) clubs, which offered troops a combination of hostel, canteen, and recreation facilities. During the latter half of 1942, they restricted access to American GIs and in order to "create a strictly American atmosphere" required the British volunteer staff to wear ARC uniforms—even if they belonged to organizations that already had uniforms.[35] For the BBC, an organization that took seriously its mission to unify the nation and which had tended to serve visiting troops with only a few special programs, the Americans' insistence on a separate network was galling.

Despite the Corporation's objections, the Americans remained firm, and in the spring of 1943 the government approved the service; the AFN commenced broadcast in Britain on July 4, 1943.[36] Its studios were based in London, and a system of low-power transmitters, located at American military bases, relayed its programs throughout the United Kingdom.[37] The BBC managed to save face by emphasizing that much of the AFN's content would consist of BBC programs that simply needed to be rebroadcast at times more convenient for the American troops.[38] A November 1945 *Band Wagon* article described the AFN's establishment as "a shining example of reverse Lend-Lease": "The BBC early declared itself an ally, made history by giving up its Government-protected monopoly, lent equipment that would otherwise be unobtainable and provided expert technical advice."[39] Internally, the BBC was far less sanguine about the AFN. A few weeks after the AFN began broadcasting, members of the BBC Interdivisional Committee on Use of Radio in Anglo-American Relations advocated for reducing the power of the network's transmitters "to the minimum necessary for US forces listening" in order to limit the number of British citizens able to hear the service. They also argued that "steps should be taken to bring home to British public that the US troops network gave a completely unfair picture of American radio."[40]

Their worries were well founded: for those who could hear it, the AFN offered a distillation of the best of America's commercial radio system. Its offerings were dominated by troop shows created by the War Office in Hollywood and commercial network favorites, including *Kay Kyser's Kollege of Musical Knowledge*, *The Hit Parade*, and *The Dinah Shore Show*.[41] BBC Variety paled in comparison. During the summer of 1943, the popular press energetically attacked the BBC's poor entertainment offerings, and the "American show-bible" *Variety* claimed that listener dissatisfaction with BBC entertainment was "feeding the fire of [the] BBC's ultimate competition": postwar commercial radio.[42]

Meanwhile, those within the Corporation who were opposed to Americanization became more inclined to speak out. In July 1943, R. A. Rendall, the Overseas assistant controller, warned that the Americans were watching to see what British reactions were to commercial "lend-lease" programming. Despite his warnings, the representation of American content on the BBC continued to increase, as exemplified by the

August introduction of yet another big-name variety show, *Charlie McCarthy* (which included a band led by Ray Noble).[43] According to Listener Research, British forces were "almost unanimous in praise of the inclusion of American variety," citing its "slicker production and its inclusion of film-star guest artists."[44] For those invested in promoting a distinctly British culture and maintaining the BBC's central role in national life, such enthusiasm did not bode well. Norman Collins, the General Overseas Service (GOS) manager, warned that the expedient of using American ideas and content in wartime would prove "disastrous" for the Corporation's future "if the BBC as a whole accepted the position that only by becoming American can we compete with the Americans."[45] Haley argued that the BBC needed to do "brave things" to counteract the popularity of American programs: "Admitting all our difficulties of man-power, and making every allowance for the fact that we are in the fifth year of war, I think we should do all we can to stimulate the production of ideas for entertainment and features."[46] Anticipating the end of subsidized American content after the war, Haley also requested an audit of all American material broadcast by the BBC in July, and in August 1944 he ordered that it be strictly limited.[47]

Much of the anxiety about Americanization revolved around the wealth of the United States, relative to Britain after years of rationing, blockade, and total war. One of the most significant causes of the BBC's poor showing in comparison to American entertainment was the Variety Department's much smaller production budget. Nevertheless, there were some exceptional BBC programs, as Adams noted when he observed, "I should, myself, place ITMA in the same class as Jack Benny and all the more credit goes to our own people that they have achieved anything so good so economically."[48]

A similar disparity in finances existed between American GIs and British soldiers, whose pay was only one-third of what the Americans earned.[49] "The sore[] point" of pay inequalities smarted even worse when women came into the mix, as Adams warned in May 1942: "This wealth, together with the personal attraction of the American soldier (largely derived from the American traditional film hero), is likely to raise a tricky problem, as the British tommy finds the girls walking out more and more with the Americans." He suggested that the BBC develop propaganda "to smooth out the various differences in pay . . . and to make them all feel part of one large force."[50]

There was little the BBC could do to "smooth out" the matter of pay differences, but it could at least mitigate anxieties about female infidelity. British authorities recognized the situation as especially damaging for the morale of British forces stationed overseas. In October 1943, Madden issued a directive to Overseas producers forbidding "any suggestion that [British] womenfolk might be getting off with someone else, particularly with troops from overseas."[51] Popular songs were a particular problem in this regard. Alarmed by the "increasing flow of numbers which suggest that girls are forgetting their sweethearts and husbands in the Forces Overseas in favour of our gallant Allies in London," the DMPC resolved to "clamp[] down" on such repertory. After extensive discussion, it banned from overseas broadcast Duke Ellington's "Baby, Please Stop and Think about Me," the lyrics of which dwelt on several scenarios of infidelity; its most controversial ruling, however, involved "Paper Doll."[52] Written by Johnny

S. Black in 1915, the song had been revived by the Mills Brothers, an African American close-harmony quartet, and became a major hit in the United States.[53] Taking on a new range of associations from the phenomenon of pinup girls, the song extolled the virtues of a paper doll over "a fickle-minded real live girl," who would not be stolen by "the flirty, flirty guys with their flirty, flirty eyes." Ignoring the song's humor (and its sexism), the DMPC banned "Paper Doll" in September "on account of the themes of feminine faithlessness."[54] When the press learned of the ban in early December, *Melody Maker* protested that the song was popular with American servicemen, whom it had not "demoralized."[55] (Of course, they did not have half a million financially flush allies stationed on their home front!) On December 13, the committee relented and raised the ban, stipulating that it could remain on air providing that no "objections [were] raised."[56]

Between October 1943 and D-Day, the number of American troops in Britain increased at a rate of more than 100,000 per month, peaking at 1.67 million at the end of May 1944.[57] While many Britons were gaining an experiential education about Americans (or, at least GIs), they also enjoyed unprecedented access to American popular music and variety in broadcast by the AFN and the BBC. Such programming did much to perpetuate an idealized vision of the entertainment provided by commercial radio in the United States. Shows like *Command Performance* were acknowledged even in America as wartime exceptions, made possible only through donated labor and government auspices; top bands and musicians played the latest music on V-discs, which were not subject to the American Federation of Musicians recording ban; variety rebroadcasts represented the cream of the national networks, not the low-budget sustaining shows of local and regional stations—and all the material was stripped of the incessant commercial messages that were woven into the fabric of American commercial radio.

Collins was right to warn that the BBC would fail if it sought to compete by becoming more American: even in the United States, listeners did not experience the version of American radio offered by the AFN. For the BBC's leadership, the solution was to articulate a clearer sense of British national style in popular music and entertainment, but this was difficult to conceptualize, particularly given the fact that American styles had long been influencing British popular music. Nevertheless, in late 1943, the BBC began to more aggressively promote British style in dance music and to feature more British songs and songwriters. Led by the Overseas Service, these actions anticipated by nearly a year Haley's efforts in 1944 to contain the Americanization of Variety and to assert the need for postwar programs that were "firmly British in character."[58]

"Pseudo-American" or "Essentially British"? Defining Britishness in Dance Music and the Dance Music Cuts of 1943–44

In September 1943, *Melody Maker* solicited a lengthy article on the state of British popular music from the music publisher Reg Connelly, who had just returned from two years abroad in the United States. Singling out the BBC house bands of Geraldo, Payne, Billy Ternent, and Ivy Benson for particular praise, Connelly asserted, "Our average standard of playing is quite as good as the Americans," a reassuring claim for a profession that usually was found lacking when such comparisons were made. The main problem of British bands, he explained, was their tendency to imitate the Americans, a criticism echoed by many. The solution that Connelly urged on bandleaders, particularly when they broadcast to North America, was to feature more "British" material, which he defined as 6/8s, waltzes, "dialect stuff—Yorkshire, Cockney, etc," and new numbers by British songwriters.[59]

The BBC embraced this approach as well. In late 1943, the Corporation took well-publicized steps to promote British songs, and it withdrew much of its support from the swing-embracing Geraldo, whom it cast as "pseudo-American," while it continued to promote the "essentially British" Payne, whose "something-for-everyone" approach included much more of the material advocated by Connelly. These shifts were rendered more visible because they occurred as part of a move that reduced the amount of dance music broadcast by the BBC, which was justified by Listener Research findings that the popularity of dance music had declined. By early 1944, the reductions led to the elimination of the Dance Band Scheme. With the 1942 ban on sentimentality and the 1943 crackdown on crooners, the scheme's demise constituted the final step away from the BBC's embrace of dance music as a populist morale builder during the early years of the war and toward a reclamation of its traditional status as a mouthpiece for British national identity and uplift.

Within the Overseas Service, where the cutbacks originated, there existed two competing perspectives on the utility of live dance music. On one side, Overseas executives identified dance music as an area where they could economize, something they were eager to do as the service continued to expand and as they sought to increase the representation of material, like orchestral music, that would "be more rewarding to the listener and to the BBC's reputation overseas."[60] In July 1943, Joanna Spicer, who after the war became a key executive in BBC television, proposed a number of cost-saving strategies: using more simultaneous broadcasts from the Home Service and Forces Programme, rebroadcasting more programs, and prohibiting Overseas producers from using expensive ad hoc bands.[61] For Spicer and Rendall, there was little difference between live and recorded dance music programs, given the limitations of shortwave reception and "bad local [listening] conditions."[62] Madden, the head of the Overseas Entertainments Unit (formerly, the EEU), disagreed. "Taken as a whole," he asserted, sessions under the Dance Band Scheme were "not expensive...and there is no real substitute for Dance Bands playing LIVE."[63]

Madden did concede that the BBC had too many contract band sessions, which limited the number of ad hoc bookings that the Corporation could make and thus its ability to represent a sufficient variety of dance music styles. Identifying Benson's band as the tipping point, he argued for its cancellation.[64] In October, the BBC cut Benson's seven sessions by half; it allowed her contract to expire in February 1944.[65] Meanwhile, Madden proposed to ease the glut by sending Geraldo on an Entertainments National Service Association (ENSA) tour of the Middle East and North Africa. Listeners at home would have a break from Geraldo, the forces stationed abroad would give Geraldo's band an enthusiastic welcome, Benson would enjoy an "honourable run" in broadcasting, and

Geraldo would return to a refreshed home audience.[66] It seemed an ideal solution for all. In mid-October, Geraldo and his band along with "a full battery of vocalists" embarked on a two-month tour. With twenty-one performers, they were the largest group yet sent abroad by ENSA.[67] The BBC broadcast recordings of his camp concerts both overseas and at home, and *Melody Maker* pronounced Geraldo's tour, which included a dramatic crash landing near Palermo, to be a "triumph."[68]

Several events transpired in late 1943 that made Geraldo's December homecoming to the BBC a far less triumphal affair than either he or Madden had expected. First, the DMPC took a firm stance in favor of British style and repertory in dance music. From at least 1942, when Madden had instituted a crackdown on "flabby entertainment" in Overseas broadcasting, Geraldo and Payne had been cast in oppositional terms. Geraldo's band, with its swing instrumentation and arrangements, was "definitely American in style" while Payne's almost orchestral instrumentation and inclusion of light classical repertory was emblematically British.[69] Their differences were valued as diversifying the BBC's offerings: Payne pleased more conservative listeners with his resistance to swing and promotion of "robust" music while Geraldo was more modern and had "greater box office value."[70]

Geraldo's and Payne's contrasting treatments of Johnny Mercer and Harold Arlen's "Accentuate the Positive" vividly illustrated their different styles.[71] The preaching style of the verse, in which the narrator "feel[s] a sermon coming on," elicited "black voice" interpretations from many white performers: indeed, the song was staged as a blackface number when Crosby sang it in the film *Here Come the Waves* (1944). Featuring his American-accented crooner Johnny Green, Geraldo rose to the challenge with an arrangement that *Gramophone* praised as outstanding—and authentic: "I would imagine that the Geraldo version is not very far from what one might hear in one of the Harlem Churches."[72] The introduction's bluesy trumpet solo, Green's dialect-tinged rendition of the verse, and the relaxed swing, rhythmic play, and call-and-response between Green and Geraldo's close-harmony vocal ensemble that shaped the chorus all demonstrated Geraldo's mastery of swing vocabularies (sound example 8.1).◐

In contrast, Payne's recording displayed many of the elements that Madden had defined as "British." Rather than a swing-style interplay of reed and brass sections, the elaborate arrangement featured strings and woodwinds: for example, the first chorus was played by a solo flute, with the bridge featuring an almost pointillistic interchange between muted trumpets, strings, and solo woodwinds. Whereas Geraldo's version was built around Green's compelling performance, Payne followed the time-honored practice of sandwiching the vocal verse and chorus between two instrumental choruses; his singers had faultless diction with no hint of an American accent, let alone "black voice." Rhythmically, the recording was square, with the rock-solid off-beats sometimes marked by a woodblock (sound example 8.2).◐ If Payne's version ignored swing idioms, it did owe a great deal to the foxtrots and symphonic jazz of Paul Whiteman, suggesting that "British style" for the BBC involved both the rejection of swing and the continuation of American symphonic jazz styles of the 1920s.

According to an August 1943 report that the BBC commissioned from Spike Hughes, Geraldo was the better bandleader.[73] Given the BBC's heightened anxiety about

American influence, however, the DMPC greeted Hughes's assessment dubiously. Certainly, Payne's "garrulous" and "pretentious" tendencies had to be watched, but "he gives the band a personality of its own which is entirely British as opposed to the many pseudo-American bands in this country." Geraldo, on the other hand, was "unduly flattered by the report." His taste and selection of material needed to be watched carefully—and he had "little imagination and relie[d] a great deal on copying American methods through gramophone records." Nevertheless, his output was "extremely good of its kind" and served to "complement" Payne's British offerings.[74] While in 1941 Watt had described Geraldo's band as "the best band on the air today," the DMPC now cast it in a supplementary, far less certain, role.[75]

The second event that weakened Geraldo's position at the BBC was growing criticism in the press that the BBC was "not encouraging British [popular] composers enough."[76] Not only did actual American songs dominate the airwaves, cinemas, and gramophones, but British songwriters had also adopted American-style lyrics and music— particularly the sentimental slush that the BBC had gone to so much effort to ban. Critics of Americanization in popular song looked to the BBC to take a stand on the issue, calling the decline in British repertory a "disgrace."[77] To more visibly demonstrate its support for British songs, the BBC announced that it would try to feature more British songs and to "encourage the unknown British song writer."[78] Payne's involvement was key. During 1943, British songs had constituted 38 percent of his repertory—a far higher share than the 20 percent or lower representation usually estimated for British songs in BBC dance programs. To encourage new songwriters, the BBC instructed Payne to "find—'if he can'—two new British songs a week." In addition, it created a (short-lived) program, *Billy Cotton's Song Shop*, which would include at least 50 percent British content, present songs by unknowns, and feature guest songwriters.[79] In practice, however, the BBC found that promoting unknown British songwriters represented too much effort for a dubious product. Although it might wish that British music would replace American commercial songs, the best it could manage was to temporarily shift the optics.

The final event that destabilized Geraldo's position at the BBC was the end of the Dance Band Scheme. Spicer concluded in November 1943 that with further dance music cuts on the GOS, the Overseas Service as a whole could no longer support the scheme, and she met with DMPC representatives to plan its orderly demise.[80] The committee agreed that the BBC could support only one house band, but deciding which band should remain was difficult. Ultimately, given the BBC's efforts to increase the visibility of British songs and dance music, Payne was more essential. His would become the sole house band, the DMPC determined, and Geraldo would be given notice when he returned from the Middle East.[81]

Madden was frustrated by the decision. With his role of overseeing all entertainment for Overseas and his close contacts with the Variety Department, he understood that the cost-cutting measures would be difficult to fulfill in practice. Moreover, Madden recognized that if Overseas replaced live performance with too many recorded programs, the BBC could face a politically damaging encounter with the Musicians' Union. Finally, he observed:

I cannot help thinking it is unfortunate that [Geraldo] is receiving notice immediately upon his return from entertaining troops in the Middle East....As far as
the Overseas Service is concerned Geraldo is likely to be the most popular band
with the listeners, since he has been there in person, and any dropping of this
band will be taking the one orchestra off the air that our Overseas Forces most
want to hear....Geraldo may consider himself to have been extremely ill-
treated—perhaps not without justification.[82]

Geraldo and his band arrived home just before Christmas, and after a rather undig-
nified tussle over who would break the news, the BBC informed him in mid-January
that his contract would end, with his nine weekly sessions reduced to four.[83] Howgill
spoke with Geraldo after the meeting and informed Haley, "It is difficult to listen to
the enthusiasm of a man whose considered opinion, based on recent experience, is
that the Forces abroad are in need of a great deal of first class live dance music,
when one knows that it is not going to be provided." Indeed, the arrival of the GFP
heralded a significant cut in dance music: while the BBC had once broadcast forty
session over the Home, Forces, and GOS wavelengths, it would now offer approximately half that amount. The nature of the sessions also changed: of the "thirteen
to fifteen sessions on the Home Service," six would be in *MWYW*, which were "not,
strictly speaking, dance music at all," and five of the nine GFP sessions would be
rebroadcast recordings, a striking repudiation of the BBC's commitment to live
performance.[84]

Melody Maker reacted to the cuts with predictable concern, asserting, "everybody
knows that dance bands are still tops with the Forces"; however, in findings that the
BBC publicized widely, Listener Research had identified a significant decline in the
popularity of dance music. Between October 1941 and October 1943, the percentage of
civilian listeners favoring dance music had decreased while the percentage of those
who disliked it had grown. It was the only programming genre so affected.[85] In 1941,
dance music was still a majority interest (with popularity figures of 53 percent), but
two years later it had become a minority interest (with popularity figures of 41 percent). While it still ranked above poetry readings and chamber music, it now fell behind
plays, musical comedies, military bands, cinema organs, documentary features, brass
bands, and religious services, which all enjoyed popularity figures that exceeded 50
percent.[86] Variety, which found favor with 75 percent of the audience, was far more reliable than dance music in the role of populist morale booster.

In a series of articles published in 1943 and 1944, "Detector" critiqued the conclu-
sions of BBC Listener Research. He did not contest the fact that dance music had declined in popularity; instead, he argued about the causes of the decline. "Detector"
pointed out that it was *"broadcast dance music,"* not live dance bands or dance music
recordings, that had declined in popularity. He blamed the BBC

for broadcasting too much corny dance music and not giving enough broadcasts
to those who could give us something better; for not knowing how to go about
the formation of the right kind of BBC resident dance bands; for putting all sorts

of absurd restrictions on dance bands; and…for the hopeless way in which the BBC allows its own announcers to compère so many dance-band programmes.[87]

Certainly, the BBC had struggled throughout the war with problems of band quality. Although the Dance Band Scheme had at least guaranteed the supply of high-quality playing in response to the call-up, it was flawed in that it could not provide variety: even good bands like Payne's and Geraldo's became stale after three years of unrelenting exposure. With the beginning of the GFP in February 1944, the reductions in dance music output and Payne's ongoing contract continued to hamper the BBC's ability to offer a diversity of bands. Swing fans, who constituted a tiny minority of civilian listeners (approximately 3 percent, according to a May 1943 survey) and a sizable portion of forces listeners (22 percent) were frustrated that swing-oriented combinations like the RAF Squadronaires and bands led by Harry Parry, Carl Barriteau, and Lew Stone rarely aired.[88] In June 1944, "Detector" received a deluge of responses to his call for the best letter explaining why *Melody Maker* readers dislike Payne. The winning letter lampooned Payne's pretentiousness and something-for-everyone approach: "When Jack Payne's band is on the air/I offer up a silent prayer./What will the maestro play today— Mozart, Brahams [*sic*] or Noel Gay."[89] Although Payne found favor with older and more conservative listeners, the BBC's promotion of British-style dance music was not succeeding with the genre's keenest fans.

The GFP's arrival heralded not only reductions in dance music but also the rationalization of dance band announcing. Bandleaders' announcements were the object of regular complaints from listeners who objected to their chattiness and informality. In an effort to correct the problem, the BBC barred most bandleaders from announcing their programs, replacing them with "professionals, i.e. Pool announcers."[90] For many critics, the solution was worse than the problem. "Detector" had complained regularly about inept BBC staff announcers, and many listeners objected especially to women's voices on the air.[91]

The announcing restrictions catalyzed an uproar about BBC dance music policy. In April, the popular bandleader Harry Roy, who had just returned from a four-month ENSA tour of the Middle East, became outraged when the BBC refused to allow any mention of his tour in the script and forbade him from delivering his customary goodbye message in a forthcoming broadcasting date. "How can you get the 'personal touch' when the BBC persists in putting on bands with the same girl announcers saying the same uninspired things[?]" he asked. Roy regarded the new policy as harmful to his reputation; in a widely publicized maneuver, he refused the April date, declared his intentions to refuse further dates, and protested the BBC's approach to dance music more generally, claiming, "The BBC is killing dance music."[92] He explained, "I entertained thousands and thousands of troops, all of whom are clamouring for dance music and more dance music. Yet the BBC attempts to produce statistics to prove that the popularity of dance bands is waning. They just don't know what they're talking about." The furor grew when Edgar Granville, MP, asked a question in Parliament as to whether Roy could be compelled to broadcast, reviving the implication that dance musicians were shirking their wartime duties while backhandedly recognizing that the entertainment they provided *was* a form of national service.[93] In response, bandleaders, music publishers, and theater organists (whose airings had been cut by 70 percent with the beginning of the GFP) united to protest the BBC's cutbacks and censorship. They claimed that the emphasis on recordings was limiting the introduction of new British tunes while the Corporation's "autocratic" policies were crushing "the individuality of dance bands."[94]

Indeed, the BBC's dance music cuts were counteracting any improvements in the representation of British music that the BBC had hoped to gain by maintaining Payne's contract. Meanwhile, Payne, whose seven weekly sessions prevented the BBC from hiring more ad hoc bands, had become increasingly uncooperative. Recognizing the situation as untenable, the BBC terminated Payne's contract in late May.[95] To fill the newly available sessions, Howgill proposed reinstating the Band of the Week. With six sessions for the week's band, continued airings for Geraldo and Payne at reduced levels, and several ad hoc sessions, the BBC would maintain a degree of continuity in its offerings while also infusing much-needed variety. Bandleaders would find it difficult to claim "neglect of dance music on the part of the BBC" or to assert "that they are not being properly represented."[96] To *Melody Maker*'s delight, the BBC adopted the plan quickly, bringing it into force in August.[97]

Although BBC dance band broadcasting appeared to return full cycle by the end of 1944, it stood in an entirely different position. At the beginning of the war, the Corporation implemented and expanded the Band of the Week scheme, which was soon supplemented by the house bands of the Dance Band Scheme, in order to fill the high-volume dance music programming demands. When it reinstated the Band of the Week scheme in 1944, a popular decision with the public, the BBC had a drastically reduced dance music output.[98] The bands featured under the new scheme represented a wide spectrum of British dance bands: the old favorite Henry Hall, the swing-oriented Stone, the sweet, Lombardo-style Maurice Winnick, and the strict-tempo favorite Victor Silvester.[99] Meanwhile, Listener Research reported an increase in the audience that was favorable to dance music, from 41 to 48 percent, lending credence to "Detector's" contention that the genre's popularity decline was largely attributable to the BBC's programming choices.[100] The problems of parsing public tastes in dance music remained, however, for the BBC continued to class strict-tempo, swing, and British-style approaches together in a single category.

In 1943 and 1944, the BBC's efforts to promote distinctly British dance music met with limited success. Even within the Corporation, opinion differed on the viability of the British idiom. Collins, who had supported the dance music cutbacks, asserted, "There is no indigenous light and dance music.... It may be held that the use of British bands to play American music is at least a move in the right direction," to which Rendall retorted, "There is *some* British dance music (if not enough and not good enough)."[101] Collins's perspective was overly gloomy: it overlooked songs from the British music hall tradition; the craft of songwriters like Ivor Novello, Noel Gay, and Jimmy Kennedy; and the entertaining stage bands of Cotton and Hylton and the sophisticated stylings of Ambrose and Carroll Gibbons, which had defined the 1930s and continued to shape dance music during the war. Moreover, Collins undervalued the ability of

British bands to assimilate "foreign" musical styles, as exemplified by Edmundo Ros's rumba band, Parry's RRC Sextet, the nascent traditional jazz movement (which revived the performance of Golden Age jazz), and the suave stylistic chameleon Geraldo. In the early months of the GFP, the BBC failed spectacularly in representing the diversity of British dance bands, and it neglected American-style swing in particular. Fortunately for swing's youthful fans, relief arrived even earlier than the August reinstatement of Band of the Week, for in June 1944, the AEFP went on the air.

"Bands across the Sea": The D-Day Invasion, Allied Radio, and American Bands in Britain

Two headlines led the issue of *Melody Maker* that went to press on June 6, 1944: "Dance Band Music on BBC Invasion Wavelength to Second Front Troops" and "Artie Shaw's Band Is in Britain." Together, they signaled the beginning of an exciting year for British popular musicians and fans. The lead article on the "invasion wavelength" reflected upon how insignificant "the purely local affairs in the world of dance music" seemed on D-Day, "one of the most memorable days in British history." Nevertheless, it was *Melody Maker's* responsibility to report on the invasion's "repercussions," which would affect "every branch of the entertainment industry"—most notably, the new wavelength now serving the invading force. In a welcome contrast to GFP and Home Service, dance music would play an important role on the AEFP.[102]

The AEFP represented more than a return to dance music, however. At a time when much of the BBC's music and entertainment policy was characterized by ambivalence about American cultural influence, the AEFP represented the apogee of cooperation between the BBC, AFN, and Canadian Broadcasting Corporation (CBC). The practical effects of this cooperation were twofold. First, more British listeners were able to hear American shows and popular music. Second, the Americans brought their top service bands and United Service Organizations (USO) stars to Britain in order to broadcast on the AEFP and perform for their troops in the United Kingdom and then Europe. Shaw's Navy Band, which was led by the tenor saxophonist Sam Donahue following Shaw's health-related discharge, represented the start of this cohort. Encountering Americans firsthand was transformative for British fans and musicians: *Melody Maker* credited interactions with American players with raising the standard of British musicianship, and they helped British enthusiasts understand their own strengths in jazz knowledge.

For outside observers, the AEFP represented a shining example of Anglo-American-Canadian cooperation; however, creating the service required complex negotiations. When U.S. military leaders officially proposed the idea to the BBC on April 28, 1944, Eisenhower insisted that "entertainment programmes...were to be apportioned in such a way that they would 'reflect the relative strength of American, British and Canadian Forces participating in the operation.'" The advantage went to the numerically superior Americans; undoubtedly, the supreme commander of the AEF recalled his troops' displeasure with the BBC. Meanwhile, the BBC's Board of Governors and many of its staff opposed sharing control of the AEFP. Churchill stepped in and informed the Corporation that if it resisted collaboration, the government would simply requisition BBC facilities for the Supreme Headquarters of the Allied Expeditionary Force (SHAEF). The BBC agreed to the idea without further debate, but it wanted leadership of the service and agreed to collaborate only until the end of the invasion. Major Maurice Gorham, newly commissioned, became the AEFP director; the American Colonel Edward Kirby, who had headed the AFN, served as liaison with SHAEF; and Madden, the "only male civilian" connected with the service, was third in command, "in charge of all integrated production." They assembled the AEFP in record time, holding the first program planning meeting on May 25, staging the first practice run on May 30, and going live on June 6.[103] Like the invasion, the new service remained secret until D-Day.

The AEFP was an immediate success. News, which was supplied by the BBC's well-regarded World News service, was central to the AEFP's mission of informing, entertaining, and "sustain[ing] the Allied troops in their stern task," but for "Detector," the program's most "noteworthy" aspect was that the AFN, following Eisenhower's strictures, supplied a large proportion of the schedule, filling it with "wonderful American bands and other artistes."[104] Listeners with an "averagely good set" could hear the AEFP almost anywhere in Britain. "It's worth putting up with atmospherics to hear something worth listening to," one civilian wrote while a member of the forces declared, "Beats the Home and Forces into a cocked hat. When I went...to an RAF station this summer, the NAAFI and dining-hall sets were tuned to the AEF permanently. They wouldn't listen to anything else."[105] Given the AEFP's popularity among its readers, *Melody Maker* began to print its schedule in December 1944.[106]

In addition to the AFN content, which included favorites like *Command Performance* and *Jack Benny* (which the BBC had stopped carrying in April), the Americans supplied top entertainers to the AEFP.[107] The most notable of these was Captain Glenn Miller, whose Army Air Force Band became the American Band of the AEF soon after its arrival in late June (figure 8.2). By November, members of the band were broadcasting thirteen shows a week, in ensembles ranging from the full forty-six-piece concert orchestra to a seven-piece jazz combo fronted by Mel Powell, along with *Strings with Wings*, featuring the string section, and a seventeen-piece swing band led by Ray McKinley. The band's membership represented the cream of white American swing bands, with string players drawn from top symphony orchestras.[108] Miller's band embodied a key difference that *Melody Maker* identified in the attitudes of British and American authorities: while the British refused to classify entertainment as war work, the Americans "regard[ed] entertainment of the troops as valuable war service" and did everything possible to provide their forces with the best performers.[109]

The other Allies were slower to create their own AEF bands. Captain Robert Farnon, a twenty-seven-year-old arranger, composer, and trumpeter, who had conducted the CBC Orchestra since 1940, arrived in September to lead the Canadian Band of the AEF.[110] The British Band of the AEF was formed in August and led by Regimental Sergeant Major George Melachrino, who had gained attention for his bandleading, singing, and violin playing at the Café de Paris early in the war as Ken Johnson's sweet music counterpart.[111] While both Melachrino and Farnon, who settled in the United

FIGURE 8.2 Glenn Miller conducting an ENSA concert in August 1944. (Photo by Felix Man/Picture Post/Getty Images)

Kingdom after the war, were well respected by their peers, Miller was the AEFP's star. Representing the cooperative spirit of the Allies, "The AEF Christmas Show" featured all three bands in relays from Paris and London to North America as well as Britain. The message of cooperation was colored, however, by the previous day's announcement that Miller had gone missing over the English Channel; Miller's arranger Jerry Gray filled in as conductor, and listeners gained another opportunity to reflect on the wartime sacrifices of entertainers.[112]

Miller and his band were not the only entertainers who risked danger to entertain the troops during the invasion. Under the auspices of the Army Entertainments Unit, the clarinetist Sid Millward and His Nit-Wits became the first swing band to arrive on the Continent—less than two weeks after D-Day.[113] Many more ENSA-sponsored bands followed in the fall: Ambrose departed for France in September, followed by Loss and Geraldo in November.[114] Others toured less publicized fronts: Vera Lynn, for example, embarked upon an arduous ENSA tour of hospitals and camps in India and Burma between March and June 1944.[115] In total war, dangers and difficulties also existed on the home front. Britain had been relatively free of air raids since mid-1942, but on June 13 the Germans launched the first V-1 flying bombs against London. As had occurred during the Blitzkrieg, the bombing cause theater attendance to dip, and many theaters closed until September, when the frequency of the flying bombs fell off.[116]

Numerous entertainers sponsored by the USO and the U.S. military stopped off in Britain on their way to Europe. Their primary duty while in the United Kingdom was performing for the more than 600,000 American troops still in the country, which limited their opportunities to broadcast on the BBC or interact with their British fans.[117] When they did, however, they invariably built goodwill. *Melody Maker* gave enthusiastic coverage to the arrivals, performances, and broadcasts of the U.S. Navy Band, Spike Jones and His City Slickers, Dinah Shore, and Miller; however, the performer who inspired the most fervent response from the British public was Crosby.

Crosby had been familiar to British audiences in recordings and films since the early 1930s. When he arrived in Glasgow on August 25, he was mobbed "by a crowd of women porters," for whom he sang "Blue of the Night" and "Glasgow Belongs to Me" before boarding the train for London.[118] He was similarly obliging four days later when, after his *Variety Band Box* taping, "thousands" of fans chanted his name outside the restaurant where he was dining in Soho: he went out onto the balcony twice to sing for the crowd, the second time singing "eight songs before they would disperse."[119] Crosby spent less than two weeks in Britain, but his graciousness endeared him to fans and critics alike. The BBC, especially Madden, who produced *Variety Band Box*, earned praise for featuring him: "They've certainly seen to it that you've heard Bing plenty during the last couple of weeks [largely on the AEFP]—and how his presence brightened up those programmes in which he guest-starred."[120]

Like Crosby, Miller's band aired mainly on the AEFP, but it was also simultaneously broadcast over the BBC Home Service in a five-week series during July and August.[121] The BBC had moved quickly to put the newly arrived stars on air, and the first hour-long airing was announced blandly without any indication that this was *the* Miller band. Rather than the expected "field day for Sousa," *Melody Maker*'s reviewer was impressed by Miller's "pleasing...microphone manner," Powell's solo in "American Patrol" ("20,000 British jazz pianists dropped in their tracks"), and a string-bolstered arrangement of "Summertime."[122] Listenership for the series peaked in the second week at more than 18 percent.[123] While sophisticated jazz connoisseurs regarded Miller as overly commercial, young fans were enthusiastic. "Countless of the young generation will, I am sure, support me if I say, thanks a million for putting Captain Glenn Miller's orchestra on the air. It is nothing short of terrific," wrote one listener.[124]

Unfortunately, swing was still a minority taste in Britain, and by the fourth week the audience for Miller's Home Service broadcasts fell to 12.8 percent.[125] In August, the BBC changed the weekly airing from its prime Thursday evening time to a Saturday afternoon slot on the GFP; in mid-October, it ended the series. The cancellation contributed to the story that Miller's band was excluded from domestic broadcast by the BBC because it considered him "not acceptable to the British public." *Melody Maker* reacted with outrage to Miller's removal, and when Miller returned to the GFP in a live broadcast from the Queensberry All-Services Club, famous British bandleaders, including Jack Hylton, Geraldo, Roy, Melachrino, and Silvester, paid public tribute to the American leader.[126] Miller continued to broadcast extensively on the AFN and AEFP while also prerecording programs. By December, when his band left for France, the AEFP had had six weeks of programming stockpiled—a preparation that proved fortuitous when Miller went missing on December 15.[127] While Miller's relations with the BBC were undoubtedly strained, his band's limited appearances on the Home Service and GFP were at least as attributable to American restrictions as to BBC bias.[128]

In contrast to their uneven relationship with the BBC, Miller and his band advanced the cause of Anglo-American cooperation with dance musicians and swing fans. In October, Miller thrilled fans by accepting a last-minute invitation to appear at the 1944 Jazz Jamboree, where the audience greeted the band with "one of the most terrific ovations I have ever heard," according to Sonin. Miller acknowledged the role of British musicians in his band's reception, claiming, "No group has done more to make our stay pleasant over here than the musicians"; at the Feldman Club later that night, he indicated that "he was pleased and surprised...to find the jazz tradition going so strong in Britain."[129] Certainly, as discussed in chapter 5, RRC had helped build the rhythm club subculture into a robust wartime scene. British hot playing had come into its own by late 1944, with the rise of small, improvising bands, such as Frank Deniz and His Spirits of Rhythm and the Dixieland-oriented Vic Lewis–Jack Parnell Jazzmen. The spaces for live jazz improvisation had also expanded—most notably at the Feldman Club, where British musicians could jam with—and learn from—visiting American luminaries, like Powell and McKinley.[130]

"Detector" attributed "the startling improvement" of many British bands to their ability to hear top U.S. bands firsthand. American bands played mostly for radio broadcasts and in ARC Clubs, where British access was limited; nevertheless, it was rare "not [to] find a knot of the more enterprising [British musicians] packed round the stand." Their most significant discoveries were in matters of ensemble playing: the American bands had "better arrangements," played with more "verve, drive or attack," and possessed a closer "attention to detail."[131] The most dramatic illustration of this was a battle of the bands, followed by a cooperative jam session, at the Queensberry All-Services' Club between the U.S. Navy Band and Jimmy Miller's RAF Squadronaires, which most enthusiasts considered to be the best British band. Donahue's Navy Band still bore the imprint of its esteemed founder, Shaw. "It was better—much better—than any American record we had ever heard....The tone and ensemble of this wonderful band in the flesh was really something we had never imagined this side of Heaven," observed Maurice Burman, Geraldo's drummer.[132] The thrilling battle aired live on the AEFP in September and was rebroadcast a month later in the Home Service as *Bands across the Sea*. "Detector" rated the Americans' reed sound to be warmer, their blend better, and their performance more relaxed. Nonetheless, the British arrangements and program compared favorably to the American, and "Detector" judged the Squadronaires' George Chisholm (who also did credit to British jazz soloing during the postbroadcast jam session) to be a better trombonist than his American counterpart. He concluded, "Of course, the BBC gave the verdict as a draw, but in truth the American Navy boys just won."[133]

It is striking that nearly all the American jazz and swing musicians who figured in the British encounters of 1944 were white. While many British and American civilian bands had embraced integration in at least a limited manner, the color bar was firmly in effect for both the U.S. military and the USO, and U.S. authorities did not include African American troops in any of its schemes for fostering Anglo-American friendship.[134] With the British jazz community's tendency to valorize black musicians, one would have expected numerous reports on visiting African American musicians, such as the communication that George Long, who played "really solid electric guitar," and his GI Band were "doing fine work...and do the boys 'jump'!"[135] That this was a nearly isolated account suggests the restrictions placed on African Americans who entertained the troops.

By late 1944, it became clear that D-Day's most significant "repercussion" for the popular music profession was the arrival of American bands, with their influence on both the playing of British musicians and the music broadcast by the BBC. By all indications, British listeners were hearing better dance music on the AEFP, Home Service, and GFP. In addition to top American bands, the BBC featured a wider range of British bands, many of which had improved noticeably. The repercussions of the "Invasion Year" would continue to resonate as the BBC assembled its postwar plans for dance music.

Conclusion

Although the dominant narrative of popular music in wartime Britain was that of American songwriters, performers, and radio producers influencing their British counterparts, there were places in which the flow reversed. Arguably, the BBC's most significant wartime musical export was *MWYW*, which came to represent the BBC's capacity for innovative programming and its organizational strengths. In contrast to the BBC's extensively researched and frequently broadcast program, industrial music in the United States remained largely a piecemeal affair, with a few wire services and radio stations offering the programs.[136] As interested Americans soon recognized, industrial music would be nearly impossible to institute in the United States on a national scale because the country was larger—and, more important, because it lacked national, public-service radio.[137]

MWYW was the exception that proved the rule, however. From 1941, the BBC relied upon American relays and radio techniques in order to refresh its tired variety programming, fill out its program schedule, and promote Anglo-American friendship. The quantity of American programs continued to increase, even during 1943 and 1944, when the BBC began to cool toward "Americanization," and its officials looked to assert a more purely British identity in their broadcasts by promoting British-style performers like Payne.[138] Nevertheless, many British listeners, particularly youth, were enthusiastic about the commercial American radio entertainment that they encountered on the AFN and AEFP while British swing fans and musicians were thrilled by their live and broadcast encounters with American performers during 1944 and 1945.

In many ways, the tensions that influenced Anglo-American cultural relations during the period were rooted in the fact that both national identities were in states of continued invention, as registered by the swaths of the United States that failed to fit the Hollywood ideal and the BBC's embrace of "rural and domestic," rather than imperial, representations of British nationhood.[139] The notion of a distinctive, class-crossing youth culture, organized around fashion, music, and media consumption, was still in formation in both nations, although the Americanized swing and sentimental vocalizing favored by the troops gave a good indication of its content. How best to program for youth as a distinct minority audience was a challenge with which the BBC would grapple well into the postwar period.

CONCLUSION

ON VE-DAY, MILLIONS of people in Britain chose to celebrate the end of the European war in public spaces. Through a complex network of microphones, the BBC offered listeners at home the chance to "mingle with the Victory crowds on city pavements, in village streets, in churches, in dance-halls, in theatres."[1] According to many accounts, the festivities were merry, yet orderly, with music, dancing, food, and bonfires to mark the occasion.[2] The day represented a liminal moment between war and (pending victory in Asia) peace, offering respite to a population that had survived total war before it began the difficult work of rebuilding. It was characterized for many by a powerful sense of community and national unity. *Melody Maker*'s account of May 8, 1945, neatly sutured the labor of musicians into the national narrative of celebration: the music heard throughout the nation and across boundaries of class was produced through the spontaneous, joyous, generous work of dance musicians.

> Frequently misunderstood, and occasionally even unjustly abused, during the war years, the dance band profession of Britain came majestically into its own on VE-Day. From one end of the country to the other, people, relaxing after nearly six years of the most terrible anxieties, wanted to dance. Everywhere—from the smallest village hall to the sumptuous restaurants of Mayfair—musicians gladly worked double, and even treble, hours to bring to the war-weary populace their chance of relaxing with dancing on this gladdest of all days.[3]

The VE-Day celebrations represented an opportunity to reflect upon the nation's values and aims. As Rose has argued, there was a populist, progressive shift in the nation's dominant culture during the war.[4] One of the key sentiments of this change was the sense that shared wartime sacrifice should lead to a better postwar future for all. These beliefs gained concrete expression in the government's Beveridge Report of December 1, 1942, which articulated the foundational concepts of the welfare state (e.g., social insurance, education, national health care), much of which was implemented in the final months of the war. William Beveridge's contention that "if the Allies could 'plan for a better peace even while waging war, they will win together two victories which in truth are indivisible'" resonated widely; the report was "an astonishing best-seller" and sold more than 630,000 copies.[5]

It is tempting to map this vision of wartime populism, unity, and democracy onto popular music and jazz broadcasting at the BBC. Indeed, the most iconic broadcasting musicians and most popular programs of the war embodied these values: Sandy Macpherson putting in long hours at the theater organ during the Phony War; dance music plucked from the privileged venues of the West End and deployed by *Music While You Work (MWYW)* into munitions factories; Vera Lynn acting as a reassuring intermediary for those separated by war in *Sincerely Yours*. Much of this music was not intellectually or aurally challenging, but it was functional: it drew listeners together into an imagined community, it boosted morale, it gave official recognition to the importance of groups involved in war service at home and abroad. For many, the act of listening to such music was an emotionally meaningful experience, whether it offered refreshment, relaxation, or a sense of companionship.

As Rose observed, however, "The pull to unity was haunted by the spectre of division and difference."[6] The values of tradition and modernity, left and right, Empire and Commonwealth, cultural chauvinism and cosmopolitanism, high and low existed in uneasy company. Popular music, which was frequently regarded as a feminized, racialized, commercialized product of modern mass culture, became the subject of vigorous debate during the war precisely because the BBC broadcast it, an act that granted the stamp of legitimacy. While "populist" performers, like Lynn with her working-class roots, enjoyed significant followings, they also had forceful detractors, who disliked hearing them over airwaves and objected to their inclusion in the BBC's representation of the nation to itself. In discussions of whether crooners and sentiment were the stuff to "give the troops," of the place of women instrumentalists and singers on the air, and of the necessity of maintaining good civilian dance bands, the BBC's staff, its critics, and its listeners were also contesting what it meant to be a good British citizen in wartime. Rather than providing the soundtrack for a unified "People's War," then, it would be more accurate to say that the BBC's broadcast of popular music exposed the differences of ideology, taste, and experience that divided the nation. More important, the debates, enabled by a democratic press and an invested listenership, also opened the possibility of "social and cultural transformations."[7]

In question here is the nature of those transformations and their implications for popular music and jazz at the BBC after the war. As was the case with the social welfare system, preparations for and discussions of the shape of the postwar BBC were a steady wartime theme.[8] According to Nicholas, "As early as 1942 some critics...had begun to consider the post-war organisation of radio, and had begun to debate such issues as what the public wanted, commercialisation, 'vulgarisation,' increased public access to the airwaves, and above all, whether or not the post-war BBC would return to 'mixed' programming."[9] In 1944, Haley promised to "take the first step towards return to normal broadcasting" within ninety days of VE-Day, and by March 1945, he was describing the postwar revival of the radio (and, soon, television) hearth in visionary terms, which obviated calls for commercial broadcasting:

> [We must] see that the entertainment that comes flooding into 12,000,000 British homes is so good, so polished, so undeniably the highest form of entertainment available at home or outside, that people will watch the clocks in the factories and shops and offices until they return home to their radio.[10]

On July 29, 1945, "VE + 82," the BBC restored regional programming in the form of six regional Home Services, instituted the national Light Programme (which replaced the domestic broadcast of the GFP), and promised to introduce the high-culture-oriented Third Programme the next year.[11]

Some aspects of popular music on the postwar BBC, such as the emphasis on airing a rota of name bands, the privileging of live over recorded performance, and an awareness of commercial competition, represented a return to normality—or at least a continuation of the priorities of the 1930s. In three major areas, however, postwar popular music broadcasting reflected changes catalyzed by the war. First, although large dance bands retained their prestige, solo singers and smaller combos, whether slick commercial swing units or amateur Dixieland-style bands, had come to the fore during the war years, heralding more thoroughgoing changes to come in Britain's music industry. Second, the BBC had developed a more nuanced understanding of its audience, recognizing the stylistic differences that ran through the broad category of dance music and the ways that taste and age divided its audience. Finally, both Britain's musicians and the BBC were still making sense of their close encounters with the American musicians who passed through Britain in 1944 and 1945 and the continued spread of American cultural influence.

"Many Varied Attractions": Popular Music for the Postwar BBC

The BBC's Light Programme began airing on July 29, 1945, two days after the Labour Party's landslide election victory. At 9:15 a.m., Macpherson sat at the BBC theater organ for a half-hour broadcast. "It seems to us a happy choice," observed the *Radio Times*, "as Sandy was called upon to do so much in the first days of the war...that he should be given a place of honour on the opening day of the new programme."[12] Haley asserted that the national Light Programme, unlike the controversial GFP, was "built-for the civilian listener," and it represented the centerpiece of the BBC's return to normality; in its populist appeal, however, it also owed a great deal to the wartime Forces Programme.[13]

Together with the regionalized Home Service and the forthcoming national Third Programme, the Light Programme would give "British listeners...the full scope and resources that broadcasting ought to cover." The Home Service retained its wartime "mixed" character and middlebrow address. Although most of its broadcast day still originated from London, the BBC aimed "to make its six regionalised Home Services alert, living things," fostering creative rivalry and local culture.[14] In the first week, only the London Regional Programme aired mainstream dance music, with other regions featured more localized fare, such as piping in Scotland and MacNamara's Ceilidhe Band in Northern Ireland.[15] The Third Programme, which began airing on September 29, 1946, would "be of a completely new pattern. It will be a programme of a high cultural level, devoted to the arts, serious discussion, and experiment."[16]

The Light Programme was to feature "plenty of light music and variety and fun and frolics," but its role at the postwar BBC was far from frivolous, for it represented a critical component of the BBC's strategy to retain its monopoly on broadcasting in the United Kingdom.[17] From 1943, Director-General Foot had recognized that the only way to stave off demands for commercial radio after the war, and to gain a renewal of the BBC's charter when it was reviewed in 1947, was to provide British listeners with a wide range of choice and "attractive programmes." Haley adopted these priorities, promoting the shape of the postwar BBC in a series of speeches throughout the last year of the war.[18] *Band Wagon* greeted the first installment of postwar choice (i.e., the Light Programme and the regional Home Services) with approval: "By this blossoming into varied attractions the BBC is making a strong bid for the renewal of its Charter."[19]

Choice was important, but the Light Programme also represented a direct response to American-style commercial radio. From early 1944, as discussed in chapter 8, Haley had prioritized reducing American content on the BBC, recognizing it as a rallying point for commercial radio advocates and knowing that it would cease to be cheaply available after the war. Even with reductions of American material on the BBC, the AEFP, with its hours of American variety and swing, remained a popular option for British listeners—until July 28, 1945, when it went off the air in a "blow to swing-fans."[20] Thus, the Light Programme, which began airing the next day, was not only the civilian replacement for the GFP but also the British, public-service replacement for the AEFP. Meanwhile, English-language commercial radio returned to the Continent, and the AFN continued to broadcast to American forces and a devoted following of more than 5 million British.[21] The BBC's charter was renewed, but the Light Programme continued to face plenty of competition.

Popular music played a critical role in the Light Programme's output. In July 1945, *Melody Maker* expressed delight in announcing that the Light Programme would "feature more dance bands and dance music than ever before" and would resume outside broadcasts from exclusive restaurants and hotels.[22] During the first week alone, it featured outside broadcasts by the swing-oriented Nat Gonella, Edmundo Ros and His Rumba Band, the variety favorite Billy Cotton, along with stalwarts of the BBC like Geraldo, Payne, and the popular old-time dance music of Harry Davidson.[23] In addition to retaining Forces-originated shows like *MWYW* and *Radio Rhythm Club* (*RRC*), the Light Programme also kept Spike Hughes's *Swing Club* and *Forces Favourites* from the GFP (adding a companion gramophone request show, *Family Favourites*) and imported several shows from the AEFP, including *Variety Band Box* and *Top Ten*, which featured Beryl Davis and the RAF Squadronaires.[24] Finally, the Light Programme's staff quietly decided that they would retain the wartime policy of Sunday dance music, although they would aim to feature sweet, rather than hot, styles and to avoid full programs of strict-tempo dance music, which was "obviously meant for dancing."[25]

Populist themes of British identity were central to one of the most hyped of the new popular music series for the Light Programme, *Write a Tune*. The series was "a competition to find new British dance tunes"; driven by listener votes, it offered a top prize of £1,000. For seventeen weeks, listeners tuned in on Monday evenings to hear Lou Preager and His Orchestra at the Hammersmith Palais de Danse perform the competing numbers: one tune from each of the twelve preliminary rounds (six weeks each for domestic and overseas submissions) won a prize of fifty pounds and a chance to move forward in the competition.[26] A total of 73,852 manuscripts were submitted, and 500,003 listeners voted on the final songs. The series' contest format, listener participation, venue, and band all fostered a participatory, populist atmosphere—and it resulted in extremely conventional contributions to the repertory. The first prize went to Elly Beadell and Nelly Tollerton for their quick waltz, "Cruising Down the River," a gloss on the waltz-song genre, which had been popular at the turn of the century and had recently been revived in the nostalgic film musical *Meet Me in St. Louis* (1944) and the Broadway juggernaut *Oklahoma!* (1943). Sonin observed, "One can merely shake one's head sadly at the corny standard which the Great British Public demands from its music....55 per cent. of all the songs sent in were waltzes....The general standard of entries was commercial in the extreme."[27]

Indeed, the wartime swing boom, the arrival of American service bands, and the regular broadcast of *RRC* had failed to broaden the tastes of Britain's dance music audience—at least when it was regarded as a whole. Fortunately, the BBC had recognized by the war's end that treating the dance music audience as a single entity was a serious mistake. An April 1945 BBC Listener Research study supported this conviction, and it influenced the direction of postwar broadcasting. Its central finding was that the tastes of the dance music public were divided sharply along lines of age while differences of class and gender were insignificant. Listeners over thirty, who represented 68 percent of the audience, tended to prefer strict-tempo dance music, sweet music, and bandleaders who had established their reputations before the war: Silvester, Henry Hall, Ambrose, and Mantovani were favorites. Younger listeners, who were a smaller public ("due to the brevity of youth!"), preferred bands that had been active or became established during the war, especially Geraldo, the Squadronaires, Joe Loss, and the Skyrockets—swing-oriented bands favored by *Melody Maker*'s readership.[28] Haley took seriously the study's contention that the dance music public needed to be envisioned as two discrete groups.[29] The BBC's tradition of broadcasting to several specific publics, and its wartime commitment to serving the forces and others war workers, who tended to be young, benefited the youthful fans of swing and jazz.

The classification of youth as a special audience justified the BBC's decision to maintain both *RRC* and *Swing Club*, along with a handful of other records programs featuring bandleaders like the American Harry James, in its postwar programming. The broadcast of jazz also benefited from the status it had acquired during the war as a "symbol of freedom." During the liberation of Europe, *Melody Maker* had featured several stories on the Nazis' opposition to jazz and the music's use in occupied Europe as a tool for resistance; in June 1945, *RRC* featured a program on the underground Hot Club of Paris.[30] The BBC had also used jazz in its transmissions to Occupied Europe. As Rex Harris observed of his 1943 broadcasts to France with Franck Bauer, "It can now be revealed that the programmes were received with joy and gratitude by many hundreds of young French men and women, to whom the strains of our signature tune, Horace Henderson's 'Happy Feet,' meant fifteen minutes of release from the ever-present shadow of the hated invader."[31]

While the BBC maintained a weekly hour of jazz records programming, it missed almost entirely the emerging live jazz revival scene. In *Melody Maker*'s 1945 poll, Vic Lewis and His Jazzmen were the undisputed winners of the best small combination prize while the semipro Freddy Mirfield and His Garbagemen and the amateur George Webb and His Dixielanders (who would become icons of the British trad movement) placed in the top five.[32] These bands and others had been nurtured by the wartime efflorescence of jam sessions, live clubs, and records recitals, for which *RRC* had provided a national voice. Although the Dixielanders appeared on *RRC*, as a now-rare live band feature, they went largely unmentioned in the BBC discussions about dance music (even when it involved "hot" bands).[33] The Corporation did better with mainstream swing, featuring a number of swing bands—and swing-oriented dance bands—favored by younger fans, such as Ted Heath, Geraldo's former trombonist, who became one of the best-regarded dance bandleaders of the late 1940s.[34]

Part of the dissonance between the BBC and the British jazz scene was that the Corporation was more invested in reviving its prewar standard of stable, "name" dance bands than in booking more innovative bands. During the war, the "bandless leader" had been a familiar figure; rather than maintaining a permanent band, he hired players from other bands when he obtained a broadcasting date. Combined with the wartime shortage of good players, the practice of forming pickup bands or augmenting for a broadcast meant that the BBC was paying "a comparatively small group of musicians who flit from studio to studio and perform under different batons, sometimes taking part in as many as four transmissions a day!" In late 1945, Michael Standing, the new director of Variety, sought to crack down on the practice and award more contracts to bandleaders who maintained regular bands, aiming to improve dance music quality.[35] In addition, the pool had become impolitic as dance musicians were demobilized from the forces: the BBC felt a responsibility to support bands employing veteran soldiers.

By early 1946, the BBC made several changes in its approach to band booking. First, it ended the Band of the Week.[36] Second, the BBC seriously considered creating a new house dance band, to be led by Geraldo, as a popular counterpart to the excellence of the BBC Symphony Orchestra. The proposed house band's organization owed a great deal to Geraldo's wartime work as house bandleader—and to Glenn Miller's Army Air Force Band, with its modular organization that permitted styles ranging from swing to strings. Although the BBC eventually rejected the scheme as prohibitively expensive, it is significant that Geraldo, whom the Corporation had classified as too American only two years before, was now cast as the best hope for BBC dance music: he was loyal, honest, and "artistically and organizationally the most capable of band leaders."[37] Ultimately, the BBC opted for a more cost-effective solution that offered a greater variety of bands (a wise choice, given the resentment that limited bookings and stale house bands had engendered during the war). Standing and his staff developed a "star" system that would feature the top twelve bands, as ranked by BBC staff, in prime evening broadcasts; four bands would broadcast regularly for two months, followed by the next four for two months, and so on. The nonstar bands would be relegated to daytime slots—but the BBC would "encourage bands in the daytime list to try and qualify for 'Star' status."[38]

By the end of the year, however, a staff member, Pat Dixon, condemned the system and its emphasis on "one man, one band." There were simply not enough good dance musicians to sustain high-quality music under the system; meanwhile, the BBC, which still undervalued the genre, kept supplying indifferent dance music while listenership fell and fans turned to the vibrant live performance scene.[39] Although the BBC had come to better understand its dance music audience, the war had not completely altered its attitude to dance music broadcasting—either in valuing innovation in the genre or in responding to the changing economics of running a band. Big bands survived longer in Britain than they did in the United States (the BBC's support most certainly helped), but even in the United Kingdom, the popular music industry was changing.

Although the BBC's postwar programming continued to frustrate the youth audience that favored "hotter" styles, the Light Programme did quite well in programming for the more conservative mainstream. It continued to feature "easy on the ears" genres, such as strict-tempo dance music, which had been cornerstones of the popular Forces Programme. Although many took pleasure in listening actively to such music, many others treated it as background. The quantity of soothing instrumental dance and light music featured on Light Programme (like the Forces before it) enabled listeners to tune in to a single radio wavelength, which would accompany them throughout their day. In fall 1945, the BBC returned Silvester's popular *Dancing Club* to the air on Monday evenings.[40] The biggest triumph for home listeners who appreciated a refreshing musical background, however, was the postwar survival of *MWYW*.

By the end of the war, *MWYW* was so popular with home audiences that "Listener Research figures [we]re at their highest for the night and week-end sessions, when comparatively few listeners are at work." As the BBC considered the program's postwar future, however, it concentrated on the needs of industry, where *MWYW* was in wide use: 9,000 "major industrial organisations" and 30,000 to 40,000 small factories relayed the service at the end of the war.[41] Despite industrialists' insistence that it not be cut, the BBC considered three daily sessions of *MWYW* too much for peacetime. It terminated the evening broadcasts, replacing them with "Uninterrupted Music," and canceled the Saturday afternoon and Sunday broadcasts.[42] Even with the reductions, eleven weekly broadcasts remained. Reynolds concluded:

It may truly be said that "Music While You Work" has become a National Institution. Primarily intended to encourage and stimulate our wartime workers its cheerful and familiar music, uninterrupted by announcements, has also established it as a favourite with home listeners. Even the title has become a symbol of a form of light entertainment that is equally suitable for the factory or the home.[43]

Another institution that survived the war was the Dance Music Policy Committee (DMPC). In addition to vetting songs and singers, the committee maintained its commitment to encouraging British style and discouraging excessive Americanism, although it recognized that it was "impossible to eradicate the American influence, which was inherent in Dance Music."[44] *Melody Maker* complained in late 1945: "Latest reason advanced by the Gargling Gestapo for banning chirpettes is that they're 'too American.' We are against the phoney-American accent, but not against American style, and who would be happier if we were sure that the powers-that-ban knew the difference."[45] In May 1946, the Music Publishers' Association protested the BBC's continued censorship of popular songs, requesting a more liberal postwar policy. The BBC remained unyielding on swung classics; however, it began focusing upon "blatant illiteracy," rather than sentimentality, as a criterion for banning.[46] By the end of 1947, the DMPC vetting process had largely become a formality; it passed almost every song submitted.[47] Nonetheless, the committee remained in place, at a reduced size, until November 1954.[48] It vetted its last singer in the late 1940s.

Finally, what of the GFP's radio girl friends? With demobilization, male variety announcers returned to the air; in December 1945, *Melody Maker*'s radio reviewer observed, "At last, we are hearing dance music announced as if the people concerned know what they are talking about."[49] Female announcers may have appealed to lonely servicemen, but they did not suit civilian dance music fans. For vocalists like Lynn and Davis, however, the war heralded a shift in which many pursued solo careers, independent of dance bands. From late in the war, Davis sang in *Top Ten*, which featured each week's American and British hits and represented the BBC's answer to the American *Lucky Strike Hit Parade*. In 1947, she traveled to the United States, where she replaced Doris Day opposite Frank Sinatra on the American series.[50] Lynn retired in the winter of 1945–46 to the country, where she lived with her husband, the former Squadronaire Harry Lewis, and their daughter, who was born in March 1946. Fortunately for her fans, Lynn's retirement was brief. In 1947, she returned to recording, the variety stage, and the BBC, where she broadcast a solo series, supported by the well-regarded music director and arranger Robert Farnon, who had formerly led the Canadian AEF Band. Lynn observed that her postwar series, which was outranked in popularity only by *Itma*, was "completely different from my wartime broadcasts, more like good general light music shows."[51] Although Lynn had worried that her heartfelt style had fallen out of fashion, she and other wartime singers enjoyed successful postwar careers not only in recording, radio, and (later) television but also in live concert tours for domestic and overseas audiences.

Touring was also important for dance bands. Among others who entertained the forces overseas, Ivy Benson and Her All-Ladies Dance Orchestra toured in Germany, and Leslie "Jiver" Hutchinson and His West Indian Band went to India. Domestic touring became more arduous as the variety circuit declined during the late 1940s, necessitating exhausting strings of one-night stands. Meanwhile, television, which resumed broadcasting in 1946, became an increasingly potent force. The transition to a more mediatized popular music industry, as well as shifting postwar tastes, favored singers like Shelton, Davis, and Lynn, who sang mainstream popular songs (often with American accents) and incorporated microphones into their technique. Stars rooted in British music hall tradition, like Gracie Fields and George Formby, retained their status as beloved institutions of British culture, but few followers emerged. While American repertory and styles continued to dominate British popular music after the war, the Ministry of Labour ban on visiting U.S. bands remained in place until 1954. There were a few exceptions, however: in 1948, Duke Ellington's band became the first American band to be permitted entry into Britain since the war, followed in 1949 by Benny Goodman's band, Charlie Parker, and Sidney Bechet—a striking representation of three competing visions of jazz and jazz authenticity.[52]

At the end of the war and in the early months of the Light Programme, however, few would have predicted the radical shifts that would reshape the music industry over the next ten years, during which austerity would remain in force at home and the British Empire would shrink abroad. The variety theaters were still running strong, television was an experimental memory, and the aim of restoring the prewar glamour of the dance bands seemed possible while an appetite for wartime nostalgia seemed absurd. Bebop, let alone skiffle or rock 'n' roll, was virtually unheard of, and the notion that in twenty years there would be a British musical invasion of the United States was unimaginable.

In its VE-Day issue, *Melody Maker* reflected upon the role that the dance music profession had played in the war, asserting in unequivocal terms that it had boosted the nation's morale:

> Never mind what the killjoys say, dance bands and dance musicians have done their full share in this war. Their job has been to keep up morale for nearly six years. Don't ask *us* how well they have succeeded for we may be biased. No, ask the factory workers, who found dance music and dance bands a factor that helped to boost up production; ask the RAF bomber crews who flew their perilous missions fortified by the dance music which came to them over the radio in their 'planes; ask the civilians who listened to radio dance bands in the blitz.[53]

Reflecting a national ambivalence about women's war work, the weekly omitted mentioning women crooners, particularly the radio girl friends who had linked the forces overseas to the homeland. However, *Melody Maker* championed to the last the validity of dance musicians' contributions in a war that had placed greater value on visible uniforms, heroism in the forces, and concrete manual labor. Its examples of the profession's contributions were striking: enabled by the medium of radio, dance musicians had served a series of distinct audiences. In this vision, wartime unity was the product of a diverse coalition rather than an organic whole.

The Second World War proved the importance of radio in modern warfare, as a disseminator of information and propaganda, force of national unity, and morale builder. As the BBC soon recognized, popular music contributed to all these aims: it linked listeners into an imagined community, conveyed ideas with a subtle touch, and, most recognizably, spread cheer and reassurance. Whereas previously the Corporation had treated popular music as a middlebrow relief from more uplifting fare, it soon recognized the critical role that such music could play in its wartime mission. To the end, the BBC worked to increase the quantity and quality of popular music and jazz broadcasting, to better understand its audience, and to offer representations of gender, nationality, race, and class that it believed would benefit the war effort.

During the war, the Corporation shifted its address from the radio hearth, with its actively listening, physically passive "tired business man," to serve a broader range of audiences and listening experiences. It came to a rapprochement with inattentive listening during the war, most tellingly demonstrated in its design of the Forces Programme and the development of *MWYW*. Although the BBC cast the Forces Programme as a special wartime accommodation for distracted listeners in the military and emphasized the industrial utility of *MWYW*, the wavelength and the series also gained a significant following among civilian listeners. *MWYW* helped middle- and working-class people to create pleasing sonic environments in their own homes, previously the terrain only of the well-off, who could afford to frequent restaurants and other leisure places that featured live background music by light orchestras and other ensembles.

BBC Listener Research played a critical role in conceptualizing the wartime audience for popular music. Through numerous factory surveys, it helped shape the experimental *MWYW* into a beacon of scientific progress while its analysis of overseas forces' correspondence supported the Empire Entertainment Unit's expansion of messages programs. Further, Listener Research helped the BBC track the popularity of dance music in order to maximize its benefits to morale. Throughout the war, it worked to refine the BBC's understandings of the audiences for dance bands and popular vocalists, arriving at the conclusion that the Corporation could not treat dance music as a monolithic entity. When it found at the end of the war that age, rather than gender or class, was the primary predictor of dance music tastes, it asserted that the BBC would ignore younger listeners to its own peril during the postwar period.

Many producers within the BBC worked valiantly during the war, both to maintain dance music standards and to represent a broader range of popular music makers. While the Variety Department turned with increasing frequency to American programs, dance music remained largely the purview of British bands. Due to the call-up, however, civilian British bands lost players and declined in quality. While Madden promoted the Dance Band Scheme, with Geraldo and Payne leading house bands to guarantee a steady supply of dance music for the BBC, Charles Chilton helped bring more fluid, jam-oriented small bands, most notably Parry's RRC Sextet, to national attention. *RRC* also made a critical intervention in the BBC's representations of race by airing serious, celebratory considerations of black creativity and presenting interracial music making on a regular basis. Meanwhile, Madden set out to represent women's important role on the British home front by featuring female announcers and crooners prominently on the General Overseas Service and GFP. Although vocal members of the home audience reviled them in 1944, the forces and many civilians overwhelmingly appreciated women crooners.

Whether the BBC legitimized dance music by calling it morale building and broadcasting it in increased quantities or sought to censor it, its decisions were accompanied by controversy in the press and among listeners. The extraordinary invective that sometimes greeted BBC decisions bespoke both the Corporation's central place in British life—and in the war effort—and the importance of popular music to its fans and critics. The 1942 ban on crooners and the actions of the DMPC demonstrated the power that the BBC attributed to popular music: it could empower or demoralize the nation at war. That the younger generations of servicemen, war workers, and teenagers disagreed with the BBC's assessment spoke to their newer conceptions of gendered and national identities. Indeed, self-consciously masculine British and American servicemen appreciated the very music that the BBC and their elders classified as effeminate, sentimental, and overly feminine. Following Allied victories in North Africa in late 1942, along with growing optimism about the course of the war, their perspective gained influence.

In many ways, popular music represented an "Other" to the BBC, which still valued its traditions of cultural uplift. Popular music could be commercial, effeminate, nonwhite, and un-British. While the ban on crooners represented at first glance the fear that slushy dance music could turn the British military and civilians at home to quivering mush before the enemy, the question of who the true enemy of British culture was remained. America was Britain's essential and courted ally, but American songs, entertainment, and—during 1944 and 1945—live performers dominated (and, on the AFN, competed with) the BBC's popular output. During the latter years of the war, the BBC worked to advance more distinctly British styles of popular music. The Corporation resisted bandleaders who slavishly copied American arrangements, and it banned singers who adopted pseudo-American accents or crooned. While the United States might have won the war in the realm of popular song, the BBC could promote British-style dance bands like Payne's, even if they really followed a style pioneered by an American, Paul Whiteman, two decades earlier. Most important, the BBC resisted American-style commercial radio, which threatened its monopoly.

Many of the BBC's wartime innovations and discoveries survived into the postwar period. Populist favorites like Lynn and Silvester went on to successful postwar careers while *MWYW* remained on the air until 1967. Geraldo, who came to prominence during the war, was regarded by the Corporation and much of the public as Britain's leading civilian bandleader at the war's end. In addition, the Corporation recognized the dance music public as composed of several audiences requiring a diversity of music. With the Third Programme to serve those who expected intellectual stimulation from the radio, the BBC could continue to serve those who wished merely to be diverted, or even to listen inattentively, on the Light Programme while, having revived prewar notions of the radio hearth, it promised both choice and riveting entertainment.

Popular music broadcasting at the BBC was marked by controversy throughout the war. Certainly, the compression of the BBC's offerings as well as shortages in resources exacerbated the "problems" of broadcasting popular music, but debate within and without the Corporation also spoke to the importance of popular music in the war effort and beyond. Rather than providing the soundtrack for a unified "People's War," popular music exposed the nation's divergent ideologies, tastes, and perspectives. During the Second World War, popular music broadcasting at the BBC allowed many to reimagine and contest the identity of "the" British listener.

Notes

DV	Director of Variety
ETRM	*Electrical Trading and Radio Marketing*
FR	File Report
GOSD	General Overseas Service Director
LRB	Listener Research Bulletin
LRD	Listener Research Department
LRWR	Listener Research Weekly Report
MM	*Melody Maker*
M-O	Mass-Observation
MOA	Mass Observation Archive
MPA	Music Publishers' Association
MWYW	Music While You Work
NSA	National Sound Archive
OB	Outside Broadcast
Oral History	Oral History of Jazz in Britain
PasB	Programmes as Broadcast
RP	*Radio Pictorial*
RT	*Radio Times*
TC	Topic Collection

INTRODUCTION

1. Letter from A. J. P. Hytch to Philip Jordan [copy of letter sent to the press], 13 June 1941, BBC WAC R27/257/2.

2. Nicholas, *Echo of War*, 12; and Scannell and Cardiff, *Social History*, 181, 184.

3. Anderson, *Imagined Communities*, 6.

4. See Humphrey Jennings and Stewart McAllister, dirs., *Listen to Britain* (1942; reissued by Image Entertainment, 2002); and Nicholas, *Echo of War*, 17.

5. *Oxford English Dictionary*, s.v. "Harmony," http://dictionary.oed.com.libaccess.lib .mcmaster.ca/cgi/entry/50102736?single=1&query_type=word&queryword=harmony&first =1&max_to_show=10 (accessed 20 May 2010).

6. *Grove Music Online*, s.v. "Harmony" (Carl Dahlhaus et al.), http://www.oxfordmusiconline .com.libaccess.lib.mcmaster.ca/subscriber/article/grove/music/50818 (accessed May 20, 2010).

7. Rose, *Which People's War?* 90.

8. Ibid., 287.

9. "Wireless in War," *Listener* (7 September 1939): 464.

10. Briggs, *History of Broadcasting*, 3:733.

11. Hall, "Notes on Deconstructing 'The Popular,'" 228.

12. Rose Macaulay, "The BBC and War Moods: I," *Spectator* (21 January 1944) [BBC clippings].

13. David Rolfe, liner notes to *I'll Play to You*.

14. LRB No. 211, 2 October 1944, BBC WAC R9/1/4.

15. H. S., "Miscellaneous and Dance," *Gramophone* (September 1942): 11.

16. Sandy Macpherson, *I'll Play to You* (Empress compact disc RAJCD 861, 1996).

17. *There'll Always Be an England* (Living Era compact disc AJA 5069, 1990).

18. Geraldo and His Orchestra, *A Journey to a Star* (Empress compact disc RAJCD 811, 1993). "Russian Lullaby" is mislabeled as "Russian Rose" on the compact disc.

19. Vera Lynn, *The Ultimate Collection* (Pulse compact disc PDS 554, 1998).

20. Silvester, *Dancing Is My Life*, 183–85; and Victor Silvester, "Yours," *Classic Years* (Prestige Elite, 2007; accessed through iTunes). The sound example features Desmond Carter and Robert Stoltz's "Don't Say Goodbye" in a similar treatment.

21. Spike Hughes, "Report on the Four BBC Contract Dance Bands and Victor Silvester's Band," 12 August 1943, BBC WAC R27/73/2.

22. Edgar Jackson, "British Jazz Makes the Grade," *MM* (15 March 1941): 3.

23. Harry Parry, *Crazy Rhythm* (Broadsword International compact disc SUN 2162, 2004).

24. Briggs, *History of Broadcasting*, vol. 3; Calder, *People's War*; Nicholas, *Echo of War*; Rose, *Which People's War?*; Scannell and Cardiff, *Social History*; Doctor, *BBC and Ultra-modern Music*; and LeMahieu, *Culture for Democracy*.

25. Jeffrey, *Mass-Observation*, 1.

26. Cain, *BBC*, 22.

27. Godbolt, *History of Jazz*, 18.

28. *Melody Maker* claimed to have a readership of 25,000. "Christmastide Greetings," *MM* (24 December 1938): 1.

29. M-O, *War Factory*, 8.

CHAPTER 1

1. MOA: TC 38/6/A, Informant to Obs. (AH), 22 March 1939.

2. Rt. Rev. Bishop of Chelmsford, "Radio Can Save the World," *RP* (12 May 1939): 7; Jan Korlstrum, "Hitler's Secret Radio," *RP* (3 March 1939): 7; and A. M. Low, "Radio in the Next War," *RP* (17 March 1939): 7.

3. Garry Allighan, "Broadcasts That Cause Trouble," *RP* (3 February 1939): 7.

4. Michael Marshall, "Dial 999 for BBC," *RP* (26 May 1939): 7.

5. Briggs, *History of Broadcasting*, 2:626; and Marwick, *Century of Total War*, 254.

6. Briggs, *History of Broadcasting*, 2:630.

7. Ibid., 645–46.

8. Jeffrey, *Mass-Observation*, 8.

9. Charles Madge and Tom H. Harrisson, *Britain by Mass-Observation* (Harmondsworth: Penguin Special, 1939), 50, quoted by Jeffrey, *Mass-Observation*, 33.

10. Giddens, *Consequences of Modernity*, 145–48.

11. Briggs, *History of Broadcasting*, 2:653.

12. Garry Allighan, "Dear Mr. Ogilvie," *RP* (6 January 1939): 7.

13. LeMahieu, *Culture for Democracy*, 227.

14. Camporesi, "Mass Culture," 4. My thanks to Michele Hilmes for lending me a copy of this dissertation.

15. Leslie Harrison, "Split-Second Presentation of American Broadcasts," *MM* (18 February 1939): 1.

16. Scannell and Cardiff, *Social History*, 269–73.

17. Leslie Perowne, 1963, BBC WAC R47/416/1, quoted by Parsonage, *Evolution of Jazz*, 259.

18. "Detector," "Recent Radio Reported,'" *MM* (10 December 1938): 4. McCarthy suggests that "Detector" was "probably" the pen name of Edgar Jackson, but Goldbolt, who lists several pseudonyms for Jackson and other *MM* critics, does not make this connection. McCarthy, *Dance Band Era*, 81; and Godbolt, *History of Jazz*.

19. Scannell and Cardiff, *Social History*, 192.

20. Bud Forder, "Geraldo Begins Something New—It's 'Up with the Curtain!'" *RP* (7 July 1939): 11.

21. "Detector," "Recent Radio Reported," *MM* (14 January 1939): 5.

22. Scannell and Cardiff, *Social History*, 10–13.

23. Anderson, *Imagined Communities*, 26, 7.

24. Scannell and Cardiff, "Broadcasting and National Unity," 159.

25. Hobsbawm, "Introduction: Inventing Traditions," 2, 9; and Cannadine, "The 'Last Night of the Proms' in Historical Perspective," 315–49.

26. LeMahieu, *Culture for Democracy*, 227.

27. Scannell and Cardiff, "Broadcasting and National Unity," 158; and Scannell and Cardiff, *Social History*, 17.

28. John Reith, *Broadcast over Britain* (London: Hodder and Stoughton, 1924), 17, quoted in Briggs, *History of Broadcasting*, 1:8.

29. Marwick, *Century of Total War*, 109–10; and LeMahieu, *Culture for Democracy*, 111.

30. LeMahieu, *Culture for Democracy*, 138.

31. Scannell and Cardiff, *Social History*, 9.

32. Scannell and Cardiff, "Broadcasting and National Unity," 158.

33. Hilmes, "Who We Are, Who We Are Not." My thanks to Michele Hilmes for providing me with a copy of her paper.

34. Reith, *Broadcast over Britain*, 173–75, quoted in Briggs, *History of Broadcasting*, 1:244.

35. Kenyon, *BBC Symphony Orchestra*, 12–49.

36. Doctor, *BBC and the Ultra-modern Problem*, 207–13.

37. Ibid., 174–75, 243–54.

38. Scholes, *Music Appreciation*, 278. Mark Katz has described a similar tendency in the United States. See Katz, "Making America More Musical through the Phonograph."

39. Scholes, *Music Appreciation*, 117; and Davies, *The Pursuit of Music*, p. 14.

40. *BBC Yearbook* (1930), 60, quoted in Scannell and Cardiff, *Social History*, 371.

41. Doctor, "'Virtual Concerts'—The BBC's Transmutation of Public Performances."

42. Nott, *Music for the People*, 116.

43. Scannell and Cardiff, *Social History*, 373.

44. Frith, "Pleasures of the Hearth," 110.

45. Scannell and Cardiff, *Social History*, 358.

46. "The BBC Has Discovered...," *RT* (10 March 1939): 11.

47. "Wireless in the Home," *Times* (1 September 1939): 8b.

48. For a discussion of the technically and bureaucratically complex history of regional broadcasting, see Scannell and Cardiff, *Social History*, 304–32.

49. Nott, *Music for the People*, 73–74.

50. Hilmes, "Who We Are, Who We Are Not," 32, 34.

51. Ursula Bloom, "What Women Listeners Want," *RP* (30 December 1938): 7.

52. Nicholas, *Echo of War*, 139.

53. Marchand, *Advertising the American Dream*, 69.

54. Hilmes, "Who We Are, Who We Are Not," 7.

55. Camporesi, "Mass Culture," 2.

56. Nott, *Music for the People*, 2–3.

57. Ibid., 19.

58. Camporesi, "Mass Culture," 2.

59. LeMahieu, *Culture for Democracy*, 118.

60. Frith, "Pleasures of the Hearth," 106, 113.

61. Ibid., 117; and Alec Mackenzie, "The Refining of Rhythm," *DT* (November/December 1920): 261.

62. Parsonage, *Evolution of Jazz*, 45.

63. McCarthy, *Dance Band Era*, 72, 74.

64. Marcelle Nicol, "After Dark in Radioland," *RP* (14 April 1939): 8.

65. "Our Radio Correspondent," "Please, Sir John, Suppress This Nightly Wailing," *Daily Dispatch* [November 1933], BBC WAC R19/585/1.

66. Parsonage, *Evolution of Jazz*, 179–80, 220; and Nott, *Music for the People*, 146.

67. Godbolt, *History of Jazz*, 118.

68. Rust, *Dance Bands*, 15; McCarthy, *Dance Band Era*, 38; and Parsonage, *Evolution of Jazz*, 134.

69. Godbolt, *History of Jazz*, 13, 54.

70. McCarthy, *Dance Band Era*, 18–20.

71. Godbolt, *History of Jazz*, 55.

72. Parsonage, *Evolution of Jazz*, 214.

73. Rust, *Dance Bands*, 53.

74. "Arranging Axioms," *MM* (30 August 1941): 2. See also Godbolt, *History of Jazz*, 70.

75. Parsonage, *Evolution of Jazz*, 214.

76. Quoted in McCarthy, *Dance Band Era*, 76.

77. LeMahieu, *Culture for Democracy*, 97.

78. Ibid.; and Nott, *Music for the People*, 155, 159. A note on currency: there were twelve pence in a shilling, twenty shillings in a pound, and twenty-one shillings in a guinea. In 1938, *Melody Maker* suggested that the average worker made three pounds per week. "Rophone," "Swing Records Too Dear!" *MM* (3 September 1938): 9.

79. Nott, *Music for the People*, 154, 169–70.

80. Richardson, *History of English Ballroom Dancing*, 89–90.

81. Frith, "Pleasures of the Hearth," 116.

82. Parsonage, *Evolution of Jazz*, 170.

83. McCarthy, *Dance Band Era*, 76.

84. Parsonage, *Evolution of Jazz*, 173.

85. Briggs, *History of Broadcasting*, 2:87.

86. Hall, *Here's to Next Time*, 84.

87. Roger Pryor Dodge, "Negro Jazz," *DT* (October 1929): 35.

88. Parsonage, *Evolution of Jazz*, 72, 194, 222.

89. Ibid., 251.

90. "Hot Jazz and Crooning," BBC ICM from DE to DV, 1 December 1933, BBC WAC R19/585/1; and "Hot Jazz and Crooning," BBC ICM from DE to DG, 7 December 1933, BBC WAC R19/585/1.

91. Scannell and Cardiff, *Social History*, 181, 184.

92. "Detector," "Recent Radio Reported," *MM* (10 December 1938): 4.

93. According to one writer for M-O, it took fifty radio airings to turn a song into a hit. MOA: FR 11A "Jazz and Dancing," November 1939, 19.

94. "Variety Department: Minutes of Meeting Held on Monday, May 4th, 1936, at 3.0 p.m. in AC(P)'s Office, Broadcasting House," BBC WAC R27/475/1.

95. "Song Plugging," BBC ICM from Mr. P. Brown to Booking Manager, 25 October 1937, BBC WAC R27/475/3.

96. "Dance Music Situation," BBC ICM from DV to C(P), 5 November 1935, BBC WAC R27/475/1.

97. See BBC WAC R27/475/1–4; and Scannell and Cardiff, *Social History*, 185–88.

98. "Anti-Song Plugging and Free Orchestrations Clause(s) as Inserted in the New Contract to Be Issued to OB Dance Band Directors, Now Being Printed," 7 August 1936, BBC WAC R27/475/1.

99. "Dance Band Directors' Association: Minutes of Meeting, Provincial Committee Held [at] Mayfair Hotel, Monday, 2 November 1936 at 11.30 a.m.," BBC WAC R27/475/2.

100. "Song Plugging," BBC ICM from PC Ex to DPA, AC(A), 4 July 1939, BBC WAC R27/475/3.

101. "Dance Band Programmes," BBC ICM from DV to PC Ex, 7 December 1939, BBC WAC R27/475/4; and Scannell and Cardiff, *Social History*, 188.

102. This was not the BBC's first attack on vocal numbers: during 1929 it had briefly banned all vocal numbers in an attempt to quash plugging. Scannell and Cardiff, *Social History*, 185.

103. "Dance Band Policy," BBC ICM from DV to ADPA, 24 February 1938, BBC WAC R27/71/3; and "Situation Regarding Dance Bands and New Regulations," BBC ICM from DV to C(P), 27 May 1937, BBC WAC R27/179.

104. "Hot Jazz and Crooning: Attached Cutting from The Daily Dispatch," BBC ICM from DG to DE, 27 November 1933, BBC WAC R19/585/1.

105. Lynn, *Vocal Refrain*, 40–41.

106. Scannell and Cardiff, *Social History*, 189.

107. Ibid., 231; Sonin, *Dance Band Mystery*, 157; and Nott, *Music for the People*, 77.

108. McCarthy, *Dance Band Era*, 77.

109. Nott, *Music for the People*, 71–76.

110. Briggs, *History of Broadcasting*, 2:45; Scannell and Cardiff, *Social History*, 233–34; and Camporesi, "Mass Culture," 68.

111. Scannell and Cardiff, *Social History*, 234.

112. Camporesi, "Mass Culture," 65.

113. Michael Marshall, "What- When- Why- Do You Listen," *RP* (21 April 1939): 7.

114. Scannell and Cardiff, *Social History*, 240–41.

115. Ibid., 191.

116. Parsonage, *Evolution of Jazz*, 259.

117. "Detector," "Recent Radio Reported," *MM* (31 December 1938): 2; and "Detector," "Recent Radio Reported," *MM* (4 February 1939): 6.

118. "Rophone," "Swing Records Too Dear!"

119. "American Relays of Dance Music," BBC ICM from Mr. L. A. Perowne to North American Representative, 11 August 1938, BBC WAC R47/3/2.

120. "Rophone," "Hot Records Reviewed," *MM* (1 October 1938): 7.

121. "Detector," "Recent Radio Reported," *MM* (1 October 1938): 7.

122. MOA: TC 38/4/F, "Leonard Feather" [interview], 28 June 1939.

123. "Detector," "Recent Radio Reported," *MM* (8 October 1938): 6.

124. "Detector," "Recent Radio Reported," *MM* (19 November 1939): 4.

125. [Sidney Petty,] "Swing Time Topics," *RP* (14 October 1938): 25.

126. Silvester, "Roll Back the Carpet," *RP* (2 December 1938): 27.

127. "Dancer's Delight," *RP* (28 July 1939): 17.

128. "Detector," "Recent Radio Reported," *MM* (17 December 1938): 4.

129. Forder, "Geraldo Begins Something New."

130. Noble, *Kings of Rhythm*, 16.

131. "Detector," "Recent Radio Reported," *MM* (10 December 1938): 4.

132. "What the Other Listener Thinks," *RT* (4 August 1939): 9.

133. Allighan, "Dear Mr. Ogilvie."

134. "What the Other Listener Thinks," *RT* (25 August 1939): 13.

135. "BBC Jittery about Sunday Dance Music," *MM* (22 October 1938): 1.

136. Leonard Meaby, "Adventures with a Portable No. 4: At the Hairdresser's, *RT* (1 September 1939): 8; and "Points from the Post," *RT* (1 September 1939): 12.

CHAPTER 2

1. "Crisis Consequences," *MM* (2 September 1939): 1.

2. Dan S. Ingman, "Your Job Now," *MM* (9 September 1939): 1–2.

3. Quoted in "It's Happening on the Home Front," *DM* (15 September 1939): 5.

4. Stevenson, *British Society*, 140.

5. Marwick, *Century of Total War*, 259.

6. Nicholas, *Echo of War*, 3–4.

7. "Both Sides of the Microphone," *RT* (22 September 1939): 3; and "Wireless in War," *Listener* (7 September 1939): 464.

8. Scott Goddard, "Broadcast Music during 1939," *Listener* (28 December 1939): 1296.

9. Memorandum on the Administration of the Broadcasting System in War, approved by the Board of Governors, 4 July 1939, quoted in Briggs, *History of Broadcasting*, 3:75.

10. "Wireless in War."

11. Briggs, *History of Broadcasting*, 3:143–49.

12. "Cassandra," "On the Air," *DM* (6 September 1939): 8.

13. "'In Tempore Belli," *Times* (7 October 1939): 4d.

14. "The Second Week," *RT* (8 September 1939): 3.

15. Briggs, *History of Broadcasting*, 3:101; and Collie Knox, "The BBC Is Creeping Back…," *Daily Mail* (6 October 1939) [BBC clippings].

16. "The Second Week."

17. Briggs, *History of Broadcasting*, 3:93.

18. "The Broadcasters," "Both Sides of the Microphone," *RT* (13 October 1939): 3.

19. "Wireless in War."

20. Briggs, *History of Broadcasting*, 3:96.

21. Collie Knox, "I Call This a Scandal…," *Daily Mail* (22 September 1939) [BBC clippings].

22. Briggs, *History of Broadcasting*, 3:96, 107; Programme Listings, *RT* (8 September 1939); Programme Listings, *RT* (15 September 1939); and Programme Listings, *RT* (22 September 1939).

23. Briggs, *History of Broadcasting*, 3:97; "Brighter Radio Again—Variety Back," *DM* (29 September 1939): 2.

24. See W. R. Anderson, "A Wireless Note," *MT* (October 1939): 712; and Knox, "I Call This a Scandal…"

25. Knox, "I Call This a Scandal…"; and Compton Mackenzie, "Editorial," *Gramophone* (December 1939): 242.

26. "Record Sales Are Booming Again," *ETRM* (November 1939): 58.

27. "Round and about This Week's Programmes," *RT* (8 September 1939): 13.

28. Sandy Macpherson, "Sandy Macpherson Thinks You Marvelous," *RT* (22 December 1939): 20; and "What the Wartime Listener Thinks," *RT* (22 September 1939): 11.

29. "Sandy's 10,000 Tunes," *Daily Mail* (20 November 1939) [BBC clippings].

30. Programme Listings, *RT* (15 September 1939).

31. "Kinema Music and BBC Broadcasts," *Kinematograph Weekly* (14 March 1940) [BBC clippings].

32. "Round and about This Week's Programmes"; and "What the Wartime Listener Thinks," *RT* (22 September 1939): 7.

33. Macpherson, "Sandy Macpherson Thinks You Marvelous."

34. Listener Research Section, "The Home Service," 11 October 1939, BBC WAC R9/9/3.

35. Knox, "I Call This a Scandal…"; and Compton Mackenzie, "Editorial," *Gramophone* (October 1939): 183.

36. Knox, "I Call This a Scandal…"; Briggs, *History of Broadcasting*, 3:108; "We Believe," *BW* (14 October 1939): 5; and Mackenzie, "Editorial," *Gramophone* (December 1939).

37. "Wartime Broadcasting," *MM* (9 September 1939): 2.

38. "Transmissions from America," BBC ICM from North American Representative to Foreign Liaison Officer, 12 September 1939, BBC WAC R47/3/4.

39. Edgar Jackson, "Swing Music," *Gramophone* (October 1939): 203.

40. "Detector," "This Month's Radio," *MM* (November 1939): 11.

41. Michael King, "Jack Hylton's Band Again," *Sunday Mail* (24 September 1939) [BBC clippings].

42. "Detector," "Our Wartime Radio to Date," *MM* (October 1939): 6.

43. "Bands for Variety Department," BBC ICM from ADPA to PC Ex, 16 October 1939, BBC WAC R27/71/3.

44. Briggs, *History of Broadcasting*, 3:108.

45. Guy Fletcher, "This Week's Radio Miscellany," *RT* (22 September 1939): 5; and "Billy Cotton's Band Playing on Six Days," *RT* (29 September 1939): 1.

46. Nott, *Music for the People*, 79.

47. "Detector," "Reviews the Carroll Gibbons and Joe Loss Broadcasts," *MM* (2 December 1939): 2.

48. "Brighter Radio Again—Variety Back"; and "The Broadcasters," "Both Sides of the Microphone," *RT* (6 October 1939): 3.

49. Jonah Barrington, "Gracie Gives Her Finest Broadcast," *Daily Express* (12 October 1939) [BBC clippings].

50. "The Gracie Tonic," *DM* (12 October 1939): 1.

51. Daily Mail Reporter, "Gracie Finds a Rhyme for Hitler," *Daily Mail* (12 October 1939) [BBC clippings].

52. "The Gracie Tonic."

53. Barrington, "Gracie Gives Her Finest Broadcast."

54. "The Broadcasters," "Both Sides of the Microphone," *RT* (6 October 1939): 3; and Knox, "The BBC Is Creeping Back…"

55. Count Ramon Vargas, "Name Bands Pay," *BW* (2 December 1939): 2.

56. McCarthy, *Dance Band Era*, 104–5.

57. Home Service PasB, 1 October 1939.

58. "West-End Wage Cutters Toe the Line," *MM* (October 1939): 1.

59. Ray Sonin, "Home Front Despatches," *MM* (October 1939): 8.

60. MOA: FR 11A, 1.

61. "All Bright on the West-End Front!" *MM* (9 December 1939): 1.

62. Quoted in "Records Are Booming," *ETRM* (December 1939): 58.

63. Bernard Buckham, "Listen in To," *DM* (4 January 1940): 15.

64. *The Oxford Dictionary of Music*, s.v. "Beer Barrel Polka," http://www.oxfordmusiconline.com.libaccess.lib.mcmaster.ca/subscriber/article/opr/t237/e1031 (accessed 11 March 2009).

65. MOA: FR 11A, 21–22.

66. Ray Sonin, "A Review of the New Songs," *MM* (October 1939): 7.

67. MOA: FR 11A, 21.

68. "Berlin or Bust," BBC ICM from AC(P) (J. Wellington) to DPA, 19 October 1939, BBC WAC R27/475/3.

69. Sonin, "A Review of the New Songs."

70. MOA: FR 11A, 22.

71. See "America Has a Headache," *MM* (November 1939): 14.

72. MOA: FR 11A, 25–26. See the introduction for a discussion of Lynn's recording of the song.

73. "Blue Note," "Jazz Is Failing to Take Its Wartime Chance," *BW* (4 November 1939): 5.

74. "Points from the Post," *RT* (17 November 1939): 14.

75. MOA: FR 11A, 23.

76. Joe Loss and His Orchestra, "Goodnight Children Everywhere," *There'll Always Be an England* (Living Era compact disc AJA 5069, 1990).

77. "Detector," "BBC Dance Music Still in a Rut," *MM* (16 December 1939): 4.

78. Stowe, *Swing Changes*, 95.

79. "Points from the Post," *RT* (17 November 1939): 14.

80. "What the Wartime Listener Thinks," *RT* (10 November 1939): 5.

81. Comment penned on Music Policy, 14 November 1939, BBC WAC R27/245/1.

82. Ralph Hill, "Radio Music in 1940," *RT* (29 December 1939): 6.

83. Programme Listings, *RT* (1 December 1939).

84. Bernard Buckham, "Listen In," *DM* (3 January 1940): 15.

85. Alec Hughes, "M-O Looks at Jazz," *BW* (22 November 1939): 2.

86. Music Policy, 14 November 1939, BBC WAC R27/245/1.

87. Hill, "Radio Music in 1940"; and Music Policy, 14 November 1939.

88. Programme Listings, *RT* (1 December 1939).

89. "We Believe," *BW* (13 January 1940): 5.

90. Forty percent of middle-class men, 24 percent of middle-class women, 8 percent of working-class men, and 15 percent of working-class women reported liking "all types" of music. Hughes, "M-O Looks at Jazz," 2.

91. "'Indefinite Series' of Guest Night Broadcasts for Henry Hall," *MM* (2 December 1939): 1.

92. *Oxford Dictionary of National Biography*, s.v. "Hall, Henry Robert (1898–1989)" (by Ian Wallace), http://www.oxforddnb.com.libaccess.lib.mcmaster.ca/view/article/40694 (accessed 28 May 2010).

93. Compton Mackenzie, "Editorial," *Gramophone* (January 1940): 282.

94. LRWR No. 17, 11 January 1941, BBC WAC R9/1/1.

95. "A Song-Plugger Makes an Epic Journey," *MM* (30 December 1939): 7.

96. Ash-Lyons, "Xmas Radio a Wash-Out!" *BW* (30 December 1939): 2.

97. Joe Loss, "What I Saw in France," *MM* (24 February 1940): 3.

98. Briggs, *History of Broadcasting*, 3:125–26.

99. General F. Beaumont-Nesbitt to Ogilvie, 2 February 1940, quoted in ibid.

100. Briggs, *History of Broadcasting*, 3:125–29.

101. "Modulator," "BEF Radio Gives Light Relief," *BW* (30 December 1939): 4.

102. Briggs, *History of Broadcasting*, 3:126–27.

103. "Wartime Broadcasting"; and "Detector," "This Month's Radio," *MM* (November 1939): 13.

104. Briggs, *History of Broadcasting*, 3:132.

105. "Horrified by Gay Sundays," *DM* (29 December 1939): 20; and Listener Research Section, "General Listening Barometer 1939/40 Report No. 24: Sunday Variety and Dance Music," 17 June 1940, BBC WAC R9/22/1.

106. Bernard Buckham, "Listen In," *DM* (23 January 1940): 18.

107. "Detector," "Review of Current Radio," *MM* (13 January 1940): 4.

108. "Sunday Policy—Home Service," DPP to DV, 20 January 1940, BBC WAC R27/172/1.

109. "The Broadcasters," "Special Programmes for the Forces," *RT* (29 December 1939): 3.

110. Programme Listings, *RT* (12 January 1940).

111. Greenway, "Balance of Music on the Forces Programme," 17.

112. Listener Research Section, "General Listening Barometer 1939/40 No. 16," 18 March 1940, BBC WAC R27/172/1.

113. Briggs, *History of Broadcasting*, 3:129.

114. Guy Fletcher, "This Week's Radio Miscellany," *RT* (3 November 1939): 7.

115. "The Broadcasters," "Both Sides of the Microphone," *RT* (19 April 1940): 8.

116. Spike Hughes, "The War Has at Least Given Us a Better BBC," *Daily Herald* (26 January 1940) [BBC clippings].

117. LRWR No. 36, 28 May 1941, BBC WAC R9/1/1.

118. R. J. E. Silvey, "Finding Out What You Listen To," *RT* (12 April 1940): 8–9.

119. Briggs, *History of Broadcasting*, 3:134; "We Believe," *BW* (10 February 1940): 6; and "Full-Time Programmes for the Forces," *RT* (16 February 1940): 3.

120. Nicholas, *Echo of War*, 49.

121. "Full-Time Programmes for the Forces."

122. "The Stuff to Give the Troops," *Listener* (15 February 1940): 308.

123. "The BBC Has Discovered...," *RT* (10 March 1939): 11; and Rose, *Which People's War?* 160–68.

124. Briggs, *History of Broadcasting*, 3:138.

125. "Special Programmes for the Forces Beginning This Week," *RT* (5 January 1940): 5.

126. "Full-Time Programmes for the Forces."

127. Charles Brewer, "What Does the RAF Listen To?" *RT* (1 March 1940): 5.

128. "Detector," "Pity the Poor Amateurs!" *MM* (23 August 1941): 3.

129. "Jazz Jamboree for the Forces," *BW* (9 March 1940): 3.

130. "Dance Music from America: Bob Crosby, 29th March, 2000–2030 BST: Forces Programme," BBC ICM from Miss Reeves to Mr. Gorham, 13 March 1940, BBC WAC R47/3/5; and "Dance Music from America: 31st March, 1830–1900 BST: Forces Programme," BBC ICM from Miss Reeves to Mr. Gorham, 20 March 1940, BBC WAC R47/3/5.

131. Guy Fletcher, "This Week's Radio Miscellany," *RT* (23 February 1940): 7; and Briggs, *History of Broadcasting*, 3:138.

132. "The Human Story behind Sandy's Half-Hour," *RT* (5 April 1940): 10; and "He Held the BBC Fort with 200 Broadcasts," *Star* (19 March 1940) [BBC clippings].

133. See the introduction for a discussion of "I'll Play to You."

134. Forces PasB, 26 February 1940, 26 March 1940.

135. "The Broadcasters," "Both Sides of the Microphone," *RT* (20 September 1940): 4.

136. "Life-Line between the People at Home and the Men Overseas," *Clip-Sheet* [Issued by the MoI for the *Exclusive* Us of Editors of Weekly Newspapers], no. 107 (21 January 1942), in Madden, Wartime Radio Diary No. 13, BBC WAC S24/54/13.

137. Crisell, *Understanding Radio*, 23.

138. Hughes, "The War Has at Least Given Us a Better BBC."

139. "We Believe," *BW* (24 February 1940): 6.

140. Silvester, *Dancing Is My Life*, 175–76.

141. "Representation of Music Publishers in Variety Programmes," BBC ICM from PC Ex to DV, 23 October 1939, BBC WAC R27/475/3.

142. "Song Plugging," BBC ICM from PC Ex to DPA, AC(A), 15 December 1939, BBC WAC R27/475/4.

143. "Dance Band Made £150 in an Hour," *Daily Sketch* (25 January 1940) [BBC clippings].

144. "Radio Song-Plugging Rife," *MM* (10 February 1940): 1. For a more detailed discussion of *Melody Maker*'s campaign and the BBC's response, see Baade, "'Victory through Harmony,'" 74–85.

145. "OB Dance Band and Studio Dance Band Programmes," BBC ICM from PC Ex to DV et al. (17 January 1940), BBC WAC R27/71/3.

146. "Song Plugging," LM 52, Issued by the Secretariat, May 1940, BBC WAC R27/475/4.

147. See *Westminster Shorter Catechism* (1674); reprinted on Faith Presbyterian Church, "Doctrine," FaithTacoma.org, http://www.faithtacoma.org/doctrine/wsc.aspx (accessed 7 July 2009).

148. "Song Plugging," LM 52, Issued by the Secretariat, May 1940.

149. MOA: FR 49 "Gramophone Records" (JC), March 1940.

150. "Lawrie Wright Defends English Song-Writers," *BW* (19 April 1940): 1+.

151. Nicholas, *Echo of War*, 82.

152. Letter from [Sir John Reith,] Ministry of Information, Senate House, to F. W. Ogilvie, DG, 21 February 1940, BBC WAC R27/213/1.

153. BBC WAC R27/213/1: Music General: Ministry of Information, 1939–1940.

CHAPTER 3

1. Wynford Reynolds, "How Music Has Speeded Up Munitions Output," *Evening Chronicle, Manchester* (9 March 1943) [BBC clippings].

2. M-O, *War Factory*, 8.

3. Foster, "Choreographing History," 14; and Outram, *The Body and the French Revolution*, 7.

4. Wollen, "Cinema/Americanism/the Robot," 49, 51.

5. Rose, *Which People's War?* 44–56.

6. Priestley, *Daylight on Saturday*, 237.

7. Marwick, *Century of Total War*, 260, 296.

8. Douglas, *Listening In*, 27.

9. Gifford, *Golden Age of Radio*.

10. Hilmes, "Who We Are, Who We Are Not," 32.

11. Gubar, "'This Is My Rifle,'" 251.

12. Giedion, *Mechanization Takes Command*, 99.

13. Taylor, *Scientific Management*, 28.

14. *Encyclopædia Britannica*, "Work, History of the Organization of," http://www.britannica.com/eb/article?tocId=9108782 (accessed 14 July 2005).

15. Soibelman, *Uses of Music*, 174–75.

16. S. Wyatt and J. N. Langdon, *Fatigue and Boredom in Repetitive Work*, Great Britain Medical Research Council, Industrial Health Research Board Report No. 77 (London: H.M. Stationary Office, 1937), cited in Soibelman, *Uses of Music*, 175–76.

17. Neil Hutchison, "Music in Factories: Preliminary Report," 26 June 1940, BBC WAC R27/257/1.

18. Taylor, *Scientific Management*, 59.

19. Rose, *Which People's War*, 109.

20. Noakes, *War and the British*, 20, n. 43.

21. M-O, *War Factory*, 18.

22. Ibid., 6. Fremlin was not identified by name in *War Factory* but is named in Kirkham, "Beauty and Duty," 16.

23. M-O, *War Factory*, 27, 30.

24. Nicholas, *Echo of War*, 3.

25. M-O, *War Factory*, 46–47. Since conscription targeted young, childless women, most female war workers escaped the added responsibilities of housework and child care.

26. Peggy Oughton, "Reactions of Factory Workers to Certain Types of Broadcast Music: Impressions of a BBC Employee in a Factory," August 1945, BBC WAC R27/257/4.

27. "Music Cheers 'Go-to-It' Sunday," *Daily Mail* (24 June 1940) [BBC clippings].

28. Letter from AC(P) to Mr. Andrew Stewart (Ministry of Information), 18 June 1940, BBC WAC R27/257/1.

29. "Music While You Work," BBC ICM from Mr. Robert MacDermott to ADPP, 25 June 1940, BBC WAC R27/257/1.

30. Foucault, *Discipline and Punish*, 138.

31. Hutchison, "Music in Factories: Preliminary Report."

32. "Music While You Work," BBC ICM from DDM to Music Ex et al., 1 July 1940, BBC WAC R27/257/1.

33. Hutchison, "Music in Factories: Preliminary Report."

34. Outram, *The Body and the French Revolution*, 8.

35. "Music While You Work," BBC ICM from Mr. Denis Wright to Mr. Hutchison (Programme Planning), 9 July 1940, BBC WAC R27/257/1.

36. "Music While You Work," BBC ICM from Hutchison to DV et al., 10 July 1940, BBC WAC R27/257/1.

37. "Music While You Work," BBC ICM from Wright to Hutchison, 9 July 1940.

38. "Music While You Work," BBC ICM from Wright to OB Executive, 22 July 1940, BBC WAC R27/257/1.

39. "BBC Military Band," BBC ICM from Music Organizer to ADPP, 23 January 1941, BBC WAC R27/257/2.

40. Giedion, *Mechanization Takes Command*, 77.

41. Guy Fletcher, "This Week's Miscellany," *RT* (30 August 1940): 5.

42. "Music While You Work," BBC ICM from ADPP to DPP, 6 December 1940, BBC WAC R27/257/1; "Music While You Work," BBC ICM from Wright (Glasgow) to ADM (Bristol), 15 February 1941, BBC WAC R27/257/2; and "Music While You Work," BBC ICM from ADPP to AC(P), 16 February 1941, BBC WAC R27/257/2.

43. "What the Other Listener Thinks," *RT* (1 January 1941): 8.

44. "Music While You Work," BBC ICM from DPP to Listener Research P[lanner?], 19 November 1940, BBC WAC R27/257/1.

45. "Music While You Work," BBC ICM from ADPP to AC(P), 16 February 1941.

46. "Music While You Work," BBC ICM from ADPP to Perowne, 2 May 1941, BBC WAC R27/257/2.

47. Wynford Reynolds, "Music While You Work," *RT* (20 June 1941): 3; and BBC WAC Artists, Wynford Reynolds, File 3A (1943–45).

48. Reynolds, "Music While You Work."

49. "Music While You Work," BBC ICM from ADPP to ADV (Bangor), 30 May 1941, BBC WAC R27/257/2; and "Music While You Work," BBC ICM from DPP to DPA, 11 May 1941, BBC WAC R27/257/2.

50. Letter from Hytch to Jordan, 13 June 1941.

51. "A Listener Research Report: Music While You Work," n.d., BBC WAC R27/257/2; and "Announcement for Music While You Work," BBC ICM, week 25, BBC WAC R27/257/2.

52. "Press Conference: Wednesday, 18th June, 1941," BBC ICM from Mr. Warren to ADM, 19 June 1941, BBC WAC R27/257/2.

53. *Music While You Work* Press Cuttings, BBC WAC 57/1.

54. "Victory through Harmony," *News Review* (26 June 1941) [BBC clippings].

55. "Music Oils Wheels of Industry," *Manchester Evening News* (7 July 1941) [BBC clippings].

56. "A Listener Research Report: Music While You Work," n.d.

57. "Music While You Work," Reynolds to DV (Bangor), 5 September 1941, BBC WAC R27/257/2.

58. "Music While You Work," BBC ICM from Reynolds to Music Department London, August 1941, BBC WAC R27/257/2.

59. "'Music While You Work," BBC ICM from Reynolds to AC(P), 5 August 1941, BBC WAC R27/257/2.

60. "Music While You Work," Reynolds to DV, 5 September 1941; and Reynolds, "The British Broadcasting Corporation, 'Music While You Work' General Directive," June 1942, BBC WAC R27/257/3.

61. Reynolds, "The British Broadcasting Corporation, 'Music While You Work.'"

62. Manufacturers could supplement the program with gramophone records, though finding suitable recordings was challenging. Although Reynolds could not make specific recommendations in BBC documents, he collaborated with Edgar Jackson, the jazz record reviewer for *Gramophone* and *Melody Maker*, in supervising Decca's "Music While You Work" series, which debuted in October 1942. Many of these recordings have been reissued on *Music While You Work*, Empress compact disc 1004 (three-compact disc set), 1994–96. "Brand's Essence," *MM* (17 February 1945): 6; and "Decca Introduce Special 'Music While You Work' Records," *Gramophone* (October 1942): 66.

63. "Committee on Industrial Publicity," Minutes of 50th Meeting, 21 April 1942, IPC 192, BBC WAC R27/262/1.

64. Reynolds, "The British Broadcasting Corporation, 'Music While You Work.'"

65. Ibid.

66. Rose, *Which People's War?* 39–41.

67. Letter to Reynolds, 28 August 1942, BBC WAC R27/263.

68. "Music While You Work Broadcast for Night Workers," BBC ICM from Reynolds to DPP, 1 May 1942, BBC WAC R27/262/1.

69. "Music While You Work: Forces Programme 10:30 p.m. August 2 Onwards," BBC ICM from Programme Organizer to Presentation Director, 11 July 1942, BBC WAC R27/257/3; and "The Night Shift," *RT* (24 July 1942): 5.

70. "Committee on Industrial Publicity," Minutes of 50th Meeting, 21 April 1942; and "Music While You Work Committee on Industrial Publicity," BBC ICM from Reynolds to AC(P), DPP, Programme Organizer (Forces), 23 April 1942, BBC WAC R27/262/1.

71. MOA: FR 1249 "Radio: Uses of Music in Factories and the BBC's 'Music While You Work,'" 21 May 1942.

72. Letter from AC(P) to Stewart, 18 June 1940.

73. "'Music While You Work' Government Factories," BBC ICM from Wynford Reynolds to C(P), 12 March 1942, BBC WAC R27/262/1.

74. "Third Anniversary of 'Music While You Work,'" *RT* (18 June 1943): 1.

75. Orpheus, "Musical Commentary," *Liverpool Evening Express* (25 February 1942) [BBC clippings].

76. "Music While You Work," BBC ICM from Reynolds to C(P), 19 January 1942, BBC WAC R27/257/3.

77. Letter to *Daily Telegraph* (7 March 1942) [BBC clippings].

78. "BBC Music Policy," draft by C(P) amended in accordance with suggestions made by DM, DDM, and Arthur Bliss, 1 April 1942, BBC WAC R27/73/1.

79. See chapter 6.

80. "BBC Music Policy," 1 April 1942.

81. "Light Music Survey," BBC ICM from Light Music Supervisor to DM, 28 December 1942, BBC WAC R27/172/1.

82. Reynolds, "'Music While You Work': Report on Experimental Programmes for Period 18th March to 30th September 1942," July 1943, BBC WAC R27/257/3.

83. Ibid.

84. Ibid.

85. "'Music While You Work': Frank Stewart and His Orchestra, Wednesday 29th April, 1942 3.0 p.m.," BBC ICM from Reynolds to DPP, ADM, 27 May 1942, BBC WAC R27/260; and "'Music While You Work': DeWolfe and His Orchestra, Wednesday 19th August, 1942 3.0 p.m.," BBC ICM from Reynolds to DPP, DM, 25 September 1942, BBC WAC R27/260.

86. "'Music While You Work': Jack Simpson and His Sextet, Wednesday 24th June, 1942 3.0 p.m.," BBC ICM from Reynolds to DV et al., 12 August 1942, BBC WAC R27/260.

87. "Music While You Work—Changes in Programme Policy," BBC ICM from MWYW Organiser to ADV, ADM (Programmes), 21 April 1944, BBC WAC R27/257/4.

88. Reynolds, "'Music While You Work': Report on Experimental Programmes for Period 18th March to 30th September 1942."

89. Ibid.

90. "'Music While You Work': Instructions for Dance Bands, Light Orchestras, Military and Brass Bands," BBC ICM from Music While You Work Organizer to DV et al., 5 April 1943, BBC WAC R27/259.

91. Ibid.; and Industrial Recreation Association, *Music in Industry*, 28.

92. "'Music While You Work': Instructions for Dance Bands, Light Orchestras, Military and Brass Bands," 5 April 1943.

93. "'Music While You Work': Instructions for Dance Bands, Light Orchestras, Military and Brass Bands," BBC ICM from MWYW Organizer to Midlands Region Programme Director et al., 23 August 1943, BBC WAC R27/259; and "'Music While You Work': Instructions for Dance Bands, Light Orchestras, Military and Brass Bands," BBC ICM from MWYW Organizer to West Region Programme Director et al., 1 November 1943, BBC WAC R27/259.

94. "'Music While You Work'—Producing and Balancing of Programmes," BBC ICM from F. W. Alexander, Head of Programme Engineering to All London P.E.'s on "Music While You Work," et al., 2 June 1943, BBC WAC R27/257/3.

95. Ibid.; and "Notes on Mr. Wynford Reynolds Talk on 'Music While You Work,'" 31 May 1943, BBC WAC R27/257/3.

96. Reynolds, "'Music While You Work': First Report for Period 5th May to 30th November 1941," 30 November 1941, BBC WAC R27/257/2. The policy was relaxed somewhat in 1944, following lobbying by cinema organists and an experimental *Music While You Work* organ broadcast, involving twenty-five firms and 92,000 workers. Reynolds, "'Music While You Work' Report on the Cinema Organ Experiment, H. Robinson Cleaver at the Organ of the Granada Theatre, Tooting, 10.30 a.m., Thursday 7 September 1944," 18 October 1944, BBC WAC R27/257/4.

97. "Notes on Mr. Wynford Reynolds Talk on 'Music While You Work,'" 31 May 1943.

98. "'Music While You Work'—Dance Music Played by Light Music Combinations," BBC ICM from MWYW Organiser to DM, 26 November 1942, BBC WAC R27/257/3.

99. "Music While You Work," BBC ICM from ADV to All Producers, 28 July 1943, BBC WAC R27/257/3.

100. "Music While You Work—Song Plugging," BBC ICM from MWYW Organiser to DM, 17 March 1944, BBC WAC R27/257/4.

101. Ibid.

102. "List of Factories, Mills, Installation Firms, and Industrial and Welfare Organisations, etc. Who Have Been Contacted by Mr. Wynford Reynolds from May 1941 up to the Present Date June, 1946," BBC WAC R27/258.

103. "'Music While You Work': Summary of Reports on Visits to Factories in December, 1944," BBC ICM from Reynolds to DPP, DM, DV, 10 January 1945, BBC WAC R27/257/4.

104. "'Music While You Work': Letter from F. Hills & Sons Ltd.," BBC ICM from MWYW Organiser to DPP, 23 April 1945, BBC WAC R27/257/4.

105. Leslie Barringer, "The Disease of Not Listening," RT (2 October 1942): 3.

106. "'Music While You Work': Important BBC Enquiry This Week," RT (4 July 1941): 3.

107. "Music While You Work," BBC ICM from Senior Superintendent Engineer to DPP, 21 August 1940, BBC WAC R27/257/1.

108. "Music While You Work," BBC ICM from Wright to OB Executive, 22 July 1940.

109. "Music While You Work," BBC ICM from Mr. Eric Dunstan to AC(P), 24 June 1940, BBC WAC R27/257/1.

110. "LRWR No. 6," week ending 24 August 1940, BBC WAC R9/1/1.

111. "Morning Programmes (8.20 a.m.–1.00 p.m.)," Listener Research Report LR/245, 23 April 1941, BBC WAC R9/9/5.

112. LRB No. 71, 2 February 1942, BBC WAC R9/1/2.

113. "Your Taste in Light Music," RT (1 September 1944): 4.

114. Reynolds, "'Music While You Work': Survey of the 5th Year of the Series," 1 June 1945, BBC WAC R27/257/4.

115. R. J. E. Silvey, "Methods of Listener Research Employed by the British Broadcasting Corporation," attached to "Paper on Listener Research for Royal Statistical Society," BBC ICM from Listener Research Director (R. J. E. Silvey) to C(P), 23 May 1944, BBC WAC R9/15/1.

116. Seton Margrave, "There Are Five 'Musts' for Popular Music," Daily Mail (Scotch Edition) (Irish Edition) (2 October 1941) [BBC clippings].

117. "'Music While You Work' Experiment, July 6th–12th: First Findings," Listener Research Director to Reynolds, 8 August 1941, BBC WAC R27/257/2.

118. Advertisement for Stentorian extension speakers by Whiteley Electrical Radio Company, Limited, ETRM (July 1941): 39.

119. Priestley, Daylight on Saturday, 25–26.

120. "Music in Factories," Pianomaker and Music Seller (August 1939): 185.

121. M-O, War Factory, 27, 9, 122.

122. "Music While You Work," BBC ICM from GOSD to Reynolds, 1 February 1944, BBC WAC R27/257/4; and "'Music While You Work'—4th Anniversary: 23rd June 1944," BBC ICM from MWYW Organiser to Director of Publicity, Deputy Editor, RT, 1 June 1944, BBC WAC R27/257/4.

123. Reynolds, "'Music While You Work': Survey of the 5th Year of the Series," 1 June 1945.

124. "The Pros and Cons of Recorded Music in the Red and Green Networks," 29 December 1942, BBC WAC R27/416/1.

125. Priestley, *Daylight on Saturday*, 25.

CHAPTER 4

1. Harry Parry, "A Musician Braves the Blitz," *MM* (21 December 1940): 15.

2. Parry narrowly failed the entry test, a disappointment that he attributed to lack of sleep. Noble, *Kings of Rhythm*, 62.

3. Parry, "A Musician Braves the Blitz."

4. "Dabbler," "Raid-io," *MM* (28 September 1940): 5; and "Eavesdropper," "Pity the Poor Leader," *MM* (7 September 1940): 9. "Detector" took a brief hiatus as the *Melody Maker*'s radio reviewer between February and October 1940.

5. "If Your Band is 'Blitzed...,'" *MM* (4 January 1941): 4.

6. "Comment," *MM* (14 September 1940): 4.

7. Don Ralfe, "'...Much to Our Surprise, the Ceiling Caved In,'" *MM* (1 February 1941): 7.

8. Rose, *Which People's War?* 2.

9. Calder, *Myth of the Blitz*, 14, 119-40. For a gloss on Calder's argument, see Ziegler, *London at War*, 163.

10. "Comment," *MM* (16 November 1940): 4.

11. "Comment," *MM* (14 September 1940).

12. *Band Wagon* also supported the dance profession, but it ceased publication in September 1940.

13. See Tucker, *Swing Shift*; and Baade, "'The Battle of the Saxes,'" 90–128.

14. Jeffery and McClelland, "A World Fit to Live In," 38.

15. Rose, *Which People's War?* 153.

16. Ibid., 181–96.

17. Leppert, *Music and Image*; and Ehrlich, *Music Profession in Britain*.

18. McKay, *Circular Breathing*, 97. See Kushner, *We Europeans?*

19. "Alien Artists and Music (Italian)," BBC ICM from DDM to AC(P), 13 June 1940, BBC WAC R27/3/1; and "Music by Alien Composers," BBC ICM from Mr. Eric Maschwitz to DDM (Bristol), 29 July 1940, BBC WAC R27/3/1.

20. Quoted in "We Protest!" *MM* (4 January 1941): 1.

21. LRD, "Broadcasting Policy," 27 August 1940, BBC WAC R9/15/1.

22. R. J. E. Silvey, "Listening in 1940," in *BBC Handbook 1941* (London: BBC, n.d.), 77–78.

23. F. H. Shera, "Broadcast Music," *Listener* (27 June 1940): 1212; and "What the Other Listener Thinks," *RT* (14 June 1940): 9.

24. Briggs, *History of Broadcasting*, 3:216.

25. Ibid., 3:217.

26. "A Smiler," letter to *RT* (21 June 1940): 9.

27. "Radio in Wartime," *RT* (21 June 1940): 3.

28. "A Listener Research Report: Are Current Programmes Too Frivolous?" Listener Research Section, Public Relations Division, BBC, LR/143, June 1940, BBC WAC R9/9/4.

29. "The Fortress of the Spirit," *Listener* (28 September 1939): 606.

30. "A Listener Research Report: Are Current Programmes Too Frivolous?"

31. Briggs, *History of Broadcasting*, 3:215.

32. MOA: FR 295 "On Jazz (Bolton)" (AH), July 1940, in MOA: FR 301A "First Weekly Morale Report: Series C (July 1940)," 27 July 1940, 44–45; and "Song Plugging," BBC ICM from ADPA to Variety Ex, 1 May 1940, BBC WAC R27/475/4.

33. LRD, "Broadcasting Policy," 27 August 1940.

34. "Contact with the Forces," BBC ICM from Mr. Roger Wilson to Mr. R. J. E. Silvey, 13 July 1940, BBC WAC R9/15/1.

35. "Authorities Hail Dancing as Vital Relaxation for Troops," *MM* (4 May 1940): 5.

36. MOA: FR 295, in MOA: FR 301A, 47.

37. Ibid., 46.

38. See "Loss's Losses," *MM* (6 July 1940): 1.

39. "Leaders Debate Call-Up of Musicians," *MM* (1 February 1941): 1.

40. "Is Entertainment National Service?" *MM* (31 August 1940): 4.

41. "Eavesdropper," "Air Bands," *MM* (6 April 1940): 3.

42. "Present Dance Band Situation," BBC ICM from Mr. Douglas Lawrence (Hereford House) to DV (Bangor), 26 February 1942, BBC WAC R27/73/1.

43. "Musicians and the RAF," *BW* (16 March 1940): 1.

44. "Ex-Ambrose Manager Leads Ace Dance Band in RAF," *MM* (6 April 1940): 1. See McCarthy, *Dance Band Era*, 143–47; and Chris Way's Anglo-American survey, *The Big Bands Go to War*.

45. "We Protest!" *MM* (28 June 1941): 2.

46. "Eavesdropper," "Dance Band Utopia," *MM* (24 August 1940): 9.

47. "Detector," "The Greatest Dance Band Airing!" *MM* (18 January 1941): 9.

48. The BBC also explored and rejected solutions including a junior dance band, composed of boys below call-up age, and an all-women's dance orchestra, the idea for which was revived when Ivy Benson signed a house band contract with the BBC in 1943. "Dance Music," BBC ICM from Philip Brown to DV, 20 March 1941, BBC WAC R27/21; and "The BBC Nearly Had a Girls' Band!" *MM* (3 August 1940): 2.

49. "Dance Bands of the Week," BBC ICM from PC Ex to Variety Booking Manager, 23 August 1940, BBC WAC R27/71/3; and "Dance Bands of the Week," BBC ICM from Variety Booking Manager to PC Ex, 28 August 1940, BBC WAC R27/21.

50. "Band of the Week," BBC ICM from ADV to C(P), 11 April 1940, BBC WAC R27/21.

51. "Air Raids No Scare Raids," *MM* (31 August 1940): 1.

52. "Air Raids," *MM* (7 September 1940): 1.

53. "Cafe Anglais...400...Berkeley Bands Out," *MM* (21 September 1940): 1.

54. "Air Raids"; and "'MM' Investigates the Air-Raids Situation,'" *MM* (14 September 1940): 1.

55. "The SitterOut" et al., "Ballroom Prospects," *DT* (October 1940): 22.

56. "Cafe Anglais...400...Berkeley Bands Out."

57. Or so it was alleged. "Comment," *MM* (21 September 1940): 4.

58. "Ambrose Is the Band of Next Week," *MM* (14 September 1940): 2.

59. "Eddie Carroll Airs in Air-Raid!" *MM* (31 August 1940): 2.

60. Briggs, *History of Broadcasting*, 3:299–300; "LRWR No. 1," week ending 20 July 1940, BBC WAC R9/1/1; and "The BBC Racks Its Brains," *MM* (12 October 1940): 9. Briggs maintained that the programs were prerecorded not because of air raids but because of the performers' busy schedules.

61. "Shows the BBC Want," *Evening News* (19 September 1940) [BBC clippings]; and "The BBC Racks Its Brains."

62. "Pick-Up," "New Commercial Records," *MM* (28 September 1940): 9.

63. "Straws in the Wind II. Influence of Air Raids on Listening Habits (Spontaneous Reports)," Listener Research Section, Public Relations Division, BBC, October 1940, LR/174, BBC WAC R9/9/4.

64. "A Listener Research Report: Air Raids and Listening," 16 October 1940, BBC WAC R9/9/4.

65. "Shows the BBC Want," *Evening News* (19 September 1940) [BBC clippings].

66. "Detector," "The BBC Racks Its Brains,'" *MM* (12 October 1940): 9; and "Straws in the Wind II."

67. *BBC Handbook 1941*, 120; and Briggs, *History of Broadcasting*, 3:297.

68. "Detector," "Fair Play for the Forces Wave-Length," *MM* (9 November 1940): 9.

69. "LRWR No. 10," week ending 26 October 1940, BBC WAC R9/1/1.

70. "Detector," "New Forces Wave Length Is Great Improvement," *MM* (15 March 1941): 9.

71. "London Niteries Blitz and Re-Open," *MM* (2 November 1940): 1.

72. Briggs, *History of Broadcasting*, 3:294–95.

73. "Blitzed!" *MM* (11 January 1941): 1.

74. "Jerry Dawson's Northern Gossip," *MM* (4 January 1941): 12.

75. "If Your Band Is 'Blitzed . . .'"

76. See Parry, "A Musician Braves the Blitz"; and Ralfe, "'. . . Much to Our Surprise, the Ceiling Caved In.'"

77. "Al Bowlly Passes," *MM* (26 April 1941): 1; "The Profession Mourns . . . Ken Johnson Killed in Blitz," *MM* (15 March 1941): 1; and "Ken Johnson: Impressive Tribute," *MM* (22 March 1941): 1.

78. Rust, *Dance Bands*, 139.

79. "What the Other Listener Thinks," *RT* (28 March 1941): 8.

80. See chapter 5.

81. After Russia's entry into World War II, the group began to support the war. D. Pritt, *From Right to Left* (1965), 245–87, quoted in Briggs, *History of Broadcasting*, 3:234, n. 3. "Bands of the Week—Overseas," BBC ICM from Variety Booking Manager to Mr. Cecil Madden (London), 22 January 1941, BBC WAC R27/21; and "BBC Bans Bandleaders for Political Opinions!" *MM* (8 March 1941): 1.

82. Quoted in "Selecting the Music," *Times* (21 March 1941): 2a.

83. "BBC Bans Bandleaders for Political Opinions!"; "Churchill Ends BBC Ban," *MM* (29 March 1941): 1; and "Feste," "Ad Libitum," *MT* (April 1941): 147.

84. "Suggestion for Second 'Bands of the Week,'" BBC ICM from Miss Osborn to (C)P, 3 October 1940, BBC WAC R27/21.

85. "Second Band of the Week," BBC ICM from ADV to ADPP, 15 October 1940, BBC WAC R27/21; and "Six Weeks at BBC for Geraldo," *MM* (19 October 1940): 1.

86. "Dance Band—London," BBC ICM from DV to C(P), 17 January 1941, BBC WAC R27/21; and "Dance Band," BBC ICM from Variety Booking Manager to ADV, 24 May 1940, BBC WAC R27/21.

87. "Eavesdropper," "Air Bands," *MM* (6 April 1940): 3; and Leonard Feather, "Signature Tune," *RT* (25 August 1939): 17.

88. Noble, *Kings of Rhythm*, 17; and LRD, "General Listening Barometer 1939/40 Report No. 53: Popularity of Dance Bands," 11 December 1940, BBC WAC R9/22/1.

89. Briggs, *History of Broadcasting*, 3:316.

90. *Oxford Dictionary of National Biography*, s.v. "Madden, Cecil Charles (1902–1987)" (by June Averill), http://www.oxforddnb.com.libaccess.lib.mcmaster.ca/view/article/40695 (accessed 9 September 2009); and "The BBC's 'American Eagle in Britain' Broadcasts at Rainbow Corner," 16 April 1944, in Madden, Wartime Radio Diary No. 20, BBC WAC S24/54/20.

91. *BBC Handbook 1941*, 112. The European Service split off from the Overseas Service in October 1941. Briggs, *History of Broadcasting*, 3:342. See chapter 7 for a more detailed discussion of Madden's work at the EEU.

92. "Geraldo's Orchestra," BBC ICM from O[verseas] P[rogramme?] P[lanning?] to Empire Executive, 17 October 1940, BBC WAC R27/21; and "Overseas Programmes: Geraldo and his Orchestra," BBC ICM from PC Ex to Variety Booking Manager, 24 October 1940, BBC WAC R27/21.

93. "Overseas Programmes: Band of the Week," BBC ICM from Madden to PC Ex, 25 October 1940, BBC WAC R27/21.

94. Madden, Wartime Radio Diary No. 18, BBC WAC S24/54/18.

95. "Dance Bands for Overseas Service," BBC ICM from Variety Bookings Manager to DV, 20 December 1940, BBC WAC R27/21.

96. Pat Brand, "Brand's Essence," *MM* (8 October 1941): 4.

97. "Jack Payne," *MM* (11 January 1941): 1.

98. "Dance Bands—Overseas, Home and Forces Programmes—Jack Payne," BBC ICM from Variety Booking Manager to PC Ex, 11 February 1941, BBC WAC R27/21.

99. "Jack Payne."

100. "The Greatest Dance Band Airing! [referring to the RAF Squandronaires, not Jack Payne]," *MM* (18 January 1941): 9; and "Jack Payne Captures Arthur Young," *MM* (25 January 1941): 1.

101. Forces PasB, 5 February 1941.

102. "Jack Payne."

103. "The Greatest Dance Band Airing!"; and "Detector," "Bouquets for Payne and Cotton," *MM* (8 February 1941): 9.

104. "Dance Band—London," BBC ICM from DV to C(P), 17 January 1941.

105. "Bands of the Week for Overseas, Home and Forces," BBC ICM from Madden to DV, 22 January 1941, BBC WAC R27/21.

106. Geraldo's and Payne's indefinite contracts were modeled upon the agreement that the Corporation had signed with Hylton for the services of Ternent's band early in the war. Ternent was still with the BBC at Bangor, broadcasting largely in Variety productions. Ibid.; and "Dance Bands—Overseas, Home and Forces Programmes—Geraldo," BBC ICM from Variety Booking Manager to PC Ex London, 8 February 1941, BBC WAC R27/21.

107. "Dance Bands—Overseas, Home and Forces Programmes," BBC ICM from Variety Booking Manager to DV, 7 February 1941, BBC WAC R27/21; "Band of the Week at Weston," BBC ICM from ADV, Weston, to Variety Booking Manager, 21 February 1941, BBC WAC R27/21; and "Band of the Week," BBC ICM from DV to Variety Booking Ex., 22 April 1941, BBC WAC R27/21.

108. See introduction for a discussion of Geraldo's adaptable style.

109. Jack Payne, "Let the People Sing," *The Other Side of the Singing Detective* (BBC compact disc 708, 1988); and Geraldo, "Let the People Sing," *British Big Bands* (ABM compact disc ABM-MCD 1185, 1999). Payne had no recording contract between July 1940 and February 1945. Brian Rust and Sandy Forbes, *British Dance Bands on Record 1911–1945 and Supplement* (Middlesex: General Gramophone Publications, 1989), 760–61.

110. "Pickup," "Tiddly Tempo," *MM* (20 April 1940): 3.

111. The versatile Geraldo also recorded "Let the People Sing" with his concert orchestra and Evelyn Laye, who starred in *Lights Up!* Geraldo, "Let the People Sing," 1CS0030507, NSA.

112. "Dance Bands Do a Good War Job," *Star* (30 December 1941) [BBC clippings]; and Rose, *Which People's War?* 156.

113. Jack Payne, ". . . So Now We Understand Each Other," *MM* (1 July 1944): 4.

114. "Corny," "Commercial Records Reviewed," *MM* (18 October 1941): 5.

115. "General Listening Barometer 1939/40 Report No. 53: Popularity of Dance Bands."

116. Columbia Records, Advertisement: "Another Columbia Star," *Pianomaker and Music Seller* (November 1939): cover; and Chris Hayes, "19. Geraldo," The Leader of the Band (vol. 1) (self-published, n.d. [before 1994]), Jazz Heritage Archives: Geraldo Folder.

117. *Oxford Dictionary of National Biography*, s.v. "Bright, Gerald Walcan- [Geraldo] (1904–1974)" (by Tony Augarde), http://www.oxforddnb.com.libaccess.lib.mcmaster.ca/view/article/31792 (accessed 11 September 2009); Bud Forder, "This Is Geraldo," *RP* (17 February 1939): 8; Noble, *Kings of Rhythm*, 12–13; and McCarthy, *Dance Band Era*, 150–51. McCarthy suggests more believably that Geraldo had traveled in Europe instead.

118. By adopting the name, it seems that Geraldo not only embraced his new identity as a tango bandleader but also took on an appealingly exotic identity that helped mask his less acceptable, "alien" identity as a London-born Jew, in an assimilationist move akin to Al Jolson's use of blackface in *The Jazz Singer*, as described in Rogin, "Blackface, White Noise."

119. "New Ideas in Dance Band Radio," *MM* (18 January 1941): 1.

120. Programme Listings, *RT* (17 January 1941): 18; and "LRWR No. 21," 6 February 1941, BBC WAC R9/1/1. Geraldo also explored classical and semiclassical repertory. "Geraldo Leading 50-Piece," *MM* (16 August 1941): 1; and Noble, *Kings of Rhythm*, 21.

121. Noble, *Kings of Rhythm*, 20.

122. Ibid., 22–23.

123. "Hello! Middle East!" *Parade* (17 May 1941): 18.

124. "Weekly Dance Band Periods Allocated," BBC ICM from ADV, Bangor, to ADPP, 6 October 1941, BBC WAC R27/71/3.

125. "Bands to Hear on the Air," *MM* (6 September 1941): 2.

126. "Detector," "Hot Stone Out in the Cold," *MM* (1 November 1941): 6.

127. "Weekly Dance Band Periods," BBC ICM from ADPP to ADV, 11 October 1941, BBC WAC R27/71/3.

128. Silvester, *Dancing Is My Life*, 177.

129. "LRWR No. 47," 16 August 1941, BBC WAC R9/1/1; and "LRWR No. 50," 6 September 1941, BBC WAC R9/1/1.

130. Spike Hughes, "Report on the Four BBC Contract Dance Bands and Victor Silvester's Band," 12 August 1943, BBC WAC R27/73/2.

131. Silvester, *Dancing Is My Life*, 149.

132. Cook, "Passionless Dancing and Passionate Reform," 133–50; and Bederman, *Manliness and Civilization*, 1–44.

133. Eric Winstone, "Personalities in Paragraph," *MM* (28 June 1941): 8; and "Dancer's Delight," *RP* (28 July 1939): 17.

134. *Modern Ballroom Dancing* Advertisement, *DT* (April 1927): 115; and Victor Silvester, "The Black Bottom," *DT* (August 1927): 503.

135. Silvester, *Dancing Is My Life*, 146, 148–49; and Winstone, "Personalities in Paragraph."

136. "Dancer's Delight."

137. Irene Raines, "London Ballroom Notes," *DT* (November 1939): 74; Irene Raines, "London Ballroom Notes," *DT* (December 1939): 153; and Irene Raines, "London Ballroom Notes," *DT* (December 1940): 147.

138. "Dancer's Delight," 17.

139. Elizabeth Cross, "Dancing in War Time," *DT* (August 1940): 651–52; and "What the Other Listener Thinks," *RT* (15 August 1941): 10.

140. "The Sitter Out," "Ballroom Notes," *DT* (April 1940): 415–17; and Eve Tynegate-Smith, "It's Not Difficult," *DT* (April 1940): 418.

141. Victor Silvester, "Dancing Club," *RT* (25 July 1941): 3.

142. "Despite Blitz a New Dance Crashes In on London," *MM* (28 December 1940): 1.

143. Victor Silvester and His Ballroom Orchestra, compèred by David Miller, *BBC Dancing Club*, [27 August] 1941, shelf mark 3343, BBC Sound Archives NSA.

144. "A Listener Research Report: Summary of Opinion of Listeners in the Forces on 1 Radio Dance Music 2 BBC Dancing Club," 21 April 1942, BBC WAC 27/73/2.

145. Silvester, "Dancing Club."

146. Ibid.

147. Silvester, *Dancing Is My Life*, 177–78.

148. "A Listener Research Report: Summary of Opinion of Listeners in the Forces on 1 Radio Dance Music 2 BBC Dancing Club."

149. Silvester, "Dancing Club."

150. "Detector," "Radio," *MM* (15 July 1944): 3.

151. Victor Silvester, "Roll Back the Carpet," *RP* (2 December 1938): 27. See the introduction for a discussion of Silvester's musical approach.

152. "A Listener Research Report: Summary of Opinion of Listeners in the Forces on 1 Radio Dance Music 2 BBC Dancing Club"; and "Detector," "Radio," *MM* (13 February 1943): 3.

153. "LRWR No. 40," 30 June 1941, BBC WAC R9/1/1.

154. Philip Brown, "And Now for Dance Music—," *RT* (22 November 1940): 5.

155. "Comment," *MM* (14 September 1940): 4.

156. Rose, *Which People's War?* 195.

CHAPTER 5

1. "Eavesdropper," "BBC Rhythm Club," *MM* (22 June 1940): 5.

2. Alec Hughes, "A Mass-Observer Looks at Jazz!" *BW* (2 December 1939): 6–7.

3. B. M. Lytton-Edwards, "Keep the Swing Flag Flying!" *MM* (October 1939): 13.

4. Briggs, *History of Broadcasting*, 3:137–39.

5. "Radio Rhythm Club," BBC ICM from Miss Maria Legge to GOSD, Gramophone Director, 7 February 1945, BBC WAC R21/121.

6. Bill Elliott, letter to *MM* (4 October 1941): 5.

7. Letter to *MM* (30 March 1940): 6.

8. "Eavesdropper," "BBC Rhythm Club."

9. See Gendron, "'Moldy Figs' and Modernists," 31–56.

10. "Radio Rhythm Club: Forces Programme: Thursday, February 11th, 1943: 6.30–7.00 pm," BBC WAC R21/121.

11. Quoted in "Brand's Essence," *MM* (5 August 1944): 4.

12. "A Rhythm Club Secretary," "Are Rhythm Clubs Worth It?" *MM* (23 November 1940): 4.

13. "BBC Launching Radio Rhythm Club," *MM* (1 June 1940): 1.

14. LRB No. 67, 3 January 1942, BBC WAC R9/1/1; and "Jazz Brains Trust," BBC ICM from ADV (London) to ADV (Bangor), 1 January 1943, BBC WAC R21/121.

15. "Radio Rhythm Club Back June 3," *MM* (15 May 1943): 1.

16. Leslie Perowne, interview by Christopher Clark, 23 February 1990, shelf mark C122/91-92, Oral History, NSA.

17. "Detector," "Radio," *MM* (27 February 1943): 3.

18. Ken Williamson, "Harry Parry and His Sextet," quoted in Frederick Laws, "Easy Guide to Jam," *News Chronicle* (5 August 1944) [BBC cuttings].

19. Moore, *Inside British Jazz*, 39.

20. See chapter 8.

21. Reynolds, *Rich Relations*, 216–17.

22. "Lauderic Caton Lost after Amazing Party Show," *MM* (8 November 1941): 1, 3.

23. DeVeaux, *Birth of Bebop*, 117–18; and Stanley Nelson, "Where Is Jazz Going?" *DT* (August 1940): 658.

24. Marwick, *Century of Total War*, 295; and Rose, *Which People's War?* 89.

25. Programme Listings, *RT* (26 November 1941).

26. "The Sitter Out," "1939 and After," *DT* (January 1940): 218; MOA: FR 295, in MOA: FR 301A, 45; and MOA: TC 38/7/A, Andy Razaf and Joe Garland, "In the Mood."

27. "Blue Note," "Jazz Is Failing to Take Its Wartime Chance," *BW* (4 November 1939): 5.

28. McCarthy, *Dance Band Era*, 149; and Joe Loss and His Orchestra, "In the Mood," *In the Mood: A Musical Tribute to the War Years* (Yesteryear compact disc GLM/Y-1-21, n.d.).

29. "Leader on Air," *BW* (3 February 1940): 16.

30. "Eavesdropper," "Good Old Young!" *MM* (2 March 1940): 3; "Eavesdropper," "The Nightingale Again!" *MM* (25 May 1940): 2; "Eavesdropper," "Ellington on the Air," *MM* (15 June 1940): 6; and letter to *MM* (2 March 1940): 6.

31. "Eavesdropper," "BBC Rhythm Club"; and Charles Chilton, interview by Jim Godbolt, 29 June 1989, shelf mark C122/71, Oral History, NSA.

32. Charles Chilton and Bill Elliott, introduction with sound examples to *RRC*, BBC Forces Broadcast [13 June 1940], Shelf mark 30B/6737, BBC Sound Archives, NSA.

33. D. Stallard Enefer, "5s. Winner," printed in "Eavesdropper," "BBC Rhythm Club."

34. "BBC Public Apology to 'Melody Maker' & Fans!" *MM* (26 October 1940): 1; and "Letters," *RT* (2 June 1944): 5.

35. Forces PasB, 5 December 1940.

36. Panassié, *Real Jazz*, 57–58.

37. DeVeaux, *Birth of Bebop*, 278.

38. "Detector," "Recent Radio Reported,'" *MM* (1 October 1938): 6.

39. *Alistair Cooke's Jazz Letter from America* (Avid Entertainment compact disc AMSC 855, 2006).

40. "Detector," "Recent Radio Reported," *MM* (28 January 1939): 6.

41. "Eavesdropper," "BBC Jam Session," *MM* (6 July 1940): 5.

42. Ibid.

43. Programme Listings, *RT* (21 July 1940).

44. *Grove Music Online*, s.v. "Shearing, George" (by Bill Dobbins), http://www.oxfordmusiconline.com.libaccess.lib.mcmaster.ca/subscriber/article/grove/music/41306 (accessed 22 October 2009).

45. Leonard Feather, "Signature Tune," *RT* (14 July 1939): 18.

46. Noble, *Kings of Rhythm*, 62; and Chilton, interview.

47. Noble, *Kings of Rhythm*, 61.

48. Chilton, *Who's Who of British Jazz*, s.v. "Parry, 'Harry' Owen."

49. Noble, *Kings of Rhythm*, 64.

50. Chilton, interview. Soon after the informal audition, Parry moved on to the Coconut Club.

51. "Dabbler," "Raid-io," *MM* (28 September 1940): 5.

52. Guy Fletcher, "Miscellany," *RT* (6 December 1940): 7; and Edgar Jackson, "Benny Goodman in the New Discs," *MM* (3 February 1940): 3.

53. Noble, *Kings of Rhythm*, 62.

54. Fletcher, "Miscellany," *RT* (6 December 1940).

55. "Detector," "Bouquets for Payne and Cotton," *MM* (8 February 1941): 9.

56. Jackson, "British Jazz Makes the Grade." See the introduction for a more detailed discussion of "I've Found a New Baby."

57. Chilton, interview.

58. Perowne, interview; and Noble, *Kings of Rhythm*, 64–65.

59. "Radio Rhythm Club Sextet Go on Records," *MM* (15 February 1941): 1; Noble, *Kings of Rhythm*, 65.

60. "Detector," "Bouquets for Payne and Cotton."

61. Edgar Jackson, "Shaw's Good Ingredients Make Poor Wax Cakes," *MM* (6 September 1941): 3; and "Detector," "A Big Bouquet for Doreen Villiers," *MM* (7 June 1941): 9.

62. Forces PasB, 25 October 1940, 17 March 1941, 30 May 1941, 29 October 1941, 12 January 1942, 30 April 1942, 22 May 1942, 2 July 1942, 6 August 1942, 15 October 1942, 26 November 1942, 7 January 1943, and 5 February 1943.

63. Bill Elliott, "1941—The Worst Jazz Year—And the Best!" *MM* (3 January 1942): 3; and Noble, *Kings of Rhythm*, 65.

64. "Harry Parry Booked for Stage," *MM* (24 January 1942): 1.

65. LRWR No. 40, 30 June 1941, BBC WAC R9/1/1; and LRWR No. 62, 29 November 1941, BBC WAC R9/1/1.

66. "Radio Rhythm Club—Amateur Half-Hour," BBC ICM from PC Ex to Variety Booking Manager, 4 April 1941, BBC WAC R21/121.

67. "Detector," "Radio Amateurs Flop," *MM* (21 June 1941): 4; LRWR No. 40; and LRWR No. 62.

68. "Detector," "What Did the US Think of This?" *MM* (19 July 1941): 3.

69. Letter to *MM* (4 October 1941): 5; and "'Detector's' Deputy's Impressions," *MM* (27 September 1941): 6.

70. LRB No. 67, 3 January 1942, BBC WAC R9/1/1.

71. Forces PasB, 28 January 1942.

72. Edgar Jackson, "The Best Jam Session Jazz Britain Has Ever Produced," *MM* (13 December 1941): 3; Peter Powell, interview by Les Back, 28 January 1999, shelf mark C122/341–44, Oral History, NSA; and "Detector," "Paying for the Privilege of Broadcasting!" *MM* (25 October 1941): 6.

73. "All Set for Our Historic Jam Session on Sunday," *MM* (15 November 1941): 1.

74. "Colossal Cavendish Coliseum Concert!" *MM* (31 January 1942): 1.

75. "36,480 Vote Their Favourites for 'Your Swing Concert,'" *MM* (10 January 1942): 1.

76. "Colossal Cavendish Coliseum Concert!"

77. Letter to *MM* (14 February 1942): 3.

78. "Colossal Cavendish Coliseum Concert!"

79. "Geraldo Postpones Big Swing Concert to Aid Charity Show," *MM* (28 February 1942): 1; and "Jack Payne Signs Grappelly," *MM* (28 February 1942): 1.

80. "Mike" [Spike Hughes], "Cashing In on Swing," *MM* (30 May 1942): 7.

81. "Detector," "What's Wrong with the Radio Rhythm Club?" *MM* (9 August 1941): 2.

82. Edgar Jackson, "Records," *MM* (10 October 1942): 3.

83. "Detector," "Radio," *MM* (27 February 1943): 3.

84. "Harry Parry Leaving Radio Rhythm Club," *MM* (5 December 1942): 1; and Chilton, interview.

85. "Radio Rhythm Club," BBC ICM from Chilton to Mrs. Neilson, 12 May 1943, BBC WAC R21/121.

86. "Harry Parry Leaving Radio Rhythm Club."

87. "Radio Rhythm Club," BBC ICM from Charles Chilton to Gramophone Director, 3 December 1943, BBC WAC R21/121.

88. See Baade, "'The Dancing Front,'" 361–62.

89. Irene Raines, "People and Places in London," *DT* (December 1943): 122; and Silvester, *This Is Jive*, 21.

90. C. Gordon Glover, "Introducing—," *RT* (22 May 1942): 5.

91. "The Broadcasters," "Both Sides of the Microphone," *RT* (23 July 1943): 3.

92. Perowne, "Calypso," *RT* (13 March 1942): 3; and Nicholas, *Echo of War*, 177.

93. Nicholas, *Echo of War*, 175.

94. Newton, "Calling the West Indies," 490–91.

95. C. Gordon Glover, "Introducing—," *RT* (12 June 1942): 5.

96. Cover, *RT* (21 November 1941).

97. Nicholas, *Echo of War*, 160, 228.

98. "Detector," "The Bands Battle," *MM* (26 July 1941): 9; and Margrave, "There Are Five 'Musts' for Popular Music."

99. Godbolt, *History of Jazz*, 162.

100. *Oxford Dictionary of National Biography*, s.v. "Preston, (Sydney) Denis (1916–1979)" (by Val Wilmer), http://www.oxforddnb.com.libaccess.lib.mcmaster.ca/view/article/75566 (accessed 16 November 2009).

101. Chilton, interview.

102. See Monson, "Problem with White Hipness."

103. "A Listener Research Report: America," 8 July 1941, BBC WAC R9/9/5.

104. Quoted in "'MM' Gets No. 1 Rhythm Club Meeting to Review the New Swing Records," *MM* (2 December 1939): 4.

105. Monson, "Problem with White Hipness," 403; and Lott, *Love and Theft*, 52.

106. Quoted in "'MM' Gets No. 1 Rhythm Club Meeting to Review the New Swing Records."

107. R. D. Ramsey, "Murder Most Foul!" *MM* (10 May 1941): 4.

108. Frank Deniz, interview by Val Wilmer, 18 August 1989, shelf mark C122/81-82, Oral History, NSA.

109. *Oxford Dictionary of National Biography*, s.v. "Johnson, Kenrick Reginald Hijmans (1914-1941)" (by Val Wilmer), http://www.oxforddnb.com.libaccess.lib.mcmaster.ca/view/article/74576 (accessed 19 November 2009).

110. Deniz, interview.

111. "A Special Representative," "Ken Johnson Will Sell Swing to the 'Swells,'" *BW* (28 October 1939): 2.

112. Powell, interview.

113. Leon Cassel-Gerald, "Who Is There to Take Ken Johnson's Place?" *MM* (22 March 1941): 5.

114. "Letters," *MM* (22 March 1941): 2.

115. Cassel-Gerald, "Who Is There to Take Ken Johnson's Place?"

116. "Both Sides of the Microphone," *RT* (21 March 1941): 2.

117. "What the Other Listener Thinks," *RT* (28 March 1941): 8.

118. Letter to *MM* (2 August 1941): 4.

119. LRWR No. 52, 29 September 1941, BBC WAC R9/1/1.

120. "Detector," "Perowne's Was the Perfect Recital," *MM* (13 September 1941): 6.

121. "Private—on the NE Coast," letter to *RT* (19 September 1941): 8.

122. Cassel-Gerald, "Who Is There to Take Ken Johnson's Place?"

123. "Both Sides of the Microphone," *RT* (21 March 1941): 2.

124. C. Gordon Glover, "This Week's Miscellany," *RT* (6 February 1942): 5; and Powell, interview.

125. Powell, interview. In addition, the West Indian–born musicians were not subject to the call-up. Dave Wilkins, interview by Val Wilmer, 9 September 1987, shelf mark C122/36, Oral History, NSA.

126. "Detector," "Radio," *MM* (6 February 1943): 9.

127. Forces PasB, 26 February 1942.

128. "Ginmill on Wax," *MM* (27 December 1941): 5. The club's name, derived from the offensive "jigaboo," functioned as "an ironic slang term of self-reference among black hipsters," a convincing explanation given that its owners, Alec and Rose Ward, were Afro-Caribbean. Andrew Simons, liner notes to *Black British Swing*, 25.

129. Godbolt, *History of Jazz*, 190.

130. "Out of the Nightclub/Into the Wax," *MM* (7 February 1942): 3; and Cyril Blake and His Jig's Club Band, "Cyril's Blues," *Black British Swing*.

131. "Dance Band OBs," BBC ICM from Mr. Cecil Madden, Criterion, to Miss Ware, Woodnorton, 18 February 1942, BBC WAC R27/71/4.

132. "Detector," "Radio," *MM* (7 August 1943): 4–5.

133. "Detector," "Radio," *MM* (5 February 1944): 3.

134. "Detector," "Spencer Williams—Ideal Jazz Broadcaster," *MM* (13 May 1944): 5.

135. Monson, "Problem with White Hipness," 403.

136. Wood had died the previous August.

137. "Brand's Essence," *MM* (7 April 1945): 4.

138. See "'Detector' Replies to Dr. Sargent," *MM* (7 March 1942): 3; and "Geraldo's Challenge to Anti-swing Brains Truster," *MM* (21 February 1942): 1.

139. "Detector," "Recent Radio," *MM* (12 December 1942): 3.

140. Warworkers Rhythm Club, Islington (seven signers), letter to *Islington Gazette* (30 June 1944) [BBC clippings].

CHAPTER 6

1. Lt.-Col., VC, letter to *Daily Telegraph* (7 March 1942) [BBC clippings].

2. Marwick, *Century of Total War*, 261.

3. Bierman and Smith, *War without Hate*, 157, 184, 197.

4. Rose, *Which People's War?* 160.

5. Dance musicians were also targets for criticism in early 1942.

6. Tom Harrisson, "Radio," *Observer* (19 July 1942) [BBC clippings]; and LRD, "A Listener Research Report: Listeners' Preferences for Home Service or Forces Programme," 13 January 1942, BBC WAC R9/9/6.

7. Letter to *Daily Telegraph* (7 March 1942) [BBC clippings].

8. Quoted in "Sloppy," *Bristol Evening News* (10 July 1942) [BBC clippings].

9. "Vera Lynn," BBC ICM from C(P) (B. E. Nicolls) to DPP, 17 March 1942, BBC WAC R19/683.

10. "Suggested Series: Six Half-Hours," [n.d.], BBC WAC R19/683.

11. Baade, "*Sincerely Yours*," 40; and Programme Listings, *RT* (11 April 1941): 21.

12. Sunday, November 30th, 1941, *Programme Parade*, BBC WAC R19/683.

13. "Our Radio Reporter," "Ambrose's Brilliant Broadcast," *BW* (20 January 1940): 11.

14. "Suggested Series: Six Half-Hours."

15. "Vera Lynn Series," BBC ICM from Mr. Howard Thomas to Director of Publicity, 3 November 1941, BBC WAC R19/683; and letter from Secretary to Thomas to Clerk of the Council, London County Council, 3 December 1941, BBC WAC R19/683.

16. Baade, "*Sincerely Yours*," 41.

17. "Detector," "BBC Goes Pure," *MM* (20 December 1941): 5.

18. "Vera Lynn," BBC ICM from C(P) to DPP, 17 March 1942.

19. "BBC Music Policy," draft by C(P) amended in accordance with suggestions made by DM, DDM, and Arthur Bliss, 1 April 1942, BBC WAC R27/73/1.

20. Briggs, *History of Broadcasting*, 3:527–55, 570, 573; and "Radio: For the Princes," *News Review* (16 April 1942) [BBC clippings].

21. MOA: FR 1087 "'Answering You': Broadcast to America: War Songs, Income Tax, Cosmetics and Clothes" (TH), February 1942.

22. "Anti Flabby Entertainment in Empire Programmes," BBC ICM from Madden, Criterion, to DEP, 11 March 1942, in Madden, Wartime Radio Diary No. 15, BBC WAC S24/54/15.

23. Nicholas, *Echo of War*, 206, 272.

24. "Analysis of Song Plugging Beginning 23rd November," BBC ICM from Norman Marshall to AC(P), 7 December 1941, BBC WAC R27/475/4.

25. "Present Dance Band Situation," BBC ICM from Lawrence to DV (Bangor), 26 February 1942, BBC WAC R27/73/1.

26. MOA: FR 795 "Songwriters: Sales of Sheet Music and Radio Broadcasts" (Annette Mills), July 1941.

27. "Present Dance Band Situation," BBC ICM from Lawrence to DV (Bangor), 26 February 1942.

28. Briggs, *History of Broadcasting*, 3:360, 530–31.

29. "Anti Flabby Entertainment in Empire Programmes," BBC ICM from Madden, Criterion, to DEP, 11 March 1942.

30. Ibid.; and "Robust Programmes," BBC ICM from Madden to Empire Presentation Manager (Aldenham), 20 March 1942, BBC WAC R27/416/1.

31. "BBC Music Policy," 1 April 1942.

32. Baade, "*Sincerely Yours*," 40.

33. "A Middle-Aged Listener," "If They Were All Her!" *RT* (30 May 1941): 6.

34. "Detector," "BBC Brains Bust!" *MM* (29 November 1941): 5; "Corny," "Commercial Records Discussed," *MM* (15 November 1941): 3; and "Corny," "Commercial Records Discussed," *MM* (29 November 1941): 6.

35. A. A. Thomson, "Laugh with Our Strolling Commentator," *RT* (28 March 1941): 3.

36. "Partnerships, Recitals, Parlour Games, and Crooning: Summary of Opinion of Listeners in the Forces," Listener Research Report, 9 May 1941, BBC WAC R41/113/1.

37. "Dance Music Policy," BBC ICM from AC(P) to C(P), 3 June 1942, BBC WAC R27/73/1.

38. "Dance Music Policy," BBC ICM from C(P) to AC(P), 17 April 1942, BBC WAC R27/73/1.

39. LRB No. 82, 18 April 1942, BBC WAC R9/1/2.

40. Harrisson, "Radio."

41. "Martial Music," *Times* (25 March 1942): 5d.

42. "Dance Music Policy," BBC ICM from AC(P) to DM et al., 7 May 1942, BBC WAC R27/73/1; and "Dance Music Policy," BBC ICM from AC(P) to C(P), 3 June 1942, BBC WAC R27/73/1.

43. Document (untitled, unsigned), c. June 1942, BBC WAC R27/73/1.

44. "Notes and News," *MT* (February 1943): 57.

45. "Mike" [Spike Hughes], "Sob-Sisters of the Air," *MM* (22 November 1941): 5.

46. "Dance Bands Do a Good War Job," *Star* (30 December 1941) [BBC clippings].

47. Rose, *Which People's War?* 79–81.

48. "Dance Music Policy," BBC ICM from AC(P) to C(P), 3 June 1942, BBC WAC R27/73/1.

49. "Dance Music Policy," BBC ICM from AC(P) to DM et al. 7 May 1942; and "Dance Music Policy," BBC ICM from AC(P) to DM et al., 20 May 1942, BBC WAC R27/73/1.

50. "Dance Music Policy," BBC ICM from AC(P) to DM et al., 7 May 1942.

51. "BBC Music Policy," 1 April 1942.

52. "Dance Music Policy," BBC ICM from AC(P) to C(P), 3 June 1942.

53. "What the Other Listener Thinks," *RT* (21 June 1941): 9; letter to *Daily Telegraph* (7 March 1942) [BBC clippings]; and "Mike," "Sob-Sisters of the Air."

54. Rose, *Which People's War?* 153–96.

55. Sinfield, *Out on Stage*, 114, 126, 74.

56. Rose, *Which People's War?* 175.

57. Ibid., 151.

58. C. Gordon Glover, "Introducing—," *RT* (3 July 1942): 5.

59. Seton Margrave, "BBC Bans Crooners," *Daily Mail* (13 June 1942) [BBC clippings].

60. "Letters," *RT* (24 July 1942): 5.

61. "Dance Music Policy," BBC ICM from AC(P) to [long list], 21 July 1942, BBC WAC R27/73/1; letter sent to music publishers, 21 June 1942, BBC WAC R27/73/1; and letter sent to dance band leaders and singers, 21 June 1942, BBC WAC R27/73/1.

62. Quoted in "Notes and News," *MT* (August 1942): 252. Space does not permit a fuller discussion of swung classics here. See Baade, "'Victory through Harmony,'" 240–44.

63. "Cleaning Up Your Dance Music," *RT* (24 July 1942): 3.

64. LRB No. 97, 1 August 1942, BBC WAC R9/1/2.

65. Vera Lynn, "The Men in the Forces *Want* Sentimental Songs...," *Sunday Dispatch* (26 July 1942) [BBC clippings].

66. "More about Slush," *Star* (23 July 1942) [BBC clippings]; and "Detector," "The 'Anti-Slush' Campaign," *MM* (8 August 1942): 5.

67. "Gutter Music," *Western Telegraph* (10 October 1942) [BBC clippings].

68. Reynolds, *Rich Relations*, 99.

69. Kirby and Harris, *Star-Spangled Radio*, 155.

70. Seton Margrave, "The Secret (BBC) Seven," *Daily Mail* (1 August 1942) [BBC clippings].

71. The committee listened to Jimmy Noone's version of the song.

72. DMPC Minutes, 31 July 1942, BBC WAC R27/74/1.

73. "Slush," BBC ICM from Miss Edmond to Assistant Director, Secretariat, 27 August 1942, BBC WAC R27/73/1.

74. "Dance Band Policy," BBC ICM from Cecil Madden to DEP, 31 July 1942, BBC WAC R27/73/1.

75. Seton Margrave, "These Lyrics Are Banned on the BBC," *Daily Mail* (8 August 1942) [BBC clippings].

76. "Music Firms Annoyed by Song Ban," *Star* (8 August 1942) [BBC clippings]; Margrave, "These Lyrics Are Banned on the BBC"; "Publishers to By-pass BBC Committee," *Daily Sketch* (12 August 1942) [BBC clippings]; and "Music Men in Revolt against Slush Ban," *DM* (11 August 1942): 5 [BBC clippings].

77. Letter from the MPA, Ltd., to Robert Foote, Joint DG, BBC, 11 August 1942, BBC WAC R27/73/1.

78. "'Slush' and Sentiment Problems for a Deputation to the BBC," *Star* (12 August 1942) [BBC clippings].

79. "What Is a 'Slushy' Song?" *Evening Standard* (12 August 1942) [BBC clippings].

80. "Definitions," *Times* (4 September 1942): 5.

81. "Dance Music Policy," report of meeting with representatives of MPA, 26 August 1942, BBC WAC R27/254.

82. "Detector," "'Slush' War: A Deadlock," *MM* (12 September 1942): 2.

83. "Publishers Meet BBC," *MM* (5 September 1942): 5.

84. LRB No. 97, 1 August 1942, BBC WAC R9/1/2.

85. "Readers Write about 'Slush,'" *MM* (15 August 1942): 3.

86. LRB No. 100, 22 August 1942, BBC WAC R9/1/2; and LRB No. 101, 29 August 1942, BBC WAC R9/1/2.

87. Harrisson, "Radio."

88. See "Overdue Purge," *Nottingham Guardian* (2 October 1942) [BBC clippings]; "A Radio Plague," *Perthshire Advertiser* (28 November 1942) [BBC clippings]; and "Crooners Still," *Evening Advertiser* (10 December 1942) [BBC clippings].

89. "Dance Music Policy and Dance Music & Variety Presentation: Gordon Crier," BBC ICM from DV to AC(P) London, 11 September 1942, BBC WAC R27/73/1.

90. DMPC Minutes, 31 August 1942, BBC WAC R27/74/1.

91. DMPC Minutes, 16 October 1942, BBC WAC R27/74/1.

92. "Corny," "Commercial Records Reviewed," *MM* (3 October 1942): 6–7.

93. "Detector," "Radio Review," *MM* (12 December 1942): 3.

94. "Detector," "Radio Review," *MM* (26 September 1942): 5; "Corny," "Commercial Records," *MM* (14 November 1942): 7.

95. "Ten Million Records Wanted," *MM* (22 August 1942): 3.

96. "Corny," "Commercial Records," *MM* (5 September 1942): 6.

97. "Film Songs and the BBC," *Walthamstow Post* (21 November 1942) [BBC clippings].

98. Stacey, *Star Gazing*, 83–84.

99. Dance Music Policy, BBC and MPA Meeting Minutes, 9 December 1942, BBC WAC R27/254.

100. DMPC Minutes, 28 August 1942, BBC WAC R27/74/1; Dance Music Policy, BBC and MPA Meeting Minutes, 16 October 1942, BBC WAC R27/254; and DMPC Minutes, 25 September 1942, BBC WAC R27/73/1.

101. Dance Music Policy, BBC and MPA Meeting Minutes, 22 January 1943, BBC WAC R27/254.

102. [Untitled], *Star*, 22 December 1942 [BBC clippings].

103. Ibid.

104. "Notes and News," *MT* (August 1942): 252.

105. DMPC Minutes, 31 July 1942, BBC WAC R27/74/1; and "Dance Bands," BBC ICM from DV to AC(P) London, 12 October 1942, BBC WAC R27/73/1.

106. [Untitled], *Star*, 22 December 1942.

107. "Notes and News," 252.

108. "Dance Band Policy: 'Hutch,'" BBC ICM from AC(P) to DV, 2 September 1942, BBC WAC R27/73/1.

109. *Oxford Dictionary of National Biography*, s.v. "Hutchinson, Leslie Arthur Julien [Hutch] (1900–1969)" (by Stephen Bourne), http://www.oxforddnb.com.libaccess.lib.mcmaster.ca/view/article/58885 (accessed 8 February 2010); and "Big Acts & Little Acts No. 15 'Hutch,'" *BW* (10 February 1940): 14.

110. See West, "Black Sexuality," 119–20.

111. "Big Acts & Little Acts No. 15 'Hutch.'"

112. "Corny," "The Story of a Hit Song," *MM* (17 January 1942): 5.

113. *Great British Dance Bands and Their Vocalists*, vol. 3 (Pulse PBX compact disc 447/3, 1999); Lynn, *Ultimate Collection*; and *The Magic of Hutch: Begin the Beguine* (Broadsword International compact disc SUN 2115, 2002).

114. DMPC Minutes, 13 November 1942, BBC WAC R27/74/1.

115. See Baade, "Between the Lines."

116. H. S., "Miscellaneous and Dance," *Gramophone* (January 1943): 8.

117. Rose, *Which People's War?* 109–10.

118. Dance Music Policy, BBC and MPA Meeting Minutes, 22 January 1943, BBC WAC R27/254.

119. "Notes and News," *MT* (February 1943): 57.

120. DMPC Minutes, 23 February 1943, BBC WAC R27/74/1.

121. Ibid.

122. For example, Carole Carr (with Geraldo and His Orchestra), "The Things We Did Last Summer," *Great British Dance Bands and Their Vocalists* (Pulse PDX compact disc 447/3, 1999); Georgina (with Geraldo and His Orchestra), "My Devotion," *A Journey to a Star*; and Bruce Trent (with Jack Hylton and His Orchestra), "I Used to Be Colourblind," http://www.youtube.com/watch?v=UkQorr3f74I (accessed 30 January 2011).

123. Evans, "The Art of Singing in Decline," *MT* (July 1943): 201.

124. For example, Beryl Davis (with Geraldo and His Orchestra), "Skylark," *We'll Meet Again: Classic Songs and Tunes from the War Years* (EMI compact disc 509999 9 68705 2 5, 2009); and Len Camber (with Geraldo and His Orchestra), "Humpty Dumpty Heart," *A Journey to a Star*.

125. "Skeleton Is His Companion," *Empire News* (14 January 1945) [BBC clippings].

126. "The Broadcasters," "Both Sides of the Microphone," *RT* (21 April 1944): 3.

127. See chapter 8.

128. DMPC Minutes, 23 February 1943.

129. Ibid.

130. "A Listener Research Report: Summary of Opinion of Listeners in the Forces on 1 Radio Dance Music 2 BBC Dancing Club."

131. DMPC Minutes, 23 February 1943.

132. The minutes for the early March meeting do not survive. The 24 May minutes reveal that Camber had been banned for nearly three months, although other documentation makes clear that he was not entirely absent from air. DMPC Minutes, 12 April 1943, BBC WAC R27/74/1; "Vocalists Are BBC Scapegoats Again!" *MM* (3 April 1943): 1; and DMPC Minutes, 24 May 1943.

133. [Untitled], *Star* (1 April 1943) [BBC clippings]. Day, the MPA chairman, was the likely source of the leak.

134. "Vocalists Are BBC Scapegoats Again!"; and DMPC Minutes, 29 March 1943, BBC WAC R27/74/1.

135. McCarthy, *Dance Band Era*, 108; and "Banned for Slush Song," *Evening News* (7 April 1943) [BBC clippings].

136. Ernest Betts, "Four Crooners to Go Off the Air," *Daily Express* (8 April 1943) [BBC clippings].

137. "Winnick Hits Out," *MM* (10 April 1943): 1.

138. DMPC Minutes, 24 May 1943.

139. "Vocalists Are BBC Scapegoats Again!"

140. Nielson had been an artists' manager at Decca for five years and worked as a song plugger for several publishers before joining the BBC. "Lady Song-Plugger Appointed BBC Dance Music Supervisor," *MM* (19 December 1942): 1.

141. "Detector," "Radio," *MM* (10 April 1943): 3.

142. [Untitled], *Star* (9 April 1943).

143. "Jack's Broadcast," *BW* (17 February 1940): 1. For example, Dolly Elsie (Billy Cotton, dir.), "You Started Something," *Great British Dance Bands and Their Vocalists*, vol. 3.

144. DMPC Minutes, 29 March 1943.

145. [Untitled], *Star* (9 April 1943) [BBC clippings].

146. [Untitled], *Star* (8 April 1943) [BBC clippings].

147. "Radio Blitz on Vocalists: Latest," *MM* (10 April 1943): 1.

148. "More Vocalists Banned by BBC," *MM* (17 April 1943): 1.

149. "Ban on Crooners," BBC ICM from Assistant Director, Secretariat, to AC(P), 30 April 1943, BBC WAC R41/113/1.

150. [Untitled], BBC ICM from AC(P) to Assistant Director, Secretariat, 4 May 1943, BBC WAC R41/113/1; DMPC Minutes, 3 May 1943, BBC WAC R27/73/2; and DMPC Minutes, 24 May 1943, BBC WAC R27/74/1.

151. DMPC Minutes, 12 April 1943.

152. DMPC Minutes, 11 October 1943, BBC WAC R27/73/2.

153. "Slush," *South London Press* (19 November 1943) [BBC clippings].

154. Briggs, *History of Broadcasting*, 3:314; Programme Listings, *RT* (29 October 1943): 7; and "Boring Broadcasts," *Star* (1 November 1943) [BBC clippings].

155. Lynn, *Vocal Refrain*, 104; and BBC WAC Personal File/Artists/Vera Lynn, 1935–1944.

156. LRB No. 172, n.d. [between 20 December 1943 and 11 January 1944], BBC WAC R9/1/3.

157. C. Gordon Glover, "Introducing—," *RT* (29 October 1943): 3.

158. "The Broadcasters," "Both Sides of the Microphone," *RT* (3 September 1943): 3.

159. Rose, *Which People's War?* 153.

160. "Detector," "Recent Radio," *MM* (25 September 1943): 3.

161. W. R. Anderson, "Round about Radio," *MT* (February 1944): 46.

CHAPTER 7

1. Briggs, *History of Broadcasting*, 3:294–95.

2. Criterion Theatre, "Show Archive," Criterion Theatre, http://www.criterion-theatre. co.uk/showarchive.php (accessed 19 April 2010).

3. Cecil Madden, "Calling Forces Overseas," *RT* (2 May 1941): 3.

4. Madden, "Messages," Wartime Radio Diary No. 31, BBC WAC S24/54/31.

5. Madden, "Calling Forces Overseas"; and Bill Grieg, "Seven Girls Keep the Empire's Soldiers Thinking of Home," *DM* (17 February 1942), in Madden, Wartime Radio Diary No. 31, BBC WAC S24/54/31.

6. "London Calling," *Parade* (8 March 1941): 10.

7. Ibid.

8. Nicholas, *Echo of War*, 235; Rose, *Which People's War?* 280, 283; and Briggs, *History of Broadcasting*, 3:493.

9. "Overseas Entertainments Unit Report on Special Programmes for Forces Overseas in 1943," in Madden, Wartime Radio Diary No. 17, BBC WAC S24/54/17.

10. The Overseas and European Services were separated fully in October 1941. Briggs, *History of Broadcasting*, 3:316, 342; and "Forces Like the Radio 'Girl Friends,'" *Evening News* (16 January 1942), in Madden, Wartime Radio Diary No. 13, BBC WAC S24/54/13.

11. In May 1941, the unit produced sixty programs weekly, twelve of which were messages programs. "London Calling," 10; and Madden, "Calling Forces Overseas."

12. See chapter 6.

13. Madden, "Sweethearts of the Forces," Wartime Radio Diary No. 17, BBC WAC S24/54/17; and Grieg, "Seven Girls Keep the Empire's Soldiers Thinking of Home."

14. Rose, *Which People's War?* 109.

15. "Women Announcers of the BBC," *RT* (18 December 1942): 7; "Lady Song-Plugger Appointed BBC Dance Music Supervisor," *MM* (19 December 1942): 1; and Baade, "'The Battle of the Saxes.'" See Baade for a fuller account of Benson's one-year tenure at the BBC.

16. "Anti Flabby Entertainment in Empire Programmes," BBC ICM from Madden, Criterion, to DEP, 11 March 1942.

17. Ibid.

18. Letter to Doreen Villiers, in Madden, Wartime Radio Diary No. 1, BBC WAC S24/54/1.

19. Madden, "AEF PROGRAMS Do Something EXTRA for the Boys," in Madden, Wartime Radio Diary No. 23, BBC WAC S24/54/23.

20. Life coined the term in July 1941. *Oxford English Dictionary*, s.v. "Pin-up," http://dictionary.oed.com.libaccess.lib.mcmaster.ca/cgi/entry/50179803?single=1&query_type=word&queryword=pinup&first=1&max_to_show=10 (accessed 23 April 2010).

21. Bierman and Smith, *War without Hate*, 42.

22. Reynolds, *Rich Relations*, 271.

23. Gubar, "This Is My Rifle," 239.

24. Hegarty, "Patriot or Prostitute?"

25. Kirkham, "Beauty and Duty," 14.

26. Rose, *Which People's War?* 143–48.

27. Madden, "Sweethearts of the Forces," Wartime Radio Diary No. 17, BBC WAC S24/54/17.

28. Overseas PasB, 9 December 1940, 17 December 1940, and 15 January 1941.

29. H. S., "Miscellaneous and Dance," *Gramophone* (February 1943): 131.

30. Joan Gilbert, "Report on Visit to Gibraltar," February 1943, in Madden, Wartime Radio Diary No. 19, BBC WAC S24/54/19.

31. "London Calling," 10.

32. Roger Wimbush, "Miscellaneous and Dance," *Gramophone* (October 1940): 118.

33. "Pick-Up," "Novel Discs for Your Shelter," *MM* (28 September 1940): 9.

34. "Two Ambrose Starlets," *MM* (17 May 1941): 6; and *Oxford Dictionary of National Biography*, s.v. "Shelton, Anne (1923–1994)" (by Derek B. Scott), http://www.oxforddnb.com.libaccess.lib.mcmaster.ca/view/article/55711 (accessed 28 April 2010).

35. "The Broadcasters," "Both Sides of the Microphone," *RT* (20 September 1940): 4; and Madden, "Calling Forces Overseas."

36. Letter to Management, BBC, 27 June 1941, in Madden, Wartime Radio Diary No. 9, BBC WAC S24/54/9.

37. Bierman and Smith, *War without Hate*, 60–62.

38. Ibid., 121, 342–43. King George VI awarded Malta's civilians with the George Cross in April 1942 to honor their bravery and resilience.

39. Letter to Mr. Hayes, 18 September 1942, in Madden, Wartime Radio Diary No. 16, BBC WAC S24/54/16.

40. "The Broadcasters," "Both Sides of the Microphone," *RT* (3 March 1944): 3. By December 1942, Canon C. F. Gillingham had taken over as Padre.

41. Overseas PasB, April 1942–March 1943.

42. Overseas PasB, 3 August 1941.

43. "Two Ambrose Starlets."

44. "Mayfair Merry-Go-Round," *MM* (19 July 1941): 1.

45. "Two Ambrose Starlets."

46. Madden, Wartime Radio Diary No. 21, BBC WAC S24/54/21.

47. C. Gordon Glover, "Introducing," *RT* (10 April 1942): 5.

48. "Corny," "Commercial Records," *MM* (5 July 1941): 4; Anne Shelton, "St. Louis Blues," *The Early Years of Anne Shelton* (Soundsrite Music Wholesale compact disc SWNCD 003, 1995); and Anne Shelton, "Kiss the Boys Goodbye," *Great British Dance Bands and Their Vocalists* (Pulse compact disc PDX 447/2, 1999).

49. "Proposed Anne Shelton Programme," BBC ICM from Mr. Alick Hayes to ADV, 27 June 1944, BBC WAC R19/1153/1; and Minutes of Meeting of Overseas Music Unit, 15 December 1941, BBC WAC R27/198/1.

50. Letter to Anne Shelton, 13 November 1941, in Madden, Wartime Radio Diary No. 13, BBC WAC S24/54/13.

51. Letter to Anne Shelton, 13 August 1941, in Madden, Wartime Radio Diary No. 9, BBC WAC S24/54/9.

52. "Anne Shelton," BBC ICM from Hayes to DEP, 7 October 1942, BBC WAC R19/1153/1.

53. "Calling the British Forces in Malta," 9 July 1944, BBC WAC R19/1153/1; and "Calling the British Forces in Malta," 25 June 1944, BBC WAC R19/1153/1.

54. "Anne Shelton," BBC ICM from ADV to GOSD, 7 July 1944, BBC WAC R19/1153/1.

55. "Proposed Anne Shelton Programme," BBC ICM from Hayes to ADV, 27 June 1944.

56. Cover, *Parade* (18 April 1942): 1.

57. "Life-Line between the People at Home and the Men Overseas: BBC Brings Comfort with Its Broadcasts of Messages"; "BBC Radio Programme," *Parade* (11 April 1942): 21; and "BBC Radio Programme," *Parade* (18 April 1942): 20–21.

58. "Broadcasts for Troops in the Middle East," document circulated by C(OS), 13 May 1942, BBC WAC R34/382.

59. "Attached Letter from Squadron Leader," BBC ICM from DEP to Mr. Davenport, 18 July 1942, BBC WAC R27/178.

60. Bergmeier and Lotz, *Hitler's Airwaves*, 187–88; and Carlton Jackson, *The Great Lili*, 22. For a fuller discussion of "Lili Marleen," the Desert War, and Andersen, Shelton, and Marlene Dietrich's associations with the song, see Baade, "Between the Lines."

61. Letter to the Editor, *Radio Newsreel* (copy), 13 September [1942], BBC WAC R27/178.

62. Letter to W. J. Brown, BBC WAC R27/178.

63. Extracts from Minutes of Programme Policy Meeting, 29 May 1942, BBC WAC R34/382; "Programme Service for Middle East Forces," BBC ICM from Mr. Goatman, Bed. Coll. to C(OS), 8 June 1942, BBC WAC R34/382; and "All-Star Programme for Forces," *Parade* (18 July 1942): 17.

64. "General Overseas Service," from General Overseas Service Manager to Middle East Director, Cairo, 27 May 1943, BBC WAC R34/382; Briggs, *History of Broadcasting*, 3:492; and "The BBC at War," *Parade* (10 July 1943): 12–13.

65. "New Radio Service for Forces," *Daily Herald* (24 October 1942) [BBC clippings].

66. "Lilli Marlene," BBC ICM from African Service Director to Adams, 1 September 1942, BBC WAC R27/178.

67. "Lilli Marlene," BBC ICM from Madden to DEP, 8 August 1942, BBC WAC R19/1153/1.

68. "Anne Shelton: 'Introducing Anne' Series," BBC ICM from Madden to DEP, 7 October 1942, BBC WAC R19/1153/1.

69. "Anne Shelton," BBC ICM from Hayes to DEP, 7 October 1942, BBC WAC R19/1153/1.

70. "Introducing Anne" [4 October 1942], BBC WAC R19/1153/1.

71. "Detector," "Recent Radio Reviewed," *MM* (24 October 1942): 8.

72. "Anne Shelton: 'Introducing Anne' Series," BBC ICM from Madden to DEP, 7 October 1942.

73. "Detector," "Radio," *MM* (24 October 1942): 8.

74. "Detector," "Radio," *MM* (7 November 1942): 6.

75. "Lili Marlene," Letter from Morris Gilbert to Thomas H. Eliot, 11 June 1943, BBC WAC R27/178.

76. Forces PasB, 18 October 1942. See Bierman and Smith, *War without Hate*, 86; and Horst Bergmeier, Rainer Lotz, and Volker Kühn, liner notes to *Lili Marleen an Allen Fronten*, 54.

77. "Anne Shelton: Signature Tune," BBC ICM from AC(P) to Miss Pratt, Programme Correspondence, 30 October 1942, BBC WAC R19/1153/1.

78. LRB No. 117, 19 December 1942, BBC WAC R9/1/2; and "Shelton Air-Series Finishes," *MM* (26 December 1942): 2.

79. George Stagg, "These Men Make the BBC Sit Up and Take Notice," *Daily Express* (5 February 1944) [BBC clippings].

80. Radio Listings, *Parade* (19 December 1942): 21.

81. "Detector," "Good BBC Programmes?" *MM* (20 March 1943): 9.

82. Cecil Madden, "Policy Directive for Variety Material Broadcast Overseas," [c. 6 October 1943], in Madden, Wartime Radio Diary No. 19, BBC WAC S24/54/19.

83. "Woe to the Victor!" *Sunday Dispatch* (5 March 1944) [BBC clippings].

84. "Every Night about This Time," *RT* (25 February 1944): 1.

85. Briggs, *History of Broadcasting*, 3:590.

86. Ibid., 3:591; and "Detector," "Radio," *MM* (4 March 1944): 5.

87. Clifford Lackey, "Let Them Croon, Say Fighting Men," *Yorkshire Evening News* (9 March 1944) [BBC clippings]; and "Women Crooners Say 'We Don't,'" *Evening News* (8 March 1944) [BBC clippings].

88. "Soft and Low," *Observer* (12 March 1944) [BBC clippings].

89. Jonah Barrington, "Radio: What BBC Changes Mean to You," *Sunday Chronicle* (6 February 1944), in Madden, Wartime Radio Diary No. 17, BBC WAC S24/54/17.

90. Briggs, *History of Broadcasting*, 3:589–91. Ultimately, the more important service for the invading forces was the Allied Expeditionary Forces Programme. See chapter 8.

91. George Stagg, "Barbara & Joan Knew What the Boys Wanted on the Air," *Daily Express* (8 January 1944) [BBC clippings].

92. "BBC 'General Forces' Programme Starts Feb. 27," *MM* (29 January 1944): 1; and LRB No. 182, 15 March 1944, BBC WAC R9/1/4.

93. Ernest Betts, "Your Preview of the Overseas," *Daily Express* (7 January 1944) [BBC clippings]; and Stagg, "Barbara & Joan Knew What the Boys Wanted on the Air."

94. "All about the General Forces," *MM* (26 February 1944): 1; and "BBC 'General Forces' Programme Starts Feb. 27," *MM* (29 January 1944): 1.

95. "BBC 'General Forces' Programme Starts Feb. 27"; and Ronald Strode, "You Will Hear Stuff They Give the Troops," *Sunday Sun* (27 February 1944) [BBC clippings].

96. Jonah Barrington, "Radio," *Sunday Chronicle* (6 February 1944), in Madden, Wartime Radio Diary No. 17, BBC WAC S24/54/17.

97. Ernest Betts, "New 'Forces' Has Brains Trust with the Pudding," *Daily Express* (28 February 1944) [BBC clippings].

98. "Listeners Say They Like the New Forces Programme," *News Chronicle* (28 February 1944) [BBC clippings].

99. LRB No. 182.

100. "Listeners Say They Like the New Forces Programme."

101. "Women Announcers," *Yorkshire Post* (7 March 1944) [BBC clippings].

102. "Women on the Air," *Daily Mail* (25 February 1944) [BBC clippings].

103. "This Is London!" *Christian World* (16 March 1944) [BBC clippings].

104. Quoted in "Notes and News," *MT* (August 1942): 252.

105. Quoted in "Detector," "Radio," *MM* (1 April 1944): 5.

106. Earl Winterton, "Crooners," *Evening Standard* (4 March 1944) [BBC clippings].

107. "Detector," "Radio," *MM* (1 April 1944): 5.

108. In the BBC WAC Press Cuttings, twenty items opposed Winterton's position and fourteen supported it. Winterton, "Crooners."

109. Quoted in "Women Crooners Say 'We Don't.'"

110. "Crooners," *Yorkshire Evening News* (15 March 1944) [BBC clippings].

111. George Stagg, "The Boys Want Bing, Vera and Deanna," *Daily Express* (1 April 1944) [BBC clippings].

112. Collie Knox, "Cut the Cackle and Get to the Forces," *Star* (17 March 1944) [BBC clippings].

113. Six Sergeants in Orkney, letter to *Aberdeen Press and Journal* (20 March 1944) [BBC clippings].

114. H. W. Seaman, "If Troops Want Crooning They Should Have It," *Sunday Chronicle and Sunday Referee* (12 March 1944) [BBC clippings].

115. At the end of the first week of the service, 32 percent thought the GFP better and 25 percent thought it worse than the Forces Programme. Two weeks later, 29 percent thought it better and 28 percent thought it worse. LRB No. 184, 27 March 1944, BBC WAC R9/1/4.

116. "Radio Critics," *Evening Chronicle* (8 March 1944) [BBC clippings]; and "Detector," "The General Forces 'Flop,'" *MM* (27 May 1944): 4–5.

117. "Sparks," "Retail Radiations," *ETRM* (March 1944): 60.

118. LRB No. 184.

119. LRB No. 186, 11 April 1944, BBC WAC R9/1/4.

120. Ibid.; and LRB No. 184.

121. "For Mr. Foot," *Star* (7 March 1944) [BBC clippings].

122. LRB No. 184.

123. Letter to *Daily Herald* (8 March 1944) [BBC clippings].

124. Norman Collins, "Lilliburlero and All That!" *RT* (23 February 1945): 3.

125. "Detector," "Radio," *MM* (20 May 1944): 3; and LRB No. 255, 7 August 1945, BBC WAC R9/1/5.

126. Collins, "Lilliburlero and All That!"

127. Sgt., RAF, letter to *MM* (10 June 1944): 6.

128. "Radio 'Hates' Analysed," *Chronicle and Echo* (11 January 1945) [BBC clippings]; Cover, *RT* (27 October 1944): 1; and Variety Booking Agent, letter to Bert Ambrose, 8 September 1944, BBC WAC Artists: Anne Shelton, File II 1944–1952.

129. Seaman, "If Troops Want Crooning They Should Have It."

130. Gordon Wellesley, dir. *Rhythm Serenade* (Columbia Pictures, 1943).

131. Gilbert, "Report on Visit to Gibraltar."

132. Letter to *Daily Telegraph* (c. March 1944), in Madden, Wartime Radio Diary No. 17, BBC WAC S24/54/17.

133. Hegarty, "Patriot or Prostitute?"

134. "Women Crooners Say 'We Don't.'"

135. "Too Much Radio Crooning," *Northern Echo* (18 March 1944) [BBC clippings]; and Madden, "Sweethearts of the Forces."

136. Rose, *Which People's War?* 2.

CHAPTER 8

1. "He's Here!" *MM* (2 September 1944): 1; and Madden, Wartime Radio Diary No. 21 S24/54/21.

2. Programme Listings, *RT* (25 August 1944); and Programme Listings, *RT* (1 September 1944).

3. Ray Sonin, "Bing Went the Strings of Our Hearts!" *MM* (2 September 1944): 3.

4. Ibid.; Madden, Wartime Radio Diary No. 21; and Anne Shelton and Bing Crosby, "Easter Parade" [27 August 1944], shelf mark 19322, BBC Sound Archives, NSA.

5. Sonin, "Bing Went the Strings of Our Hearts!"

6. Reynolds, *Rich Relations*, 431.

7. Nicholas, *Echo of War*, 168.

8. Reynolds, *Rich Relations*, 41; Nicholas, *Echo of War*, 172; and LRD, "A Listener Research Report: 'America,'" 15 April 1942, BBC WAC R9/9/6.

9. Nicholas, *Echo of War*, 180; and quoted by Reynolds, *Rich Relations*, 42.

10. Camporesi, "Mass Culture," 142–56.

11. "Use of Radio in Anglo-American Relations," BBC ICM from AC(OS) to C(OS), 12 March 1942, BBC WAC R34/188.

12. Camporesi, "Mass Culture," 158, 166.

13. Reynolds, *Rich Relations*, 146–58.

14. See chapter 4.

15. Nicholas, *Echo of War*, 180.

16. Camporesi, "Mass Culture," 22; and "Detector," "Scotland Listens to the AFN," *MM* (25 November 1944): 6–7.

17. Maurice Gorham, *Broadcasting and Television since 1900* (1952), quoted by Camporesi, "Mass Culture," 23.

18. Quoted in "Detector," "Radio," *MM* (21 August 1943): 4–5.

19. German Propaganda Leaflets Dropped in British Lines in Italy to Undermine Troops' Morale, in Madden, Wartime Radio Diary No. 23, BBC WAC S24/54/23.

20. Reynolds, *Rich Relations*, 41; and "American Output," BBC ICM from DPP to C(P), 29 July 1942, BBC WAC R34/188.

21. Programme Listings, *RT* (13 June 1941): 8.

22. "American Output," BBC ICM from DPP to C(P), 29 July 1942; Programme Listings, *RT* (21 December 1941): 9; Programme Listings, *RT* (28 December 1941): 7; Programme Listings, *RT* (11 January 1942): 7; and Programme Listings, *RT* (26 January 1942): 7.

23. LRD, "A Listener Research Report: Listening Conditions, the Forces Programme Generally and Particular Types of Output in the Forces Programme," 27 January 1942, BBC WAC R9/9/6.

24. "BBC Use of Material from the USA," BBC ICM from AC(P) to A[ssistant?] D[irector?] O[verseas?] C[ontinuity?] D[epartment?], 26 February 1942, BBC WAC R34/188; and Letter from Overseas Liaison Unit to Lieutenant Buttles, USA Army Headquarters, 18 April 1942, BBC WAC R23/913.

25. Dunning, s.v. "Command Performance," *On the Air*.

26. "Use of Radio in Anglo-American Relations," Minutes, 11 May 1942, BBC WAC R34/687; and "Detector," "US Sponsored Shows over the BBC," *MM* (28 June 1941): 4.

27. Reynolds, *Rich Relations*, 166.

28. "Programmes for American Troops in England," BBC ICM from Assistant Director Features to Assistant Director Talks, 10 August 1942, BBC WAC R34/913.

29. "Programmes Likely to Be of Interest to USA Troops in This Country (Sept 27th–Oct. 3rd [1942])," BBC WAC R34/913.

30. Programme Listings, RT (2 October 1942): 19; and "Detector," "Recent Radio Reviewed," MM (17 October 1942): 8.

31. "Detector," "Recent Radio Reviewed," MM (17 October 1942): 8.

32. Reynolds, Rich Relations, 167.

33. Camporesi, "Mass Culture," 22.

34. Quoted by Reynolds, Rich Relations, 167.

35. Reynolds, Rich Relations, 158–60.

36. Ibid., 168; and Briggs, History of Broadcasting, 3:645.

37. Briggs, History of Broadcasting, 3:645.

38. "The Broadcasters," "Both Sides of the Microphone," RT (2 July 1943): 3.

39. Gale Pedrick, "In the American Way," BW (November 1945): 28.

40. Minutes of Interdivisional Committee on Use of Radio in Anglo-American Relations, 30 July 1943, BBC WAC R34/687.

41. "Detector," "Radio," MM (17 July 1943): 3; and Pedrick, "In the American Way," 29.

42. "Detector," "Radio," MM (21 August 1943): 4–5; and "American Show-Bible Bears Out 'MM' Criticism of the BBC," MM (24 July 1943): 5.

43. Camporesi, "Mass Culture," 166; and "Detector," "Radio," MM (21 August 1943): 4–5.

44. LRB No. 161, 18 October 1943, BBC WAC R9/1/3.

45. Camporesi, "Mass Culture," 168.

46. "American Programmes in Home Service," BBC ICM from Editor-in-Chief to C(P), 10 February 1944, BBC WAC E1/109.

47. Camporesi, "Mass Culture," 169–70.

48. "Northern Ireland Region," BBC ICM from DPP to C(P), 21 May 1942, BBC WAC R34/913.

49. Reynolds, Rich Relations, 152.

50. LRD, "A Listener Research Report: 'America,'" 7 February 1944, BBC WAC R9/9/7; and "Northern Ireland Region," BBC ICM from DPP to C(P), 21 May 1942.

51. "Policy Directive for Variety Material Broadcast Overseas," from Madden [c. 6 October 1943], in Madden, Wartime Radio Diary No. 19, BBC WAC S24/54/19.

52. "Points Arising from DMPC Meeting: Monday, October 25th," BBC ICM from Programme Organizer to DPP, 26 October 1943, BBC WAC R27/73/2; and DMPC Minutes, 25 October 1943, BBC WAC R27/74/1.

53. "BBC Anti-slushers Ban No. 1 US Hit," MM (4 December 1943): 1.

54. Dance Music Policy: Report of 6th Meeting with Representatives of the MPA, 31 September 1943, BBC WAC R27/73/2.

55. "BBC Anti-Slushers Ban No. 1 US Hit."

56. DMPC Minutes, 13 December 1943, BBC WAC R27/74/1.

57. Reynolds, Rich Relations, 103.

58. Basil Nicolls, quoted by Camporesi, "Mass Culture," 173.

59. Reg Connelly, "Homecoming Thoughts," MM (18 September 1943): 3.

60. "Dance Band Sessions: Overseas Services," BBC ICM from AC(OS) to AC(P), 25 February 1944, BBC WAC R27/73/2.

61. "Overseas Services (Oxford Street)—Use of Dance Bands," BBC ICM from Mrs. Spicer to Madden, 30 July 1943, BBC WAC R27/71/4; "Overseas Services (Oxford Street)—Use of Dance Bands," BBC ICM from Spicer to Madden, 12 August 1943, BBC WAC R27/71/4; and

"Dance Band Contracts," BBC ICM from Spicer to Programme Contracts Director, 12 August 1943, BBC WAC R27/71/4.

62. "Dance Band Sessions: Overseas Services," BBC ICM from AC(OS) to AC(P), 25 February 1944.

63. "Overseas Services (Oxford Street)—Use of Dance Bands," BBC ICM from Madden to Spicer, 31 July 1943, BBC WAC R27/71/4.

64. "Dance Bands Policy and Suggestion," BBC ICM from Madden to DV, 30 July 1943, BBC WAC R27/73/2.

65. See Baade, "'The Battle of the Saxes.'"

66. "Dance Bands Policy and Suggestion," BBC ICM from Madden to DV, 30 July 1943.

67. "Geraldo and His Whole Band Are Going to Entertain Middle East Troops," *MM* (11 September 1943): 1.

68. "Geraldo's Triumph," *MM* (20 November 1943): 1; and Dean, *The Theatre at War*, 465.

69. "Anti Flabby Entertainment in Empire Programmes," BBC ICM from Madden, Criterion, to DEP, 11 March 1942; and "This Dance Music," *London Calling* (21 January 1943): 2. Although ethnicity was never mentioned—even obliquely—in BBC documents and the press, one wonders whether Geraldo's Jewishness made it easier to classify him as less "all-British" than Payne.

70. "Anti Flabby Entertainment in Empire Programme," BBC ICM from Madden, Criterion, to DEP, 11 March 1942; and "Brains Trust and Dance Music," BBC ICM from Howard Thomas to Lawrence, 20 February 1942, BBC WAC R27/71/4.

71. Geraldo and His Orchestra (3 Boys and a Girl, vocals), "Accentuate the Positive," *You Must Remember This: The Happy Album* (Conifer Records compact disc 75605 52261 2, 1996); and Jack Payne, "Accentuate the Positive" (The Crackerjacks, vocal), *Dance Band Recollections of 1945* (Empress compact disc RAJCD 876, 1996). Both versions were released in May 1945.

72. H. S., "Miscellaneous and Dance," *Gramophone* (May 1945): 145–46.

73. Spike Hughes, "Report on the Four BBC Contract Dance Bands and Victor Silvester's Band," 12 August 1943, BBC WAC R27/73/2.

74. AC(P) "Spike Hughes' Report on the Four BBC Contract Dance Bands and Victor Silvester's Band" [note], 31 August 1943, BBC WAC R27/73/2.

75. "Dance Band—London," BBC ICM from DV to C(P), 17 January 1941, BBC WAC R27/21.

76. "Dance Band Sessions," BBC ICM from Madden to AC(OS), 22 November 1943, BBC WAC R27/73/2.

77. Letters to *Bournemouth Daily Echo* (21 January 1944) [BBC clippings]; and "As 'The Performer' Sees It," *Performer* (2 December 1943) [BBC clippings].

78. BBC ICM from AC(OS) to C(OS), 16 November 1943, BBC WAC R27/71/4; and Ralph Woolfe, "Will the BBC Really Give a Chance to Unknowns?" *Empire News* (12 December 1943) [BBC clippings].

79. "British Songs," *Yorkshire Post* (24 November 1943) [BBC clippings]; "Encouraging British Tunes," *Bournemouth Daily Echo* (1 March 1944) [BBC clippings]; and "Lament by the Song Writers: Blame the BBC," *Daily Mail* (5 November 1943), BBC WAC R27/13/1.

80. "Dance Band Programmes in the Overseas Services," BBC ICM from Spicer to AC(OS), 4 November 1943, BBC WAC R27/71/4.

81. "Dance Band Programmes in the Overseas Services," BBC ICM from Spicer to AC(OS), 11 November 1943, BBC WAC R27/71/4; and "Dance Band Sessions," BBC ICM from Madden to AC(OS), 22 November 1943, BBC WAC R27/73/2.

82. "House Band (Overseas Services)," BBC ICM from Madden to DV, 1 December 1943, BBC WAC R27/71/4.

83. "Geraldo Home after Plane Crash Drama," *MM* (1 January 1944): 1; and "Drastic Cut in Geraldo Airings," *MM* (12 February 1944): 1.

84. "Dance Music Output," BBC ICM from AC(P) to Editor-in-Chief, DG, 21 January 1944, BBC WAC R27/73/2.

85. "Drastic Cut in Geraldo Airings." According to Listener Research 25 percent of the audience disliked dance music in 1941; by 1943, 35 percent disliked it. LRB No. 162, 26 October 1943, BBC WAC R9/1/3.

86. Silvey, "Methods of Listener Research Employed by the British Broadcasting Corporation."

87. "Detector," "Radio," *MM* (12 February 1944): 3.

88. "A Listener Research Report on Broadcast Dance Music," [May 1943], BBC WAC R27/73/2.

89. "Detector," "Jack Payne: The Winning Letter," *MM* (24 June 1944): 5.

90. "Variety Programmes for the Overseas Services—Presentation," BBC ICM from Overseas Presentation Director to ADV, 9 February 1944, BBC WAC R27/71/4.

91. See chapter 7.

92. "Harry Roy through with Broadcasting!" *MM* (22 April 1944): 1.

93. "Harry Roy and BBC," *MM* (6 May 1944): 1.

94. "Bandleaders' Call for Unity as Dance Music Faces Crisis," *MM* (27 May 1944): 1; "Popular Music Forces in Big Anti-BBC Drive," *MM* (3 June 1944): 1; and "Band Leaders to Fight BBC 'War' on Swing," *DM* (3 June 1944) [BBC clippings].

95. "Dance Bands," BBC ICM from AC(P) to C(P), 10 March 1944, BBC WAC R27/73/2; "Dance Music: Jack Payne," BBC ICM from DV to AC(P), 24 April 1944, BBC WAC R27/73/2; and "Payne Cuts Airings for New Activities," *MM* (19 June 1944): 1.

96. "Jack Payne and Dance Music Output," BBC ICM from AC(P) to DG, 26 May 1944, BBC WAC R27/73/2.

97. "Engagements Offered to Dance Bands," BBC ICM from Programme Contracts Director, 55, P[ortland] P[lace,] to DV, 9 June 1944, BBC WAC R27/73/2; and "BBC 'Band of the Week' Restarts," *MM* (12 August 1944): 1.

98. [Untitled], *Evening News* (16 October 1944) [BBC clippings].

99. "BBC 'Band of the Week' Restarts."

100. LRB No. 215, 30 October 1944, BBC WAC R9/1/4.

101. "American Music Programmes," BBC ICM from GOSD to AC(OS), 1 June 1944, BBC WAC E1/109.

102. "Dance Band Music on BBC Invasion Wavelength to Second Front Troops," *MM* (10 June 1944): 1.

103. Briggs, *History of Broadcasting*, 3:648–52; and Madden, Wartime Radio Diary No. 22, BBC WAC S24/54/22.

104. Briggs, *History of Broadcasting*, 3:650; "Dance Band Music on BBC Invasion Wavelength to Second Front Troops"; and "Detector," "Praise for the BBC," *MM* (17 June 1944): 3.

105. "Detector," "You All Like the AEF Programmes," *MM* (18 November 1944): 4–5.

106. "Your AEF Programme Schedule," *MM* (9 December 1944): 2.

107. "Detector," "No More for Benny!" *MM* (15 April 1944): 3; and Madden, Wartime Radio Diary No. 21.

108. Simon, *Glenn Miller and His Orchestra*, 346, 367–69; and "AEF to Get Glenn Miller Every Day," *MM* (11 November 1944): 2.

109. "Brand's Essence," *MM* (10 June 1944): 6.

110. David Ades, "Robert Farnon: A Legend of Light Music" (2005), Robert Farnon Society website, http://www.rfsoc.org.uk/rf_bio.shtml (accessed 11 April 2010).

111. Count Ramon Vargas, "Melachrino Goes on the Air," *BW* (13 April 1940): 5.

112. Programme Listings, *RT* (22 December 1944); and "Glenn Miller Is Missing," *MM* (30 December 1944): 1.

113. "Dance Musicians in the Invasion," *MM* (24 June 1944): 1.

114. "Ambrose to Entertain Troops in France," *MM* (2 September 1944): 1; "Joe Loss and Band Leaving for France," *MM* (28 October1944): 1; and "Geraldo for France and Belgium," *MM* (4 November 1944): 1.

115. Lynn, *Vocal Refrain*, 111.

116. "Musicals for West End Again," *MM* (9 September 1944): 1.

117. Reynolds, *Rich Relations*, 393.

118. "He's Here!" *MM* (2 September 1944): 1.

119. Sonin, "Bing Went the Strings of Our Hearts!"

120. Ernest Dudley, "Are You Listening?" *Sunday Pictorial* (10 September 1944), in Madden, Wartime Radio Diary No. 20, BBC WAC S24/54/20.

121. "Glenn Miller in Britain," *RT* (28 July 1944): 5.

122. Laurie Henshaw, "Glenn Miller on the Air," *MM* (22 July 1944): 3.

123. LRB No. 203, 8 August 1944, BBC WAC R9/1/4.

124. "Letters from Listeners," *RT* (11 August 1944): 5.

125. LRB No. 204, 14 August 1944, BBC WAC R9/1/4.

126. "BBC Cold-Shoulders AEF Stars," *MM* (30 September 1944): 1; and "British Leaders Pay Tribute to Glenn Miller as Protest against BBC," *MM* (7 October 1944): 1.

127. "The Mystery of Glenn Miller," *MM* (6 January 1945): 1.

128. "AEF to Get Glenn Miller Every Day."

129. "The Best Jazz Jamboree Ever!" *MM* (21 October 1944): 1; and "Brand's Essence," *MM* (21 October 1944): 4.

130. "Brand's Essence," *MM* (9 September 1944): 6–7.

131. "Detector," "Good US Influence on Local Boys," *MM* (4 November 1944): 9.

132. "Brand's Essence," *MM* (15 July 1944): 4; and "Squadronairs – 1[,] Geraldo – 2[,] Barriteau – 3," *MM* (13 May 1944): 1.

133. "Detector," "Good US Influence on Local Boys," 9; and Marshall, "Brand's Essence," *MM* (16 September 1944): 6.

134. Reynolds, *Rich Relations*, 229.

135. "Brand's Essence," *MM* (19 August 1944): 6.

136. Industrial Recreation Association, *Music in Industry*, 15–17, 34–35.

137. Beckett, *Music in War Plants*.

138. Camporesi, "Mass Culture," 141–66.

139. Reynolds, *Rich Relations*, 431; and Nicholas, *Echo of War*, 235.

CONCLUSION

1. "The Broadcasters," "Both Sides of the Microphone," *RT* (10 May 1945): 4.

2. BBC, WW2 People's War: An Archive of World War Two Memories—Written by the Public, Gathered by the BBC, http://www.bbc.co.uk/ww2peopleswar/ (accessed 12 May 2010). A search for "VE Day" and "Music" reveals more than 3,000 entries.

3. "Dance Bands in Forefront of Nation's Victory Rejoicing," *MM* (19 May 1945): 1.

4. Rose, *Which People's War?* 25.

5. Stevenson, *British Society*, 455–56.

6. Rose, *Which People's War?* 286.

7. Ibid., 292.

8. Calder, *People's War*, 545.

9. Nicholas, *Echo of War*, 275.

10. W. J. Haley, "The Two New Programmes," *RT* (27 July 1945): 1; and "Radio in Family Life," *Glasgow Herald* (15 March 1945) [BBC clippings].

11. Haley, "The Two New Programmes."

12. "The Broadcasters," "Both Sides of the Microphone," *RT* (27 July 1945): 4.

13. Haley, "The Two New Programmes."

14. Ibid.

15. Programme Listings, *RT* (27 July 1945): 9.

16. Haley, "The Two New Programmes."

17. Janet Leeper, "BBC Prepares Change-Over," *BW* (July 1945): 73.

18. Briggs, *History of Broadcasting*, 3:716–17, 722.

19. Leeper, "BBC Prepares Change-Over."

20. "AEF Programme Off the Air in July," *MM* (26 May 1945): 1.

21. Pedrick, "In the American Way," 29; and "Commercial Radio Again!" *MM* (14 July 1945): 1.

22. "More Bands on the Air in New BBC Programmes," *MM* (28 July 1945): 1.

23. Programme Listings, *RT* (27 July 1945).

24. "The Broadcasters," "Both Sides of the Microphone," *RT* (27 July 1945): 4.

25. "Sunday Dance Music," BBC ICM from Mr. Gorham to DV et al., 30 July 1945, BBC WAC R27/72/1.

26. "Sensational Chance for British Songwriters in £2000 Air-Contest," *MM* (14 July 1945): 1; and Programme Listings, *RT* (27 July 1945): 13.

27. "70,000 Songs in H'Smith Palais £2,000 Air-Contest," *MM* (1 December 1945): 2.

28. LRD, "Dance Band Preferences: Spring 1945," LR/3393, 20 April 1945, BBC WAC R9/9/9.

29. Note by DG on LR/3393, Dance Band Preferences: Spring 1945, to Senior Controller, 27 April 1945, BBC WAC R9/15/1.

30. "Jazz *versus* the Gestapo," *RT* (8 June 1945): 7.

31. Rex Harris and Max Jones, "V-E Collectors' Corner," *MM* (12 May 1945): 1.

32. "'MM' 1945 Poll Results," *MM* (1 September 1945): 3.

33. Godbolt, *History of Jazz*, 207.

34. "Dance Bands," BBC ICM from DV to Mr. Wellington et al., 3 October 1945, BBC WAC R27/72/1; and "Dance Band Broadcasts," BBC ICM from DV to Wellington et al., 25 January 1946, BBC WAC R27/74/1.

35. "Dance Bands," BBC ICM from DV to Wellington et al., 3 October 1945.

36. Ibid.

37. "BBC Dance Orchestra," BBC ICM from Acting Controller (Entertainment) to DG, 4 December 1945, BBC WAC R27/72/1.

38. "Dance Bands," BBC ICM from DV to Wellington et al., 3 October 1945.

39. "Dance Music," BBC ICM from Mr. Pat Dixon to ADV, 10 October 1946, BBC WAC R27/72/2.

40. Irene Raines, "People and Places in London," *DT* (November 1945): 81.

41. Reynolds, "'Music While You Work': Survey of the 5th Year of the Series," BBC WAC R27/257/4.

42. The workweek at the time included Saturday mornings.

43. Reynolds, "'Music While You Work': Survey of the 5th Year of the Series."

44. DMPC Minutes, 31 January 1945, BBC WAC R/27/74/1.

45. "Dynamo," "Radio Flashes," *MM* (22 December 1945): 8–9.

46. "Dance Music Policy," report on eighth meeting with representatives of the MPA, 8 May 1946, BBC WAC R/27/74/1.

47. "DMPC," BBC ICM from DV to Assistant Controller (Entertainment), 30 December 1947, BBC WAC R27/74/2.

48. Music General, DMPC, file 3 (1951–54), BBC WAC R27/74/3.

49. "Dynamo," "Radio Flashes," 8–9.

50. Edward Chase, liner notes to *Beryl Davis*.

51. Lynn, *Vocal Refrain*, 136–37.

52. Godbolt, *History of Jazz*, 236–38.

53. "Ring dem Bells," *MM* (12 May 1945): 1.

Bibliography

BBC WRITTEN ARCHIVES CENTRE, CAVERSHAM

Radio Files

R9/1/1: Audience Research/Bulletins, Sound/1–68 (1941)
R9/1/2: Audience Research/Bulletins, Sound/69–121 (1942)
R9/1/3: Audience Research/Bulletins, Sound/122–73 (1943)
R9/1/4: Audience Research/Bulletins, Sound/174–225 (1944)
R9/1/5: Audience Research/Bulletins, Sound/226–273 (1945)
R9/9/3: Audience Research/Special Reports, Sound and General, file 3 (1939)
R9/9/4: Audience Research/Special Reports, Sound and General, file 4 (1940)
R9/9/5: Audience Research/Special Reports, Sound and General, file 5 (1941)
R9/9/6: Audience Research/Special Reports, Sound and General, file 6 (1942)
R9/9/7: Audience Research/Special Reports, Sound and General, file 7 (1943)
R9/9/9: Audience Research/Special Reports, Sound and General, file 9 (1945)
R9/15/1: Audience Research/Head of Audience Research Department/Wartime Listener Research Policy (1939–49)
R9/22/1: Audience Research/HAR: Variety Radio (1937–57)
R19/585/1: Entertainment "Jazz" (1933–46)
R19/683: Entertainment/Vera Lynn Programmes (1941–53)
R19/1153/1: Entertainment/Anne Shelton Programmes (1942–44)
R21/121: Gramophone Correspondence/Radio Rhythm Club (1941–49)
R27/3/1: Music General/Alien Composers, file 1 (1939–40)
R27/21: Music General/Band of the Week (1940–45, 1955)
R27/71/3: Music General/Dance Bands, file 3 (1938–41)
R27/71/4: Music General/Dance Bands, file 4 (1942–44)

R27/72/1: Music General/Dance Music, file 1 (1945)

R27/72/2: Music General/Dance Music, file 2 (1946)

R27/73/1: Music General/Dance Music Policy, file 1 (1941–42)

R27/73/2: Music General/Dance Music Policy, file 2 (1943–44)

R27/74/1: Music General/Dance Music Policy Committee, file 1 (1942–46)

R27/74/2: Music General/Dance Music Policy Committee, file 2 (1947–50)

R27/74/3: Music General/Dance Music Policy Committee, file 3 (1951–54)

R27/172/1: Music General/Light Music, file 1 (1939–43)

R27/178: Music General/Lili Marlene (1942–47)

R27/179: Music General/Limitation of Vocal Numbers in Dance Band Programmes (1937–41)

R27/198/1: Music General/Meetings/Overseas Service Minutes, file 1 (1941–43)

R27/213/1: Music General/Ministry of Information, file 1A (1939–40)

R27/245/1: Music General/Music Policy, file 1A (1930–43)

R27/254: Music General/Music Publishers Association, file 1 (1942–54)

R27/257/1: Music General/Music While You Work, file 1 (1940)

R27/257/2: Music General/Music While You Work, file 2 (1941)

R27/257/3: Music General/Music While You Work, file 3 (1942–43)

R27/257/4: Music General/Music While You Work, file 4 (1944–47)

R27/258: Music General/Music While You Work/Factory Visits A–Z (1941–53)

R27/259: Music General/Music While You Work Instructions (1941–55)

R27/260: Music General/Music While You Work/Orchestral Reports (1942)

R27/262/1: Music General/Music While You Work/Public Bodies A–Z, file 1 (1940–46)

R27/263: Music General/Music While You Work/Technical P.A. (1942)

R27/416/1: Music General/Overseas Service, file 1 (1936–42)

R27/475/1: Music General/Song Plugging, file 1 (June 1935–October 1936)

R27/475/2: Music General/Song Plugging, file 2 (November–December 1936)

R27/475/3: Music General/Song Plugging, file 3 (July 1937–[November] 1939)

R27/475/4: Music General/Song Plugging, file 4 (December 1939–45)

R34/188: Policy/American Material in Programmes, file 1 (1940–44)

R34/382: Policy Forces/Broadcasts to the Forces/Middle East (1941–46)

R34/687: Policy/Propaganda/Inter-Divisional Committee on Use of Radio in Anglo-American and Imperial Relations (1942–44)

R34/913: Policy/United States Army Programmes for Americans in Great Britain (1942–43)

R41/113/1: PCS (Listeners' Letters)/Music—Popular, file 1 (1931–44)

R47/3/2: Relays "America Dances," file 2 ([July–August] 1938)

R47/3/4: Relays "America Dances," file 3 (1939)

R47/3/5: Relays "America Dances," file 4 (1940–63)

R47/416/1: Relays/Jam Sessions from America (1938–63)

Artist Files, Countries, and Special Collections

Artists: Wynford Reynolds, file 3A (1943–45)

Artists: Anne Shelton, file 2 (1944–52)

E1/109: Countries/America/American Material in Programmes (1941–48)

Personal File/Artists/Vera Lynn (1935–44)

S24/54/1–38: Special collections/Madden/Wartime Radio Diary

BBC Programs as Broadcast

Home Service (October 1939)

Forces Programme (February–March 1940, December 1940, February–March 1941, January–February 1942, October 1942)

Overseas Programme (December 1940–January 1941, August 1941, April 1942–March 1943)

MASS OBSERVATION ARCHIVE, THE UNIVERSITY OF SUSSEX

File Report 11A "Jazz and Dancing." November 1939

File Report 49 "Gramophone Records" (JC). March 1940

File Report 301A "First Weekly Morale Report: Series C." July 1940

File Report 795 "Songwriters: Sales of Sheet Music and Radio Broadcasts." July 1941

File Report 1087 "'Answering You': Broadcast to America: War Songs, Income Tax, Cosmetics and Clothes" (TH). February 1942

File Report 1249 "Radio: Use of Music in Factories and the BBC's 'Music While You Work.'" May 1942

Topic Collection 38 "Music, Dancing & Jazz 1938–41." 4/F, Swing (XXVII)

Topic Collection 38 "Music, Dancing & Jazz 1938–41." 6/A, History of Jazz and Dancing: Notes (XLI)

Topic Collection 38 "Music, Dancing & Jazz 1938–41." 7/A, Sheet Music 1940-41: Samples of Song Sheets and Sheet Music

NATIONAL SOUND ARCHIVE

Geraldo (Evelyn Laye). "Let the People Sing." Shelf mark 1CS0030507

BBC Sound Archives

Chilton, Charles and Bill Elliott. Spoken introduction with sound examples. *Radio Rhythm Club*. BBC Forces Broadcast. [13 June 1940]. Shelf mark 30B/6737

Shelton, Anne and Bing Crosby. "Easter Parade." [27 August 1944]. Shelf mark 19322

Silvester, Victor and His Ballroom Orchestra. Compèred by David Miller. Excerpt from *BBC Dancing Club*. [27 August] 1941. Shelf mark 3343

Oral History of Jazz in Britain

Chilton, Charles. Interview by Jim Godbolt. 29 June 1989. Shelf mark C122/71

Deniz, Frank. Interview by Val Wilmer. 18 August 1989. Shelf mark C122/81-82

Perowne, Leslie. Interview by Christopher Clark. 23 February 1990. Shelf mark C122/91-92

Powell, Peter. Interview by Les Back. 28 January 1999. Shelf mark C122/341-44

Wilkins, Dave. Interview by Val Wilmer. 9 September 1987. Shelf mark C122/36

PERIODICALS

Band Wagon: An Independent Weekly Newspaper. 14 October 1939–19 April 1940.

Band Wagon: The Journal of Leisure, published monthly. July 1945–November 1945.

Daily Mirror. 6 September 1939–23 January 1940.

Dancing Times. November/December 1920–November 1945.

Electrical Trading and Radio Marketing. November 1939–March 1944.

Gramophone: Incorporating Vox, The Radio Critic and Broadcast Review. October 1939–May 1945.

Listener. London: British Broadcasting Corporation, 7 September 1939–27 June 1940.

Melody Maker. 3 September 1938–2 December 1939.

Melody Maker, incorporating *Rhythm.* 9 December 1939–22 December 1945.

Musical Times. London. October 1939–February 1944.

Parade. Cairo. 8 March 1941–10 July 1943.

The Pianomaker and Music Seller. August 1939–November 1939.

Radio Pictorial. 14 October 1938–28 July 1939.

Radio Times. 10 March 1939–27 July 1945.

The Times. London. 1 September 1939–4 September 1942.

BOOKS AND ARTICLES

Anderson, Benedict. *Imagined Communities: Reflections on the Origin and Spread of Nationalism.* London: Verso, 1983; revised and extended, 1991.

Baade, Christina. " 'The Battle of the Saxes' ": Gender, Dance Bands, and British Nationalism in the Second World War." In *Big Ears: Listening for Gender in Jazz Studies.* Edited by Sherrie Tucker and Nichole Rustin. Durham, NC: Duke University Press, 2008.

———. "Between the Lines: 'Lili Marlene,' Sexuality, and the Desert War." In *Music, Geopolitics and Violence.* Edited by Susan Fast and Kip Pegley. Hanover, NH: Wesleyan University Press, forthcoming.

———. " 'The Dancing Front': Dance Music, Dancing, and the BBC in World War II." *Popular Music* 25, no. 3 (2006): 347–68.

———. *"Sincerely Yours—Vera Lynn:* Performing Class, Sentiment, and Femininity in the 'People's War.' " *Atlantis, A Women's Studies Journal/Revue d'Etudes sur les Femmes* 30, no. 2 (2006): 36–49.

———. " 'Victory through Harmony': Popular Music and the British Broadcasting Corporation in World War II." Ph.D. diss., University of Wisconsin–Madison, 2002.

BBC Handbook 1941. London: BBC, n.d.

Beckett, Wheeler. *Music in War Plants.* Washington, DC: War Production Drive Headquarters, War Production Board, 1943.

Bederman, Gail. *Manliness and Civilization: A Cultural History of Gender and Race in the United States, 1880–1917.* Chicago: University of Chicago Press, 1995.

Bergmeier Horst J. P., and Ranier E. Lotz. *Hitler's Airwaves: The Inside Story of Nazi Radio Broadcasting and Propaganda Swing.* New Haven, CT: Yale University Press, 1997.

Bergmeier, Horst, Ranier Lotz, and Volker Kühn. Liner notes. *Lili Marleen an Allen Fronten: Das Lied, seine Zeit, seine Interpreten, seine Botschaften.* Bear Family Records compact disc BCD 16022 GL, 2005.

Bierman, John, and Colin Smith. *War without Hate: The Desert Campaign of 1940–1943.* New York: Penguin Books, 2004.

Briggs, Asa. *The History of Broadcasting in the United Kingdom.* Vol. 1, *The Birth of Broadcasting.* London: Oxford University Press, 1961.

———. *The History of Broadcasting in the United Kingdom.* Vol. 2, *The Golden Age of Wireless.* London: Oxford University Press, 1965.

———. *The History of Broadcasting in the United Kingdom.* Vol. 3, *The War of Words.* London: Oxford University Press, 1970.

Cain, John. *The BBC: 70 Years of Broadcasting.* London: British Broadcasting Corporation, 1992.

Calder, Angus. *The Myth of the Blitz*. London: Jonathan Cape, 1991.

Calder, Angus. *The People's War*. New York: Pantheon Books, 1969.

Camporesi, Valeria. "Mass Culture and the Defense of National Traditions: The BBC and American Broadcasting 1922–1954." Ph.D. diss., Florence: European University Institute, 1993.

Cannadine, David. "The 'Last Night of the Proms' in Historical Perspective." *Historical Research* 81, no. 212 (2008): 315–49.

Chase, Edward. Liner notes. *Beryl Davis: Alone Together*. Flare Royce compact disc 221, 2000.

Chilton, John. *Who's Who of British Jazz*. 2nd ed. London: Continuum, 2004.

Cook, Susan C. "Passionless Dancing and Passionate Reform: Respectability, Modernism, and the Social Dancing of Irene and Vernon Castle." In *The Passion of Music and Dance: Body, Gender and Sexuality*. Edited by William Washabaugh. Oxford: Berg, 1998.

Crisell, Andrew. *Understanding Radio*. London: Routledge, 1986.

Davies, Sir Walford. *The Pursuit of Music*. London: Thomas Nelson & Sons Ltd., 1935.

Dean, Basil. *The Theatre at War*. London: George G. Harray and Co., 1956.

DeVeaux, Scott. *The Birth of Bebop: A Social and Musical History*. Berkeley: University of California Press, 1997.

Doctor, Jenny. *The BBC and Ultra-modern Music, 1922–1936: Shaping a Nation's Tastes*. Cambridge: Cambridge University Press, 1999.

———. "The BBC and the Ultra-modern Problem: A Documentary Study of the BBC's Dissemination of Second Viennese School Repertory, 1922–1936." Ph.D. diss., Northwestern University, 1993.

———. "'Virtual Concerts'—The BBC's Transmutation of Public Performances." Paper presented at Britannia (Re-) Sounding: Music in the Arts, Politics, and Culture of Great Britain, The North American British Music Studies Association First Biennial Conference, Oberlin, Ohio, June 2004.

Douglas, Susan J. *Listening In: Radio and the American Imagination, from Amos'n' Andy and Edward R. Murrow to Wolfman Jack and Howard Stern*. New York: Random House, 1999.

Dunning, John. *On the Air: The Encyclopedia of Old-Time Radio*. New York: Oxford University Press, 1998.

Ehrlich, Cyril. *The Music Profession in Britain since the Eighteenth Century: A Social History*. Oxford: Claredon Press, 1985.

Foster, Susan Leigh. "Choreographing History." In *Choreographing History*. Edited by Susan Leigh Foster. Bloomington: Indiana University Press, 1995.

Foucault, Michel. *Discipline and Punish*. Translated by Alan Sheridan. New York: Vintage Books, 1977.

Frith, Simon. "The Pleasures of the Hearth: The Making of BBC Light Entertainment." In *Formations of Pleasure*. London: Routledge and Kegan Paul, 1983.

Gendron, Bernard. "'Moldy Figs' and Modernists: Jazz at War (1942–1946)." In *Jazz among the Discourses*. Edited by Krin Gabbard. Durham, NC: Duke University Press, 1995.

Giddens, Anthony. *The Consequences of Modernity*. Stanford, CA: Stanford University Press, 1990.

Giedion, Sigfried. *Mechanization Takes Command: A Contribution to Anonymous History*. New York: Oxford University Press, 1948.

Gifford, Denis. *The Golden Age of Radio*. London: B. T. Batsford, 1985.

Godbolt, Jim. *A History of Jazz in Britain, 1919–50*. London: Quartet Books, 1984.

Greenway, Robert. "A Balance of Music on the Forces Programme." B.A. thesis, University of York, 2007.

Gubar, Susan. "'This Is My Rifle, This Is My Gun': World War II and the Blitz on Women." In *Behind the Lines: Gender and the Two World Wars*. Edited by Margaret Randolph Higonnet et al. New Haven, CT: Yale University Press, 1987.

Hall, Henry. *Here's to Next Time: The Autobiography of Henry Hall*. London: Odhams Press, 1955.

Hall, Stuart. "Notes on Deconstructing 'The Popular.'" In *People's History and Socialist Theory*. Edited by Raphael Samuel. London: Routledge, 1981.

Hayes, Chris. "19. Geraldo." *The Leader of the Band*. Vol. 1. Self-published, n.d. [before 1994]. Jazz Heritage Archives: Geraldo Folder.

Hegarty, Marilyn E. "Patriot or Prostitute? Sexual Discourses, Print Media, and American Women during World War II." *Journal of Women's History* 10, no. 2 (1998): 112–36.

Hilmes, Michele. "Who We Are, Who We Are Not: Broadcasting and National Identity in the US and Great Britain, 1920–1940." Unpublished paper, Department of Communication Arts, University of Wisconsin, 1998.

Hobsbawm, Eric. "Introduction: Inventing Traditions." In *The Invention of Tradition*. Edited by Eric Hobsbawm and Terence Ranger. Cambridge: Cambridge University Press, 1983.

Industrial Recreation Association. *Music in Industry: A Manual on Music for Work and for Recreation in Business and Industry*. Chicago: Industrial Recreation Association, 1944.

Jackson, Carlton. *The Great Lili*. San Francisco: Strawberry Hill Press, 1979.

Jeffrey, Tom. *Mass-Observation: A Short History*. Mass-Observation Archive Occasional Paper no. 10. University of Sussex Library, 1999.

Jeffery, Tom, and Keith McClelland. "A World Fit to Live in: The *Daily Mail* and the Middle Classes 1918–39." In *Impacts and Influences: Essays on Media Power in the Twentieth Century*. Edited by James Curran, Anthony Smith, and Pauline Wingate. London: Methuen, 1987.

Katz, Mark. "Making America More Musical through the Phonograph." *American Music* 16, no. 4 (1998): 448–75.

Kenyon, Nicholas. *The BBC Symphony Orchestra: The First Fifty Years, 1930–1980*. London: British Broadcasting Corporation, 1981.

Kirby, Edward M., and Jack W. Harris. *Star-Spangled Radio*. Chicago: Ziff-Davis, 1948.

Kirkham, Pat. "Beauty and Duty: Keeping Up the (Home) Front." In *War Culture: Social Change and Changing Experience in World War Two Britain*. Edited by Pat Kirkham and David Thoms. London: Lawrence and Wishart, 1995.

Kushner, Tony. *We Europeans? Mass-Observation, 'Race' and British Identity in the Twentieth Century*. Aldershot: Ashgate, 2004.

LeMahieu, D. L. *A Culture for Democracy: Mass Communication and the Cultivated Mind in Britain between the Wars*. Oxford: Clarendon Press, 1988.

Leppert, Richard. *Music and Image: Domesticity, Ideology and Socio-cultural Formation in Eighteenth-Century England*. Cambridge: Cambridge University Press, 1988.

Lott, Eric. *Love and Theft: Blackface Minstrelsy and the American Working Class*. New York: Oxford University Press, 1993.

Lynn, Vera. *Vocal Refrain*. London: W. H. Allen, 1975.

Marchand, Roland. *Advertising the American Dream: Making Way for Modernity, 1920–1940*. Berkeley: University of California Press, 1985.

Marwick, Arthur. *Britain in the Century of Total War: War, Peace and Social Change 1900–1967*. London: Bodley Head, 1968; reprint, Harmondsworth, Middlesex: Penguin Books, 1970.

Mass-Observation. *War Factory: A Report*. Edited by Tom Harrisson. London: Victor Gollancz, 1943.

McCarthy, Albert. *The Dance Band Era: The Dancing Decades from Ragtime to Swing: 1910–1950.* London: Studio Vista, 1971.

McKay, George. *Circular Breathing: The Cultural Politics of Jazz in Britain.* Durham: Duke University Press, 2005.

Middleton, Richard. *Studying Popular Music.* Philadelphia: Open University Press, 1990.

Monson, Ingrid. "The Problem with White Hipness: Race, Gender, and Cultural Conceptions in Jazz Historical Discourse." *Journal of the American Musicological Society* 48, no. 3 (1995): 396–421.

Moore, Hilary. *Inside British Jazz: Crossing Borders of Race, Nation, and Class.* Aldershot: Ashgate, 2007.

Newton, Darrell. "Calling the West Indies: The BBC World Service and *Caribbean Voices.*" *Historical Journal of Film, Radio and Television* 28, no. 4 (2008): 489–97.

Nicholas, Siân. *The Echo of War: Home Front Propaganda and the Wartime BBC, 1939–45.* Manchester: Manchester University Press, 1996.

Noakes, Lucy. *War and the British: Gender, Memory and National Identity.* London: I. B. Tauris, 1998.

Noble, Peter. *Kings of Rhythm: A Review of Dance-Band and British Dance-Band Personalities.* London: Dunlop Publications, n.d. [1944].

Nott, James J. *Music for the People: Popular Music and Dance in Interwar Britain.* Oxford: Oxford University Press, 2002.

Outram, Dorinda. *The Body and the French Revolution: Sex, Class and Political Culture.* New Haven, CT: Yale University Press, 1989.

Panassié, Hugues. *The Real Jazz.* New York: Smith and Durrell, 1942.

Parsonage, Catherine. *The Evolution of Jazz in Britain, 1880–1935.* Aldershot: Ashgate, 2005.

Priestley, J. B. *Daylight on Saturday.* New York: Harper and Brothers, 1943.

Reynolds, David. *Rich Relations: The American Occupation of Britain 1942–1945.* London: Phoenix Press, 1995.

Richardson, Philip J. S. *A History of English Ballroom Dancing (1910–54).* London: Herbert Jenkins, 1945.

Rogin, Michael. "Blackface, White Noise: The Jewish Jazz Singer Finds His Voice." *Critical Inquiry* 18, no. 3 (1992): 417–53.

Rolfe, David. Liner notes. *I'll Play to You.* Sandy Macpherson, theater organ. Empress compact disc RAJCD 861. 1996.

Rose, Sonya O. *Which People's War? National Identity and Citizenship in Britain 1939–1945.* Oxford: Oxford University Press, 2003.

Rust, Brian. *The Dance Bands.* New Rochelle, NY: Arlington House, 1974.

Rust, Brian, and Sandy Forbes. *British Dance Bands on Record 1911–1945 & Supplement.* Middlesex: General Gramophone Publications, 1989.

Scannell, Paddy, and David Cardiff. "Broadcasting and National Unity." In *Impacts and Influences: Essays on Media Power in the Twentieth Century.* Edited by James Curran, Anthony Smith, and Pauline Wingate. London: Methuen, 1987.

———. *A Social History of British Broadcasting.* Vol. 1, *Serving the Nation.* Oxford: Basil Blackwell, 1991.

Scholes, Percy A. *Music Appreciation: Its History and Techniques.* New York: M. Witmark and Sons, 1935.

Silvester, Victor. *Dancing Is My Life: An Autobiography.* London: Heinemann, 1958.

———. *This Is Jive.* Bournemouth: Hardy Press, 1944.

Simon, George T. *Glenn Miller and His Orchestra*. New York: Thomas Y. Crowell, 1974.

Simons, Andrew. Liner notes. *Black British Swing*. Topic Records compact disc TSCD781, 2001.

Sinfield, Alan. *Out on Stage: Lesbian and Gay Theatre in the Twentieth Century*. New Haven, CT: Yale University Press, 1999.

Soibelman, Doris. *Therapeutic and Industrial Uses of Music: A Review of the Literature*. New York: Columbia University Press, 1948.

Sonin, Ray. *The Dance Band Mystery*. London: Quality Press, 1940.

Stacey, Jackie. *Star Gazing: Hollywood Cinema and Female Spectatorship*. London: Routledge, 1994.

Stevenson, John. *British Society 1914–45*. New York: Penguin Books, 1984.

Stowe, David W. *Swing Changes: Big-Band Jazz in New Deal America*. Cambridge: Harvard University Press, 1994.

Taylor, Frederick Winslow. *Scientific Management*. 1911. Reprint, New York: Harper and Brothers, 1947.

Tucker, Sherrie. *Swing Shift: "All-Girl" Bands of the 1940s*. Durham, NC: Duke University Press, 2000.

Way, Chris. *The Big Bands Go to War*. Edinburgh: Mainstream Publishers, 1991.

West, Cornell. "Black Sexuality: The Taboo Subject." In *Race Matters*. Boston: Beacon Press, 1993.

Wollen, Peter. "Cinema/Americanism/the Robot." In *Modernity and Mass Culture*. Edited by James Naremore and Patrick Brantlinger. Bloomington: Indiana University Press, 1991.

Ziegler, Philip. *London at War, 1939–1945*. New York: Knopf, 1995.

SELECTED DISCOGRAPHY

Alistair Cooke's Jazz Letter from America. Avid Entertainment compact disc AMSC 855. 2006.

Black British Swing. Topic Records compact disc TSCD781. 2001.

British Big Bands. ABM ABMM compact disc 1185. 1999.

Dance Band Recollections of 1945. Empress compact disc RAJCD 876. 1996.

Geraldo and His Orchestra, 3 Boys and a Girl (vocals), "Accentuate the Positive." *You Must Remember This: The Happy Album*. Conifer Records compact disc 75605 52261 2. 1996.

Geraldo and His Orchestra. *A Journey to a Star*. Empress compact disc RAJCD 811. 1993.

Great British Dance Bands and Their Vocalists. Pulse PBX compact disc 447/2–3. 1999.

In the Mood: A Musical Tribute to the War Years. Yesteryear compact disc GLM/Y-1–21. no date.

Jazz in Britain, 1919–1950. Proper Records compact disc Properbox 88. 2005.

Lynn, Vera. *The Ultimate Collection*. Pulse PDS compact disc 554. 1998.

Macpherson, Sandy. *I'll Play to You*. Empress compact disc RAJCD 861. 1996.

The Magic of Hutch: Begin the Beguine. Broadsword International compact disc SUN 2115. 2002.

Music While You Work. Empress compact disc 1004. 1994–99.

The Other Side of the Singing Detective. BBC compact disc 708. 1986.

Our Gracie: The Best of Gracie Fields. Decca compact disc 5324560. 2010.

Parry, Harry. *Crazy Rhythm*. Broadsword International compact disc SUN 2162. 2004.

Shelton, Anne. *The Early Years of Anne Shelton*. Soundsrite Music Wholesale compact disc SWNCD 003. 1995.

Silvester, Victor and His Ballroom Orchestra. *Slow, Slow, Quick, Quick, Slow*. Empress compact disc 890. 1998.

There'll Always Be an England. Living Era compact disc AJA 5069. 1990.

We'll Meet Again: Classic Songs and Tunes from the War Years. EMI compact disc 509999 9 68705 2 5. 2009.

SELECTED FILMOGRAPHY

Jennings, Humphrey, and Stewart McAllister, dirs. *Listen to Britain.* 1942; reissued by Image Entertainment, 2002.

Wellesley, Gordon, dir. *Rhythm Serenade.* Columbia Pictures, 1943.

Index

Page numbers in italics indicate illustrations.